THE SITE OF THE SOCIAL

THE SITE OF THE SOCIAL

a philosophical account of the constitution of social life and change

theodore r. schatzki

the pennsylvania state university press

university park, pennsylvania

Library of Congress Cataloging-in-Publication Data

Schatzki, Theodore R.
    The site of the social : a philosophical account of
the constitution of social life and change / Theodore R.
Schatzki.
        p.   cm.
Includes bibliographical references and index.
ISBN 978-0-271-02292-5 (pbk : alk. paper)
1. Sociology—Philosophy. 2. Social change. I. Title.

HM585 .S33 2002
301—dc21   2001036464

It is the policy of The Pennsylvania State University Press to use acid-free paper for
the first printing of all clothbound books. Publications on uncoated stock satisfy the
minimum requirements of American National Standard for Information Sciences—
Permanence of Paper for Printed Library Materials, ANSI Z39.48–1992.

For Nora, aka Rosie

CONTENTS

ACKNOWLEDGMENTS

This book was born of the realization that the concluding chapter of my previous book slighted the role of materiality in social life.

The initial opportunity to organize the ideas contained herein was afforded by an invitation to teach at a 1997 National Endowment for the Humanities (NEH) Summer Institute on Intelligibility and Background Practices at the University of California, Santa Cruz. I thank the directors of the Institute, Hubert Dreyfus and David Hoy, for the invitation and the Institute's participants for their considerable feedback. First composition of much of the manuscript occurred during the 1997–98 academic year while I was a guest scholar at the Max Planck Institute for the History of Science in Berlin. I wish to thank the director of Department Three, Hans-Jörg Rheinberger, for this opportunity. The close-knit network of the Institute proved to be an extraordinarily stimulating environment in which to pursue intellectual work, and I am grateful to the other members of Department Three for their feedback and camaraderie and to the Institute for its much-appreciated support services. Part of the 1997–98 year was also spent at the Free University, Berlin, with a research fellowship from the Alexander von Humboldt Foundation. I heartily thank both the foundation, for the renewal of my fellowship, and my host at the Free University, Albrecht Wellmer, for sage advice, invigorating conversations, and an exceptionally thought-provoking seminar on Heidegger and Robert Brandom. Finally, I wish to thank the Advanced Study Program of the Winterthur Library for a research fellowship that supported archival research on the Shakers at the library. This venue proved to be a propitious location at which to become acquainted with the minutiae of the Shaker medicinal herb industry.

In one form or another, parts of this manuscript have been presented at the NEH Summer Institute, a Pittsburgh Central Division meeting of the American Philosophical Association, the University of Bielefeld, the European University at Saint Petersburg, the Free University, Berlin, the Max Planck Institute for the History of Science, the University of Illinois at Urbana-Champaign, and the University of Kentucky. Among the many individuals who have offered valuable feedback, I especially want to thank Rudiger Bittner, John Carvalho, Bert Dreyfus, Michael Hagner, Mark Hansen, Hubert Henrichs, Oleg Kharkhordin, Hans-Jörg Rheinberger, Joe Rouse, Eike von Savigny, Henning Schmidgen, Vadim Volkov, and Albrecht Wellmer. Additional thanks for useful suggestions go to the two referees that The Pennsylvania State University Press secured for the book, Todd May and Stephen Turner. For guidance in working through Shaker archive material, I thank Jerry Grant and Virginia McEwen at the Shaker Museum and Library, Randy Folger at Pleasant Hill, and the librarians at the Winterthur Library. Thanks, too, to John Murray for helpful comments on what I wrote about the Shakers.

Intellectual works owe much to the support of local contexts. I thank former Arts and Sciences Dean Richard Edwards (who will be missed) for a fellowship leave in 1997–98; Suzanne, Andreas, and Anna Brose for their lovely apartment in Berlin, which was also a splendid place to write; Nora Moosnick for her love, companionship, and willingness again to travel; and Louis, whose enthusiasm for life makes every day a joy.

PREFACE

This book is about the constitution of social life: the nature of social existence, what it consists in, and the character of its transformation. The work's most general claim is that the best way to approach these topics is to tie social life to something called "the site of the social." The social site is a specific context of human coexistence: the place where, and as part of which, social life inherently occurs. To theorize sociality through the concept of a social site is to hold that the character and transformation of social life are both intrinsically and decisively rooted in the site where it takes place. In turn, this site-context, I claim, is composed of a mesh of orders and practices. Orders are arrangements of entities (e.g., people, artifacts, things), whereas practices are organized activities. Human coexistence thus transpires as and amid an elaborate, constantly evolving nexus of arranged things and organized activities.

Analyzing the social through the concept of a site offers several advantages over rival social ontological paths. Individualist ontologies have never quite disposed of the suspicion that those features of individuals that they take to be constitutive of social affairs are intrinsically tied to an embedding milieu or medium that cannot, without remainder, be analyzed simply as more individuals. Prominent among these features of individuals are mental conditions and actions. Conceptualizing the character and transformation of social life as bound to a site theorizes this embedment. At the same time, it accommodates the individualist insight that individuals and constellations thereof are causally responsible for the progress of social affairs.

Site ontologies are not, of course, the only accounts that take wing on the intuition that social life transpires in an embedding milieu or medium. Diverse anti-individualisms over the past century and a half have articulated variants of this thesis, usually on the background of the ideas of G. W. F. Hegel, Emile Durkheim, or Ferdinand de Saussure. Such anti-individualist, or "socialist," accounts suffer, however, from a tendency toward hypostatization: of wholes, emergent levels of description, or abstract structures. Site approaches, by contrast, flourish on the ground of the ideas of Martin Heidegger and Ludwig Wittgenstein and shun reified individual-shaping phenomena in favor of a continuously churning enveloping horizon of organized human activity. In addition, both individualist and socialist analyses fall prey to the scientific urge to build simplifying, diagrammatic models of social life. They thereby neglect key dimensions of social existence. Site ontologies undertake a more descriptive, even phenomenological marking and conceptualization of pervasive features of social existence, which can be extended almost indefinitely.

As noted, furthermore, the site of the social, according to my more specific account, is a mesh of practices and orders: a contingently and differentially evolving configuration of organized activities and arrangements. This account shares an emphasis on organized activity with other site ontologies, for example, those of Pierre Bourdieu, Charles Taylor, and Ernesto Laclau and Chantal Mouffe. Compared to these ontologies, however, my account more successfully resists the drive to totalize, recognizes greater multifaceted change in social life in addition to greater contingency and openness, and/or perceives more clearly both the significance of arrangements and the contribution of entities other than people to the character and progression of social affairs. In doing so, my account seeks to give substance to Michel Foucault's vision of history as a thoroughly contingent and severely fragmented affair.

As the master figure organizing this treatise's account of the social, the distinction between arrangements and practices runs throughout the book. Its prominence is further reflected in the fact that two of the bodies of literature through, and per confrontation with, which the book's account of the social site develops are what I call "theories of arrangements" and "practice theories." The principal exponents of these two lines of thought are, on the one hand, Foucault, Bruno Latour, Michel Callon, and the teams of Laclau and Mouffe and Gilles Deleuze and Félix Guattari, and, on the other, Bourdieu, Taylor, Hubert Dreyfus, and Anthony Giddens.

Because practice theory has gained visibility in recent years as both a path

of thinking and a label,[1] nothing needs to be said about it at the present juncture. The appellation "arrangement theorists," by contrast, is an uncommon
moniker and should be explicated. This term denotes a group of thinkers
who take arrangements of entities to be the principal compositional feature of
social life. According to these theorists, human coexistence takes place as and
amid arrangements of human beings and other phenomena, so that the nature
of social life is tied to fundamental features of such arrangements. The analyses, accordingly, that arrangement theorists offer of particular social phenomena, such as disciplinary societies, science, technology, states, and democracy,
feature the arrangements that compose these phenomena.

Of course, the word "arrangements" does not appear in these thinkers' primarily French texts. The relevant expressions are instead *dispositifs* (Foucault),
agencements (Deleuze and Guattari), and *réseaux* (Latour and Callon). These
expressions are regularly translated as apparatus, assemblage, and network, although one of Deleuze's translators argues that Foucault's and Deleuze's terms
are better rendered as "assemblage" and "arrangement," respectively.[2] Latour,
Callon, and Laclau and Mouffe also routinely write in English and employ the
words "network"[3] or "discourse." Regardless of the "proper" translation of these
terms, they designate a common figure: Social things organized in configurations, where they hang together, determine one another via their connections, as combined both exert effects on other configurations of things and are
transformed through the action of other configurations, and therewith constitute the setting and medium of human action, interaction, and coexistence.
Together, these thinkers highlight the elementariness of what might be called
the labyrinthine "configurational order" of the social: the involuted lacing of
human and other phenomena into extensive arrangements that determine as
well as bind together their characters and fates.

Orders, practices, and different categories of social ontology are not the

[1] See Theodore R. Schatzki, Karin Knorr-Cetina, and Eike von Savigny, eds., *The Practice Turn in Contemporary Theory* (London: Routledge, 2001).
[2] See Gilles Deleuze, *Negotiations * 1972–1990,* trans. Martin Joughin (New York: Columbia University Press, 1995), 196 n. 9. Joughin notes that Deleuze himself has translated "arrangement" as *agencement.*
[3] Latour confirms the affinity of these terms in a glossary he and Madeleine Akrich wrote to set out key expressions of actor-network theory. He employs the words "set up" and "setting" to designate what he and Callon otherwise call a "network," defines the denoted phenomenon as "assemblies of actants," and then adds that the French word for this phenomenon is *dispositifs.* Madeleine Akrich and Bruno Latour, "A Summary of a Convenient Vocabulary for the Semiotics of Human and Nonhuman Assemblies," in *Shaping Technology/Building Society: Studies in Sociotechnical Change,* ed. Wiebe J. Bijker and John Law (Cambridge, Mass.: MIT Press, 1992), 259–64, here 259.

only axes around which the current book revolves. Other issues centrally organizing my discussions are the contrast between nominalism and contextualism,
the opposition between humanism and posthumanism, and the conceptualization of social change.

Nominalism versus contextualism is a key issue for all accounts of social life,
especially those seeking to chart the forms and determinants of social change.
Nominalism contends that the character and transformation of sociality can be
explained solely through the properties of and relations among the particular
entities that compose social life. It thereby opposes *contextualism,* which argues
that these matters must be referred to a context, different from these entities,
in which the latter exist. By "context," I mean, provisionally, a setting or backdrop that envelops and determines phenomena. The distinction between nominalism and contextualism becomes palpable when applied to the phenomenon
of social orders qua arrangements. It then becomes a distinction between those
theories that maintain that the character and transformation of arrangements
are beholden to nothing but properties of and transactions among the components of arrangements and those accounts that declare these matters to depend
on a context in which arrangements subside. Examples of contexts typically
cited in this regard are economic systems, social structures, hierarchical distributions of power or capital, webs of meaning, discourses, and social practices.

Individualist ontologies are nominalist in character. Socialist and site ontologies, by contrast, work with one or more of the phenomena just cited. According to ontologies of the latter sorts, although the character and transformation
of social orders are tied to the existing state of arrangements, they are so only
in conjunction with the systems, structures, and webs that envelope orders.
Nominalists deny the existence of such robust contexts. For them, such phenomena as systems and structures either do not exist or are, at bottom, merely
configurations of arrangements. Indeed, the only "contexts" that nominalists
recognize in social life are components and features of arrangements other
than (but relevant to) the particular components and features they currently
investigate.

The opposition between nominalism and contextualism dates from the
1800s. The front between humanism and posthumanism has become increasingly prominent in contemporary thought. "Humanism" has no precise meaning. Generally speaking, it is a broad cultural stance, arising in Europe during
the 1500s and 1600s, which enunciates the pathos of human existence and cel-
ebrates human beings as thinkers, creators, and actors. Among the prominent

forms that this cultural movement has assumed in intellectual thought are
(1) an epistemological humanism that privileges the human subject-mind as
the exclusive place of knowledge; (2) a psychological version that considers
humans to be masters of both their psyches and the phenomena of meaning
and intentionality; (3) a value humanism that proclaims that humans give
themselves political-ethical values and do not receive them from God, the
chain of being, the order of the cosmos, or the inherent structure of reason;
(4) an agential variant that trumpets human agency as both the highest form
of agency and the type of greatest significance to life on earth; and (5) a definitional version that argues that the being of humanity is such that human life
essentially contrasts with or differs absolutely from animality or mere animal
life. My concern in the present book is primarily with agential humanism
and indirectly with its definitional cousin. Various "posthumanist" analyses,
including several prominent theories of arrangements or of practice, stress
the causal significance of entities other than humans for social life, challenge
the claim that humans alone are agents, threaten to dissolve human agency
into the actions of nonhuman entities, and/or attribute central features of
human agency to the agencies of other entities. Posthumanist distrust of "the
human," like its embrace of nonhumans as compatriots in social life, is an
important intellectual development with which analyses of social life must
come to terms. This is why the lines and interface between humans and other
entities form a key axis of investigation beginning partway through the book;
why nature becomes a pressing object of inquiry at subsequent stages; and also
why my discussion periodically confronts recent work in science studies, which
is perhaps that area of contemporary humanistic-social scientific theory most
occupied with these issues. I argue that posthumanists are wrong to debunk
the integrity, unique richness, and significance of human agency.

The third ontological issue to which I pay significant attention is the
conceptualization of social change. Some theorists who hold that explanation
is the telos of social inquiry have singled out social change as the prime object
of social investigation. Whether or not this position is tenable, social change
is a crucial phenomenon. I do not, however, offer a general account of social
explanation. Nor do I outline a framework for explaining social change that
is any more detailed or systematic than the general dictum that explaining
change involves summarily documenting (and accounting for) the agencies
that brought it about. Instead, I focus on two other matters. The first is prefiguration, or the ways that the social present channels forthcoming action.

The fact that social becoming and change take place through agency makes this a crucial area of investigation. The second topic is the consequences my ontology holds for the forms and mechanisms of becoming and change. Although the issue of the forms that change takes is at least coeval with that of how to explain change, it is somewhat neglected. The thesis that all social life transpires as part of a nexus of practices and arrangements implies that social changes are metamorphoses in such nexuses and their components. I describe some of the forms that such metamorphoses take, as well as several mechanisms through which they transpire. My discussion of change also engages an issue that has enjoyed great prominence since social thought arose: the relations between society and nature, in particular, the relations between social and natural change.

These are some of the ontological issues to which the present work attends. All social ontologies face, in addition, the issue of justification. How can a particular ontology be justified as superior, better, or more preferable than others? An ontological account can be defended in at least three ways: through arguments against its rivals, through demonstrations of its compatibility with the social world, and through its ability to underwrite first-rate social investigation. The first strategy articulates theoretical arguments. The second presents plausible descriptions of empirical phenomena in the terms of the ontology, thereby using these phenomena as examples to illustrate the latter. The third strategy provides insightful descriptions, explanations, and interpretations of social affairs on the basis of the ontology. Whereas the first procedure reveals the deficiencies of alternatives, the second and third exhibit, respectively, the plausibility of one's own account and the advantages of approaching social life through it. The more of these strategies implemented, the stronger an ontology stands defended.

Empirical phenomena play a different role in the justification of ontologies than in the vindication of explanatory theories. Ontologies are not explanatory theories. They describe basic characters, compositions, and structures. They do not specify general frameworks for explaining social phenomena, though they do provide explanatory resources and can also ground general pronouncements about explanation. A defender of a particular explanatory theory marshals empirical examples to support it. She or he cites phenomena that this theory alone can explain or that it explains "better" than do its rivals. Empirical phenomena also support an explanatory theory when they corroborate the predictions it generates about the future or about still-undocumented phenomena.

In these ways, empirical phenomena constitute evidence for a theory. Onto-logical accounts do not qua ontological provide explanations or predictions. Empirical phenomena cannot, as a result, serve as evidence for them. Such phenomena are instead employed to demonstrate the compatibility (or in-compatibility) of the account with social life. An ontology is compatible with social life when it can describe social phenomena in its own terms. Different ontologies, however, can usually supply descriptions of the same phenomenon. Consequently, compatibility (the ability to handle particular examples) can only confer plausibility. It cannot provide evidence for or confirm or prove an ontology. This does not imply, however, that empirical illustration is an insignificant task.

The current book implements the first two justificatory strategies. Theoret-ical arguments against alternatives are presented in Chapter 3, and empirical illustration occurs throughout the text. I do not, however, pursue the third strategy: showing that an ontology underwrites excellent social inquiry. To begin with, the present text is a work in ontology. It aims to discuss the enter-prise of social ontology and to defend a particular ontological approach. Fully implementing the third strategy involves explaining the consequences of the ontology for description, explanation, and interpretation, presenting research that heeds these consequences, and defending the value of this research. It also requires detailed exploration of the epistemology of social investigation (and of the considerable literature on this topic). Pursuing this strategy would, consequently, explode the boundaries of the present book. Nonetheless, I carry out this strategy to a limited extent. The book's ontology, for example, informs its description of select phenomena. These descriptions thus exemplify what social description—reportage, in Runciman's terms[4]—looks like in my account. In particular, the detailed description of day trading in Chapter 3 illustrates what multiscalar description of social phenomena involves. The discussions of agency and change in Chapters 2 and 4 also mention implications of the ontol-ogy for social explanation.

Another reason I prescind from implementing the third strategy is that, although underwriting excellent research is a mark in favor of an ontology, which ontology-research packages satisfy this criterion—at all or best—is severely contentious. The implications of different ontologies for the conduct of social investigation can diverge so radically that judgments about which

[4] W. G. Runciman, *A Treatise on Social Theory*, vol. 1 (Cambridge: Cambridge University Press, 1983).

investigations exemplify "fruitful," "insightful," or "excellent" research are hopelessly crossed. Such discord is well known to anyone familiar with the "antiscientistic" implications that some thinkers (e.g., those in the *Verstehen* tradition writ large) have wrung from their conceptions of human existence. A theorist can outline consequences that her or his ontological ideas hold for the conduct of social investigation, and investigators can (even) respect them. But theoretical and methodological differences will fuel perpetual disagreement about the value of the resulting research. Hence, the third justificatory strategy is somewhat less decisive than the first two. I do not mean to imply that specifying epistemological and methodological implications and conducting investigations on their basis are not important tasks. I am only explaining why they are not carried out in the present work.

Finally, the third and, for me, main reason for declining to implement the third strategy is that I want, instead, to spend time discussing the aforementioned ontological issues that bear on or are implicated in both social ontologies generally and my own ontology in particular.

As stated, I defend my social ontology through descriptions of empirical phenomena that illustrate and lend it plausibility. Two examples, in particular, are developed in the following, both in great detail: the medicinal herb business at the Shaker village of New Lebanon, New York, in the mid-nineteenth century, and contemporary day trading on the Nasdaq market. The division of labor between these two examples is the following. I first use the Shaker example in Chapters 1–3 to develop, illustrate, and corroborate theoretical contentions about the character of social arrangements, the nature of practices, the contextualization of arrangements in practices, and the site of social life. The day trading example is introduced midway through Chapter 3 and initially used to exemplify—in a summarizing manner—the sum of contentions defended to that point. In the remainder of the book, the two examples are employed in tandem to develop and illustrate theses about nature, agency, prefiguration, change, and natural history.

Because theoreticians typically marshal diverse empirical phenomena to illustrate their theoretical propositions, my focus on two examples contrasts with standard practice. The advantage of working with two examples is that they can be developed in greater detail. The Shaker example is used to develop and to illustrate a series of theoretical claims through cumulative descriptions that expand or deepen previous ones. The day trading example is used to substantialize these claims all at once as a package. In comparison to the procedure of drumming up numerous examples, this modus operandi provides at once greater substantiality, sharpened perspicuity, and above all enhanced clarity of understanding. Because the theoretical account in its entirety is substantialized in the same phenomena instead of being scattered across many, the meaning and implications of theoretical propositions are plainer and enjoy greater concreteness. The cumulative descriptions of the Shakers make the structure of theoretical propositions clearer and more tangible, whereas the concentrated depiction of day trading provides an overview of how the entire theoretical edifice works out concretely. In short, substantiality, perspicuity, understanding, and grasp are all enhanced when select empirical phenomena serve as foci where the theory *as a whole* can be concretized, elaborated, and corroborated.

Accordingly, I affirm Barry Barnes's claim that social theory is sterile in the absence of carefully investigated empirical examples. He writes:

> Social theory needs at all times to keep in touch with the states of affairs it purports to describe or explain. This is not just a matter of checking predictions.... It is essential as the means of giving theory meaning: if instances and examples of the use of theoretical concepts are never supplied then it remains unclear, indeed wholly indeterminate, what significance theoretical concepts—and hence theory—might have. Theory without some kind of exemplification is no theory at all.[5]

The present book's methodology takes this plea seriously and adds that theoretical propositions attain *greater* meaning, determinacy, and clarity when they are worked out and illustrated through extremely detailed examples.

Investigating a pair of examples might be thought to bring with it the danger that peculiarities of the cases skew the account or subtend false generalization. Circumventing this peril is one motivation for multiple examples and comparative methods. This danger, however, above all imperils research in history and social science that formulates, defends, and explains empirical generalizations. It is considerably less a threat to the enterprise of social ontology, whose accounts are constructed much more on the basis of theoretical considerations and general intuitions than on the basis of particular empirical examples. If anything, social ontology is far more concerned with reconnecting to empirical phenomena than with over-relying on particular ones.

---

[5] Barry Barnes, *The Elements of Social Theory* (Princeton: Princeton University Press, 1995), 61.

Nevertheless, this worry does correctly suggest that any account that works with a small number of examples must choose its examples carefully.

Governing my selection of the Shaker medicinal herb business and Nasdaq day trading was the desire that the examples contrast in multiple dimensions. The Shaker business, to begin with, was simpler than the Nasdaq market. Harmony and consensus, moreover, reigned in Shaker activities, whereas competition and even conflict characterize Nasdaq trading. The Shaker business, furthermore, was as spatially localized, well-bounded, and contained in specific small communities as Nasdaq trading is spatially scattered, rapidly expanding, and extended through many communities and groups. The Shaker example hails, in addition, from an earlier historical era. This is important given the sometimes-enunciated thesis that the contemporary world is much more systematically organized than are its predecessors. Finally, Nasdaq trading incorporates cybernetic phenomena, unknown in the Shakers' time. Because of these contrasts, the two examples, taken together, go far toward substantiating the contention that the book's ontological theses apply to social life in general. At the same time, because the examples are two, my discussion can enjoy the benefits of unearthing details.

An additional word should be appended about my use of the Shaker business. As noted, Chapters 1–3 employ the Shaker example by itself to develop and illustrate basic ontological theses. I feature the Shakers thus because social life (like almost everything else) is highly complex, and any simplification permits fundamentals to show forth more clearly. Shaker life was simpler, in many regards, than both social life outside their villages and social life today. Not only was the Shakers' attempt to banish the pervasive tentacles of sexuality relatively successful, but their affairs proceeded with uncommon openness and frankness and, in addition, were blessed with diminished conflict. Indeed, the Shakers keenly sought to exile sexuality, impede conflict, and maximize community harmony. Because of this attenuation of disruptive and complicating phenomena in comparison to social life elsewhere, Shaker orders and practices display basic features of the social site unusually clearly, thereby enhancing access to them. The dilution of disruptive and vexing phenomena does not, moreover, affect the ontological fundamentals that their lives are called on to illustrate.

Some readers might think that the relative simplicity of Shaker life makes it a rather poor focus for developing a general account of social existence, one that is also supposed to illuminate, among other things, complex contemporary

societies. I affirm that contemporary social life is subject to forms of organization and change that were not instantiated in Shaker life. This truth is exemplified in the Nasdaq trading example. The manifold differences between today's
complex, open, and multiply integrated societies and the Shakers' small, semi-
closed, and separate communities, however, do not vitiate employing the latter
for the purposes of theory development. I do not claim that Shaker life is rep-
resentative of or even congruent with contemporary life. I suggest only that the
simplicity of their lives makes it easier to espy and to present basic ontological
features of social existence. Examples of such ontological fundamentals are that
human coexistence is suspended in a mesh of practices and orders and that
orders are established within the sway of practices. Nor do I contend that all elements and principles required to describe and explain contemporary life appear
in the Shaker example. Basic ontological features simply specify the general
nature of the elements and principles of social organization and change that
characterize any given period or region of human geohistory. This specification
is, moreover, compatible with whatever differences do or do not mark elements
and principles at different times and places. Indeed, the ontology might be
thought of as a scaffolding that the description of geohistorically disparate
phenomena fills in. In this regard, my claim vis-à-vis the contemporary world
is simply that the elements of and principles for adequately describing and
explaining this world are elements and principles of the *complex, open, and multiply integrated* mesh of practices and arrangements that composes the present-
day site of the social.

The plan of this book is as follows. Chapter 1 analyzes social order. It begins
by criticizing three prominent conceptions of social order: regularity, stability,
and interdependence. It then argues that social order should be conceived of,
instead, as arrangements of the entities that enter social life. At this point,
I introduce the Shaker medicinal herb industry and describe the orders that
composed the industry at New Lebanon in the 1850s. Utilizing this example,
the remainder of the chapter scrutinizes central dimensions of arrangements:
relations, positions, and meanings. In Chapter 2, the focus switches to social
practices. After elucidating the contrast between social nominalism and contextualism, the chapter outlines the nature of practices. A practice, it contends,
is a collection of activities that are linked through an array of understandings,
rules, and "teleoaffectivities." The chapter continues with a demonstration that
practices form a crucial context in which social orders are established. The

book's engagement with posthumanism commences thereafter with a defense of the constitutive, causal, and prefigurative priority of human actions over objects.

Chapter 3 follows with my account of the site of the social. It first outlines, as background, two types of social ontology—individualist and socialist—and offers arguments against these. The succeeding section introduces the category of site ontology and contrasts the notion of a site with several field concepts prominent in recent social analysis. It then argues that the site of social life is a mesh of orders and practices and shows how this account of the social site surpasses those found in rival site ontologies. Following this, I introduce the book's second empirical focus: Nasdaq day trading. A description of this phenomenon provides an illustrative summary of the theoretical claims advanced to this juncture. The chapter finishes with an analysis of the society-nature divide, whose conclusion is that the legitimate distinction between the social site and nature does not mark a division between two substantive realms.

The final chapter investigates social change and becoming as affairs of agency, human and nonhuman. Confronting several outstanding posthumanist lines of argument, it first vindicates the intactness and unique richness of the human type of doing. The succeeding section investigates how the site of social life prefigures the paths taken by the human activity that perpetuates and alters it. I dispute the widespread practice of analyzing the prefiguration of activity as the delimitation of fields of possibility (physically possible actions and feasible options). Prefiguration, I contend, is a variegated phenomenon, wherein courses of action are qualified in many further ways such as harder and easier, promising of ruin or gain, and prescribed and proscribed. The next section sets out prominent forms and mechanisms of change in orders, practices, and practice-order complexes. The final section outlines a novel concept of natural history. In portraying natural history as the development of humankind's entanglement with nature, this conception contrasts with that notion of natural history, dominant in contemporary evolutionary and ecological theory, which treats human history as a natural process. A concluding coda sketches investigative paths that the foregoing analyses open.

SOCIAL ORDERS

Order is a basic dimension of any domain of entities. Things tend not to form random aggregates of continuously metamorphosing matters, but instead to hang together as clusters of interrelated determinate stuff. Order is the basic disposition of a domain of entities, the way that things are laid out or hang together in that domain. Conceived this abstractly, moreover, order is neutral vis-à-vis atomistic and holistic construals of any given field. Whether a domain, say, is composed of elements externally joined in larger molecular conglomerates or is a space of varying intensities and unarticulated continua from which determinate phenomena precipitate, order is the basic layout of matters in that domain, a layout embracing their relations, specifications, and boundaries.

Social thought has long concerned itself with social order, the layout of social life. For example, the constructive portion of Plato's *Republic,* the inaugural work of social inquiry, begins with a question of order. Given that human settlements are founded on the need to exchange goods to overcome the individual's lack of self-sufficiency, how must labor be divided so that people's combined efforts maximize the quantity and quality of their possessions and consumables? Plato's account of the best division of labor addresses fundamental features of the ordering of human groups. It begins with the specifications that humans are creatures of need and that objects are satisfiers of those needs, and with the presumption that humans and nonhumans are joined through three relations: exchange, consumption, and use. It then argues that the best satisfaction of needs is secured if labor is apportioned in line with the principle that people perform that job to which their skills are most suited. Plato thereby advocates a particular distribution of activities among people who share specific needs, possess varying talents, and relate to one another through social transactions of certain kinds. He thus favors a particular social order, a particular way that social things—people, jobs, consumables, and use objects—should hang together.

Theoretical interest in social order is more commonly said to commence in the modern era, above all with Thomas Hobbes's *Leviathan.* As is famously recounted, Hobbes gave the search for order a particular orientation. Plato had distinguished a city of health, where only the necessities of life were satisfied, and in a temperate manner, from an inflamed city, which pursues desires beyond necessity and seeks to satisfy them luxuriously. Noting that few people are likely to be satisfied with the simpler, more moderate lifestyle, Plato conjectured that the fevered city eventually instigates war to procure the larger territories needed to feed its habits. Much as in Jean-Jacques Rousseau's *The Social Contract,* an intact functional social order precedes and makes possible the pursuit of armed conflict. War would be impossible without the prior establishment of the economic relations and division of labor that compose the transfamilial social ordering from which the desires subtending it can grow.

Hobbes, by contrast, so portrayed humankind's natural endowment—the faculties, capacities, desires, and passions that nature allots to any functional human being qua individual creature—that war is the inevitable consequence of the joining of individuals in all social orders that lack a certain ingredient. According to Hobbes, human beings are roughly equal in mind and body, and this equality implies that they have like hope of attaining their individual ends. This latter equality, in turn, brings them into opposition when their ends and preferred means coincide or are mutually incompatible, and, therewith, into war as soon as they grasp that oppugnancy is their shared situation. Not only does that which underlies war exist independently of social order (except perhaps familial orders) rather than, as in Plato, developing once social order is established. The constant threat of the eruption of conflict also undermines the establishment of social orders, including the simple exchange relationships and division of labor that Plato ascribed to his primitive cities of health. In the state of nature, Hobbes wrote, neither industry, nor culture, nor navigation, nor building, nor knowledge, nor society exists. Indeed, taken to its logical conclusion, this view implies that in the state of nature there can occur only that desperate attempt at individual provisional self-sufficiency that Plato seemed to consider impossible or, perhaps, nonhuman.

War results from the competition and diffidence (and love of glory) that naturally attend the physical commingling of similarly endowed and similarly minded individuals in a world of scarcity. It seems, consequently, inevitable. The issue for Hobbes, then, was how to guarantee peace or at least nonovertly violent human coexistence. Social order, equated with this state of affairs, became a social good. Hobbes therewith bequeathed to modern thought its typical concern with social order. Moreover, by proposing that the means of achieving the desired condition is the consolidation of force in the hands of a central sovereign, Hobbes handed to modern thought the now-familiar idea that social order is the province of politics and government.

Things more or less stood here throughout the heyday of the modern natural law tradition, from the mid-1600s to the early 1800s. Even today, social order is widely understood both inside and outside the academy as nonovertly violent human coexistence. The rise of modern social science prepared the ground, however, for more cognitive-ontological and less political notions of order. Although the emergence of organized social studies was tied to concerns of state, it spawned accounts of the components, structures, and principles of social life that no longer overtly addressed what today would be identified as questions of political theory. As attention to these matters gained momentum and depth in the twentieth century, the idea that social order—the basic structure, organization, or layout of social life—constitutes a distinct social scientific issue gained steam. A prominent theorist has even recently dubbed the nature of ontological-cognitive order the central problem of social thought, explicitly contrasting this asseveration with Talcott Parsons's famous declaration of the centrality of the neo-Hobbesian problem of normative order.[1]

Still today, however, nonpolitical order often goes unarticulated as a distinct issue. Theorists regularly ponder the basic features of social life, but the trenchancy of Hobbes's legacy obstructs appreciation that such reflections are, among other things, explorations of order. What, nonetheless, reveals that theory is in fact concerned with social order, and that different accounts of basic social features encompass disparate depictions of it, is the widespread unconsidered theoretical use of the term "order(s)" as a fundamental reference point. Three examples illustrating three senses of social order convey something of this situation.

In chapter 5 of *The Rules of Sociological Method*, Emile Durkheim argued that a complete explanation of a social fact must cite the fact's cause and function, where "function" means the useful results that the fact produces for society as a whole. In summarizing his position, he wrote: "Consequently, to explain a social fact it is not enough to show the cause on which it depends; we must also ... show its function in the establishment of social order."[2] Functionality is defined relative to society, the social whole: The function of a social fact is the contribution it makes to putting "society in harmony with itself and with the environment external to it." If society is construed as a sum-total of social facts, then because a social fact is a collective way of thinking, feeling, and acting, the function of a social fact is its contribution to a harmonious and adaptable interweaving of collective ways. Although, consequently, Durkheim left the term unanalyzed, he conceived of social order as the stability of the social whole, the harmonious ordering of collective practices.

As a second example, consider Erving Goffman's notion of the interaction order.[3] The interaction order is a sui generis realm of human meaning and

---

[1] Anthony Giddens, *The Constitution of Society* (Berkeley and Los Angeles: University of California Press, 1984), 35; cf. Dennis S. Wrong, *The Problem of Order: What Unites and Divides Societies* (New York: Free Press, 1994), chap. 1; Jeffrey Alexander, *Theoretical Logic in Sociology*, vol. 1: *Positivism, Presuppositions, and Current Controversies* (Berkeley and Los Angeles: University of California Press, 1982), 92.

[2] Emile Durkheim, *The Rules of Sociological Method*, trans. Sarah A. Solovay and John H. Mueller (New York: Free Press, 1938), 97.

[3] Erving Goffman, "Presidential Address: The Interaction Order," *American Sociological Review* 48 (1983): 1–17. For an analysis tying Goffman's ideas to wider concerns about order, see Anne Rawls, "The Interaction Order Sui Generis: Goffman's Contribution to Social Theory," *Sociological Theory* 5 (fall 1987): 136–49.

action, which possesses its own processes and constraints and is the principal site where selves are constituted. This realm is an integral and semiautonomous field of human endeavor distinct from all institutional frameworks, whose procedures, rules, and limitations resist the encroachment of social structures. Goffman's denomination of this realm as an "order" exemplifies the currently popular use of the expression "order" to designate a structured realm of action (cf. "a country's economic order"). The idea that society or social life is composed of a number of orders wields this conception.

A third example occurs in a contemporary book on the philosophy of social science, on whose pages the unexplicated expression "social order" repeatedly appears. Describing Jürgen Habermas's thesis that the dynamics of social systems such as economy and polity are detached from cultural rules, norms, beliefs, and interactions, James Bohman writes that "some aspects of social order, specifically material reproduction, may become 'uncoupled' from the normative or cultural order."[4] Two different senses of "order" appear here. "Social order" stands for the total organization and arrangement of social life, which is also sometimes called "the social order." This phrase is extremely prevalent. "Normative or cultural order" designates the domain of normatively governed action, thus a structured realm of action in the sense in which Goffman spoke of an "interaction order."

In contemporary social investigation, one thus finds alongside order conceived of sociopolitically as nonovertly violent coexistence a variety of socio-ontological conceptions such as the stability of society, structured realms of action, and the total state of social life. Common to the first two, though not the third, of these nonpolitical conceptions is the idea that order pertains to the composition of social affairs, more specifically, to the "hanging together" (*Zusammenhang*) of the phenomena that compose social life. I point this out because of my remark at the beginning of this chapter that order is the way that things are laid out or hang together in some domain.

Section 1 of this chapter examines several conceptions of social order. It does not consider all the sorts of order that have been attributed to social affairs. It concentrates, instead, on interpretations of social order qua generic ontological-compositional feature of the layout of social life that can characterize, in principle, any component or space-time swath of social existence. This focus entails that I do not further consider such notions as structured

[4] James Bohman, *New Philosophy of Social Science* (Cambridge, Mass.: MIT Press, 1991), 168.

realms of activity or the total state of social life. The first of these notions cannot be attributed, for example, to momentary encounters, people's beliefs, or joint ventures, whereas the second is not a conception of a generic feature of the layout of social life.

Before proceeding, I should acknowledge that John Law, among others, has recently urged theorists to substitute talk of ordering for talk of order. His reason is that, *pace* the social theoretical tradition, social life contains no complete, perduring, autonomous, and final organizational forms, that is to say, orders.[5] Organizations and orders are in reality precarious, unstable, and transitory beings. "Ordering," by contrast, designates the dynamic processes that organize-order social existence. In Law's eyes, substituting talk of ordering for that of order not only directs attention to these processes, but also acknowledges that they never achieve definitive and lasting results.[6] Law is correct that becoming is an omnipresent feature of social reality and that being qua fixity, or abidingness, is a transitory feat. This truth counsels abandoning the expression "order," however, only within the penumbra of earlier functionalist, structuralist, and structure-functionalist notions of well-defined and well-organized enduring wholes. The notion of order can be retained, even as Law's emphasis on processes is hailed, if the incompleteness and transitoriness of orders are affirmed. Holding onto the notion of order also requires recognizing that, because orders are proteanly incomplete, explanatory strategies developed to account for orders qua enduring beings might no longer apply without emendation. Taking process-becoming seriously problematizes not just orders as fixed entities but also traditional forms of explanation.

1. THREE CONCEPTIONS OF SOCIAL ORDER

To provide a sense of contrast and context, I now examine three key conceptions of order qua generic ontological feature of social affairs: regularity/pattern, stability, and interdependence.

[5] See John Law, *Organizing Modernity* (Oxford: Blackwell, 1994), 1–2, 101; also John Law, "Notes on the Theory of the Actor-Network: Ordering, Strategy, and Heterogeneity," *Systems Practice* 5, 4 (1992): 379–93.

[6] See also Ernesto Laclau and Chantal Mouffe, *Hegemony and Socialist Strategy: Toward a Radical Democratic Politics* (London: Verso, 1985), chap. 3. They call order and ordering "discourse" and "practice," respectively.

Perhaps the most prominent conception is regularity and pattern, where "regularity" and "pattern" connote repetition of the same. According to this conception, social order is the repetition of given components of social life—beliefs, actions, rules, institutions, and so on. Its sway as conception of order is so immense that the seasoned theorist Jeffrey Alexander, when introducing the problem of order as one of the two main axes around which he analyzes post–World War II sociological theory, offhandedly writes that "[a] second major issue needs to be presupposed. I will call this the 'problem of order.' Sociologists are sociologists because they believe there are patterns to society."[7] Consider three further examples.

In *Social Theory: Its Situation and Its Task,* Roberto Unger describes social order as "frozen politics."[8] He means that order is the persistence of both routine actions and the conceptual-institutional frameworks sustaining them that results from people simply not paying attention to routines and frameworks. The routines involved concern conflicts over the mastery and use of resources, while the frameworks sustaining them have two dimensions: imaginary assumptions about the possible as well as desirable forms of human association, and institutional arrangements and practices. Unger's pithy phrase underscores the potential politicization of all features of social existence, routines and frameworks alike. By implication, however, his phrase defines order as unchanging routines and frameworks: the repetition of given routines and the abidingness of extant sets of imaginative preconceptions and institutional setups. Unger takes such persistence to be conceptually unproblematic. Indeed, like the principle of the conservation of momentum in physics, stasis is the default state of a social "system" that does not perturb itself through self-reflection.

More recently, Dennis Wrong has defined the problem of order as the issue of what holds society together. He also claims that "order" means regularity, predictability, and system.[9] These contentions seem to imply that the establishment of regularity and predictability holds society together, a thesis that nicely joins ontological and political order. Wrong also asserts, however, that the definition of social order as regularity and predictability is "otiose," because the concern with and search for regularity and predictability are common to

---

[7] Jeffrey Alexander, *Twenty Lectures: Sociological Theory Since World War II* (New York: Columbia University Press, 1987), 11.

[8] Roberto Mangabeira Unger, *Social Theory: Its Situation and Its Task* (Cambridge: Cambridge University Press, 1987), 11.

[9] Wrong, *The Problem of Order: What Unites and Divides Society,* 37.

all sciences. This definition, consequently, does not distinguish social order from the sorts of order found in other domains. Wrong advocates, accordingly, a Hobbesian rendering of social order as the absence of universal conflict conjoined with the cooperative pursuit of collective goals. It turns out, however, that on his account cooperative Hobbesian order is not distinct from regularities and predictability: The cognitive and motivational/affective phenomena that secure both the absence of violence and the cooperative pursuit of collective goals also explain regularities and predictability. Examples of these phenomena are shared understandings and expectations, emotional attachments, and the desires to win approval and to avoid disapproval. This explanatory conjoining of political and ontological orders suggests that the establishment of nonviolent human coexistence not just presupposes, but also is constituted partly by, ontological orderings of social affairs in the form of regularities. Notice, incidentally, Wrong's pairing of regularities and predictability. Redolent of older positivist schemes that linked regularity, prediction, and explanation, this juxtaposition errs if it implies that the scope of social predictability is limited to the bounds of social regularities.

Finally, the 1992 *Encyclopedia of Sociology* contains no entry for "social order." The entry for "social organization," however, describes a phenomenon of considerable scope: "Social organization is nonrandom *pattern* within human populations that comprise society by sharing the main aspects of a common existence over time as well as nonrandom *patterning*, the human and interhuman activities through which patterns are formed, retained, altered, or replaced."[10] Organization is pattern, together with the processes responsible for pattern. The author's equation of pattern with regularity is revealed in a subsequent assertion that the opposite of organization (disorganization) cannot be discord or opposition because these can exhibit regularity as readily as union can. Disorganization is, instead, chaos, formlessness, and idiosyncratic behavior. So interpreted, organization seems to be a conception of social order qua pervasive ontological-compositional feature of the layout of social life.

A second prominent conception of order is stability. This conception is strongly associated with functionalism and its scions, though it actually has wider scope. Conceiving society as a whole, and comparing this whole (in successive scientific historical eras) to biological organisms, complex machines,

---

[10] Herman Turk, "Social Organization," *Encyclopedia of Sociology,* ed. Edgar F. Borgalla (New York: Macmillan, 1992), 1894–1907, here 1894.

and cybernetic systems, this conception analyzes social order as harmonious functioning, that is, as equilibrium or slow directional change: Order reigns when society as a whole functions harmoniously and is, as a result, stable. An example from Durkheim was presented above. Stability must not be assimilated to regularity. Whereas order as regularity/pattern highlights repetition of the same, order as stability spotlights the integrity of large-scale social formations. Indeed, although a stable social formation likely exhibits persistence in key institutions and subsystems, it can also tolerate transformations of, realignments among, and turbulence in its components so long as the overall pattern of relatedness among them upholds the equilibrium or slow directional change of the whole. Of course, the scope of internal change compatible with harmony is limited. Change in one sector or component must be either compatible with existing conditions in others or compensated for by alterations in them.

When applied to smaller-scale phenomena such as interactions, recreational practices, and local school boards, stability shades into regularity/pattern: The stability of simpler phenomena lies less in harmonious functioning than in continuation of the same—the same interaction, the same games and diversions, and the same offices and events. A good example of this principle is found in the actor-network theory of Latour and Callon. Treating the stability of social life as the stability of networks of humans and nonhumans, this theory conceptualizes the latter stability as the obstruction of both change and development in network components and their activities. To be sure, continuation of the same is not quite the same as repetition of the same (just as a continuum differs from a series of points). Nonetheless, the stability of smaller-scale phenomena is a function of sameness. Stability is clearly differentiated from regularity only when the complexity of a social phenomenon is sufficiently great that its components can adjust to changes in other components and thereby maintain overall equilibrium or slow directional change. The distinction between stability and regularity is as blurred as the spectrum from complexity to simplicity is continuous.

A third conception of order is the interdependence of things social, preeminently the actions of individuals and groups. Because interdependence can be analyzed in various ways, for example, as ties, reciprocity, and coordination, this conception is admittedly somewhat of a grab bag. Indeed, regularity and stability are relatively precise notions in comparison to it. Interdependence is distinct from these first two notions because it does not imply any degree of regularity, pattern, or harmonious functioning. When, moreover, order is equated with interdependence, it can just as much characterize a single event, say, a unique encounter on the street, as it can a complete domain of activity, for instance, the richly interlaced activities that compose an economy. Exemplifying this analysis are Anthony Giddens's and Jürgen Habermas's distinctions between social and system integration.[11] Neither theorist, it should be noted, calls integration a conception of order. Giddens, in fact, characterizes social order as "the transcending of time and space in social relationships."[12] (This characterization is a version of the regularity conception that equates order with the space-time extension of practices and of the sets of rules and resources that govern them. The role Giddens accords routinization in the transcendence of time-space also points toward this equation.) Their analyses of integration nonetheless illustrate order qua interdependence.

In Giddens's hands, integration is the degree of action interdependence that is implicated in the reproduction of particular interlocked practices. By "interdependence," he means "regularised ties, interchanges, or reciprocity."[13] The differentiation of social from system integration marks the distinction between interdependencies in face-to-face interactions and those in relations among social systems or collectivities. Order, accordingly, can characterize phenomena ranging from unique encounters among individuals to spatially-temporally extended practices embracing many actors to extensive space-time swaths of social life.

For Habermas, "integration" designates a specific type of interdependence, namely, coordinated action. As a result, his rendering of the distinction between social and systems integration denotes two avenues over which action is coordinated: through the harmonization of "action orientations" and through the functional intermeshing (*Vernetzung*) of the unintended consequences of action.[14] The first mechanism is a descendent of Durkheimian normative consensus, the second a version of Parsonian systems. For both Giddens and Habermas, consequently, integration pertains to how actions hang together, thus to social order.

---

[11] Both distinctions derive from David Lockwood's "Social Integration and System Integration," in *Explorations in Social Change*, ed. George K. Zollschan and W. Hirsch (London: Routledge, 1964), 244–57.

[12] Giddens, *The Constitution of Society*, 35, 87.

[13] Anthony Giddens, *Central Problems in Social Theory: Action, Structure, and Contradiction in Social Analysis* (Berkeley and Los Angeles: University of California Press, 1979), 76–77.

[14] Jürgen Habermas, *The Theory of Communicative Action*, vol. 2: *Lifeworld and System: A Critique of Functionalist Reason*, trans. Thomas McCarthy (Boston: Beacon Press, 1987), 117.

According to the three above conceptions, order is a trait of the hanging together of things that potentially characterizes the entirety of social life. About order as regularity/pattern, for example, Barry Barnes exclaims, "But the existence of pattern in human social life is evidently not an optional extra. Always and everywhere, human beings, in peace and war, cooperation and conflict, relate to one another in systematically patterned ways. Always and everywhere, the relations between human beings are linguistically and cognitively, culturally and practically ordered. Order at this level is deeply sociologically interesting."[15] Parallel quotes could be cited about stability and interdependence. Stability, for instance, is accorded all-inclusive reach in the functionalist and structural-functionalist dictums that (1) societies are the basic large-scale units in social life, (2) the maintenance of harmonious functioning orders the subsystems and key components of societies, and (3) the principles that thereby govern these subsystems and components in turn organize activity in them.

I want now, through critical examination of the just-discussed conceptions, to develop several conditions for an adequate conception of social order.

Challenging the conception of social order as regularity or pattern are arguments against its scope. One such argument can be extracted from Ludwig Wittgenstein's celebrated analysis of concepts.[16] Wittgenstein denied that all instances of those concepts introduced into usage other than through explicit definition share properties by virtue of which they qualify as such instances. His example was the concept of a game. Being a game does not involve essential properties. Any two games share certain features while differing in others, and the sets of features that two games do and do not share vary among pairs of games. Overlaps among these sets ensure, nonetheless, that games resemble one another and form, as a group, a family whose members bear what Wittgenstein called "family resemblances" to one another.

Traditional analyses of concepts supposed that all instances of a given concept share particular properties (essence). According to these analyses, such instances form a regularity in the sense of repetition of the same. Wittgenstein turned the tradition on its head: Instances of a concept do not universally share any property. They do not, therefore, form a regularity. If, accordingly, patterns are conceived of as regular arrangements, a concept's instances fail to

---

[15] Barry Barnes, *The Elements of Social Theory* (Princeton: Princeton University Press, 1995), 66–67.

[16] Another argument is contained in Jacques Derrida's dissolution of regularity into sequences of smallish difference; see, for example, *On Grammatology*, trans. Gayatri Chakravorty Spivak (Baltimore: Johns Hopkins University Press, 1974).

form a pattern. Of course, they do constitute an "irregular pattern," which expression suggests the need for an alternative conception of order.

By virtue of shared features and resemblances, the activities called "games" form a family distinct from others. This hanging together of particular activities to form such a family is a phenomenon of order. Wittgenstein's remarks demonstrate, consequently, that regarding, at least, social affairs, order per se cannot be equated with regularity. The order exhibited in the family of games is not regularity, repetition of the same, but similarity, a thicket of family resemblances among activities. It follows that an adequate conception of order must encompass nonregularity in addition to regularity; that is to say, it must encompass entities hanging together in ways other than as the same (in this case, as similar). Regularity does appear in Wittgenstein's analysis in the guise of the same word ("game") being used to name these varied activities. (Subsets, moreover, of the family of games do share properties—call these "subregularities.") However, the repetition of the word cannot draw the medley of similar activities into the embrace of sameness. It simply demarcates the range of phenomena about which the issue of regularity versus nonregularity arises.[17]

Wittgenstein's analysis of concepts stands stead for a wider theme in his work, namely, that the impression of sameness (or of generality) typically conceals a reality of relevant differences (or particulars). Theorizing undoubtedly involves a drive to generalize. In, for example, the human sciences, however, generalizations too often veil the wide variety of factors that shape the activities, processes, or formations they are about. Wittgenstein is reported to have made this specific point about, inter alia, the variety of reasons why children play and the range of causes for punishment.[18] He similarly criticized Sigmund Freud's dream theory for seeking a single explanation for the entire manifold of dream phenomena and Sir James Frazer for offering a single form of

---

[17] This is why I interpret Wittgenstein's considerations as narrowing the scope of regularity as opposed to reconceptualizing regularity as something other than repetition of the same. What suggests the latter, reconceptualization interpretation is the fact that, according to Wittgenstein, the state of the world that corresponds to a regularity (repetition) of language (i.e., the use of the word "game") is a set of activities that do not collectively share any property. One might interpret this situation as implying that regularity is something like Derridean "sameness over difference." What it actually entails, however, is that the reconceptualization interpretation is self-defeating because it presents Wittgenstein's reconceptualization as employing the conception it is supposed to reconceive: The regularity involved is still a repetition of the same.

[18] Ludwig Wittgenstein, *Conversations on Aesthetics, Psychology, and Religious Belief*, ed. Cyril Barrett (Oxford: Blackwell, 1966), 49–50.

explanation for "primitive" magic rituals.[19] None of these remarks implies the absence of regularities in social life. They do suggest, however, that regularities enjoy far more attenuated scope than is usually supposed. The constitution and determination of the phenomena falling under a given term or descriptive phrase of natural language ("game," "dream," "punishment," "obeying authority") are so varied that these phenomena, as a group, are unlikely to exhibit regularities in these matters—only subregularities that encompass subsets of them. Consequently, Wittgenstein's remarks on concepts not only suggest that order per se is not regularity; in combination with the wider theme of the heterogeneous determination of phenomena, they also imply that the notion of regularity cannot characterize the full range of ways that components of social life hang together.

Foucault nicely illustrated this thesis, in a manner that dovetails with Wittgenstein's remarks and further substantiates their social theoretical relevance. In his early work, Foucault examined modern Western discourses on illness, living beings, language, and wealth and sought, among other things, to ascertain their unity. In *The Archaeology of Knowledge,* he recounted that he initially attempted to conceive this unity via sameness; for instance, as consisting in all texts of a given discourse examining the same objects or employing the same concepts, theories, or discursive infrastructures. This attempt only revealed, however, the dispersion, that is, irreducible diversity, of objects and concepts. This discovery suggested, in turn, that the unity of a discourse does not lie in the repetition of the same objects and concepts, but instead in the possession of delimited diversities of them. For example, what defined the discourse on illness was a particular range of matters discussed in medical texts and the particular spectrums of concepts and theories that these texts employed. This state of affairs does not imply that medicine was free to study anything at all and to use any and all concepts and theories in its investigations. Dispersions of objects and concepts exhibit "orders in the appearances of their elements, correlations in their simultaneity, assignable positions in common spaces, reciprocal functioning, and/or linked and hierarchized transformations";[20] and these orders, correlations, and the like are governed by

[19] Wittgenstein, *Conversations on Aesthetics, Psychology, and Religious Belief,* 43, 47–48; and Ludwig Wittgenstein, "Remarks on Frazer's *Golden Bough,*" in *Philosophical Occasions,* ed. James C. Klagge and Alfred Nordmann, trans. John Beverslvis (Indianapolis: Hackett, 1993), 119–55.

[20] Michel Foucault, *The Archaeology of Knowledge,* trans. A. M. Sheridan-Smith (New York: Harper & Row, 1976), 37.

rules, which Foucault defined as the conditions to which dispersions submit. Consequently, the unity of a discourse lies in the determinate delimitation of the ranges of objects, concepts, and so on in which it trucks.

Just as Wittgenstein discovered dispersion where the (philosophical) tradition had presumed regularity, Foucault uncovered variety where the (intellectual history) tradition had presumed sameness. This parallel reinforces not just the suggestion that the supposition of sameness often obscures relevant differences, but also the claim that order per se is not regularity. The fact that various texts constituted the discourse of illness was an aspect of the ordering of social affairs, even though no regularity of discourse elements united these texts.

Wittgenstein's remarks on concepts apply broadly to concepts of natural language. It might be feared, consequently, that their implications for order hold for a great variety of scientific enterprises and, if taken seriously, challenge the search for regularities even in the natural disciplines, where regularities are well established. Ordinary language, however, bears different relations to the social and natural sciences. Because this topic is too large to address here, I simply assert, first, that the natural sciences employ unrevised natural language concepts of physical objects and states of affairs only if scientific developments have not undermined these concepts' scientific credentials; and second, that regularities in this branch of knowledge are largely expressed in technical terms. The social sciences, by contrast, have not expelled natural language concepts for social phenomena, despite their efforts to emulate their scientific brethren in this regard. Indeed, in this division of learning, most regularities are formulated with such concepts. Examples are religion, government, exchange, law, action, and medical text. This difference implies that Wittgenstein's discernment of dispersion behind the veneer of sameness has far greater relevance for the social than for the natural disciplines.

In addition, the classification tasks that concepts of any sort perform have immense importance in social life and, hence, special significance for social inquiry. Every action, for instance, presupposes a conceptual sorting of the phenomena that populate the setting of action or are that with which the actor is concerned. The continuous advance of daily commerce with the world is likewise informed by a sorting organized around natural language concepts, regardless of whether and how subconscious cognitive processes implement this partitioning. Speech acts, moreover, are central to the organization of social life, and most such acts employ common concepts. For all these reasons, then, the course of daily life, and thus the orders that everyday activities perpetuate or bring about, rests on natural language concepts and likely reflects the family resemblance structure of these concepts' instances. Orders perpetrated or brought about through actions premised on or explicitly employing fuzzy categorization are bound to exhibit the same fuzziness.

In sum, social order should not be equated with regularity or pattern in social phenomena. An adequate conception of social order must encompass both regular and irregular orders.

The second conception of order, however, is no more satisfactory. Stability, recall, is the harmonious functioning, that is, equilibrium or slow directional change of a social whole, paradigmatically, society. The fortune of this analysis of order rises and falls with the fate of its operative concepts, for example, equilibrium, slow directional change, and society as a whole. Recent thought, however, has not been kind to these concepts. Consider one line of criticism. In the 1960s, a number of theorists censured functionalism for failing to give precise "empirical meaning," as it was sometimes put, to the concepts of equilibrium and continuous directional change.[21] One problem was that these concepts presuppose the integrity of societies as wholes; and the virtually universal empirical impossibility of pinpointing the boundaries of allegedly distinct societies challenges the integrity of these social wholes. Just where, for instance, does American society or the American economy begin and Canadian society or economy end? Elsewhere, I have myself provided a version of such an argument against Habermas's (Parsonian) depiction of an economy as a system of success-oriented purpose-rational actions that is (1) coordinated in a nonconsensual manner over money and (2) differentiated over feedback out of the totality of social actions in fulfillment of the function of maintaining the material substrate.[22] As I showed, none of the concepts employed in this analysis (e.g., purpose-rationality, money, and feedback) can rigorously demarcate an economy from its "environments," for instance, households and bureaucracies. Even when, moreover, the problem of boundaries can be overcome, as in now

[21] See, for instance, George Homans, "Bringing Men Back In," *American Sociological Review* 29, 5 (December 1964): 809–18; also Jürgen Habermas, *The Logic of the Social Sciences,* trans. Shierry Weber Nicholson and Jerry A. Stark (Cambridge, Mass.: MIT Press, 1988), pt. 2.

[22] Theodore R. Schatzki, *Social Practices: A Wittgensteinian Approach to Human Activity and the Social* (New York: Cambridge University Press, 1996), chap. 6.

extinct cases of somewhat geographically isolated "primitive" societies, the difficulty of specifying what equilibrium and slow directional change mean remains. For example, Thomas Schelling's suggestion that equilibrium be operationally defined as stasis in key social measures (e.g., gross national product, divorce rate, immigration) either transforms the dilemma into one about proper measures or reinforces antifunctionalist arguments by fragmenting equilibrium into an array of subequilibriums as multiple as the range of major social measures.[23]

Such problems rob stability of its usefulness in conceptualizing social order, at least when stability is treated as a feature of either whole societies or large-scale sectors and subsystems thereof. It remains possible to tie social order to the stability of smaller-scale phenomena such as neighborhood parties, sporting events, and culinary practices. As noted, however, stability converges with regularity and pattern at these lesser scales. The stability of culinary practices, for instance, consists largely in the persistence of particular activities and the use of the same foodstuffs and equipment. Because of this convergence, the arguments of Wittgenstein and Foucault against the presumption of sameness equally confute any rooting of social order in the stability of small-scale social phenomena.

The decline of functionalism and its progeny in the 1970s and after brought with it the demise of stability as a purported feature of large-scale social formations. Today, theorists are much more likely to emphasize the flux and becoming that pervade such formations. Flux and becoming, however, infect much more than large- (and small-) scale social phenomena alone. Even the being of the entities that hang together to constitute the orders that characterize such phenomena succumbs to it. Being is stable, generally, if what things are and which state(s) of affairs a given arrangement of things constitutes remain the same over time. Social orders are inherently unstable, and frequently de- and restabilized, in these regards.[24] What a thing of social life is, for instance, cannot be fixed. A garden rock, say, can suddenly become a paperweight and at a later moment a weapon, just as the sky can be the home of the gods at one time, a window onto the universe at another, and the medium of aeronautical and aerospace transportation at still a third. In general, both what things are

---

[23] Thomas C. Schelling, *The Strategy of Conflict* (Cambridge, Mass.: Harvard University Press, 1960).

[24] This thesis, as well as the remainder of this paragraph, is inspired by the discussion of the impossibility of hegemonic suturing in Laclau and Mouffe, *Hegemony and Socialist Strategy: Toward a Radical Democratic Politics*, chap. 3.

and the state(s) of affairs a given configuration of things constitutes depend on the things involved and their properties in conjunction with how people act toward and understand them. The vicissitudes of the transformation of properties, together with the diversity and lability of actions and conceptual schemes, ensure that everything is ontologically mutable. Hence, in addition to regularity and irregularity, an adequate conception of social order must encompass stability *and* instability—now understood as endpoints on a continuum and not as fixed opposites (see Chapter 4).

The third conception of order under scrutiny is interdependence, paradigmatically, among actions. Although this conception, like regularity and stability, is overly narrow, it points toward a key feature of a more satisfactory conception. A central issue for conceiving order as interdependence is the level of generality at which to interpret interdependence. As outlined, whereas Habermas works with a particular interdependence, coordination, Giddens interprets interdependence more broadly as regularized ties, interchanges, or reciprocity. Indeed, he contrasts dependence with autonomy. This contrast suggests that "interdependence" umbrellas all relations among individuals or collectives that make it the case that one unit's choice and pursuit of goals are not utterly self-determined and unaffected by the choices and pursuits of other units. Whether Habermas's coordination or Giddens's regularized ties, interchanges, and reciprocity is a better explication of integration, the notion common to them, is a question best left to the reader. What needs to be emphasized in the present context is that Giddens's analysis of integration as regularized ties and so on reinforces the intuition that social order has something to do with the inter-relations of things social *in general.* For regularized ties and so on is a species of the genus inter-relation, and integration is a particular form of social order construed as the layout of social life. This parallel, regular ties are to inter-relations as integration is to social order, suggests that social order must be conceived to be at least as capacious as the phenomenon of inter-relations in toto. Notice that this suggestion also points up a shortcoming of interdependence as a conception of order. Interdependence connotes mutual dependence. One-way dependencies, too, however, are a dimension of social order.

This critical canvassing yields the following conditions for an adequate conception of social order: It should countenance irregularity as a phenomenon of order; it should tolerate instability as such a phenomenon; and it should admit the full range of relations among social entities as pertinent to order.

2. Social Order as Arrangements

The current section offers an abstract specification of order and social order, which Section 4 concretizes and illustrates. Recall the intuition informing my initial characterizations. Order, I wrote, is a domain's state of determination-inter-relation: how determinate entities are laid out and hang together. This intuition ties order to a particular generic state of affairs, namely, that how things stand with one entity has to do with how they stand with others. It also converges with Bernard Waldenfels's definition of order as a "regulated nexus of this and that" (*geregelter Zusammenhang von diesem und jenem*).[25] By "regulated," Waldenfels means nonarbitrary (*nicht-beliebig*). Waldenfels's definition, too, equates order with the generic state of affairs, things hanging together. Whereas Waldenfels, however, limits orders to nonarbitrary arrays, I prefer to conceptualize order as nexuses of any sort. For the notion of a nexus (*Zusammenhang*) already contains the idea of linked existence. Waldenfels's restriction excludes haphazard and fortuitous couplings of things as instances of order, despite the fact that things still hang together when they are linked haphazardly and arbitrarily. Waldenfels also interprets "regulated" more content-fully as entailing a structure of order (*Ordnungsgefüge*), examples of which include schema, pattern (*Muster*), form, *eidos,* and formula. According to him, as a result, the layout of a nexus's elements realizes or conforms to a "structure" analytically distinct from it. This specification, as well, builds too much into the idea of order. In a nexus, things can hang together in a unique way that instantiates nothing at all: The "structure" of such a nexus is its particular contingent de facto layout or reticular composition, not any schema, pattern, or formula. Similarly, changes in how things hang together need not conform to a schema, pattern, or formula. They can be contingent and unique transformations dependent on nothing but the de facto state of inter-relatedness from which they start. Notice that, to the extent that notions such as schema, pattern, form, and formula suggest regularity, Waldenfels has unwittingly assimilated order to regularity.

Order is the hanging together of things, the existence of nexuses. Ordering, furthermore, is the hanging together of things, the establishment of nexuses. Another way of capturing this is to equate orders with *arrangements* of things and ordering with *arranging*. An arrangement of things is a layout of them in

---

[25] Bernhard Waldenfels, *Ordnung im Zwielicht* (Frankfort am Main: Suhrkamp, 1987), 17.

which they relate and are positioned with respect to one another. To be "positioned" is to take up a place among other things, a place that reflects relations among the things involved. As discussed in Section 4, however, position must not be understood merely as a spatial phenomenon. Although material entities occupy spatial positions that depend at least partly, if not entirely, on their spatial relations, an entity's position is more multiple than that. Stars and their planetary systems, for example, are positioned not just spatially with respect to one another, but also, for example, as the source of heat and as the recipients of charged particles. Members of a flock of birds likewise form a spatial distribution, at the same time that their different calls and colorings position them differentially in mating rituals as well as in signaling and fleeing behaviors. Accompanying, to take a final example, the spatial arrangement of life in a desert commune is both the mutual positioning of commune members in a motley of activities, intrigues, and joint ventures and their positioning vis-à-vis artifacts, organisms, and things in a variety of use, appreciation, and contemplation activities. "Position," in short, is an abstract term denoting where an entity fits in a nexus. As emerges below, positions always depend on the events and activities that encompass, or are carried out by, the components of arrangements.

An order is an arrangement in which entities also possess meaning and identity. By "meaning," I mean what something is and by "identity" who (if anything) it is. Identity is a subgenus of meaning, one that is accorded its own name in conformity with both the traditional distinction between what and who and the consignment of the latter status to persons. Every entity has meaning, that is, is something or other, although its meaning can be multiple, unstable, and constantly changing. Its meaning (and/or identity) is as much, moreover, a reflection of its relations as its relations reflect its meaning. For instance, being the president of a university determines a person's relations with other individuals (dictating letters, calling meetings, entertaining donors), just as that person's relations (undermining the chancellor, greeting staff affably, and growling at faculty) fill out his or her identity as corrupt, pleasant, or curmudgeonly president. Relations, positions, and meanings are bound holistically together, none enjoying priority over the others.

The idea of an arrangement bears great resemblance to Ernesto Laclau and Chantal Mouffe's notion of a discourse. I sketch their notion so as, through contrast, to clarify arrangements further. Laclau and Mouffe conceptualize discourses as totalities of systematically and inter-relatedly meaningful actions, words, and things. They use the word "positions" to designate the meanings involved, more precisely, to denote entities qua bearers of these meanings. Positions, moreover, are defined neo-Saussuringly through their differences from one another. They also constitute being, what entities are.[26] Discourses, consequently, are structured totalities of systematically related, being-articulating positions. They are a type of order as I have defined the term, one whose components are positions (entities with meaning) and whose relations are the differences (among positions) from which meaning devolves. Already one difference between discourses and arrangements should be apparent: The components of arrangements, unlike those of discourses, need not be systematically related.

An arrangement is a hanging together of entities in which they relate, occupy positions, and enjoy meaning (and/or identity).[27] In the preface, I mentioned the contrast between nominalist and contextualist accounts of the character and transformation of social life. According to nominalist theories of arrangements, the meanings and positions of the components of arrangements depend solely on properties of as well as relations between these components. The preface also stated that Chapter 2 contends, by contrast, that the layouts, positions, and meanings of social entities derive in part from a context composed of social practices. By "context," I mean, roughly, a setting or backdrop that envelops entities and helps determine their existence and being. The notion of context highlights an ambiguity in Laclau and Mouffe's account. As indicated, taking the functional place of relations in their analysis are Saussurian differences. Are, however, differences among positions, taken as a group, a prearticulated field in which particular entities take up residence and thereby acquire meaning? Or are they constitutive of and thus inseparable from particular meaningful entities? The former interpretation tracks de Saussure's separation of signifieds and signifiers: his claim that the identity of any signified or signifier

---

[26] Laclau and Mouffe, *Hegemony and Socialist Strategy: Toward a Radical Democratic Politics,* 108.

[27] This fuller formulation should dispel any fear that my analysis of social order as arrangements is truistic. In many contexts, "order" is more or less synonymous with "arrangement" (cf. the entry for "order" in *Webster's Third New International Dictionary*). As a result, analyzing social order as how things are arranged in social life might seem intuitively obvious and trivial to many social theorists, at least as an analysis of something kin to what Parsons dubbed "factual" (as opposed to normative) order, that is, accessibility to logical thought, the opposite of randomness (Talcott Parsons, *The Structure of Social Action*, vol. 1: *Marshall, Pareto, and Durkheim* [New York: Free Press, 1949], 91). The additional content that reference to relations, positions, and meaning provides alters the epistemological status of my analysis.

devolves from its differences from all other signifieds and signifiers, respectively; and the resulting thesis that signifiers gain meaning through association with particular signifieds. Like the first interpretation of Laclau and Mouffe's differences, these doctrines entail that material entities gain meaning through association with prearticulated knots in fields of conceptual-semantic difference. The alternative interpretation of Laclau and Mouffe's sets of Saussurian difference ties semantic differences to the particular meaningful entities between which they exist. In this interpretation, a position is the position it is because of these differences. These two interpretations radically differ because the first permits disparate entities to assume the same sets of meaning, whereas the second contends that meanings are inseparable from the particular things they imbue.

An arrangement is a nexus of entities in which they relate, occupy positions, and possess meanings. As my examples indicate, this conception of order applies more widely than to social affairs alone. A conception of social order requires, accordingly, greater specificity. Elsewhere I have urged that social existence be construed as coexistence and that coexistence be understood as human lives so hanging together that they, together with their relations, form contexts in which each transpires individually.[28] Context-forming configurations of lives characterize all social phenomena, from chance meetings on the street and local city council meetings to the world credit market and international crime syndicates. Indeed, a phenomenon is social to the extent that it embraces or pertains to so-configured lives. An account, incidentally, of the hanging together of lives with which social existence is here being equated is presented in Chapter 3.

The hanging together of lives is itself an arrangement. Although it is possible, consequently, to define social order as such nexuses, it is unpropitious to define social orders as arrangements simply of human lives. The context-forming arrangements into which coexisting humans are woven encompass artifacts, other living organisms, and things in addition to people. As discussed in upcoming chapters, entities of these first three sorts are as much components and determinants of the layout of social life as are people. It is more advantageous, therefore, to leave the hanging together of lives as the analysis of what coexistence is, and to demarcate social orders as all arrangements of entities, through and amid which human coexistence—the hanging together

---

[28] Schatzki, *Social Practices: A Wittgensteinian Approach to Human Activity and the Social,* chaps. 1 and 6.

of lives—transpires. Social orders are thus the arrangements of people, artifacts, organisms, and things through and amid which social life transpires, in
which these entities relate, occupy positions, and possess meanings. Notice that
orders of this sort are inherent in sociality. In embracing or pertaining to a configuration of mutually contextualizing lives, any social phenomenon (a system,
institution, group, or fleeting interaction) encompasses a human coexistence-
mediating (and -constituting; cf. Chapter 3) arrangement of humans and nonhumans in which nonhumans enjoy meaning, people assume meanings and
identities, and entities of both sorts relate and occupy positions.

I should add a word about what entities compose the arrangements through
and amid which social life transpires, drawing in the conceptions of arrangements wielded by the other arrangement theorists mentioned in the preface
(Foucault, Latour and Callon, and the team of Deleuze and Guattari). My
remarks are preliminary because this issue is rejoined in greater detail in Chapter 3. I just indicated that the entities concerned are people, artifacts, living
organisms, and things. By "people" (or "humans"), I do not simply mean
members of the species *Homo sapiens,* but living, sentient members of this
species to whom actions and mental conditions as well as self-consciousness,
gender, and identity are ascribed. Artifacts, moreover, are products of human
action, whereas living organisms are life forms other than humans, and things
are nonliving entities whose being is not the result of human activity. All these
notions require elaboration or refinement.

Objects of these types also populate the sociotechnical networks of the
actor-network theory of Callon, Latour, and Law (though these theorists tend
to classify entities into two types, actors and nonactors, and Latour has also
sought to collapse practically all objects into a single type, hybrids). Both
sociotechnical networks and arrangements as I conceive of them are configurations of objects. By contrast, neither Foucault's apparatuses nor Deleuze and
Guattari's assemblages are composed of objects alone. Foucault's apparatuses
are composed, for example, of discourses, nondiscursive behaviors, and archi-
tectures.[29] (For my purposes here, discourses can be understood as ensembles
of statements, propositions, and their presuppositions.) The assemblages that
Deleuze and Guattari espied in social life, moreover, are unions of power
regimes and regimes of enunciation. Regimes of power are configurations of

---

[29] Michel Foucault, "The Confession of the Flesh," in *Power/Knowledge,* ed. and trans. Colin Gordon
(New York: Pantheon, 1980), 194–228, here 194.

people, artifacts, and things, together with their actions, passions (what they suffer), and interminglings, whereas regimes of enunciation are systems of statements (*enoncés*), where statements are primarily uses of marks and sounds that express what the authors called "incorporeal transformations."[30] Deleuze and Guattari, incidentally, also associated regimes of power and regimes of enunciation with "what is done" and "what is said," respectively, thereby drawing their position close to that of Foucault.[31] In any event, apparatuses and assemblages embrace not just heterogeneous objects, but metaphysically disparate entities: objects, things done (actions), things said (statements), and abstract entities (propositions and incorporeal transformations). Laclau and Mouffe exhibit similar catholicism in conceptualizing discourses as configurations of actions, words, and things.

Just what is bound up with these different categorical construals of the arrangements through and amid which social life transpires becomes clear as my discussion proceeds. Here I simply point out that social arrangements, as I conceive of them, are arrangements of substances (humans, artifacts, living organisms, things), where by "substance" I mean, in the spirit of Aristotle's *Categories,* an abiding object that bears properties. As discussed in the following two chapters, this conception of arrangements does not entail that entities of other categories—above all, the actions of substances—lack considerable import for social life. Chapter 2 contends, for instance, that social orders are established in practices, themselves organized open sets of *doings* and *sayings.* It is best, however, to conceive arrangements as embracing entities of a particular metaphysical category. Doing this facilitates more careful consideration both of the different roles categorically disparate beings play in social life and of the relations of actions and words to ordered substances.[32]

---

[30] As the translator of *A Thousand Plateaus* indicates, this conception of a statement is extremely close to Foucault's; Gilles Deleuze and Félix Guattari, *A Thousand Plateaus: Capitalism and Schizophrenia,* trans. Brian Massumi (Minneapolis: University of Minnesota Press, 1987), xviii.

[31] Deleuze and Guattari, *A Thousand Plateaus,* 504. Compare Michel Foucault, "Questions of Method," in *The Foucault Effect: Studies in Governmentality,* ed. Graham Burchell, Colin Gordon, and Peter Miller (Chicago: University of Chicago Press, 1991), 73–86, here 75.

[32] I acknowledge Deleuze and Guattari's intriguing attempt to analyze substances as distillates of continuously metamorphosing multiplicities. See above all the discussion of haecceities in *A Thousand Plateaus,* plateau 10. For the initiate, let me point out, however, that their analysis there presupposes the notion of a body, thus problematizing the success of their attempt to eliminate substances. What is on one level of reality (one "stratum," in their language) a body is on the subjacent level a substance. A discussion of this topic would also have to consider the ontological status of "particles," the allegedly form-less and thus nonsubstantial entities that populate the "basement" stratum ("the plane of consistency"). See *A Thousand Plateaus,* 254.

Social orders are arrangements of entities through and amid which human existence transpires, in which the entities involved relate, occupy positions, and enjoy meanings. This notion fulfills the earlier-adumbrated conditions for an adequate conception of order. Arrangements, to start with, are not inherently regular. Entities can be, and often are, arranged irregularly, as in an English garden. Arrangements are also not inherently stable. Relations, positions, and meanings, like the arrangements of which they are aspects, are labile phenomena, only transitory fixations of which can be assured. As Laclau and Mouffe argue, any attempt at "hegemonic" articulation—a fixation of the positions of a given discourse that at once leaves no entity unpositioned, identifies entities wholly with their assigned meanings, and resists any attempt to impress the meanings of a different discourse on entities—is doomed to failure. This conception also meets the third condition, that of treating the full range of relations as pertinent to order, for all relations among entities contribute to their positions in arrangements: As discussed in Section 4 of this chapter, spatial, causal, intentional, and prefigurational relations, among others, help determine positionality. The notion of an arrangement is thus sufficiently abstract to encompass any ordering of the entities that enter social existence. At the same time, the upcoming discussion of the dimensions of order gives the notion sufficient content to dissipate the fear that it is too abstract to be useful for theoretical and empirical purposes.

The notion of arrangements also absorbs the more restricted notions of order as regularity/pattern, stability, and interdependence. These three notions actually mark *dimensions* of order, that is, possible characteristics of arrangements. A given arrangement can be regular or irregular, stable or unstable, and these in different regards and to different degrees. Arranged entities can also be symmetrically or asymmetrically dependent. It might be objected at this point that the delimitation of a single notion of order is pointless because social life is better approached with a variety of such notions that can be called on as need or usefulness for empirical analysis dictates. The fact that the notion of arrangements absorbs alternatives, however, suggests that one can have one's cake and eat it too. It does make sense to scrutinize social affairs with a battery of order concepts such as regularity, stability, and interdependence. At the same time, these concepts mark dimensions of a more inclusive notion of order as arrangement. Thus they can be wielded coordinately as part of a single approach operating with a unified conception, not just ad hoc and in combinations dictated by empirical exigency or taste.

The inclusiveness of this conception of social order can be summed up in a terse comparison of the different notions' construals of disorder. On the assumption that disorder is the lack of order, the lack of regularity is, of course, irregularity. That of stability is instability or flux, whereas the absence of interdependence is one-way dependence or independence. Irregularity, flux, and asymmetrical dependence are possible features of arrangements (no arranged entity, however, is independent of all others). What, then, is the opposite of arrangements? Isolation, dissociation, solitariness. It is impossible, however, to imagine a human being in this condition, utterly unpositioned vis-à-vis others through arrangements of which they are parts. Even Robinson Crusoe and Theodore Kaczynski were so positioned. Disorder, in other words, amounts to derangement. A life of disorder would be one of unfathomable distress.

3. HOUSES OF CELESTIAL INDUSTRY

This section introduces one of the two empirical phenomena through which the analysis of the social site in the remainder of this book is developed: the medicinal herb business at the village of New Lebanon, New York, in the mid-1850s.[33] I first provide general information about the Shakers before describing the arrangements that helped compose this phenomenon.

Established in 1787, New Lebanon was one of seventeen Shaker villages of any appreciable size. It was also one of the two earliest. Although total membership in the United Society of Believers never topped 3,600,[34] its villages flourished in the decades between 1810 and the American Civil War. Thereafter the Society suffered steady economic decline, brought about by a number of factors including the growth of U.S. industry, improvements in transportation, an accelerating attrition of male members, an intensifying inability to attract converts, the increasingly lower literacy and commitment of those who did join, a decline in the quality of leadership, widespread fires, and mistakes as well as fraudulent and criminal dealings in the management of money. All but two of the villages were closed by the mid-1900s.

[33] The expression "celestial industry" comes from William Hepworth Dixon, *New America* 2 (New York: AMS Press, 1971 [1867]), 71.

[34] William Sims Bainbridge, "Shaker Demographics, 1840–1900: An Example of the Use of U.S. Census Enumeration Schedules," *Journal for the Scientific Study of Religion* 21 (1982): 352–65. The largest size any village reached was around 550 souls at New Lebanon in 1860.

A Shaker "village" was not a village typically conceived—with a center surrounded by residential, agricultural, hunting, industrial, and/or recreational areas—but a network of communes called "families." These families were socioeconomic units[35] existing under the auspices of religious authority and experience. A given village was composed of anywhere from two to eight such families, each family comprising between thirty and ninety individuals and serving as the social, economic, and personal center of its members' lives. A prominent feature of every family was its dwelling house, around which were arrayed at a relatively close distance various structures devoted to temporal concerns (e.g., shops, washhouses, barns, infirmaries, and kitchen gardens) and at a greater distance from which lay the family's fields and mills. The different families composing a given village normally lay short distances apart and were named in a manner (e.g., East Family, North Family) indicating geographical direction from the chief family. The latter, in turn, was typically situated at the center and called the "Church" Family because it housed the village's ministry and meetinghouse, home of Sunday services. As suggested, a Shaker's identity was tied, first, to his or her family.[36] Family members ate together in a central hall, met daily for religious and social ends, ran agricultural and manufacturing enterprises in teams, and entertained their closest personal relationships with one another.

As for government, each family had two elders and two eldresses who disposed of religious and disciplinary affairs and appointed the deacons and deaconesses in charge of the temporal enterprises. Each family also had trustees responsible for handling money, exercising legal control of the family's property, and conducting business with both the outside world and other families and villages. The elders, eldresses, and trustees were appointed by the ministry, whose jurisdiction was the village as a whole. Composed of two men and two women, this ministry tended to the village's religious-spiritual affairs and exerted general oversight over its temporal ones. The ministry, in turn, was appointed by the central ministry, which was housed in the Church Family at New Lebanon, New York. As this manner of determining leaders suggests, Shaker government was autocratic. Not only did the line of command move

---

[35] For discussion of the economic significance of the family, see Metin M. Cosgel, Thomas J. Miceli, and John E. Murray, "Organization and Distributional Equality in a Network of Communes: The Shakers," *American Journal of Economics and Sociology* 56, 2 (1997): 129–44.

[36] For discussion, see Stephen J. Stein, *The Shaker Experience in America* (New Haven: Yale University Press, 1992), 149.

decisively from the top downward, but the ministers and elders and eldresses pronounced the "general good" of the village and family, toward which most common Believers were faithfully oriented. Few democratic procedures, accordingly, were found anywhere in Shaker life. As befits, furthermore, a theocratic parental regime, daily life was subject to painstaking regulation through the occasionally revised "Millennial Laws." This codex covered most, though variable, areas of religious and temporal existence, including government, confession, tools, meals, language, animals, doorways, reading material, relationships between men and women, the organization of the day, and the furnishing of rooms.

Religion was central to Shaker life. Religious doctrines grounded their most basic practices and goals, including celibacy, equality of the sexes and races, communism, confession of sins, separation from "the world" (as the Shakers labeled non-Shakers), and pacifism.[37] Shaker religious practices also became famous in their day, in no small part because of their Sunday worship meetings, the scene of the whirling, ecstatic dances that gave them their (popular) name. Religion, however, was not confined to Sunday and other meetings. Religious aims and beliefs, as well as religion-based admonitions, permeated all Shaker secular ("temporal") domains of practice.

As just mentioned, two central practical principles governing Shaker life were celibacy and communism. (The Shakers replenished their numbers through conversion and the adoption of orphans.) Celibacy was enforced though an extensive division of the sexes embracing, among other things, physical separation (e.g., separate entrances, staircases, work buildings, and eating, not to mention sleeping quarters); elaborate regulation of interactions (e.g., injunctions not to touch or speak to one another, instructions both to confess "special feelings" for members of the opposite sex and to report compatriots' failures to report themselves); and separate lines of work (e.g., spinning, weaving, cooking, cleaning, knitting, sewing, seed and herb preparation work for the sisters; shop, mill, stable, and fieldwork for the brothers).[38] As for communism,

---

[37] For discussion, see Edward Deming Andrews, *The People Called Shakers,* new enlarged ed. (New York: Dover, 1963), chap. 6.

[38] As suggested in the preface, the Shakers seem to have succeeded reasonably well in banishing sexual relationships from their villages. For discussion, see Louis Kern, *An Ordered Love* (Chapel Hill: University of North Carolina Press, 1981), pt. 2. One piece of evidence for this claim is the relatively low number of members expelled or apostatized because of such relationships. To say that the Shakers were successful in this regard, however, is not to assert that believers were immune to carnal or romantic thoughts and inclinations. A Shakeress wrote in 1906, for example: "Of course, we

the Shakers believed that common property helped enforce joint interest and union among Believers. It should be noted that the United Society was the longest-lived dual sex communist experiment in modern, if not all of Western history.

I spoke in the preface of the harmony that reigned in Shaker villages. The Shakers ate in silence, spoke in plain language, were rarely observed either to raise their voices or to bicker, and allegedly never gave commands to one another. According to one sympathetic visitor, although the Shakers had a definite "look,"[39] their lives were not steeped in gloomy asceticism. The expressions he used to describe them were, instead, "self-restraint," "discipline," "quiet," "sober," "considered," and "conscientious."[40] An English visitor at Mount Lebanon in 1866 (the name changed from New Lebanon in 1861 with the opening of a post office) idyllically summarized their demeanor as follows: "The people are like their village; soft in speech, demure in bearing, gentle in face; a people seeming to be at peace, not only with themselves, but with nature and with heaven."[41] Although, finally, the Shakers did not enjoy luxury, their material needs were well met: They ate well and benefited from, for instance, excellent medicines and linens. A remarkable number of Believers lived beyond the age of eighty.

Stated summarily, the "average" Shaker was enmeshed in three all-encompassing teleoaffective regimes. The first and foremost was religious faith in salvation through Shaker existence, the faith that Shaker union was the heavenly kingdom. The second was the extensive governing hierarchies that stretched from the central ministry downward. The third was the surety and camaraderie of shared property, communal life, and general harmony (which

---

were forbidden to speak to them [the men] unless it was absolutely necessary, but it was surprising to see how often it seemed to be necessary. At dusk we rode home over the rough wood road, and … fell asleep to dream confusedly of plunging steers, maple candy, trees, swings, and fascinating young brethren" (Sister Marcia [Bullard], "Shaker Industries," *Good Housekeeping* 43 [1906]: 33–37, here 37). The point is that there is not much evidence of sexual and romantic *relationships*, except perhaps among teenagers, most of whom left the village when given the opportunity on coming of age. Of course, the subjugation of sexuality required relatively continuous and strenuous effort via self-monitoring and confession, among other things, and this exerted its toll. Another reason the Shakers maintained their villages relatively free of sexual transactions was that individuals who did or wanted to "get into the flesh" were free, and usually required, to leave. On this entire subject, see also Lawrence Foster, *Religion and Sexuality: Three American Communal Experiments of the Nineteenth Century* (New York: Oxford University Press, 1981), chap. 2.

39 W. D. Howells, *The Undiscovered Country* (Boston: Houghton, Mifflin, & Co., 1888), 322.
40 W. D. Howells, *Three Villages* (Boston: James R. Osgood & Co., 1884), 108.
41 Dixon, *New America*, 86.

is not to say that dissonance and dissidents were absent[42]). A Shaker's religious faith rendered his or her existence at the "bottom" of the governmental hierarchies acceptable or insignificant, while also imparting a sense of over-riding purpose and duty to daily temporal life. The governing hierarchies meted out specific orientations and directives to behavior, established spiritual and personal goals for individual Shakers, and reassured Believers of both their progress and their need for further progress toward ultimate ends. Together with religious faith, these hierarchies established discipline and the rule of life. Communitarianism, finally, was a formative backdrop of most everyday activities and interactions, as well as a key determinant of the peculiar Shaker experience of human sociality.

Shaker temporal enterprises were carried out principally under the aegis of this third teleoaffective regime, imbued also with the spirit of religious faith but largely uncoupled from the superintendence and stern love of the hierarchies. The religious basis of Shaker agricultural and manufacturing practices must be emphasized. The potent Shaker embrace of labor derived from a religious injunction to save the earth (the secular sphere). Abjuring the familiar Christian tenet that labor is a form of punishment, the Shakers instead considered it to be a means of sanctification. Labor, in fact, was almost a religious act. In Dixon's words,

> these toilers ... consider their labour on the soil as a part of their ritual, looking upon the earth as a stained and degraded sphere, which they have been called to redeem from corruption and restore to God. ... On being received into the union, [one] no longer regards the earth as a spoil to be won, but as a pledge to be redeemed. By man it fell, by man it may be restored. Every one chosen of the Father has the privilege of aiding in this redemption; not only by the toil of his hands, by the contrivance of his brain, but by the sympathies of his soul; covering the earth with verdure, filling the air with perfume, storing the granary with fruit.[43]

---

[42] This is the place to add that the main reason for apostasy, other than the desire to pursue sexual-romantic desire, was the inability to submit to hierarchical existence and to accept diminished individuality. On this topic, see Foster, *Religion and Sexuality: Three American Communal Experiments of the Nineteenth Century.* See also Stein, *The Shaker Experience in America.*

[43] Dixon, *New America*, 83–84, 103–4. Andrews writes, a bit more prosaically, that "manual labor was glorified from higher motives. It was good for both the individual soul and the collective welfare, mortifying lust, teaching humility, creating order and convenience, supplying a surplus for charity,

Indolence, consequently, was a relatively small problem in Shaker villages (though its low incidence, like that of sexual relationships, was in part the product of measures taken to prevent it). At the same time, visitors and Shaker leaders alike reported that Believers did not overwork. Shakers worked only so far as was necessary to further the project of sanctification and salvation, which in their eyes did not mean infinitely. As a result, their "combined industry did not degenerate into a rigidly regulated system ... [or] regimentation."[44] Despite this moderation and the religious underpinning of business practices, their business successes seem to have occasionally inflamed the profit motive in the forepersons and trustees running them, especially as the religious and secular orders slowly grew apart during the nineteenth century. All Shaker industries that sold to the world were profit oriented in the sense that they sought earnings with which to (1) support community projects and (2) purchase items and labor that were either needed in daily life or required in the various enterprises (e.g., raw materials and people with particular skills). For some forepersons, however, profit seems to have gained particular allure as a means of enhancing their individual status through the success of their enterprises.

Work was not just religiously infused and occasionally diverted toward the vainglorious pursuit of profit. It was also a communal effort. All Shakers performed manual labor, including the elders, eldresses, and ministers. Believers also usually rotated the jobs they carried out as their main occupation on a weekly or monthly basis. Rotation freed individual Shakers from burnout and strain in particularly taxing jobs. It also equipped them with multiple skills, which in turn subtended maximal efficiency and flexibility in their finite cooperative communities. Job rotation was used, further, as a form of discipline.[45] At the same time, individuals with highly specialized skills often continued for years to concentrate on a single trade. In many regards, consequently, the Shakers were models of cooperative efficiency. As indicated, however, the system was not democratic. Who did what when in a given business was determined by the deacon in charge; and to which enterprise a given person was

---

supporting the structure of fraternity, protecting it from the world, and strengthening it for increasing service" (*The People Called Shakers,* 104).

44 Andrews, *The People Called Shakers,* 107.

45 For a discussion of the social functions of labor in Shaker villages, see Suzanne Thurman, "'No Idle Hands Are Seen': The Social Construction of Work in Shaker Communities," *Communal Societies* (fall 1998).

assigned as his or her current chief place of labor was the decision of the family's elders and eldresses (in consultation with the deacons and deaconesses and in cognizance of a person's talents, record, and preferences—Shakers could apply to be reassigned). Another feature of this system was the relative absence of motives for individual gain. As E. V. Smalley wrote in a letter to *The New York Times,* "In place of stimulus of individual gain, there is the public spirit of the community, which spurs all laggards, and strong religious conviction of duty that makes all the members work together harmoniously."[46]

Shaker enterprises were decided successes. They supplied the villages with quality artifacts and foods in abundance; produced sturdy, handsome, and reliable items that were sought after and often renowned in the world; and secured profits sufficient to underwrite village maintenance and expansion. These accomplishments, which distinguished Shaker villages from other, shorter-lived nineteenth-century communist experiments,[47] can be credited to various factors, including the cooperative spirit with which their industries were blessed, the ability to shift people into particular industries when needed, the absence of wages, the quality of their products, Believers' incentives to be inventive, and the religious faith that sustained dedication, care, and hard work and guaranteed that the imperatives to order and to improve governed Shaker enterprises.

Individual families ran their own enterprises. As a result, business overlap and specialization occurred both in and between villages. Families in a given community sometimes united to run joint businesses and to maintain common stores for their goods. Among the many industries that served both Shaker villages and the outside world were tanning, broom making, seeds, coopering, milling, hat making, chair making, and the preparation of medicinal herbs and extracts. Other industries such as printing, shoemaking, tailoring, wagon making, furniture making, and food production provided mainly for the Shakers.

Many Shaker wares came to be as renowned for quality as their Shaker producers and merchants became well-known for honesty and fairness. The

---

[46] Quoted in Richard Ely, *The Labor Movement in America* (New York: Thomas Y. Crowell & Co., 1886), 31. The date of the letter is not given.

[47] Edward Deming Andrews stresses that the longevity of the Shaker communist scheme was grounded in its effectual practical organization (*The Community Industries of the Shakers* [Albany: State University of New York Press, 1933], 13.) For further evidence, in this case of the role that market acumen played in helping secure longevity, see John E. Murray and Metin M. Cosgel, "Market, Religion, and Culture in Shaker Swine Production, 1788–1880," *Agricultural History* 72, 3 (1998): 552–73.

understanding of work as sanctification strongly contributed to this state of affairs. Another factor was a utilitarian attitude toward knowledge, science, and technology. These were not sought for their own sake; in fact, such pursuit was condemned as trivial.[48] The Shakers eagerly sought, acquired, and used knowledge and technology whenever doing so promised to improve their agricultural or manufacturing practices or the products thereof. They kept abreast of theoretical and technological developments in the mechanical and agricultural sciences; the apprentice system was widely used; individual Shakers were encouraged both to acquire technical and mechanical skills and to develop native aptitudes; and the latest machines were avidly put to work. In the pursuit of useful knowledge, moreover, those running agricultural or manufacturing businesses conducted frequent experiments. The Shakers were also inventive folks, "per pound" apparently among the most inventive known to history. Although extreme claims have been made for the range of items they invented, they indisputably improved such devices as washing machines, threshing machines, seed planters, nails, and pens and invented or "invented" such items as the flat broom, the clothespin, the circular saw, the seed packet, and, most likely, the vacuum pan (for boiling herbs). Numerous observers agreed that one reason for this inventiveness was the fact that the benefits of innovation, in the form of release from strenuous activity and time freed for other pursuits, rebounded directly to the inventor and his or her colleagues. In the words of the Englishman Arthur Baker, the Shaker system showed that "nothing so much stimulates the inventive genius of a group as a system which enables them to reap the benefits of their own talent, and to save their own labour by whatever labour-saving devices they introduce."[49]

The Shaker medicinal herb business was one of the most extensive Shaker enterprises and also one of the nationally, and even internationally, most famous Shaker product lines. It was a pioneer in the pharmaceutical field, eventually ceding its markets to larger industrial factory operations in the last four decades of the nineteenth century. The business began inconspicuously.[50]

[48] "This life is short at the longest, and ought not to be spent in acquiring any kind of knowledge which can not be put to a good use" (Seth Y. Wells, *Remarks on Learning and the Use of Books*, 10 March 1836, Edward Deming Andrews Memorial Shaker Collection, Winterthur Library, Winterthur, Del., manuscript no. 808; quoted with permission of The Winterthur Library, Joseph Downs Collection of Manuscripts and Printed Ephemera.)

[49] Arthur Baker, *Shakers and Shakerism* (London: New Moral World Series, 1896), 16.

[50] The most informative histories of the Shaker medicinal herb businesses are contained in Galen Beale and Mary Rose Boswell, *The Earth Shall Blossom: Shaker Herbs and Gardening* (Woodstock,

In the 1780s and 90s, herbs were gathered in the wild for use in the villages, a practice that continued with regard to certain herbs for the entire life of the industry. The first mention of separate herb gardens occurs around 1800. First mention of a garden at New Lebanon, home of the largest herb operation in the middle decades of the century, occurs in 1812. During the 1810s, the New Lebanon business was operated only to raise money to purchase other medicines and therefore grew very slowly. After Eliab Harlow and Garrett Lawrence reorganized the enterprise in 1822 on a "systematic and scientific basis,"[51] it expanded rapidly. By the end of the decade, with major operations at a number of villages, the Shakers were the major suppliers of medicinal herbs to the nascent pharmaceutical trade in the United States. By 1831, New Lebanon was sending shipments around the world (California, England, France, Australia), and during this decade villages engaged in the herb business issued the first catalogues. At this time, the first medicinal herbal extracts were also manufactured, thereby adding a technical chemical component to an already formidable nexus of field and shop practices and orders. Business increased at this point: All villages producing herbs raised new herb buildings and acquired up-to-date machinery, most extensively at New Lebanon in the 1840s and 50s, the apogee of the Shaker pharmaceutical industry. In 1856, the "physics garden" at that village composed fifty acres and scores of herbs. Over 350 herbal products were offered for sale in a number of forms: as loosely packed dried herbs in tins and cylinders; as paper-wrapped bricks of pressed herbs; as ointments and powders in ceramic jars; as extracts, juices, oils, syrups, and solutions in glass vials; and as pills. The preeminence of New Lebanon in the medicinal herb industry was partly due to the inventive genius of two men, the physician Garrett Lawrence and the chemist James Long (the latter likely conceived of and developed the process of distilling herbs in a vacuum).

The herb industry did not weather the Civil War well. Signs of decline multiply after the war: The last herb catalogue was issued at Mount Lebanon, for

Vt.: Countryman Press, 1991), chaps. 2 and 7; Edward Deming Andrews and Faith Andrews, *Work and Worship Among the Shakers* (New York: Dover, 1974), chap. 2; and Amy Bess Miller, *Shaker Herbs: A History and a Compendium* (New York: Clarkson N. Potter, 1976). A short history of the New Lebanon business is found in Isaac Youngs, *A Concise View of the Church of God and of Christ on Earth Having Its Foundation in the Faith of Christ's First and Second Appearing*, New Lebanon, N.Y., 1856–60, Edward Deming Andrews Memorial Shaker Collection, Winterthur Library, Winterthur, Del., manuscript no. 861.

51 See William Proctor, "New Lebanon; Its Physics Gardens and Their Products," *American Journal of Pharmacy* 18 (1852): 88–91.

example, in 1873. The Shaker enterprises were especially eclipsed by the large commercial pharmaceutical concerns that emerged during these decades, including the patent medicine industry in the 1870s. The Shakers' industry limped along nonetheless, particular villages specializing in the production of one or a tiny number of profitable herbal medicines, and several villages belatedly launching the production of particular proprietary medicines as a less labor-intensive way of making money.[52] By the 1890s, however, the industry was more or less finished, apart from the production of a few marquee products such as the famous Norwood's Tincture of Veratrum Viride (made at Mount Lebanon until around 1934).

During the 1840s and 50s, the industry at New Lebanon exacted the involvement of between ten and twenty-five people.[53] A distinct sexual division of labor reigned. Men did most of the outside work, though men and women, joined by boys and girls, sometimes collected wild herbs together. Women did some of the inside work, above all cleaning and packaging but also extraction (until 1841 at New Lebanon, when the men assumed this task). Men, in particular, physicians, were also in charge of the overall enterprise. Demand for medicinal herbs, moreover, came almost exclusively from physicians. The Shakers' reputation for quality served them well in this market, for physicians were wary of lower quality or fraudulent medicines and many were allegedly satisfied only with Shaker herbs and herbal products.[54] Demand was so great that the herb enterprises were forced to buy extensively from the world, including European sources. (The large quantity of labels, bottles, jars, vials, and so on also had to be obtained from outside sources.) The prominence of Shaker products in this market was so pronounced that a plausible claim can be made that their medicinal herb businesses were both the first forms and direct precursors of large-scale pharmaceutical operations in the United States.[55] As one commentator said in the mid-1950s to his colleagues in the

[52] See J. Worth Estes, "The Shakers and Their Proprietary Medicines," *Bulletin of Historical Medicine* 65 (1991): 162–84.

[53] This estimate is based on a figure Benson J. Lossing gives ("The Shakers," *Harper's New Monthly Magazine* 15 [June–November 1857]: 164–77 [reprinted in Don Gifford, ed., *An Early View of the Shakers: Benson John Lossing and the Harper's Article of 1857* (Hanover and London: University Press of New England, 1989), 29–57]; 173).

[54] On the other hand, big city physicians made the brick form in which Shakers sold herbs the "food of merriment" when they were first sold in Boston. See Isaac Hill, "The Shakers," *Farmer's Monthly Visitor* 2, 8, 31 August 1840, pp. 113–18.

[55] There is some lack of clarity about the founding of the rival medicinal herb firm of Tilden & Co., which was located across the Lebanon Valley from New Lebanon. Whereas Miller dates the firm to

pharmaceutical industry: "It appears that the Shakers pioneered, or at least contributed much to the manufacture of our pharmaceuticals such as extracts, inspissated juices, essential oils, distilled and fragrant waters, and other products. . . . In the thinking of most of us the drug manufacturing industry in this country was almost unheard of until after the Civil War. On the other hand the Shakers had approached the peak of their herb and drug industry prior to this time."[56]

At New Lebanon in the mid-1850s, the production component of the medicinal herb business, under the overall charge of the trustee Edward Fowler, was stationed in three buildings.[57] The two principal buildings were the herb house and the extract house. The business, incidentally, also had field and marketing components, which are generally ignored in the following. The herb house, a former granary, was a good-sized building measuring 120 feet in length and roughly 40 feet in width. It boasted two stories along with a basement and an attic. A person entering the building on the first floor encountered the business office, the packing room, the papering room, and several storerooms. The business office was where James Vail kept records. In the packing room, the province for a time of Jethro Turner, pressed herbs were prepared for sale, while in the papering (or print) room, the province of Samuel

---

1824 (*Shaker Herbs: A History and a Compendium*, 30), Andrews and Andrews place its start in 1847–48 (*Work and Worship Among the Shakers*, 68).

[56] Charles Lee, "The Shakers as Pioneers in the American Herb and Drug Industry," talk given to the American Pharmaceutical Association, 1959, Edward Deming Andrews Memorial Shaker Collection, Winterthur Library, Winterthur, Del., manuscript no. 1203, 8, 12; quoted with permission of The Winterthur Library, Joseph Downs Collection of Manuscripts and Printed Ephemera. Compare the earlier words of a colleague in the pharmaceutical line: "The Shakers propagated medicinal plants as early as 1825, long before such cultivation became widely spread in the United States. They also devised the famous system for taking down medicinal extracts 'in vacuo,' and their vacuum apparatus was a model for the great medicine industry of today" (George Niles Hoffman, "Mt. Lebanon Medicine Makers—The Shakers," *Pharmaceutical Era* [July 1920]: 229). In fact, however, it remains unclear whether the New Lebanon Shakers or the aforementioned firm of Tilden & Co. invented the famous vacuum extract process.

[57] The primary sources of the following description of the medicinal herb production orders are Benson J. Lossing, "The Shakers," 164–77 (repr. in Don Gifford, ed., *An Early View of the Shakers*, 29–57); William Proctor, "New Lebanon; Its Physics Gardens and Their Products;" *Herb Medicine Department Records*, 1869, Emma B. King Library, Shaker Museum and Library, Old Chatham, N.Y., manuscript no. 4456; *Center Family Journal*, New Lebanon, 1848–57, Emma B. King Library, Shaker Museum and Library, Old Chatham, N.Y., manuscript no. 8831; *Account Book*, New Lebanon, 1860–62, Edward Deming Andrews Memorial Shaker Collection, Winterthur Library, Winterthur Del., manuscript no. 839; Alonzo Hollister, *Daily Journal of Extract Business Kept by A. G. H.*, New Lebanon, 1856–60, Shaker Manuscripts, Series III: B 19, Western Reserve Historical Society, Cleveland.

Johnson, labels for the packaged herbs came off a printing press. (Labels were also printed by the C. V. Benthuysen Company of New York, as were catalogues and receipt books.) Packaged herbs were stowed in the storerooms, as were the various supplies the business required such as paper, boxes, and tins.

The heavier machinery was found in the basement. Chief among these were the presses,[58] one of them hydraulic, which compressed the herbs into the block forms in which they were primarily sold. These blocks were three to six inches in length and two inches thick on average, and as they came off the presses auxiliary apparatuses received them. The presses were attached by rotating shafts to the power system, a horse that tread in circles, also located in the basement. In the second floor and attic, the sisters dried the herbs and roots. Doing this involved laying the green leaves and roots "on sheets of canvas, about fourteen inches apart, supported by cords"[59] and opening the many windows whenever possible to ensure good circulation of air. Ringing the rooms on the second floor were large, tight bins in which dried herbs were stored before being brought below for chopping and pressing. In the rooms on this floor, the sisters also picked over and cleaned the green herbs as they arrived from the gardens and woods. A water pipe conducted water there for this purpose. Other equipment employed in the industry, for instance, the cutting machines used initially to chop dried herbs into smaller pieces, was installed either in the basement or in a room on the first floor immediately above the horse power. The herb house was a bustling place, its customary staff of ten rising to twenty or more as need demanded. It was also surrounded by several outhouses, one of which contained a kiln for drying. Hoisting works and scales, finally, were attached to the outside of the house for the purpose of raising the green herbs and roots to the second floor.

The extract house, the province of the chemist James Long and his assistant as well as successor Alonzo Hollister, was the site where extracts, ointments, oils, and some of the business's powders were produced. It contained a far

---

[58] So claims Proctor. Lossing, by contrast, implies that the pressing was done on the first floor, though his text is not clear on this point. Proctor's description, incidentally, is not unproblematic. For instance, he writes that a steam boiler stood at one end of the basement. According to Alonzo Hollister, about whom more will be said shortly, (1) the first steam boiler used in New Lebanon was installed in the extract house when it was built in 1850, and (2) horse power was introduced to the herb building in September 1852 (Hollister, *Daily Journal of Extract Business Kept by A. G. H.*). Before the latter date, consequently, and thus at the time when Proctor visited New Lebanon in 1851, it is possible that a steam boiler powered the presses and cutting machines. It would have been odd, however, to later replace more advanced technology with its less up-to-date predecessor.

[59] Lossing, "The Shakers," 172.

greater variety of machinery than did the herb house and was a bit smaller in size, thirty-six by one hundred feet. Erected in 1850, it was as up-to-date as any contemporaneous U.S. pharmaceutical business. Operations there revolved about the laboratory, where the herbs and roots were boiled and pressed and their juices extracted. This room contained kettles (for boiling herbs and roots), grated cylinder presses, or "fluid extract barrels" (for extracting juices from boiled herbs and roots under pressure), stills, "steam chests," and iron-skirted copper pans (for boiling down the extracted juices or the solutions formed by steeping bark), benches (on which to place pans), shelves (for bottles), and a large boiler (for producing steam; it was so large that it was installed before the building's frame was constructed). For the purpose of boiling, moreover, some juices were conveyed to the huge copper vacuum pan mentioned above, which was located on the second floor. The water used in these operations was conveyed to the building via pipes from a spring one-eighth of a mile distant. The laboratory must have been a scorching place to work in the summer.

The presses used in the extract operations were distributed between the first and second floors. On the first floor, in a room adjoining the large laboratory, the crushing mill that mashed raw herbs to smaller sizes was operated. On this floor, too, I surmise (judging from the shape of the building), stood a grist-mill for cracking seeds, a pug mill and power press for crushing herbs, and a cutting machine for initial reduction. Activities carried out at the herb house were duplicated in its extract counterpart because the production of extracts and ointments and the preparation of herb blocks required many of the same operations. On the second floor in a room next to the one housing the vacuum pan also stood the powdering mills ("chasers"), which reduced the crushed herbs and roots to fine powder. All these presses and mills, together with the vacuum pan, were powered by a steam engine, which stood in the basement and to which they were connected by a series of shafts, wheels, and belts. An air pump was used to evacuate the vacuum pan and stills. On the first floor, in addition, was the preparation room, where the sisters, with occasional help from the brothers, poured and placed the extracts, powders, and ointments into earthen, glass, tin, and wooden containers of varied sizes and shapes. They also washed used containers that had come back from the industry's customers. Considerable space, moreover, had to be devoted to the storage of the business's products and implements (e.g., balances, pails, dippers, measures, graduated glasses, bottles, jars, bottles, tin boxes, alcohol). The herb house, finally, also had a drying kiln, probably located outside, as well as a place where herbs were mixed with alcohol in barrels to macerate. For several years in the late 1850s, it might be added, some of the village's boys slept in the building's attic.

The medicinal herb industry made use of a third building as well, the dairy house, where the finishing room was located. Here the sisters cut labels and packaged as well as labeled the already prepared medicines for sale. This structure was a building-of-all-trades, because it also housed the tailoresses in addition to dairy operations.

4. DIMENSIONS OF ARRANGEMENTS

Social orders are the ensembles of entities, through and amid which social life transpires—the arrangements of people, artifacts, organisms, and things that characterize human coexistence. All social life is marked by social orders. In such orders, moreover, entities relate, enjoy meaning (and identity), and are positioned with respect to one another. All social life exhibits, as a result, relatedness, meaning, and mutual positioning. I emphasize that the following discussion of relations, meaning, and positionality is not intended to examine these ponderous topics in great depth. It addresses them only in the detail required to fill out my analysis of social orders and to prepare the ground for upcoming discussions of both the relations between practices and orders and the site of social life.

SOCIAL RELATIONS

Relations among the components of arrangements form a complex, polychromatic dimension of social order. These relations are social relations to the extent that they help constitute social life. Before describing four basic relations among components, three conceptions of social relation must be set aside.

Logicians analyze relations abstractly. Anything expressible in the formula aRb, thus anything that connects, conjugates, or juxtaposes entities, counts as a relation. Given my construal of "social" as pertaining to coexistence, any conjoining of items is a social relation, logically, if it helps constitute a state of human coexistence. This notion of relation is simply too abstract to be of much use. In specifying nothing further about the identity or nature of social relations than what is already contained in the concept of the social, it permits an infinite number of states of affairs to qualify as social relations. It thus fails to provide a content-full specification of the character of such relations. There is nothing conceptually amiss in characterizing social relations in this manner and thereby construing the social site as home to an infinite number of orders. Doing so, however, does not further the cause of social analysis. A social relation must not be construed *merely* as anything expressible in the formula aRb that helps constitute human coexistence.

Many social theorists have restricted the appellation "social relation" to relations among people. One prominent subgroup of these theorists—embracing structuralists, systems theorists, and some Marxists—construes the people involved not as concrete individuals, but as types thereof. One paradigm category of such types is roles. According to theorists of this sort who work with this category, social relations hold between roles, and the totality of relations characteristic of particular social phenomena such as an institution (e.g., the Catholic Church) or a social sector (e.g., an economy) is the texture of relations that hold among the roles that individuals occupy in that institution or sector. In this sense of "relation," Karl Marx wrote: "Society does not consist in individuals, but expresses the sum of relations within which these individuals stand."[60] (An example of the sort of relation he had in mind is Capitalist-Formally Free Worker.)

The paramount problem with abstract relations of this sort (and with the social structures composed of systems of them) is that it is not certain that they exist outside the minds and texts of analysts.[61] Consider, for instance, the relation, elder-common believer. What evidence is there that such a relation exists and that the concept of it is not simply a convenient way of thinking-via-simplification of the messy plexus composed both of interactions between elders and common Believers (individually or in groups) and of the understandings, rules, thoughts, emotions, and ends bound up with these interactions? Contrary to the claims of some theorists,[62] there are no events whose explanation necessitates or even recommends the postulation of abstract social relations as entities with powers of determination. The details of particular

---

[60] Karl Marx, *Grundrisse,* trans. Martin Nicolaus (New York: Vintage, 1973), 265.

[61] It should be counted part of Lévi-Strauss's eminence that he squarely faced this problem in relation to his own structures and bit the bullet. See Claude Lévi-Strauss, *Structural Anthropology,* trans. Claire Jacobson and Brooke Grundfest Schoepf (New York: Basic Books, 1963).

[62] A fine example is found in Roy Bhaskar, *The Possibility of Naturalism* (Atlantic Highlands, N.J.: Humanities Press, 1979), chap. 2.

actions and interactions, and of their situations and wider contexts, suffice for explanatory purposes. Nor can these abstract relations be experienced empirically. What can be directly observed or perceived (I leave this notion unanalyzed) are elders, their charges, and many, though not all, of the actions and interactions that join them. Because the elder-common believer relation is neither a source of determination nor an object of experience, there is insufficient ground to countenance its existence. I do not deny that it might, nonetheless, make sense to speak of "the" relation between elder and common believer. Perhaps such a relation is a collection of generalizations about the individuals occupying these roles; perhaps it is an "ideal type" with which an investigator can pry apart the structure of social reality; perhaps it is a topic written about in Shaker and academic texts. I do not attempt to adjudicate this issue.

Another group of theorists restricts the term "social relation" to interactions among particular human beings. Most directly associated with the loose collection of thinkers labeled "symbolic interactionists," this conception enjoys widespread acceptance. One of its virtues is that it gives the term "social relation" greater empirical concreteness. It is, however, too narrowly focused, and in two regards. First, not all relations among people that are of importance for the setup and progress of social affairs are interactions. Citizens, for example, stand in various relations to the rulers of their municipalities, states, and countries, regardless of the extent to which these relations assume the form of, or consist in, interactions. Shakers, for example, wherever they lived, stood in varied relations to the individuals composing the central ministry in New Lebanon. These relations were not reducible, however, to whatever direct interactions individual Shakers might have had with the ministers and could exist even in the complete absence of such interactions. The holding of these relations was also not just a matter of some *totality* of interactions, involving many individuals, which linked particular Shakers to the distant ministers via extended sequences. Individual members' thoughts about and attitudes toward the ministers also, for instance, helped constitute such relations. Second, this circumscription of "social relation" neglects the various connections both among nonhumans and between humans and nonhumans that contribute to human coexistence. Working together in the extract house, James Long's and Alonzo Hollister's lives were closely entwined through more than whatever direct interactions transpired between them. Their lives also hung together via connections between, for example, the boiler on the one hand and the presses, mills, and vacuum pan on the other, and between Long's tinkering with one device and Hollister's constant repairing of another. Indeed, remarkably many states of coexistence among human beings embrace concrete connections involving nonhumans. *Social* relations, consequently, cannot be restricted to relations among humans alone.

An adequate account of social relations must satisfy at least two desiderata. First, it must construe relations as links among particular entities, as opposed to types or hypostatized abstractions. Second, it must cover the full range of connections among components of arrangements through which human lives hang together, not just links that join humans directly.

The following are four principal sorts of social relations. I do not aver that these are the only sorts, only that they are pervasive and crucial.

Causal Relations
For purposes of the present discussion, I treat causality as the relation of bringing about. Two forms of this relation are paramount in social arrangements.[63] The first is one entity's actions *making* something *happen*. The second is one entity's actions or conditions *leading to* another entity's action(s). To say that actions/conditions lead to actions is to say that the latter respond to the former. Causal relations hold among entities by virtue of action: either by virtue of action having some effect or by virtue of something triggering action.

The first sort of causal relation is intuitively obvious. It is instantiated among humans whenever a person's action(s) directly brings some state about, as when a loud shout startles another person or a blow to the head draws blood. It is also instantiated whenever people intervene in the world and bring about changes there. Long and Hollister, for instance, were constantly arranging things, taking them apart, moving them around, and so forth. All these interventions in the world were causal operations on it. Similarly, the doings of nonhumans alter and leave their marks on both humans and other nonhumans. Chopping machines too often lopped off digits, and horses and steam powered the presses.

The second sort of causal relation is instantiated among humans when something about one person, for instance, what he does, what he says, or the events that befall her, are something to which another person reacts. In a conversation, for example, persons respond to one another's assertions and gestures:

[63] For detailed discussion of types of causal relations prominent in social life, see my essay, "Social Causality," *Inquiry* 31, 2 (1988): 151–70.

Particular assertions and gestures are the causes of further actions in the sense that they lead to these further actions. This causality differs from the making happen sort. If I loudly shout a question at you, I might make you shake, but I do not make you answer. My asking the question is, instead, something to which you respond with an utterance, gesture, or disregard. It leads to your action and thereby brings it about.

It is worth elucidating this second type of causality further. When someone makes something happen, what happens, as it were, just happens. The actor is responsible for what occurs, and what happens itself does nothing in order to happen (causal consequences of action complicate this formulation). When, on the other hand, something leads to someone's action, the person who responds carries responsibility for the effect: He or she *does* something that constitutes the response and usually could have acted differently. These facts might lead some to deny that the leading to, or inducement, relation is a type of causality. What leads to an action, however, also bears responsibility for the action; that is to say, it—and not just the actor—has a hand to play in this here action being performed in this here situation. This fact justifies the appellation "causality." At almost any moment, people are up to something, pursing ends and carrying out projects. On encountering or learning about this or that, they hold up their activity, pursue different courses of action, alter plans, and so on. What I call the phenomena that "lead to" actions are the phenomena that induce people to hold up, divert, alter. These phenomena cause changes in the flow of action.

For the present, I leave open whether this second causal relation, paradigmatically instantiated in one person's actions leading to another's, is instantiated between humans and nonhumans or between nonhumans. I think it is, but the issue is under what conditions. The two types of causal relation, by the way, also underwrite the idea of causal chains of action, which are series of actions each member of which is a response to its predecessor or to a change in the world that its predecessor brought about.[64]

Spatial Relations
The entities that compose an arrangement are all physical entities (though not merely physical entities). As such, they compose an objective spatial ordering

---

[64] For further discussion, see Georg Henrik von Wright, *Explanation and Understanding* (Ithaca: Cornell University Press, 1971), chap. 4, and my essay, "Social Causality."

embracing diverse relations, such as further from, closer to, in the vicinity of, next to, between, inside, and outside. It is not pertinent to the current discussion to inquire whether these relations are better analyzed absolutely or relatively. It is, nonetheless, apposite to recall that until the 1960s (and arguably even after) the physical relationships of humans to the earth and its gravitational field founded the objective physical spatiality of social orders. Physical spatial relations are not, however, the only sort inhabiting social life.

The entities that compose social orders also assume positions in spatialities of nonphysical sorts. Broaching this topic anticipates a theme of the following chapter, namely, that social orders answer to contexts that help position their constituents. Vis-à-vis space, what I have in mind is twofold. To begin with, physical space underlies other objective spaces. An example is the distribution of human activities (in physical space), which some geographers call "activity space." Activity space is not a physical matrix because its constituents are actions. Its objectivity nonetheless derives from the locations in physical space where activities take place. More categorically disparate is, second, something that can be called "activity-place space." Spaces of this sort are composed of places and paths, where a place is defined as a location to X (where X is an action), and a path is defined as a place of a particular sort, namely, a place to get from one location to another. An activity-place space is a matrix of places and paths where activities are performed. These places and paths are invariably stationed, furthermore, at particular entities. Insofar, consequently, as these entities are physical beings, places and paths are anchored in physical space. The objects found, say, in the laboratory of the extract house anchored a variety of places, for example, a place to macerate herbs, a place to boil them, and a place to reduce the resulting liquids. This fact is reflected in the names given to and the definitions of these objects: maceration barrels, kettles, evaporation pans. (Think also of the bedroom, kitchen, or office.)

A further feature of activity-place space is that, to the extent that the activities that are to occur in a given locale are interdependent, sequenced, and nested, the places where these activities are to take place are similarly interdependent, sequenced, and nested. Indeed, rooms, buildings, and housing complexes, even whole communities and urban expanses, are laid out with an eye to such activity-place relations. The laboratory's kettles, stills, and chests were laid out with an eye to what would be done with them, how these activities interconnected, and thus what places these entities would anchor in the activity-place space of the laboratory. For instance, the place to draw liquors from the fluid extract barrels needed to be convenient, sufficiently expansive, and so anchored as to permit the smooth transition from extraction to reduction of the liquors via boiling. In 1861, accordingly, the eight barrels were set on a bench near the iron-skirted copper pans to allow the liquor to be drawn off underneath.[65] To the objective spatial relations of physical entities must be added activity-place spatial relations of objects of use.[66]

Intentionality

Two entities can be related by way of one of them performing actions toward or having thoughts, beliefs, intentions, and emotions about the other. In philosophical parlance, the second is that toward which the first is directed by virtue of one or more of its mental states or actions. When an entity is directed toward an object in this way, it can be said to stand in an "intentional" relation to this object. Intentional relations are social relations when they help compose human coexistence. Although the nature of mentality/activity is an abstruse philosophical problem of immense significance, it need not be addressed for the purposes of analyzing social orders. The language of mentality and activity is the principal medium of the everyday propositional understanding that people have of themselves and others. As a result, any reader of this text, and any analyst of social life, is familiar with the ideas (1) that people perform actions and have understandings, thoughts, emotions, and so on; and (2) that these actions, understandings, thoughts, and emotions are about or directed toward things. This familiarity permits deployment of these notions in the following. An issue of greater relevance that is touched on Chapter 4 is the range of entities that can be in these conditions.

Prefiguration

By "prefiguration," I mean how the world channels forthcoming activity. Chapter 4 examines this phenomenon in detail, in particular, how at any moment the site of the social prefigures the flow of activity by qualifying the possible paths it can take. For present purposes, prefiguration can be equated with a

---

[65] *Account Book,* New Lebanon, 1860–62, entry for 31 May 1861.

[66] For further elaboration of activity-place space, see my essay, "Spatial Ontology and Explanation," *Annals of the Association of American Geographers* 81, 4 (1991): 650–70. For two of the rare examples of social analyses that work with some notion of activity-place space, see Anthony Giddens, "Time, Space, and Regionalization," in *Social Relations and Spatial Structures,* ed. Derek Gregory and John Urry (London: Macmillan, 1985), 265–95; and Edward Soja, *Postmodern Geographies* (London: Verso, 1989), chap. 6.

more familiar phenomenon, constraint and enablement. The present state of social affairs prefigures forthcoming activity by constraining and enabling it.

The figure of enablement-constraint has acquired immense prominence in recent years. Lying behind its rise in fortune is the desire to identify another form of determination in social life than causality. This desire has especially seized those theorists who want to square the conviction that abstract structures possess powers of determination with the realization that according such structures causal powers vis-à-vis human action denies the individual and collective agencies to which the historical record steadfastly attests.[67] Conceiving of these powers as the enablement and constraint of agency leaves room for structure and agency alike. The figure of enablement-constraint is not, however, limited to reconceptualizations of structure. Foucault's notorious concept of power, for instance, is defined through it. "The exercise of power," he wrote, "is not simply a relationship between partners, individual or collective.... It is ... always a way of acting upon an acting subject or acting subjects by virtue of their acting or being capable of action. A set of actions upon other actions."[68] What this means is that the relationship proper to power is government, where "To govern ... is to structure the possible field of action of others."[69] Power, accordingly, consists in actions of one or more persons enabling and constraining the actions of others.

In writing that power extends into the "capillaries" of social life, Foucault telescoped enablement and constraint into the minutest nooks of human activity. What enables and constrains actions, however, is not actions alone. Artifacts, organisms, and things, typically in combination and as arranged, also do so. More generally, the different components of arrangements enable and constrain one another's activities. Prefiguration, consequently, is a fourth category of relation among such components and a fourth type of social relation. Notice that prefiguration is a relation among the components of arrangements and not one between abstract structures and actions. The ubiquity of the mutual enablement and constraint of such components, individually and

---

[67] Among the "neo-abstract structuralists" caught in this vice are Pierre Bourdieu, Anthony Giddens, and Roy Bhaskar. See, for example, Pierre Bourdieu, *Outline of a Theory of Practice*, trans. Richard Nice (Cambridge: Cambridge University Press, 1976); Giddens, *Central Problems in Social Theory*; and Bhaskar, *The Possibility of Naturalism*.

[68] Michel Foucault, "The Subject and Power," afterword to Hubert L. Dreyfus and Paul Rabinow, *Michel Foucault: Beyond Structuralism and Hermeneutics* (Chicago: University of Chicago Press, 1982), 208–27, here 219, 220.

[69] Foucault, "The Subject and Power," 221.

collectively, bespeaks the propitiousness of Foucault's infamous claim that power is everywhere.

An arrangement's components are linked through a tangle of causal, spatial, intentional, and prefigurational relations. This means that entities form arrangements by virtue of taking up or occupying relations of these sorts (usually a combination of them). Long, Hollister, and the extract machinery, for example, formed an arrangement via relations of all these sorts, as did this arrangement together with the machinery for and the personnel at work chopping herbs in the adjacent room, as did this larger arrangement together with the sisters, their vials, jars, and labels, and the preparation room in the dairy house. The fact that arrangements link in larger arrangements raises the issue of the demarcation of arrangements. Definite causal, spatial, intentional, and enablement/constraint relations exist among people, artifacts, organisms, and things. The dispositions of these relations do not themselves, however, institute specific arrangements: The set of relations that existed among the personnel, artifacts, organisms, and things of the New Lebanon pharmaceutical industry did not entail that these entities and relations were intrinsically marked out into specific arrangements with definite boundaries—for instance, the three nested arrangements mentioned two sentences above. The specification of these three arrangements was an act of choice on my part; and someone else could identify different arrangements at the herb industry without falsifying the reality composed of the tangle of relations that existed among the industry's personnel, artifacts, organisms, and things. In other words, the materiality as and through which social life transpires is not—as far as relations alone are concerned—intrinsically broken into specific arrangements. The demarcation of specific arrangements is, instead, relative to the interests and purposes of the demarcator. This relativism parallels an oft-noted feature of causal judgment: Whereas a range of factors invariably "contributes" to the occurrence of a given fact, identifying which factor was "the cause" is a matter of interest- and context-driven judgment.[70]

In the following chapter, it emerges that the existence of distinct arrangements depends on a third thing—practices—in addition to relations and interests/purposes. This fact attenuates the above relativism. For the time being, I note that arrangements cannot be arbitrarily demarcated. Just as causal judgment,

---

[70] This structure of causal judgment is most famously discussed in H. L. A. Hart and A. M. Honore, *Causation in the Law* (New York: Oxford University Press, 1959). See also Samuel Gorovitz, "Causal Judgements and Causal Explanations," *Journal of Philosophy* 62, 23, 2 December 1965, pp. 695–711.

in identifying the cause of an event, must choose from among the factors at work, so, too, must delimitations of arrangements attend to relations among entities (though not to these alone). Relations, moreover, are so distributed as to compose contours, densities, regions, and constellations. Although such phenomena do not determine unique boundaries, the analyst interested in registering reality must respect them when demarcating arrangements.

BEING

As indicated, the components of an arrangement boast meanings and/or identities that derive in part from relations (and in part from practices). Indeed, an arrangement comprehends a realm of inter-related meanings that encompasses all its elements. The current section engages two issues. The first is the nature of social meaning, identity, and position. The second is the question, What establishes meaning? Consideration of the second issue spills over into subsequent chapters.

Meaning, Identity, Position

By "meaning," I mean what something is and by "identity" who someone is. As indicated, identity is a subtype of meaning that is dignified with its own name in line with humanist convictions that people are metaphysically disparate from nonhumans. As I understand matters, entities with an identity are entities that have an understanding of their own meaning.[71] Entities that enjoy meaning but not identity are something, but they have no understanding of this. This construal of identity entails that the meaning of an entity with identity is binary in a way that the meaning of one without it is not. What I mean is that a person's identity embraces two analytically distinguishable and possibly divergent components: that person's meaning and that person's understanding of his or her meaning. The fact that identity possesses these two components opens the possibility of people's self-understandings diverging from the identities attributed to and foisted on them by or through others. To forestall misunderstandings, moreover, I add that nothing in the following presumes that members of the species *Homo sapiens* alone can have identities. Identity is part of a package of mentality and activity attributed to people.

---

[71] This definition bears obvious and intended affinity to Heidegger's definition of *Dasein* as the being constituted by an understanding of (its own) being. See Martin Heidegger, *Being and Time,* trans. John Macquarrie and Edward Robinson (Oxford: Blackwell, 1978), second introduction.

Whether other entities partake of identity is a matter of how similar they are to us, how we interact with them in living with them, and the results of empirical research.

Consider Alonzo Hollister. His identity was manifold. He was extractor, experimenter, repairman, wild herb picker, builder (of buildings and air pumps), and keeper of inventories, among other things. There is good evidence that other Shakers took him to be all these things, and I see no reason not to think that he, too, understood himself in these ways. Of course, these meanings did not exhaust his identity. He was also writer of theological texts, recorder of testimonials, author of pamphlets and monographs, copier of visions, narratives, and poems, brother, member of the second order of the Church Family of New Lebanon, and eventually elder, as well as worshiper, dancer, consumer of hearty Shaker meals—and of course Shaker.[72] (Although this name was originally coined by outsiders as a term of derision, the Shakers eventually embraced it.) Similar statuses composed the meaning, that is identity, of the sisters who worked in the dairy house. Someone such as Nancy Dow, for instance, was bottle washer, packer, labeler, picker of wild herbs, on the one hand, housecleaner, grape picker, carpet darner, and repairer of a particular man's clothing, on another, as well as sister, member of the Church Family, worshiper, dancer, consumer, and Shaker. Of course, not all components of Hollister's or Dow's identity were relevant or lived while they worked in the medicinal herb industry. While at work, Hollister was, and understood himself as being, the various things initially listed above. It would have made little sense for him, and he would not have got very far if he had tried, to be dancer or hearty consumer. Apparently, however, there was abundant opportunity to be theologian while on the job: "And there was considerable opportunity to read & write—particularly mornings & evenings & Sabbath days—& other times, when resting, or waiting to begin a job, or watching the liquor in the pan evaporating."[73]

Identity is clearly a complicated affair. Each Shaker who participated in the medicinal herb business, however, possessed a chief identity qua such participant. This is made clear in the records the families kept. In 1857, the Center (Second Order Church) Family Journal listed the individual brethren's and

---

[72] See Diane Sasson, "A 19th-Century Case Study: Alonzo Giles Hollister (1830–1911)," *Shaker Quarterly* 17 (1989): 154–72, 188–93.

[73] Alonzo Hollister, "Reminiscences of a Soldier of the Cross," Shaker Manuscripts, Series X: B 31, Western Reserve Historical Society, Cleveland. Quoted in Sasson, "A 19th-Century Case Study: Alonzo Giles Hollister (1830–1911)," 160, and requoted with permission of the Western Reserve Historical Society.

sisters' primary occupations. Six brethren were connected to the herb industry. Long was identified as "Chemist & Extract maker" and Hollister as "Clerk and Herb packer." As explained in the previous section, the elders and eldresses, deacons and deaconesses, and trustees of a given family assigned individual Shakers to particular temporal businesses, where the responsible deacons (deaconesses) and forepersons would further assign them to particular tasks. Who an individual was, what both the individual and others took her or him to be, centered around these assignments. The fact that diarists and "journalists" routinely referred to brethren and sisters as "the farmers," "the masons," "the broom makers," and so on further reveals this state of affairs. In addition, particular Shakers, typically brethren, were tinkers, designers, and engineers for all a family's operations and not just for particular industries. At Hancock, Massachusetts, in the 1850s, for example, George Whiting was chief designer of machines, apparatuses, and products for the Church Family.

Many of the above meanings-identities are what in sociological discourse were once, and are still today sometimes, called "roles." I do not attempt to ascertain the extent to which people's meanings-identities can be adequately conceptualized as roles. I should acknowledge, however, that my notion of meaning resembles contemporary conceptions of subject positions. Giddens develops one such conception as a substitute for the notion of a role. A social position, he writes, is "a social identity that carries with it a certain range (however diffusely specified) of prerogatives and obligations that an actor who is accorded that identity ... may activate or carry out."[74] By contrast, the essential aspect of a meaning, on my understanding, is not whatever prerogatives and obligations might be associated with it. Although prerogatives and obligations were associated with being chemist, wild herb picker, consumer of food, worshiper, recorder of testimonials, and so on, these prerogatives and obligations were not just diffuse and changing, but also *derivative* from these meanings.[75]

The notion of identity qua understood meaning also bears a strong resemblance to poststructural conceptions of subject positions. The grandfather of

[74] Giddens, *Central Problems in Social Theory*, 117. On 115–17, Giddens summarizes criticisms of the notion of a role. See also the analysis of positions as sets of rights and duties in Wendy Hollway, "Gender Difference and The Production of Subjectivity," in *Changing the Subject*, ed. J. Henriques et al. (London: Methuen, 1984), 227–63.

[75] In some of her work, Judith Butler seems to treat positions as bundles of norms, where norms pertain to intelligibility and not to propriety: To occupy a position is something like being intelligible as such and such. I believe this conception approximates my own, though I am wary of conceptualizing norms as axes of intelligibility. Butler, in any event, does not develop the conception explicitly. See Judith Butler, *Bodies That Matter: On the Discursive Limits of "Sex"* (New York: Routledge, 1993).

such conceptions is Foucault's notion of the "positions of subjectivity," which help compose the enunciative modalities of a discourse.[76] For Foucault, a subject position is a position that a person can occupy vis-à-vis objects and object domains. One prominent type thereof is perceptual positions such as listener, seer, and observer. Another is information-network positions such as teacher, trainer, student, questioner, describer, and sender or recipient of observations or theoretical propositions. According to Foucault, subject positions are discursive statuses that are made available to people insofar as they participate in discursive practices.

Foucault's association of subject positions with discourse has undergirded subsequent poststructural analyses of subject positions as discursive phenomena. There are, of course, many divergent interpretations of discursivity. These interpretations divide, moreover, on the relations of discourse to language and to practices. Setting aside the many issues that arise in this complicated terrain, I want only to point out that people's meanings-identities must not be treated principally as linguistic phenomena. They are, instead, practice phenomena with linguistic aspects. There are two typical ways that practical subject positions are taken to be linguistic entities.

The first way is to treat subject positions as words. As explained, Laclau and Mouffe analyze discourses as constellations of meaningful actions, words, and objects. Just as Foucault's discourses hold open enunciative positions for people, those of Mouffe and Laclau hold out subject positions for actors.[77] Although Laclau and Mouffe do not fully clarify the concept, it seems at times that a subject position is a word that belongs to a particular discourse and that is applied to people whose actions are also part of that discourse.[78] The meanings of people should not, however, be collapsed to words. Just what Hollister was as inventor, wild herb picker, consumer, and the like was not fully captured by his and others' application of certain words to him. Indeed, even though meanings and the words designating them were closely associated in Shaker life, his being these things did not require that any particular words be used to describe him.[79]

---

[76] Foucault, *The Archaeology of Knowledge*, pt. II, chap. 4.

[77] Laclau and Mouffe, *Hegemony and Socialist Strategy*, 114–22.

[78] See also Chantal Mouffe, "Feminism, Citizenship, and Radical Democratic Politics," in *Feminists Theorize the Political*, ed. Judith Butler and Joan Scott (London: Routledge, 1992), 369–84.

[79] This observation raises an issue that an epistemology of social investigation based on the ontology defended in this book would have to address: how an investigator identifies meaning, that is to say, the meanings of the components of arrangements. Indeed, such an epistemology would have to

A second overly discursive interpretation of identity is to treat the occupation of subject positions as a purely discursive affair. A good example is found
in Bronwyn Davies and Rom Harré's analysis of positioning as a conversational
phenomenon.[80] According to Davies and Harré, occupying positions is a matter of how people take up and are located in positions both in their own and
others' talk and in their own and others' interpretation of others' speech acts
and talk. The authors offer a superlative analysis of this discursive constitution,
emphasizing the story lines people draw on in talking and interpreting. A person's identity, however, is not just conversationally constituted. Rather, it is
constituted in the full range of actions that he or she performs or that are
performed toward him or her. What Hollister was as extractor, wild herb
picker, and consumer is not adequately conceived of as something established
through his and other Shakers' speech acts and interpretations thereof. Being
these things was, instead, a dense reality that he and other Shakers lived and
understood as they carried on Shaker practices and fitted into various arrangements. Meaning and identity are determinations of being that are established
in the full complexity of the flow of social life. They are neither merely words
(or concepts) that designate these determinations nor discursive products that
arise solely from the talk and conversation that occur as part of this flow.

My focus to this point has been the meanings-identities of people. The
meanings of artifacts, organisms, and things are less complex. The copper
evaporating pans, for example, were principally containers for boiling down
the juices or solutions formed by steeping and boiling herbs and roots. Their
being this required that they also be a number of other things, such as instruments attached to the boiler and equipment periodically in need of cleaning.
The extract operations did not always go smoothly, moreover, so they were also
at times contraptions in need of repair or equipment requiring a new coat of
varnish. Given the keen Shaker interest in improving and adopting the latest
technology, the copper pans were also artifacts to redesign and improve. At

---

explain how an investigator can identify not just meanings, but also relations and positions as well
as practices and "bundles of practices and arrangements" (see Chapter 3). Summarily stated, my
position is that all these phenomena are revealed in actions and in the language people use to talk
about their lives. Incidentally, because the people described in the current text—Shakers and day
traders—use English and are part of Western culture, I did not face problems in identifying phenomena of the above sorts that characterize(d) their lives. The epistemological issues become more
pressing in "cross-cultural" cases.
80 Bronwyn Davies and Rom Harré, "Positioning: The Discursive Production of Selves," *Journal for the
Theory of Social Behavior* 20, 1 (1990): 43–63.

first wooden cylinders lined with sheet copper tacked to the wood and sol-
dered at the edges ("steam chests"), they later were skirted with iron because
the earlier design was not good at containing steam.[81]

Few living organisms other than humans figured in the medicinal herb operations. The primary such entity was the herb-house horse, who powered the
herb block presses. This creature was also, among other things, something in
need of periodic reshoeing, something after which to clean up, and something
whose pace could at times of peak activity impede production. Rats, furthermore, were an occasional nuisance. The storerooms stockpiling dried herbs were
convenient nests, and rats figured in herbal operations as pests to be cleaned
up after in the storerooms and to be chased away when they became too copi-
ous. Rats also inhabited Shaker water systems and found additional entrée into
the herb and seed operations as, for instance, the cause of water backups.[82]

The main things, finally, figuring in the medicinal herb industry were the
herbs and roots themselves. They were purely things, however, only at the
stage where they were gathered in the wild or harvested in the gardens, thereafter in stages becoming increasingly artifactual (see Chapter 3). Qua things
they were, in the first place, belladonna, dandelion, fennel, bayberry, cicuta,
mandrake, boxwood, wormwood, witch hazel, cramp bark, hardhack leaves,
bugle, and so on. In addition, they were searched-for entities, cultivated beings,
the objects of painstaking garden attention, and things to be dried.

These cumulating examples suggest several important points, familiar to
readers of poststructural accounts of identity. The first is that what something
is is relative to where it fits into given arrangements. Hollister was extractor in
so far as he fit, and fit in particular ways, into the arrangements of the herbal
medicine industry. So enmeshed, other Shakers—involved or uninvolved in
the industry, at the extract house or elsewhere—understood him thus and
acted toward him in particular ways. Similarly, an apparatus was a copper
evaporating pan, the rats were causes of water backups, and the herbs were
mandrake as well as sought-after plants insofar as they figured in the industry's
arrangements in particular ways. Of course, the rats were likely to be such
causes and the herbs were likely to be mandrake, bugle, and the like insofar as

---

[81] This is reported by Hollister in *Daily Journal of the Herb Extract Business Kept by A. G. H.,* pages following entry marked "November 1860."

[82] Elisha Myrick noted that he had to dig up the drain to the cellar sink of the herb house at Hancock
to clear out the rubbish that the rats had carried there (*A Diary Kept for the Convenience of the Herb
Department by Elisha Myrick,* Edward Deming Andrews Memorial Shaker Collection, Winterthur
Library, Winterthur, Del., manuscript no. 837, entry for 20 November 1856).

they figured in other arrangements as well, for instance, those of the clothes-washing industry or of botanical taxonomy. Still the general point holds: Meaning and identity arise (in part) from where an entity fits into the mazes of relations that characterize the arrangements of which it is a part.

Second, the converse also holds: Where something fits into these plexuses depends (in part) on its meaning. It is because Hollister was extractor that he conducted experiments, operated certain machinery, mixed herbs with alcohol, occupied certain activity-places in the extract house, possessed certain beliefs about activities in the rooms adjacent to the laboratory, and forbade the boys who slept in the attic to enter the laboratory. Similarly, it is because these substances were cicuta, dandelion, belladonna, and so on that they were stored in tins, vials, and boxes, subjected to steaming and boiling, in turn yielded juices, and enabled Hollister to distill particular products while also preventing him from speeding up operations.

As this bidependence makes clear, meaning and identity must, third, be distinguished from position. An entity's position in a given arrangement is its location in that arrangement's plexus of relations. I indicated above, but it bears repeating, that positionality is not a spatial affair alone. An entity's position lies not just in what it is next to, what it is near to or far from, and of what it is inside or outside. It also lies in a variety of other matters that are to varying degrees inflected with spatiality: the components and aspects of the arrangement the entity causes; the components and aspects that cause it; how it is understood, thought about, emoted, and acted toward by other components of the arrangement; how it itself is intentionally directed (if at all) toward features of the arrangement; and what of the arrangement it enables and constrains as well as how the arrangement enables and constrains it. Positionality is clearly so complex that its full details are never plumbed. The present point, however, is that because meaning derives in part from position and position derives in part from meaning, the two must be distinguished. Contemporary theorists who analyze identity as an amalgam of "subject positions" run the risk of reducing identity to location in a network (i.e., position), instead of properly construing identity and position as codependent.

The above examples illustrate, fourth, that meaning and identity are invariably multiple. Hollister, as discussed, was many things, even in the extract business, and he also understood himself multiply. The machinery, rats, and herbs, too, were varied things, though they did not understand themselves so—or any way. Despite this multiformity, identity is sometimes organized, fifth, around central axes. Laclau and Mouffe write convergently of "nodal points," which are subject positions of relatively greater fixity around which a person's other more ephemeral subject positions accumulate. Any concept of a central axis of identity must be construed dually in line with the binary nature of identity. In the first place, someone's identity derives partly from his or her position in arrangements and, in turn, is partly responsible for his or her position there. To the extent that these dependencies hold, how someone is positioned, and how identity helps determine this, might revolve around particular meanings. I think that after Long's departure in 1861, for example, Hollister's secular identity centered around being extractor. To say that it "centered" around this is to say that at least most of the other identities he assumed in the medicinal herb business depended on his being extractor. Examples are experimenter, repairer, builder of machinery, and keeper of journals and inventories. In the second place, insofar as who someone is is who he understands himself to be, a person's chief identity is what, if anything, he understands himself principally to be. Clearly, people can vary greatly in both the degree to which their identities are centered in this second sense and in how many centers their identities enjoy. Vis-à-vis the medicinal herb business, for instance, Hollister likely thought of himself principally as extractor, though elsewhere it seems likely (and even in the extract business it could have been the case) that he understood himself chiefly as theologian, member of the Church Family, and believer in the teachings of Mother Ann.

It should be obvious, finally, that meaning and identity are labile phenomena. What Hollister, the copper evaporating pans, the horse, and the herbs were, altered with context, circumstance, and changing events, both predictably and unpredictably. Indeed, as above all Laclau and Mouffe have emphasized, meaning is and can never be fixed.

The Determination of Being

As indicated, the second issue for the present section, the determination of being, can be fully dealt with only over the course of upcoming chapters. Here I lay the groundwork for my analysis by, first, spelling out the account of meaning found in Laclau and Mouffe and, then, baldly stating the alternative I defend. To facilitate comparison, I begin with a description of another Shaker order.

The first floor of the herb house was home to an array of machinery: three herb presses, several cutting machines and grinders, and a printing press for producing labels. These were not located in a single room. The herb presses were in one room, the printing press in another. Adjoining the pressing room was a storeroom where the pressed herbs, after being removed from the apparatus that received them as they slid off the presses, were placed in further devices that maintained their form. The pressed herbs were papered and labeled in a prep room. This room contained various papers and glues, a wooden cupboard-like piece of furniture where the labels for each product were separately stored, and a variety of shelves, tables, and cupboards. The grinding and herb press rooms contained various entities in addition to the aforementioned equipment, such as tins of dried herbs, boxes of cut herbs, containers of empty vials for ground herbs, holders for filled vials, and tables, shelves, and chairs. Brethren were in charge of these activities, one in the print room, two or more in the pressing room, and another doing the chopping. The sisters helped out with the packaging.

As indicated in Section 2, Laclau and Mouffe analyze meaning neo-Saussuringly by reference to difference. What something is lies in the differences between it and all other components of its discourse. What, for example, the herb house's hydraulic press was, lay in the differences between it and the other implements and artifacts there, hence in its differences with the printing press, the herb block collecting apparatus, the chopping machines, the labels, the glue, the tins, and so on. Its meaning also lay in the differences between it and (1) the brethren and sisters who operated this machinery; (2) the different activities these individuals carried out; (3) the herbs and roots; (4) the rooms of the herb house and their walls, doorways, ceilings; and (5) the words uttered and written in these activities and places. Just what this hydraulic press was, consequently, rang out of the sum total of differences between it qua element of the herb house setup and all other objects, actions, and words that were part of this setup. Of course, what each of these other entities was similarly rang out of the totality of differences between it and all other components of the arrangement.

Accounts of meaning of this neo-Saussurian sort were a familiar fixture in twentieth-century thought. The relation of meaning to difference that they promulgate, however, is problematic. What, for example, were the meaning-instituting differences between the hydraulic press and the printing press? Many differences existed between them, not all of which determined meaning.[83] The

---

[83] In section 2, I pointed out an ambiguity in Laclau and Mouffe's account: Are the differences that establish meaning differences among meaningful entities ("positions," or "moments") or differences among the meanings of those entities? For the purposes of the following argument, I assume the

machines were located in different rooms, for instance, but this seems more a result than a determinant of what they were. The hydraulic press was larger and more complicated, but again this seems more to be a product than a determinant. So, too, does the fact that the one was consistently operated by one brother, the other by another. Myriad further differences seem unrelated to meaning, for example, that the two devices were constructed at different times. In short, a great number of differences among an arrangement's components are products of or incidental to their meanings.

That difference between the hydraulic press and the printing press that seems most directly to have determined what the hydraulic press was, is the fact that the hydraulic press was used to press herbs, while the printing press was used to print labels. What sort of difference is this? It is, of course, a difference in function, or use. That is to say, however, it is a difference *in the meanings of* these two machines. In this example, therefore, meaning does not derive from difference. Rather, it is the other way around: This particular difference, as a difference *in* meaning, derives from the meanings involved. It follows that what the hydraulic press was must have depended on something other than difference. Given that the (central) meaning of a machine is its function, the obvious conclusion is that what the hydraulic machine was somehow arose from human activity. This conclusion instantiates, however, a wider thesis, namely, that the meanings of the entities amid and through which humans coexistently live derive from activity. This idea is shared by thinkers as diverse as Martin Heidegger, Ludwig Wittgenstein, and John Dewey; it marks an intellectual tradition, extending from the early parts of the twentieth century to the present, that contrasts with, inter alia, the Saussurian stream.

Of course, the meaning of the hydraulic press was multiform. At different moments and in different situations, it was something that needed repair, something run by the horse power in the basement, something requiring periodic cleaning, something obstructing the view of the meeting outside between the elder and the trustee Edward Fowler, and so on. These meanings, too, did not derive from any differences between the hydraulic press and, for example once again, the printing press. Both, to begin with, required repair and cleaning. What is more, that the hydraulic press was something run by the horse power in the basement did not derive from any differences, say, between the

---

former. One implication of assuming this is that any and all differences that exist among meaningful entities can be relevant to an analysis of their meaning.

shafts, wheels, and pulleys that connected it with the horse and the lever that connected the printing press with the humans powering that press. Its being such a thing derived, instead, from the causal and spatial relations embodied in the setup of shafts, wheels, and pulleys. Furthermore, and similarly, its meaning as obstacle derived from its actually obstructing the view, not from the difference between its doing this and the printing press's not doing so. Similar conclusions result if the thesis that meaning devolves from differences is tested against differences between the hydraulic press, on the one hand, and entities of categorically different sorts on the other (herbs, brothers, actions, words).

These examples point toward a general conclusion. As suggested, the meaning of a component of an arrangement derives partly, and in some cases primarily (e.g., being run by horsepower), from its position in the arrangement—its location in the plexus of actual relations among the arrangement's components. Differences, consequently, are not what determine what that component is. Indeed, its differences with other components result from its and their positions. Similarly, some meanings of some components of an arrangement, for example, a machine's function, derive from the activities performed by other components, that is to say, people. (This phenomenon is examined more carefully in the next chapter, where it also emerges that the determination of meaning by position usually depends on human activity.) Once again, differences are results, not determinants, in this case of actual activities. It follows that meaning does not, as a general matter, arise from difference. Rather, it arises from *actuality:* actual relations among entities, and what these entities actually do. Because, moreover, semantic difference presupposes meaning, it, too, is a product of actuality. These conclusions show that de Saussure, in proclaiming that the identity of an individual signifier or signified lies in its differences from all other signifiers and signifieds, respectively, wrongly—and lamentably—convinced generations of linguistic and sociocultural theorists of the semantic-ontological significance of difference. Meaning, as a general rule, can never derive from difference, for there are no differences among things without there being things—which differ because of what the one and the other are. In particular, semantic linguistic differences cannot exist without the existence of multiple positions and uses (or activities), whose differences consist of what the one is and what the other is not being the same. (The same point can be put in terms of other proffered *explanantia* of meaning, e.g., intentions, signifieds, signs, or truth/assertability conditions.) Differences, in short, are abstractions that cannot reconstruct the states of actuality from which they are lifted and apart from which they are nothing.

The following chapter advocates an account of meaning that stands in the Heideggarian-Wittgensteinian-Deweyian tradition mentioned above. According to this account, what something is is, fundamentally, what it is understood to be. Understandings, moreover, are carried in social practices and expressed in the doings and sayings that compose practices. In particular, what something is understood to be in a given practice is expressed by those of the practice's doings and sayings that are directed toward it. Meaning, consequently, is carried by and established in social practices. Practices, furthermore, embody organizations, which circumscribe the meanings and arrangements set up and otherwise encompassed in them. Meaning is not a matter of difference, abstract schema, or attributional relativity, but a reality laid down in the regimes of activity and intelligibility called "practices."

PRACTICES

Now and again, I have suggested that social orders are not self-standing or self-propagating configurations, but that they instead exist and evolve only in some context encompassing them. The current chapter argues that this context is a nexus of social practices. To say that the social orders through and amid which human coexistence transpires are established in this nexus is to say that the relations, meanings, identities, and positions of their components (as well as changes in these) are beholden to certain organized bundles of human activity. This state of affairs entails, in turn, that human lives hang together, not just through social orders, but also through social practices. As discussed in the following chapter, the overall site specific to human coexistence is a mesh of orders and practices.

1. CONTEXTS AND SOCIAL NOMINALISM

The expression "context" has assumed virtually mythic allure in recent decades of social and humanistic theory. Like the word "practice," it has become an expression with which a theorist can point toward an encompassing and richly, perhaps indefinitely textured something—local circumstances, the wider situation, a surrounding space, or receding horizon—in whose hands lie the being and determination of his or her specific object of attention. This intuition of indelible embedment is the opposite side of the equally pervasive and insistent antiatomism of recent years, which contends that nothing is what it is when considered in isolation: If things are not self-determining or ontologically free-standing, determination and being must be referred elsewhere. Context, at bottom, is simply that portion of what is that something is beholden to for its character and existence, the sum-total of everything other than itself that determines these. By "determination," I should explain, I do not mean causal determination alone, but any manner in which something contributes to the being, existence, or transformation of something else. Unfortunately, too often the word "context" has become a wand for empty gestures, a word a theorist marshals to acknowledge the absence of self-sufficiency and self-determination and to point toward the surrounding force field of determination without inquiring further into the precise identity of this force field or its determining modus operandi.

The two chief contemporary philosophical sources of the term's fascination are the texts of Jacques Derrida and Ludwig Wittgenstein. Derrida argues that no text is self-standing.[1] Rather, every text exists only in a context of other texts. Taking seriously the meaning of the Latin root *com* (of which con is a variant)—together, with, joint, or jointly—Derrida goes a step further and contends that every text *is* a context: What a text is derives from and, in turn, helps determine what the other texts in whose context it exists are. Texts

---

[1] On the following, see, for example, Jacques Derrida, *Of Grammatology*, trans. Gayatri Chakravorty Spivak (Baltimore: Johns Hopkins University Press), 1976; Jacques Derrida, "Différance," in *Margins of Philosophy*, trans. Alan Bass (Chicago: University of Chicago Press, 1982), 1–21.

compose a texture by way of their labyrinthine references to one another, and what a text is is caught in this web of references. Derrida maintains, further, that anything that exists in a context is a text. This thesis makes clear that by "text" he means not script alone, but any articulation of intelligibility, that is to say, of being. "Textuality," accordingly, is a web of intelligibility-being. Because, finally, this web always "exceeds" whatever articulations it has received, the meaning of something always outruns extant articulations of it. Together, then, the theses that texts are contexts and that anything existing in a context is a text entail that any articulation of intelligibility is part of the web of intelligibility and that anything intelligible (anything that is) is so within this articulated but inexhaustible and never-settled web. Later Wittgenstein, by contrast, focused primarily on language and contended that linguistic meaning is not the product of a fixed principle or relation (e.g., reference), which determinatively, inexorably, and stably assigns meanings to words. Rather, the meaning of a word depends on the circumstances of its use, for instance, the activities as part of which it is used, what is going on in the immediate setting of use, the history of its usage, who speaks or writes and to whom, and what stands fast as "self-evident" for the people involved.[2] Together, these and other phenomena constitute the context in which words are meaningful. Meaning, accordingly, varies across context, that is to say, with different specifications and combinations of these phenomena.

A context has three general aspects. The first is that it "surrounds" or "immerses" that of which it is the context. It is best to avoid the word "outside" here, for this expression connotes a definite or at least clear division between regions. "Surrounds" and "immerses" more adequately capture the phenomenon of being caught in something broader that embraces and holds in its grasp. Things are entangled or suspended in contexts, as a physical body is suspended in an electromagnetic field, a fish is immersed in water, and a Shaker is caught up in the practices of his or her village. Intuitively, moreover, that in which something is caught or immersed is larger, broader, more encompassing in some sense than the thing grasped. Greater expansiveness, in turn, suggests that a given context usually embraces a multiplicity of entities. Although in a formal sense each nonself-sufficient entity enjoys its own context, what are content-fully identified as the contexts of particular entities are

[2] See Ludwig Wittgenstein, *Philosophical Investigations,* 3d ed., trans. G. E. M. Anscombe (London: Macmillan, 1957).

typically phenomena, media, or domains in which numerous, sundry, and often inter-related entities or phenomena exist.

Contexts, second, have powers of determination. They determine the entities or phenomena caught in them. They can do so, moreover, in any combination of the varied genre of determination. A context might, for instance, causally shape the beings in it. The medicinal herb industry at New Lebanon, for instance, was a context in which the attitudes of individual Shakers toward co-workers, the industry, the Second Order of the Church Family, and work itself were molded—by the events that occurred there, the regimens to which workers were subjected, the assertions of compatriots, the actions of forepersons, deacons, and trustees, and so on. It was also a context in which medicines were manufactured and packaged. A context might, further, ontologically determine ("institute") the entities in it. What a given piece of machinery, for instance, was rested largely on what was done with it, thus on the activities carried out at the extract and herb houses. Similarly, who the workers in this business were derived in part from these activities in conjunction with, for instance, the places that working in this industry and working *tout court* occupied in Shakers' lives. Contexts, furthermore, can also prefigure, that is (until Chapter 4) enable and constrain what occurs in them. Assignments of tasks and the organization of medicinal herb production activities constrained what individual Shakers could do during the course of the day, at the same time that they enabled certain innovations in procedure, equipment, and organization. A context can also, finally, confer value and significance on entities and events in it. Because the Shakers valued harmony in all walks of their existence, strife was often disparaged as a threat to unity, and quarrels were handled as occasions to stop and think through problems. At the same time, because Shaker government was hierarchical and reached down into the affairs of individual businesses, strife could also be disparaged as a threat to authority and quarrels exploited as occasions to discipline reprobates. I note that the expression "powers" carries no theoretical significance as I use it. To say that context possess powers of determination is to say simply that context determines. It is not also eo ipso to attribute to it structures or mechanisms.[3]

The third aspect of context is its own composition. A context is not a diaphanous atmosphere or medium, a substanceless ground of substance similar to light in ancient Greek interpretations of light as an invisible ground of

---

[3] I have in mind here the sort of analysis of causal powers initiated in Rom Harré and Edward Madden, *Causal Powers* (Oxford: Blackwell, 1975).

visibility. A context has composition, the precise character of which varies with the entities and phenomena that exist in context. In the examples of the previous paragraph, for example, medicinal herb activities, their organization, the entire business, and Shaker culture more generally each served as the context of some feature of the business. In the paragraph on Derrida and Wittgenstein, moreover, texts, the web of intelligibility, activities, events, specific individuals, histories, and "obviousnesses" made up the contexts in which intelligibility is articulated or words are meaningful. Given the endlessness of the range of entities and phenomena that can determine the character, existence, or transformation of things, the character and composition of contexts are endlessly varied.

Within this diversity, a distinction can be drawn between two categories of context: those whose components are the same in type as the entities contextualized in them and those whose components typologically differ from what is embedded. When a context is made out of entities of the same sort as those of which it is the context, I call it a *texture*. When this stuff differs, I call it a *contexture*. In the aforementioned examples, texts form textures. Indeed, this is the point of context in Derrida: A text is only as part of a texture, an ensemble of texts. The web of textuality, moreover, is alternately a texture or a contexture depending on whether things or articulations of intelligibility are taken as the contextualized entities. Activities, events, identities, histories, and obviousnesses, by contrast, compose a contexture. They differ in nature from the words and the meaningfulness of words that they determine, and they also differ among themselves. The Shaker examples contain a mix of textures and contextures. Textures and contextures, it should be emphasized, are different beasts. Textures are more of the same, wider expanses of entities of the same sort as those selected for attention. Indeed, a set of entities in a texture is a cut from, a sector of, a wider cognate tapestry. By contrast, contextures, together with what exists in them, form regionalized compositions with crosscategorical powers of determination. Entities in a contexture are less a cut of a fabric than the focal point of surrounding estates.

An additional and particularly important type of context is that of sites, in a special sense of this word. Sites, in general, are *where* things exist and events happen. From the start, it is important to hold at bay the spatial connotations of the expression "where." Spatial sites are only one genre of site. To delimit those sites that are contexts, moreover, three senses of "site," of "where" something is or happens, must be distinguished.

A site is, first, the location where something is or takes place. Something's spatial site, for instance, is its location in space. It is where in space it is or occurs and can, thus, be found. The spatial site of an activity, for instance, is where in physical, activity, or activity-place space it is located. Location, however, is not a spatial matter alone. All entities and phenomena that exist or occur in broader phenomena and regions have locations in those phenomena or regions. It is at these locations that they can be found. The site where humans come of age, for instance, is not just where in physical space the occurrences constituting this extended event transpire, but also where in the life-course of a person this event is located. Similarly, both the storage of pressed herbs and Hollister's experiments with belladonna had particular locations, or sites, in the activities of the herb business, and Long's apostasy in 1860 occupied a particular location in the history of the business. Appearances notwithstanding, these examples do not simply double spatial sites with temporal ones. Locations are defined wherever there are multiplicities, and the nature of the location reflects the character of the multiplicity. As becomes clearer later in this chapter, for example, Hollister's activities occupied a *teleological* location in the herbal medicine production practices.

Second, where something is is the wider scene in which it occupies a site in the first sense. In this second sense of "where," physical space is the site where phenomena occupy physical spatial locations, and physical, activity, or activity-place spaces are the spatial sites where activity occurs. Nonspatial versions of this second type of site also exist, for instance, the extended and articulated phenomena or realms in which things exist or occur. In this sense, one site of humans' coming of age is the life-course of human beings; one site of herb storage and Hollister's experiments was the activities of the medicinal herb business; and one site of Long's apostasy was the history of this business. I write "one site" because, just as something can have multiple sites in the first sense, it can simultaneously exist or take place in various wider scenes. Hollister's experiments, for instance, not only were part of medicinal herb production activities at New Lebanon, but also occurred in the history of nineteenth-century U.S. pharmaceutical manufacture.

The final type of site is more rarefied. Where something is is, third, that extended and articulated phenomenon or realm of which it is intrinsically a part. Something's site in this sense is that phenomenon or realm (if any) *as* part of which it is or occurs. This sense of "where" shares with the second the intuition of wider scene, and it shares with the first and second senses the idea that where something is is the place it is found. Site-ment in this third sense is also a central feature of that type of context I call "site": a context is a site when at least some of the entities that occur in it are inherently components of it. That is to say, for something to be or to occur in a site context is for it to be or to occur *as* a constituent part of its context. (Henceforth, the word "site" is used to designate such contexts.) For example, space, in an absolutist conception of it, is the site of spatial locations because spatial locations exist only as part of the space defining them. (Space is not a site on a relational construal.) For reasons that are clarified in Section 3, moreover, the medicinal herb production activities and not, say, the history of nineteenth-century U.S. pharmaceuticals, were the site for Hollister's experimental activities. Notice that not all textures and contextures are sites. A space walk, for instance, occurs in the context of solar bombardment against which precautions are taken, but it does not occur as part of that bombardment. The walk also occurs in the context of the sleeping and eating practices on orbiting spaceships with which it must be coordinated, but it does not occur as part of those practices. A site is a special sort of context, the strongest and, to my mind, most interesting type. For it is the one type where entities are intrinsically part of their own context.

In social theory, contextualism is the position that the character and transformation of social affairs are beholden to contexts. Typical examples of such contexts are abstract structures, systems of action, worldviews, social practices, and fields of various sorts. Standing opposed to this general way of thinking is social nominalism. Social nominalism has two components. The first is the intuition that there are no contexts in social life; there are only the entities that contextualists contend exist only in contexts. If, for example, a contextualist like myself opines that social orders exist only in particular contexts, a nominalist such as the actor-network theorist Callon (Latour, too) replies that all that exists are the orders themselves. If a contextualist such as the practice theorist Bourdieu maintains that actions are bound to delimited fields of possibility, a nominalist such as the science scholar Andrew Pickering claims that there are no constraints in the social (see Chapter 4). It is evident, however, that the first component of nominalism is not adequately defined as the denial of context. Nominalists such as those just cited might not deny all contexts, only certain types. Someone like Callon who argues that society is a constellation of networks can also believe that each network exists only in the context of others; and someone like Pickering who denies constraint can still think that scientific activities occur in the context of machines, instruments, social relations, theories, and the like ("culture," in his terms).[4] As a result, I define the first component of social nominalism, more specifically, as the thesis that there are no *contextures* in social life. Individual networks might exist only in the context of other networks, but they are not suspended in further contexts that differ in nature from them. Based on this first component, Callon, but not Pickering, qualifies as a nominalist.

The second component of social nominalism is particularism. Particularism maintains that all that exists are constellations of particulars. Its purest versions claim that particulars alone exist, whereas its more moderate versions admit the existence of relations among particulars. According to positions of both sorts, constellations of particulars and relations are not immersed in contextures; the only admissible contexts are further textures of inter-related particulars. It is in this sense of particularism, I believe, that Foucault claimed that "one must be nominalistic" when analyzing power.[5] Power, he explained, should not be hypostatized as a structure, institution, or unity that holds social life in its embrace. To speak of power is, instead, to speak of the state of force relations that hold among social particulars (where a force relation is a molding of possible actions): "power must be understood in the first instance as the multiplicity of force relations immanent in the sphere in which they operate and which constitute their own organization."[6] "Power" thus designates the reticular force relation organization of particulars in the social. Indeed, the social *is* this reticular organization of particulars.

Social theoretical nominalism, consequently, is a particularism that denies all contextures. Not all social particularisms are nominalist in this sense, because it is possible to argue that particulars of one sort (e.g., people) occur in the contexture of particulars of another sort (e.g., things of nature). So defined, moreover, social theoretical nominalism diverges from what metaphysicians and epistemologists call "nominalism." Philosophical nominalism is, roughly, the denial of abstract entities, the classic examples of which are forms and universals. Social theoretical nominalism converges with philosophical nominalism insofar as it denies the existence of abstract contextures. It diverges, however, in not restricting the particulars, constellations of which are all there is to social reality, to concrete particulars. By "concrete," I simply mean experiential.

[4] Andrew Pickering, *The Mangle of Practice: Time, Agency & Science* (Chicago: University of Chicago Press, 1995), 3.
[5] Michel Foucault, *The History of Sexuality,* vol. 1: *An Introduction,* trans. Richard Hurley (New York: Vintage, 1980), 93.
[6] Foucault, *The History of Sexuality,* 1: 92.

(Although the latter term is anything but clear cut, it is not necessary in the present context to make it more precise.) According to some brands of individualism, for instance, the actions and mental conditions that are considered to help compose social life are abstract entities. Still, many social nominalisms are philosophically nominalist. If actions are construed, instead, as concrete beings, Foucault's account of power is an example.

An important contemporary exemplar of social nominalism is actor-network theory. Actor-network theory treats the reality amid which humans live as an immense labyrinth of interconnected networks. A scientific laboratory, for instance, is a network of scientists, inscriptions, instruments, and visual displays. It is connected with the networks that are other labs and also with the networks that are governments, corporations, medical facilities, and so on. These networks, which make up reality, are composed of entities of four basic types (humans, artifacts, organisms, and things), though Latour and Callon, as noted, also treat such entities as instances of two sorts, actor and intermediary (see Chapter 4). The networks that compose reality thus form textures through their connections, wider constellations of networks serving as the contexts in which individual networks exist.[7] Indeed, whenever actor-network theorists employ the term "context" affirmatively, what is thereby designated is just more networks. Clarifying this is facilitated by first explicating their well-known notion of blackboxing.

Any element in a network is itself a network of further elements, which for the purposes of activities conducted in the first, higher-order network is treated as a single entity. For instance, Hollister, the hydraulic press, and the power system horse were each a network of further entities (bodily systems and processes in the case of Hollister), which the herb business workers treated as individual beings during normal operations at the extract house. Similarly, the physicians who purchased herbal medicines did not treat the extract business as a network of people, machines, herbs, and organisms, but instead as a unit from which they could request and receive desired products. The practice of treating networks as units is called "blackboxing." Its occurrence shows, by the way, that the maze of interconnected networks that actor-network theory takes reality to be is hierarchically organized.

[7] For a clear statement, see Michel Callon, "Society in the Making: The Study of Technology as a Tool of Sociological Analysis," in *The Social Construction of Technological Systems: New Directions in the Sociology and History of Technology*, ed. Wiebe E. Bijker, Thomas Hughes, and Trevor Pinch (Cambridge, Mass.: MIT Press, 1987), 83–103, here 95.

Callon and Law write that, formally, content is whatever actors attend to, whereas context is whatever they successfully relegate to the background via blackboxing. In any particular case, however, what is specifically addressed or relegated are networks or their components.[8] According to actor-network theory, furthermore, just as constellations of networks form textures for individual networks, an individual network is a texture for its own components. Because, however, there is no other stuff to reality than entities of the above four, or two, types, actor-network theory's acknowledgment of context does not extend to contextures. And because a network is a constellation of particulars, reality at bottom is just one immense array of interconnected sets of particulars. As Latour writes, "networks are immersed in nothing."[9]

It is probably obvious, but bears brief discussion, that the most famous form of social theoretical nominalism is the broad ontological position known as "individualism."[10] Ontological individualists (e.g., Max Weber, F. A. Hayek, and Alfred Schütz) maintain that social phenomena are nothing more than constellations or constructions of individual persons (and artifacts). To say that social phenomena are constellations of individuals and artifacts is to say that such phenomena consist in or of such constellations (including features thereof such as actions and mental states). To say that social phenomena are constructions of individuals is to say that social phenomena are instituted (i.e., constituted in their being and thereby made the case) by individuals' mental states and actions. Because the second thesis instantiates the first (it construes social phenomena as consisting of constellations of mental states, notions, and also artifacts), further discussion of individualism in this section and the following chapter treats individualism as maintaining the constellation thesis. As with social nominalism generally, the individualist front divides into two factions: those maintaining that social phenomena are constellations of individuals (including actions and mental states) and artifacts alone and those averring that such phenomena are constellations of individuals together with relations

---

[8] Michel Callon and John Law, "On the Construction of Sociotechnical Networks: Content and Context Revisited," in *Knowledge and Society: Studies in the Sociology of Science Past and Present,* ed. Lowell Hargens, Robert Alun Jones, and Andrew Pickering (Greenwich, Conn.: JAI Press, 1989), 57–83, cf. 62, 78.

[9] Bruno Latour, *We Have Never Been Modern,* trans. Catherine Porter (Cambridge, Mass.: Harvard University Press, 1993), 128. See also idem, "On Actor-Network Theory: A Few Clarifications," *Soziale Welt* 47 (1996): 369–81, here 370.

[10] For discussion of various flavors of individualism, see the essays collected in John O'Neill, *Modes of Individualism and Collectivism* (London: Heinemann, 1973).

among them. In either view, overarching social formations such as economies, ethnic groups, and international crime syndicates do not, strictly, form contextures in which individuals carry on their lives. To speak of an overarching social phenomenon is, instead, simply an abbreviating way of speaking of a constellation of individuals. Social reality is at bottom a texture of interconnected individuals and artifacts, and social formations are sectors or slices of this texture (which are typically spatially, and also sometimes temporally, discontinuous). They are more of the same, more interconnected individuals, and do not, as a result, form a contexture in which individuals live. By contrast, some, though not all, forms of social theoretical "socialism" (cf. Chapter 3) are contexturalist. More specifically, all positions that attribute powers of determination vis-à-vis people to those social formations that they maintain are irreducible to collections of individuals earn this epithet. Individuals, in these views, are caught in such phenomena as states (G. W. F. Hegel), social facts (Emile Durkheim), totalities of structures (Louis Althusser), and modes of production (Karl Marx), which mold or prefigure mental states and actions. Social formations, consequently, form a contexture in which people live their lives. Actions, in addition, form a texture in which individuals conduct their daily affairs.

An important component of the social theoretical nominalism of individualism is what Charles Taylor calls "monologism." Monologism analyzes knowledge and language as properties of individuals. This analysis, Taylor explains, leads monological theories to deny background contexts, in particular, the "clearing" as Heidegger conceived of it.[11] According to Heidegger, the clearing is an opening in which entities can be. As such, it is categorically different in nature from entities (the infamous "ontological difference"). In *Being and Time,* Heidegger contended that the clearing is opened by *Dasein*'s existence, above all by the dimensions of this existence called *Befindlichkeit* and *Verstehen,* attunement and understanding. In his later philosophy, language came to play the crucial role in this regard. Monologism's denial that there is any clearing or background beyond the particular entities that are[12] rests on the claim that the dimensions of *Dasein* that supposedly constitute this clearing are really

[11] Charles Taylor, "Lichtung or Lebensform: Parallels Between Heidegger and Wittgenstein," in his *Philosophical Arguments* (Cambridge, Mass.: Harvard University Press, 1995), 61–78.

[12] See also Theodor Adorno's attack on Heidegger, which still bears careful study today: Theodor Adorno, *The Jargon of Authenticity,* trans. Knut Tarnowski and Frederic Will (Evanston: Northwestern University Press, 1973).

nothing more than psychological properties of the individual people who, con-textualism alleges, exist in the clearing alongside other entities. In particular, social theoretical individualism maintains that individuals do not subsist in a "clearing" because the phenomena such as language that allegedly constitute that contexture are in fact nothing but (convergent) properties of individuals.[13]

A principal argument of the current chapter is that social practices form the context in which social orders are established. More specifically, I contend that practices form the contexture and also, in part, the site of social arrangements. Together, moreover, practices and orders make up the site of human coexis-tence: Human lives hang together through a mesh of interlocked practices and orders, as a constitutive part of which this hanging together occurs. Before elucidating these claims in this and the following chapter, it is necessary to clarify the character of social practices.

2. WHAT IS A SOCIAL PRACTICE?

To some extent, the current section summarizes the account of social practices that was developed and defended against alternatives in my previous book.[14] It also, however, presents several substantial revisions and clarifications of my earlier position, above all concerning know-how, general understanding, "teleo-affective structure," and normativity. I propose neither to contrast this account with competing theories of practice nor to demonstrate its superiority to them. Arguments against analyses of the social site that follow from certain practice theories are presented in the succeeding chapter.

My starting point is an intuition I associate, I hope not wrongly, with Charles Taylor, namely, that social life is plied by a range of such practices as negotiation practices, political practices, cooking practices, banking prac-tices, recreation practices, religious practices, and educational practices. Shaker life, for example, included, inter alia, religious practices, cooking practices,

---

[13] Taylor argues, by contrast, that the language and knowledge that constitute the background cannot be reduced to properties of the entities that exist against it. In his well-known essay, "Interpretation and the Sciences of Man," Taylor articulates the same argument in the form of a defense of the nonreducibility of intersubjective and common meanings to the attitudes and beliefs of individual people. Reprinted in Charles Taylor, *Philosophy and the Human Sciences: Philosophical Papers* 2 (Cambridge: Cambridge University Press, 1985), 15–58.

[14] Theodore R. Schatzki, *Social Practices: A Wittgensteinian Approach to Human Activity and the Social* (New York: Cambridge University Press, 1996), chaps. 4 and 5.

medicinal herb production practices, chair production practices, trading practices, medical practices, and educational practices. As these examples suggest, a practice is a "bundle" of activities, that is to say, an organized nexus of actions. Any practice, consequently, embraces two overall dimensions: activity and organization.

As these examples further suggest, the activities concerned are ones of humans. In writing this, I implicitly cross swords with actor-network's extension of the categories of actor and action to entities of all sorts. I also contravene, more directly, those theorists who contend that practices comprise the actions of various entities and not those of people alone.[15] I insist, however, that it is both cogent and imperative to distinguish organized constellations of human activity in social life. It is cogent because human actions in fact hang together in the ways that I take to be definitive of practices. It is imperative because, as later discussed, the specific character of social life is to a remarkable extent attributable to these bundled activities. This is a point about determination, I should add, not a moral claim. I do not mark off nexuses of activity embracing human activities alone with an eye to ethical concerns. At the same time, I do not deny the existence of nonhuman agency. Its home, however, is social orders and not social practices as I conceive of them (see Section 4 and Chapter 4). Practices are the bundled activities that one type of component of social orders performs.

Theorists who employ the expression "practice" to refer to human activity are divided about the phenomenon that the term designates. In writing that a practice is an organized constellation of actions, I treat practices as integral blocks. The idea that practices are integral activity bundles is widespread among theorists of practice, including Giddens, Taylor, Bourdieu (and Rouse). Some theorists, however, use the expression "practice" or "practices" to refer to a domain of human activity. Such theorists, who include Bourdieu (*sic*), Dreyfus, and Robert Brandom, may or may not have further views about the partitionment of this overall domain into packages of activity. Brandom, for instance, conceptualizes practices as the domain of normatively governed human activity, the domain of activities to which considerations of propriety—

---

[15] I have in mind Joseph Rouse, *Engaging Science: How to Understand Its Practices Philosophically* (Ithaca: Cornell University Press, 1996), chap. 5; Pickering, *The Mangle of Practice*. Pickering distinguishes between practices, which are repeatable sequences of activities, and practice, which is the "cultural extension" of science (the extension of its skills, machines, theories, social relations, and practices in the first sense). This extension, he claims, is as much the result of material as of human agency.

oughtness, entitlement, commitment, and correctness—apply.[16] He does not, however, conceive of this domain as broken into particular packages, that is to say, integral nexuses of activity. Dreyfus, by contrast, conceives of practices as the domain of purposeful skilled activity. As discussed in the following chapter, he unlike Brandom does think of this domain as divided into units, which are associated with what he calls "local worlds." In my account, practices are open, temporally unfolding nexuses of actions. The nature of the overall arena that practices help compose is examined in the following chapter.

The point of the qualifiers "open, temporally unfolding" is that fresh actions are continually perpetuating and extending practices temporally. The actions involved, moreover, are, first, bodily doings and sayings. Bodily doings and sayings are actions that people directly perform, where by "directly" I mean that people perform them not by way of doing something else. In this regard, they are "basic actions," to use Arthur Danto's term.[17] Examples are waving, running, jumping, turning knobs, handing someone something, pouring liquid into a barrel, throwing the horse's oats in the corner, uttering words, and writing script. I label them "bodily" to emphasize that they are things people do with their bodies, including whatever prosthetic parts and extensions (e.g., canes) bodies possess. Waving, running, pouring, throwing, uttering, and so on are things people directly do with their arms, legs, mouths, and the like. Sayings, moreover, are a subset of doings, in particular, doings that say something (usually about something). So defined, sayings need not involve language: Shakes of the head, waves of the hand, and winks can all, given the context, say something. The identity of sayings, I should add, lies in what is said. Just as numerically distinct acts can be the same doing, numerically distinct acts can say the same thing and thus be the same saying.

Doings and sayings "constitute" further actions whenever performing them amounts, in the contexts in which they are performed, to carrying out those actions. In a particular context, for instance, waving a hand might constitute greeting someone; in a different context, it might amount to requesting that someone come over. Greeting and requesting—as much as waving—are actions that people perform.[18] Because, furthermore, a "basic action" can be

---

[16] See, for example, Robert Brandom, "Freedom and Constraint by Norms," *American Philosophical Quarterly* 16 (1979): 187–96; more recently, Brandon, *Making It Explicit: Reasoning, Representing, and Discursive Commitment* (Cambridge, Mass.: Harvard University Press, 1994).

[17] Arthur Danto, "Basic Actions," *American Philosophical Quarterly* 2 (1965): 141–48.

[18] I note, terminologically, that the actions that bodily doings and sayings "constitute" in particular contexts are the same actions that are carried out in those contexts "by way of" the performance of those doings and sayings.

simultaneously performed in multiple contexts, it can constitute multiple higher-order actions. Subsets of these actions often form series, each member of which is what the performance of the previous member amounts to in some further context. Hollister's waving his hand, for instance, might constitute requesting that his assistant come over, which itself might constitute his continuing to lord it over him that morning, which itself might constitute upholding proper discipline in the herbal medicine business, and so on.[19] In addition, the leaving off of certain doings and sayings can amount in particular situations to performing particular actions, for example, refusing to answer.

A practice is a set of doings and sayings. Because these doings and sayings almost always constitute further actions in the contexts in which they are performed, the set of actions that composes a practice is broader than its doings and sayings alone. I use the expressions "task" and "project" to impose some order on this wider set. Different doings and sayings often constitute the same action. In the herb production practices, for instance, any of the following actions might have been constituted—on different occasions—by different sets of doings and sayings: getting the herbs up to the drying rooms, drying them, storing them, transporting them downstairs, and pressing them. I call such actions "tasks." The performance of tasks often consists of aggregated doings and sayings. On a particular occasion, for example, getting herbs into the drying rooms might have consisted of pulling on the hoist, bending over, lifting the basket of herbs, turning, and handing the basket to a co-worker. Tasks, in turn, constitute still higher-order actions; many tasks that particular or aggregated doings and sayings constitute themselves constitute, singly or in groups, further actions. For example, both getting the herbs into the drying rooms and drying them are parts of the activity of preparing them for pressing. I label those actions that consist of tasks "projects." A practice thus embraces a set of hierarchically organized doings/sayings, tasks, and projects; and at any given *durée,* a participant in the practice is likely, though not necessarily, to be carrying out actions of all three types. I add that a particular action term (e.g., "pressing") can designate a task in some contexts and a project in others.

It is important to stress that the doings and sayings that compose a practice

---

[19] This situation is sometimes known as the "accordion effect"; cf. Joel Feinberg, "Action and Responsibility," in *Philosophy in America,* ed. Max Black (London: Allen and Unwin, 1965), 134–60. For extensive discussion, see the careful exposition in Alvin Goldman, *A Theory of Human Action* (Princeton: Princeton University Press, 1970), chap. 2.

need not be regular.[20] A practice's actions, above all its tasks and projects, do invariably exhibit regularities. A practice, however, also embraces irregular, unique, and constantly changing doings/sayings, tasks, and projects. Herbal production practices involved the regular performance of such doings as pulling hoists, placing green herbs and roots on drying sheets, picking up these sheets, turning them over, pouring the dried herbs and roots into tins, lifting these tins, placing them in cupboards, and so on. The production practices further encompassed the regular performance of such tasks as getting herbs up to the drying rooms, drying them, storing them, and transporting them downstairs to be pressed. But the practices also encompassed (1) unusual and circumstantially determined doings and saying that on occasion constituted these regularly performed tasks; (2) a variety of infrequent and irregular doings and sayings, occasioned by breakdowns and dangers, which constituted such sporadic tasks and projects as repairing engines and chaser spindles, extinguishing a fire in the boiler room, thawing frozen water pipes, and checking the purity of the quassia to see whether Long tampered with it before apostatizing; and (3) new doings and sayings that constituted extant tasks, as well as existing and new doings and sayings that constituted novel tasks, where the newness involved resulted from innovations in and reorganizations of the practice's operations. Medicinal herbs, for instance, were not always sold in pressed block form. The introduction of this innovation required the performance of a great variety of new doings and sayings that constituted existing (e.g., packaging) as well as novel (e.g., pressing) tasks. Practices thus comprise regular, occasional, rare, and novel doings/sayings, tasks, and projects.

Cutting across the different actions that a person performs at any moment is the ontological primacy of one of them. To explain this, I must first briefly consider the governance of action. Elsewhere I have argued that human activity is governed by something called "practical intelligibility."[21] Practical

---

[20] Contra, for example, Rouse, *Engaging Science,* chap. 5. Stephen Turner provides a further example. In his book-length critique of certain practice theories, he argues long and persuasively against explaining agreement, disagreement, and similarities in behavior by reference to shared mental objects with causal powers (e.g., tacit knowledge). He calls such mental objects "practices." He also suggests that his arguments imply that the term "practices" can designate only regularities in behavior. He thereby overlooks the possibility that a practice is an evolving domain-site of activity. See Stephen Turner, *The Social Theory of Practices: Tradition, Tacit Knowledge, and Presuppositions* (Cambridge, Mass.: Polity Press, 1994); the suggestion is on 117.

[21] For more detailed discussion of the account of action sketched in this and the following paragraphs, see Schatzki, *Social Practices,* chaps. 2 and 4.

intelligibility is what makes sense to a person to do. It governs action by specifying what an actor does next in the continuous flow of activity. It also *causes*
activity in the senses of formal and final—but not efficient—causality: It
specifies *what* a person does; and the specification of what to do is usually
oriented toward specific ends. Now, people usually perform the actions that
are signified to them as the ones to perform. Moreover, they carry out those
actions by way of performing doings and sayings, the performance of which in
the circumstances amounts to the performance of the specified actions. If, for
example, mixing alcohol with belladonna is signified to Hollister as what next
to do, he might forthwith pick up a jug of alcohol, walk over to the barrel of
belladonna, and pour it in. I should stress that practical intelligibility is an
individualist phenomenon: It is always to an individual that a specific action
makes sense. Features of individuals, moreover, are what principally determine
what makes sense to them to do. Examples of such features are a person's ends,
the projects and tasks he or she is pursuing, and affectivity.[22] To the extent that
nonindividualist phenomena, for example, practices, determine practical intelligibility, they do so by molding such features.

The arguments of the present book do not require that practical intelligibility be further clarified. I might, nonetheless, explain that practical intelligibility is not the same as rationality. Its making sense to someone to X is not
the same phenomenon as its being (or seeming) rational to that person to do
so. Although the particular actions signified as the ones to do next are often
also the ones that the counsels of rationality single out, practical intelligibility
and rationality can diverge. Similarly, practical intelligibility is not the same
phenomenon as normativity. What makes sense to someone to do is not the
same as what is, or seems to the actor to be, appropriate, right, or correct.
Although, once again, the particular actions that practical intelligibility specifies might also be normatively enjoined, and although it can make sense to
someone to X in part because X-ing is enjoined, intelligibility and normativity
can and do diverge. Of course, intelligibility, as just indicated, does not swing
free of normative stricture. Participating in a practice is operating in an arena
where certain actions and ends are prescribed, correct, or acceptable on certain
occasions. As a result, the practical intelligibility that informs participants'

---

[22] The features of individuals that determine practical intelligibility are in fact mental conditions. The
ends, projects, and tasks that a person pursues, for instance, are objects of her or his desires and
intentions. Explaining in greater detail just how mentality determines practical intelligibility would
take the current discussion too far afield. See Schatzki, *Social Practices*.

activity can be partially determined by normativity and subject to the normative judgment and sanction of others. Falling under normativity, however, is
a different matter than intrinsically being a normative phenomenon. Note,
finally, that its making sense to someone to X is a phenomenon different from
that person's making sense of his or her own or someone else's action as X.
Practical intelligibility is, in the first place, practical.

What people, at almost any moment, are *in the first place* doing is whatever
at that moment makes sense to them to do. When conducting experiments
with belladonna, for example, Hollister lifted beakers, peered into vats, turned
knobs, and carried around pans (etc.). It is not likely, however, that what he
was doing, first, was lifting beakers, peering into vats, turning knobs, and
carrying about pans. Nor is it likely that he was beginning a new phase of the
experiment, repeating the same procedure for the seventh time that day, over-
loading the engine, or using the last load of belladonna brought in last month.
He might, in fact, have been doing all these things; and on some occasions (for
instance, breakdowns and moments of reflection) one or more of these actions
might have been what was signified to him to do. But what he was far more
likely doing, that is to say, what was far more likely being signified to him to
do, was such actions as mixing alcohol with the belladonna liquor, checking
to see whether the evaporation process was complete, turning on the steam,
and bringing the macerated belladonna to the press.[23] (Even though I cannot
explain this here, I note that this primacy is tied to which mental conditions
his doings and sayings expressed at the time.) The actions that a person in the
first place performs can be of many categorical sorts, including doings and general projects. Usually, however, what is signified to someone is some action, the
performance of which involves the performance of a doing or saying that she or
he can spontaneously carry out because it is part of his or her bodily repertoire.

Before continuing, I want to comment on the distinction between doings
and sayings. Uttering words is as much a doing as is squatting on one's heels.
For deep reasons, however, which it is safe to say no one has yet fully fathomed,
on most occasions uttering words says something in a way that squatting only

---

[23] Readers familiar with analytic philosophy of action will recognize here a pendent to the widespread
thesis that intentions (or being intentional) are crucial to defining what actions a person performs.
For very different versions of this proposition, see G. E. M. Anscombe, *Intention* (Ithaca: Cornell
University Press, 1957); Donald Davidson, "Intending," in his *Essays on Actions and Events* (New
York: Oxford University Press, 1980), 83–102; John Searle, *Intentionality* (Cambridge: Cambridge
University Press, 1983), chap. 3.

rarely—and with the help of special arrangements—does. This difference is the difference between discursive and nondiscursive actions. Practices are a motley of actions of both sorts, and it seems to me an error to grant priority to either type. I asseverate this because the formidability of the linguistic turn in recent decades has led some theorists to overvalue the significance of discourse in social life. One form this overvaluation assumes is that of conceptualizing practices as collections of sayings alone. Perhaps the clearest example of this is Jean-François Lyotard's construal of language-games as constellations of sayings.[24] Another, considerably more subtle form, is slipping from a conception of discourse, or of discursivity, as articulated intelligibility to formulations that both privilege language in this articulation and neglect the role that nonlinguistic, nonsaying doings play therein.[25] Foucault, it seems to me, strikes the proper balance in treating behaviors and discourses, thus nondiscursive and discursive acts, alike as components of apparatuses. Deleuze and Guattari are similarly ecumenical. An account of practices must not just mark the distinction between doings and sayings, but also grant each its proper due in both the perpetuation of practices and the articulation of intelligibility.

As indicated, practices are *organized* nexuses of actions. This means that the doings and sayings composing them hang together. More specifically, the doings and sayings that compose a given practice are linked through (1) practical understandings, (2) rules, (3) a teleoaffective structure, and (4) general understandings. Together, the understandings, rules, and teleoaffective structure that link the doings and sayings of a practice form its organization.

By "practical understandings," I mean certain abilities that pertain to the actions composing a practice. Above all, three such abilities are germane to practices: knowing how to X, knowing how to identify X-ings, and knowing how to prompt as well as respond to X-ings. All participants in a practice are

---

[24] Jean François Lyotard, *The Postmodern Condition: A Report on Knowledge,* trans. Geoff Bennington and Brian Massumi (Minneapolis: University of Minnesota Press, 1979), for instance, xxiv, 15–17; Jean-François Lyotard and Jean-Loup Thébaud, *Just Gaming,* trans. Wald Godzich (Minneapolis: University of Minnesota Press, 1985), for example, 93–94, 99; cf. the notions of a regime and of a genre in Jean-François Lyotard, *The Differend: Phrases in Dispute,* trans. Georges van den Abbeele (Minneapolis: University of Minnesota Press, 1988), for instance, xvi.

[25] For an example, see Bronwyn Davies, "The Concept of Agency: A Feminist Poststructualist Analysis," *Social Analysis* 30 (1991): 42–53. Even as exceptional a theorist as Judith Butler sometimes succumbs to this temptation. In a recent work, for example, she argues that (1) individuals are intelligible only if they are subjects, and (2) subject is a "linguistic category," such that being an individual is a "linguistic occasion" (Judith Butler, *The Psychic Life of Power* [Stanford: Stanford University Press, 1997], 10–11).

able to perform, identify, and prompt some subset of the practice's doings, sayings, tasks, and projects. I should clarify that knowing how to X, where X is a nonbasic action, is knowing which of the doings and saying of which one is capable (i.e., that are part of one's spontaneous bodily repertoire) would, in the circumstances, constitute X-ing. When X, by contrast, is a basic action such as lifting a beaker or reading graphical displays on a computer screen, knowing how to X is a motor- or perceptual-cognitive skill. To say that two or more doings or sayings are "linked" by practical understanding is to say that they express the same understanding. What qualifies two people's understandings of X as the same is that (1) either person's performances of doings and sayings as X-ings are intelligible to the other as X-ings; and (2) either person's judgments of which doings and sayings constitute X-ings are intelligible to the other (provided, in both cases, that they share knowledge of action circumstances and of the actor or judger's mentality and action history).[26] In this way, the doings and sayings that composed Shaker medicinal herb production practices were linked by an interdependent pool of practical understandings of grinding, macerating, drying, storing, mixing, labeling, feeding, and printing labels. In expressing these understandings, I might add, the doings and sayings involved constituted the actions just listed.

Hence, by "practical understanding," I do not mean a sort of know-how that, according to several prominent theorists of practice, lies behind much, if not all, human behavior in its finely tuned sensitivity to immediate setting and wider context. Examples of what I have in mind are Bourdieu's habitus, otherwise called practical sense ("having a feeling for the game"), and Giddens's practical consciousness ("tacitly grasping a rule"), both conceptualizations the phenomenon of knowing how to go on highlighted in Wittgenstein's *Philosophical Investigations*.[27] Habitus and practical consciousness are alleged either always (Bourdieu) or often (Giddens) to determine what people on particular occasions do. As a result, these phenomena also allegedly provide

---

[26] Shared understanding does not exclude disagreements about whether a given doing or saying amounts to an X-ing. Actors typically diverge in their knowledges of the action circumstances and of the actor's or judger's state of mind and past actions; these differences underpin divergent judgments. Even when, moreover, they share knowledge of these matters, what is known might underdetermine whether the doing or saying was an X-ing, again leaving open the possibility of disagreement. There are also the proverbial borderline cases arising from the "fuzzy" character of concepts and understanding.

[27] See Pierre Bourdieu, *The Logic of Practice*, trans. Richard Nice (Stanford: Stanford University Press, 1990), chaps. 3–5; Anthony Giddens, *The Constitution of Society* (Berkeley and Los Angeles: University of California Press, 1984), chap. 1.

explanations of the particular actions involved. Practical understanding, in my account, resembles habitus and practical consciousness in being a skill or capacity that underlies activity. It differs in almost never determining what makes sense to people to do, in almost never, therefore, governing what people do. Practical understanding instead executes the actions that practical intelligibility singles out. I might add that know-hows of Bourdieu's and Giddens's sorts in reality lack the multiplicity required for attributing to them the determination of the specific actions people carry out. They also fail, consequently, to explain these actions. Invoking them simply marks conceptually that people's actions instantiate proficiencies at getting about in particular arenas. In applying, moreover, not just to specific actions, but to anything or much that actors might do in those arenas, they fail—once again—to explain *particular* actions.[28]

The second phenomenon that links the doings and sayings of a given practice is a set of rules. By "rules," I mean explicit formulations, principles, precepts, and instructions that enjoin, direct, or remonstrate people to perform specific actions. To say that rules link doings and sayings is to say that people, in carrying out these doings and sayings, take account of and adhere to the same rules. Examples of rules that were at work in the herb production practices are recipes for medicines and the following injunctions: that trustees alone carry out transactions with the world, that trustees need not tell others in the business the actual prices paid and received for supplies and medicines, that "physics gardens" be laid out in square form, that rubbish not be left around the workhouses, that implements be in their proper places on Saturday night and as far as is consistent every night, and that the press horse not be called by a given or Christian name.[29] Notice that one way normativity shapes what makes sense to people to do is through rules. Although, incidentally, it should be obvious, it bears saying (given the attention lavished on rules in

---

[28] For details, see my essay, "Practices and Actions: A Wittgensteinian Critique of Bourdieu and Giddens," *Philosophy of the Social Sciences* 27, 3 (1997): 283–308. Similar comments do not apply to Dreyfus's notion of coping skills, which boast a teleological structuring that outfits them with the necessary explanatory multiplicity. This teleological structure resembles what I call "teleological chains." See Hubert Dreyfus, *Being-in-the-World: A Commentary on Heidegger's Being and Time, Division I* (Cambridge, Mass.: MIT Press, 1991), chaps. 3, 5, and 11.

[29] These rules, culled from the 1843 *Millennial Laws* (reprinted in Edward Deming Andrews, *The People Called Shakers* [New York: Dover, 1963], 243–89), applied to a variety of Shaker practices and not those of medicinal herb production alone. Although additional rules specific to herb production must have existed, the primary sources contain scant evidence of them (apart from remonstrations from deceased ministers conveyed through "instruments," i.e., mediums). More can be gathered from these sources about the next two dimensions of practice organization.

recent decades) that rules of the present sort are not explicitizations of previously unarticulated understandings. Nor are they tacit or implicit formulas or contents (as in, say, Giddens). Rather, they are formulations interjected into social life for the purpose of orienting and determining the course of activity, typically by those with the authority to enforce them.

Linking the doings and sayings of a practice is, third, a teleoaffective structure. A "teleoaffective structure" is a range of normativized and hierarchically ordered ends, projects, and tasks, to varying degrees allied with normativized emotions and even moods. By "normativity," I mean, first, oughtness and, beyond this, acceptability. The indefinite range of end-project-task combinations contained in a practice's teleoaffective structure and realized in participants' doings and sayings are either ones that participants ought to realize or ones that it is acceptable for them to do so: A practice always exhibits a set of ends that participants should or may pursue, a range of projects that they should or may carry out for the sake of these ends, and a selection of tasks that they should or may perform for the sake of those projects. Participants, moreover, typically carry out end-project-task combinations that are contained in the practice's teleoaffective structure; that is to say, normativized ends, projects, and tasks determine what is signified to them to do. As indicated, coordinated with this teleological structuring are emotions and moods that participants should or may enjoy. Practices vary greatly in both the complexity of their teleological structuring and the depth of their affective ordering. Western cooking practices, for instance, are typically heavy on teleological and light on affective structure, whereas Western rearing practices display considerably more of the affective. To say that doings and sayings are linked by a teleoaffective structure is to say that they pursue end-project combinations that are contained in the same teleoaffective structure.

For the sake of clarity, I should explain that a teleoaffective structure is not a set of properties of actors. It is, instead, the property of a practice: a set of ends, projects, and affectivities that, as a collection, is (1) expressed in the open-ended set of doings and sayings that compose the practice and (2) unevenly incorporated into different participants' minds and actions. For example, the fact that different sequences of tasks could be pursued for the sake of producing extract medicine was an aspect of the teleological organization of the production practices and expressed only in the doings and sayings of multiple workers over time. Some workers, moreover, carried out (and grasped) certain such sequences, while others such as Hollister carried out (and understood) most of them. Helping to establish the distinction between end-project combinations as elements of a practice's structure and as incorporated/expressed in participants' mind/actions, are cross-references and inter-relations among them. For example, the task of getting herbs to the drying room implicitly refers to the task of drying them, even though someone can carry out the former task without carrying out (or even knowing about) the latter. Neophytes, finally, come to perform actions that express elements of a practice's structure by joining in the practice's activity through learning as well as instruction and correction.

Teleoaffective structures are not just distinct from properties of participants. They also are not equivalent to collectively willed ends and projects (e.g., the general will or the we-intentions of a group). Ends, for instance, need not be conscious goals, that is to say, states of affairs that people consciously seek to realize. A person need not be thematically aware—at any time—of the teleological end points that determine what makes sense to him or her to do. Nor are such structures, ontologically speaking, the same as, though they are closer to, Giddens's rule-resource structures, which both mediate and are reproduced in activity. Teleoaffective structures are recurring and evolving effects of what actors do together with what determines this. They themselves, however, do not govern activity. Activity is governed by practical intelligibility, which is itself determined by mental conditions, many of which formed during the processes of learning and being trained and instructed to carry on the practices involved. It follows that the normativity that characterizes a practice's teleoaffective structure shapes what makes sense to people to do by way of the example, instruction, and sanction to which neophytes (and veterans) are subject and in the context of which certain mental conditions arise in these individuals.

The Shaker herb production practices exhibited a number of ends, including making a profit, maximizing profit, meeting demand, keeping the machinery functional, and maintaining sufficient stock. In pursuit of these ends, an array of projects and tasks either was supposed to or could acceptably be carried out, for example, all the activities of hoisting, storing, drying, experimenting, heating, and the like mentioned to this point. When carrying on production practices at the herb, extract, or dairy houses, the workers' doings and sayings expressed tasks-projects-end(s) combinations that fell within the practice's teleoaffective structure. Of course, while at work, people could also perform doings and sayings that composed other practices, for example, those of rebellion, self-promotion, or sexual dalliance; that is to say, these houses of work could be the site (in the second sense of this term) where Shakers carried out multiple practices, not all of which were compatible with those of herb production. Furthermore, the emotions and moods that Shaker herbal medicine workers were supposed or permitted to exhibit were considerably less firmly delimited than were teleological hierarchies. Shakers were supposed, for example, to maintain a certain degree of piety and measuredness in their demeanor. No one minded, moreover, if herb workers felt lazy on very hot days and somewhat bored or dull when faced with the same projects and tasks for days on end. In line, finally, with the utilitarian spirit pervading these practices, workers collectively experienced anxiety in the face of setbacks as well as satisfaction when the business went especially well.

I wrote in Chapter 1 that one of the teleological regimes permeating Shaker life was hierarchical authority. Hierarchical control was built into the teleoaffective structure of the herbal medicine practices because the obligatoriness and/or acceptability of certain teleological chains were tied to specific identities. For example, it was not for everyone participating in these practices, but only for those understood to be foremen, that teleological chains issuing in the assignment of people to projects and in the remonstration of people for nonexecution of their assignments were obligatory or acceptable. Hierarchical authority is not the only phenomenon, however, of which the articulation of teleoaffective structure (and rules) around specific identities is an aspect. It is also a facet, for example, of the division of labor. In the previous chapter, I wrote that a person's identity depends partly on where he or she fits into social arrangements. It now emerges that it is also tied to the practices in which he or she participates, whose organizations are articulated around identities available to participants.

Inclusion of profit among the ends of this practice indicates that the ends, projects, and emotions that compose a practice's teleoaffective structure can be the object of controversy. I indicated in Chapter 1 that the profit motive seems to have got the better of certain Shaker deacons and forepersons, and that this situation was the subject of some remonstration and conflict in Shaker villages. The fact that the pursuit of profit was controversial did not dislodge it from its position as one of the overall ends of the herb production practices. However much some Shakers disliked it, workers continued to carry out tasks and projects whose performance subtended this aim. As this shows, the status of oughtness or acceptability does not preclude controversy.

The existence of normative controversy also points toward the issue of what the contents of a given teleoaffective structure are. Which ends, projects, tasks, and emotions are obligatory or acceptable in a practice is open-ended. What I mean is that a definitive list cannot be drawn up of these items, and this for two reasons. First, a teleoaffective structure is indefinitely complex. This indefiniteness is partly due to the indefinite variety of circumstances in which any practice is carried out and partly due to the fact that there are always more projects, tasks, and even ends that participants can acceptably carry out (e.g., novel ones hitherto untried or unconceived; the only limits here are those of participants' imaginations). Open-endedness arises, second, from the situation that what is acceptable (or obligatory) in a practice is often subject to discussion and contention, and the results of such disputes are indeterminate before they are completed. What is acceptable (or obligatory) is also sometimes tied to the decrees of authorities, which are likewise indeterminate until issued. In addition, Rouse has pointed out, against those who tie normativity to community response, that who is a member of a community is not settled in advance of the moments when community response is to determine correct or incorrect performance.[30] Similarly, contestation and conflict can attend who is a participant in a given practice and who is admitted as a partner in conversations about what is and is not acceptable (or obligatory) there. In my view, incidentally, anyone in principle can participate in a discussion of the normative content of a practice. It is only to be expected, however, that participants in the practice have more to offer on this topic than nonparticipants. Not only, moreover, are the outcomes of these discussions indeterminate before their conclusion. They need not end in consensus and can, in principle, always be reopened.

These facts do not imply that practically any end, project, or task can be part of any teleoaffective structure and, as a result, that the teleoaffective structures of practices—and therewith practices themselves—cannot be distinguished. The existence of a teleoaffective structure is a factual matter. Aside from cases where a specific designated authority pronounces normativity, a teleoaffective structure exists when general agreement reigns about what is and is not acceptable in a practice (i.e., in a comprehensive activity that people understand themselves to be carrying on). Disputed, unclear, contentious, and not yet attempted or conceived teleoaffective orders are all addressed, debated,

---

[30] Rouse, *Engaging Science,* 139, 144–45.

and conceived against the background of this agreement. Of course, the scopes of such agreements are not immutable. They evolve along with innovations, changes in circumstances, and the results of disputation. But this evolution entails only, in general, that background agreement is moving and, in particular, that contestation alters the background against which further contestation occurs. Furthermore, although participants can disagree about whether background agreement reigns, their opinions on the matter do not determine its existence or absence. What determines this is whether people see eye to eye in most cases. The existence of disagreement of such magnitude that people do not largely concur and are split into two or more conflicting camps entails that the practice has been destroyed, is dividing into two or more different practices, is about to coalesce, or never existed—despite appearances—in the first place.

Similarly, who the participants in a practice are is only contingently related to people's opinions on the matter. Anyone who performs actions that are part of a nexus of activities organized by a collection of interlinked understandings, rules, and teleoaffective structure is by that fact alone a participant in that practice. This fact proscribes neither the contentiousness of judgments about who is a participant nor the use of explicit criteria (if any) to admit people into the practice. It does entail, however, that people can be wrong about who the participants are and that some participants might be barred from debates about the contours of normativity there. The point is Wittgenstein's: Normativity bottoms out in the holding of certain facts.[31] The facts that these facts might not hold and that people might have different opinions about whether they do does not alter this rootedness.

Brandom has recently offered thoughts about membership that seem to make this account of the contents of teleoaffective structures problematic.[32] He claims that membership in a community is a normative status: To be a member of a community means that one *ought* to conform to the normativity plying its practices. He avers this, moreover, as part of an argument against that subset of so-called regularity accounts of normativity that analyze what is correct and incorrect, and appropriate and inappropriate, by reference to regularities of communal assessment. Brandom's point in maintaining this is that these analyses covertly—and illicitly—make appeal to normative notions.

I acknowledge that participation in a practice entails a normative status

---

[31] Cf. the famous remarks at Wittgenstein, *Philosophical Investigations*, par. 217.
[32] Brandom, *Making It Explicit*, 37–42.

of the sort Brandom claims, namely, being obliged to act in accord with the practice's teleoaffective structure. One of the issues I just broached was, *Which* individuals are participants and obliged thus? My answer was: all those—in the past, present, or future—whose doings and sayings express elements of the practice's organization (Chapter 4 discusses the temporal dimension of practice organization). Being a participant is not, therefore, *defined* as a normative status, that is to say, as being someone who ought to conform to normativity. Being a participant is a factual matter, the obtaining of which *implies* that one ought to do what is obligatory and acceptable (this implication simply reflects the fact that the organization of a practice is normative).[33]

Hence, although I rely on regularities of assessment, that is to say, general agreement in demarcating the contents of teleoaffective structures, my account of this demarcation is not subject to Brandom's arguments. Because participation is not defined as a normative status, I do not "smuggl[e] normative notions illicitly into what purports to be a reductive, nonnormative theory."[34] (I also certainly do not essay a "reductive" account of normativity that specifies sufficient conditions, in nonnormative terms, for a "content," that is to say, a rule, end, task, or emotion, having normative force.) Moreover, my notion of a participant does not presuppose any ontologically suspect social formation, a charge Brandom levels at the conception of communities found in community regularity theories. Finally, I do not tie the contents of teleoaffective structure to the assessments of participants alone. As noted, anyone in principle is a legitimate partner in discussions about the scope of these structures. I simply claim that, *as a matter of fact,* people generally agree about what is obligatory and acceptable in and connected with the activities they carry on; that, as a result, there exist practices with distinct teleoaffective structures in which subsets of people participate; and that the more precise demarcation of these structures rests on discussion, conducted above all among those who participate in these practices and are, thus, already conforming to these structures. Indeed, this seems to me a version of the general position that Brandom advocates, namely, that normativity is instituted in practical attitudes and that contents are conferred in social practices.

[33] I should add that, because I do not analyze practices as regularities of action, my claim here is not targeted by an argument Brandom levels at "simple" regularity theories of norms concerning the distinction between those people in whose activities the norms are implicit and those on whom the norms are binding; cf. Brandom, *Making It Explicit,* 26–30.
[34] Brandom, *Making It Explicit,* 38.

I wrote in the previous chapter that two of the teleoaffective regimes infusing Shaker life were religious conviction and sense of community. These regimes illustrate the fourth component of practice organization, general understandings. As explained, the Shakers viewed labor as a sanctification of the earthly sphere. Because of this, they sometimes demonstrated unusual tenacity and dedication in their temporal pursuits. Indeed, a reader of these enterprises' journals and diaries cannot overlook the zealous perseverance of some (not all) workers.[35] The tenacity and dedication of these workers manifested a general understanding that Shakers had of their work and, thus, of themselves. This understanding qualifies as a further component of the organization of the medicinal herb production practices because a variety of the doings and sayings that composed these practices expressed it. For the same reasons, the sense of common enterprise, concern, and fate that is central to people forming a commune also helped compose these practices' organization. This general understanding was expressed in some of the same steadfast, determined actions that expressed an understanding of work as religious sanctification. It was further manifested in the friendly, courteous, and decent manner of interaction widely noted of—though hardly universal among—the Shakers, as well as in the tendency of workers at the herb and extract houses to uphold and not to contravene the rules and teleological organization of the production practices. Of course, neither the religious nor the communitarian understanding was unique to the medicinal herb practices. They were *general* understandings that helped organize most Shaker temporal practices. Notice that pervasive understandings of this sort are expressed in the manner in which people carry out projects and tasks, in this case, the fervent dedication with which herb production activities were sometimes pursued, as well as the usually friendly and courteous cast of interaction. Such understandings, however, can also be expressed in doings and sayings (as opposed to their manner of performance), as when Shakers spontaneously broke out in song at the workplace, when they formulated the religious bearing of their labor in speech, or when all the men in a village joined together to carry out some project such as raising the extract house.

[35] This reader found especially stunning the repeated long nights and extremely early morning risings of the herbalist Elisha Myrick in the early 1850s, as documented in Elisha Myrick, *Day Book Kept for the Convenience of the Herb Department by Elisha Myrick Harvard Church*, Hancock Shaker Village, Hancock, Mass. (covering 1849–52); and Elisha Myrick, *A Diary Kept for the Convenience of the Herb Department by Elisha Myrick*, Edward Deming Andrews Memorial Shaker Collection, Winterthur Library, Winterthur, Del., manuscript no. 837 (covering 1853–57).

In sum, a practice is a temporally evolving, open-ended set of doings and sayings linked by practical understandings, rules, teleoaffective structure, and general understandings. It is important to emphasize that the organization of a practice describes the practice's frontiers: A doing or saying belongs to a given practice if it expresses components of that practice's organization. This delimitation of boundaries entails that practices can overlap. A particular doing, for instance, might belong to two or more practices by virtue of expressing components of these different practices' organizations. The doings and sayings that were performed when the extract house steam engine was repaired, for example, might have been moments of both the production practices at New Lebanon and certain Shaker power system practices that cut through different Shaker industrial practices and were carried out at different villages. As this language of "cutting through" suggests, practices crisscross and interweave, thereby forming densely interwoven mats. Another way that practices overlap is for a given organizational component to belong to more than a single practice. Examples are the Shaker rules earlier cited, which applied broadly across practices; the pursuit of profit, which characterized numerous Shaker industrial practices; the task of printing labels, which was carried out in a number of temporal practices; and the sense of religious sanctification that attached to temporal concerns generally. (Common organizational elements, it might be noted, help link practices into ensembles.) The distinctiveness of different practices lies in the distinctiveness of the *package* of doings and sayings plus organization that each is: a particular set of doings and sayings expressing a particular array of cross-referencing and interconnected abilities, rules, teleoaffectivities, and understandings. This implies that *which* practices exist in social life is the empirical issue of which such packages factually subsist there.

Practices, as I have described them, are social phenomena. This is because, first, participating in them entails immersion in an extensive tissue of coexistence that embraces varying sets of people. A participant in a practice coexists not just with those with whom she interacts, but also eo ipso with various sets of other participants, including the collection of all participants. In carrying on medicinal herb production practices, for example, Hollister coexisted with all those who worked at extracting juices, all those who dried herbs, all those who pursued profit through the production of medicinal herb products, and all those who obeyed the injunction not to call the horse by a name. Practices are social, second, because, as stated, their organization is expressed in the nexuses of doings and sayings that compose them, as opposed to the individual doings and sayings involved.

Before explaining how practices establish arrangements, one final distinction is in order. What I have been calling "practices" are a particular category of practice, "integrative practices." As the name suggests, integrative practices are complex entities joining multiple actions, projects, ends, and emotions. Social life is also plied by a second type of practice, "dispersed practices," which are considerably simpler than their integrative kin. Examples of dispersed practices are describing, ordering, questioning, reporting, and examining. As these examples suggest, dispersed practices center around a single type of action. In labeling them "dispersed," I call attention to the fact that certain activities circulate through different sectors of social life, retaining more or less the same shape in those different sectors. In different arenas and integrative practices of Shaker life, for example, questioning and ordering occurred and remained more or less the same. One must take care, however, when offering examples of dispersed practices. At the same time that a dispersed practice of questioning coursed through and remained the same in different Shaker domains, a very different-looking activity of questioning was carried on in Shaker confessional practices. The existence of a dispersed practice of X-ing does not preclude the existence of X-ing activities that are specific to particular integrative practices and that differ from both their dispersed cousin(s) and one another.

In contrast to the doings and sayings that compose integrative practices, those composing a dispersed practice of X-ing are usually linked by a practical understanding of X-ing alone. These doings and sayings express abilities to carry out X-ings and to recognize X-ings and perhaps also to prompt and respond to X-ings. In carrying out their dispersed practice of questioning, for example, Shakers performed doings and sayings that expressed abilities to question, recognize questions, and respond to them (e.g., answering). Unlike integrative practices, however, dispersed practices are typically rule free. They rarely, moreover, possess teleoaffective structure. Indeed, the absence of such structure is what makes it possible for them to exist in varied walks of life.

The webs of interweaving practices in which humans exist and coexist embrace integrative and dispersed practices. While integrative practices overlap, interweave, and also conflict (see Chapter 3), dispersed practices course through them. At any time and place, social life transpires in a nexus of dispersed practices-woven-into-wedded-or-conflicting integrative ones.

3. How Practices Establish Orders

The thesis that social practices are the contexture in which social orders are established faces two adversaries. The first disputes that orders are contexturalized at all, whereas the second promotes phenomena other than practices as the contextures of order. I have no general argument against the claims of nominalism. My rejoinder to theories such as those of Latour and Callon is a demonstration that, yes, orders do subsist in a contexture that helps found them. Arguments to that effect are found in this section. A further tack is to unearth difficulties with particular contexture-denying theories, a path to be taken later.

Similar strategies can be pursued against competing contexturalist accounts. In this instance, however, I want also to confront one chief competitor, Deleuze and Guattari's theory of social assemblages as presented in their book *A Thousand Plateaus.*[36] Doing so helps clarify the entire issue of arrangements and contextures. Deleuze and Guattari's theory stands for a pervasive twentieth-century school of thought that explains the progress of social affairs by reference to abstract structures. Inspired by de Saussure's separation of *la parole* from *la langue,* this school maintains that abstract structures inform and/or constrain both human activity and the phenomena it brings about. What makes Deleuze and Guattari particularly pertinent in the present context is that they

---

[36] Gilles Deleuze and Félix Guattari, *A Thousand Plateaus: Capitalism and Schizophrenia,* trans. Brian Massumi (Minneapolis: University of Minnesota Press, 1987). Page references to this book henceforth appear in the text. In the current work, by the way, I attend solely to a particular phase of Deleuze and Guattari's production: *A Thousand Plateaus.* The other texts I principally draw on are two of Deleuze's that immediately flank this work, *Dialogues* (with Claire Parnet) and *Foucault.* This focus means that I practically ignore part 1 (*Anti-Oedipus*) of the two-part work, *Capitalism and Schizophrenia,* of which *A Thousand Plateaus* is part 2. The reason for this selectivity is that, whereas *Anti-Oedipus* is very much a critical confrontation with psychoanalysis, *A Thousand Plateaus* offers a general metaphysics that not only is largely independent of (though anticipated in many regards by) its companion, but largely rewrites the analyses found in *Anti-Oedipus* of topics the two works address in common. What is more, the theory in *A Thousand Plateaus* is considerably richer and both more systematic and far-reaching than the account developed in *Anti-Oedipus.* I do not, in any event, aim to interpret Deleuze and Guattari comprehensively. All in all, dealing with *Anti-Oedipus* and its differences with *A Thousand Plateaus* would overburden my narrative. For adepts, I should add that *A Thousand Plateaus* is treated more or less as a unified work presenting a systematic metaphysics. I acknowledge that its chapters (plateaus) might not fit together smoothly and that, in many regards, it is a highly personal effort. Nonetheless, it does clearly have systematic intent, as plateaus 3 and 15 demonstrate. Given, moreover, that *A Thousand Plateaus* is just one of many players in the present work, I do not confront its (alleged) inconsequence and eccentricity.

developed an account of assemblages that directly rivals my account of arrangements and argued that assemblages are contextualized in abstract structures
that considerably differ from the contexture in which arrangements, I claim,
are immersed (i.e., practices). I describe their views in some detail on the
assumption that the reader is unfamiliar with them.

According to Deleuze and Guattari, reality boasts various "strata." These
strata are populated by "assemblages," and entities of two types compose the
assemblages that populate any given stratum. The technical names for these
types are "content" and "expression." On the social stratum, contents are people, artifacts, and things, whereas expressions are statements. (Because Deleuze
and Guattari usually spoke of persons and artifacts alone, I henceforth forsake
mention of things.) On any stratum, moreover, assemblages are constellations
of contents and of expressions. On the social stratum, in particular, assemblages
are composed of regimes of power (constellations of contents) and regimes
of enunciation (constellations of expressions). Contents and expressions alike
also, once again on any stratum, have forms and matters. Forms are organizations and orders of functions and finalities, whereas matters are the materialities that forms organize and order. In a social field, (1) forms of content are
organizations of the functions, statuses, and relations of people and artifacts;
(2) matters of content are the materialities that acquire one or more of these
functions, statuses, or relations; (3) forms of expression are organizations of
what meaningful entities express; and (4) matters of expression are materialities that express something.

To illustrate this conceptual armature, Deleuze and Guattari distilled an
example from Foucault's *Discipline and Punish*.[37] In this example, forms of
content are prison, school, barracks, and factory. These are functional organizations of persons and artifacts as formations of power. The correlative matters
of content are particular bodies and materials. In being organized, say, by the
prison form, these matters become such contents as prisoners, wardens, guards,
cells, surveillance towers, punitive actions, and internalized self-surveillance.
The prison regime of power, consequently, is an organized constellation of
these entities.[38] The form of expression of the enunciation regime associated

[37] The following reading merges the slightly varying accounts found in *A Thousand Plateaus*, 66–67,
and Gilles Deleuze, *Foucault*, trans. and ed. Seán Hand (Minneapolis: University of Minnesota
Press, 1988), 31, 33, and 47.
[38] Brian Massumi claims that a regime's form of content (in his terms, "form of containment") is an
organization of already existent contents, whose individual forms (in his terms, "orders of qualities")

with the prison power regime is penal law. It is a finalizing organization of expressibles as a system of enunciation. The correlative matters of expression are used, performed, or uttered marks, gestures, and sounds, which in being organized by the penal law form are statements pertaining to delinquency, for example, its nature, its genesis, its infractions, and the sentences accruing to it. The penal law regime of enunciation is, thus, a collection of statements about delinquency.[39] In sum, the concrete assemblage that Deleuze (and Guattari) extracted from Foucault's text is a prison-penal law configuration: the interlaced confinement, surveillance, and punishment of people in prisons (a regime of power) in association with an ensemble of statements about delinquency (a regime of enunciation).

Any social assemblage is a regime of power and a regime of enunciation. What combines the two into a single assemblage is the fact that they presuppose each other. The one cannot exist without the other. (I believe that this entails that the forms organizing these two regimes are also mutually presupposing.) What, in turn, underlies the reciprocal presupposition of the two regimes is the fact that they are actualizations of governing schemas. Regimes of these two sorts presuppose each other when they are actualizations of one and the same abstract schema, each of whose "substantializations" necessarily consists of a regime of each sort. As actualizations of something that can be actualized only in dual form, regimes of power and enunciation, together with their forms of content and expression, presuppose each other.

are distinct from that form of content. This assertion is ambiguous. A prisoner is not a prisoner independently of the prison form of content (and the penal law form of expression). A human body is a prisoner only as organized by this form. So Massumi is wrong if the individual forms he has in mind are prisoner, warden, cell, and the like. (His example of students and schools suggests that he means this.) On the other hand, the bodies that are prisoners, cells, and so on have invariably already been coded as various contents *in different assemblages* on the same or subjacent stratum, for instance, as father, worker, and human being. Human beings, for example, are organized units of bodily systems and processes on the stratum subjacent to the social field (in Deleuze and Guattari's words, the "external milieu"). In this regard, Massumi is correct, for the bodies that become prisoners are always already human beings. I further agree with him that a "function" of a regime's form of content is to organize the affects (capacities) of that regime's contents. See Brian Massumi, *A Reader's Guide to Capitalism and Schizophrenia* (Cambridge, Mass.: MIT Press, 1992), 25–26, 152 n. 36.

[39] Deleuze's analysis of statements has not received attention or commentary to any degree commensurate with its depth of insight and suggestiveness. This analysis, more or less presupposed in A *Thousand Plateaus,* is developed at length in Deleuze's earlier book, *The Logic of Sense,* trans. Mark Lester with Charles Stivale (New York: Columbia University Press, 1990). For a thoughtful account of this analysis, see John M. Heaton, "Language-Games, Expression, and Desire in the Work of Deleuze," *Journal of the British Society for Phenomenology* 24, 1 (1993): 77–87.

Deleuze and Guattari called these schemas "abstract machines." An abstract machine is an essential organizational factor on any stratum of reality. It is pure Matter-Function (141), a "diagram" of nonformal matters and nonformal functions (511), which is "substantialized" by specific assemblages on its stratum. In its role as diagram, an abstract machine defines the "unity of composition" (or "program") of the stratum involved (71). This means that it generally specifies the materialities on which that stratum's assemblages draw (the "exterior milieu"), the contents and expressions that these materials become, and the forms that organize these contents and expressions as assemblages. The abstract machine itself, however, knows no distinction between content and expression. Its "functions are not yet 'semiotically' formed, and [its] matters are not yet 'physically' formed" (141). Nonformal matters and nonfinalized functions precede the division into content and expression, and they possess "traits" of content and expression only in the sense that their concretion always involves this distinction. It is in the assemblages that substantialize an abstract machine that nonformalized materials are divided into matters of content and expression, nonformalized functions become forms of content and expression, and the therewith resulting entities are organized in parallel regimes. Indeed, this is part of what it means to say that assemblages "substantialize" machines. Hence, the regimes of content and of expression that in tandem effectuate abstract machines presuppose each other because they actualize a diagram whose substantializations necessarily effect a division into content and expression. As Deleuze elsewhere asserted, "It is precisely because the [abstract machine], in both its matter and its functions, disregards form that it is realized on the basis of a central differentiation which, on the one hand, will form visible matter, and on the other will formalize articulable functions."[40] Multiple assemblages, furthermore, can substantialize one and the same diagram; any abstract machine can be effectuated multiply. Indeed, assemblages vary in how "adequately" they substantialize machines (71).

These contentions can be illustrated, once again, with the example Deleuze and Guattari drew from *Discipline and Punish*. The abstract machine at work in the social field described in that book is panopticism. Its diagram, its pure Matter-Function, is "to impos[e] a particular taste or conduct on a multiplicity of individuals."[41] When this diagram is substantialized in a particular

---

[40] Deleuze, *Foucault*, 38. See also the statement in Gilles Deleuze and Claire Parnet, *Dialogues,* trans. Hugh Tomlinson and Barbara Habberjam (New York: Columbia University Press, 1987), 71.

[41] Deleuze, *Foucault,* 72. In *A Thousand Plateaus,* Deleuze and Guattari seem to characterize the

assemblage, it divides into a prison (or barracks or school, etc.) form of content that organizes persons and artifacts and a penal law (or training or education, etc.) form of expression that organizes statements. The materials that are so organized are particular bodies, objects, and uttered or written sounds and marks. As actualizations of the same panoptic machine, moreover, these regimes and forms are mutually presupposing. Deleuze claimed, additionally, that in *History of Sexuality, Volume 1* Foucault discerned a second diagram at work in nineteenth-century Western societies, namely, "controlling and administering life in a particular multiplicity."[42] This diagram has two pure functions, an "anatomo-politics" and a "bio-politics," whose pure matters are a particular body and a particular population, respectively.

It is worth interjecting that, in claiming that prisons and penal law presuppose each other, Deleuze and Guattari, despite their reliance on Foucault, departed radically from him. Prisons and penal law are certainly related. The story that *Discipline and Punish* tells, however, is one of small, circumstantial, and sometimes interconnected shifts and transformations, the end result of which is a contingent complex in which prisons, penal law, delinquency, and surveillance hang together. One great insight of that work is that history is made in minute, happenstance, at times converging and at other times diverging moves, the consequences of which could just as easily have turned out otherwise than they did (see Chapter 4). There is no room in this picture for mutual presupposition. If X presupposes Y, X *cannot* exist without Y. This is a very strong requirement. X might depend on Y without being unable to exist without Y, in which case the relation between them is the weaker one of dependence. In *Discipline and Punish,* the prison and penal law regimes are described as mutually dependent, in that the particular form each took depended on the particular shape of the other. For Foucault, however, this was a matter of contingent joint historical fate, not mutual presupposition.

An abstract machine, in determining a social stratum's unity of composition, grounds the forms that organize regimes of power and enunciation: the functions, statuses, relations, and expresseds that characterize concrete assemblages. I write "grounds" instead of something stronger because abstract

---

panoptic diagram as "the unspecified multiplicity of human beings to be controlled" (530–31 n. 39). In a further essay, moreover, Deleuze describes it as: "To see without being seen, applicable to any multiplicity" ("Desire and Pleasure," in *Foucault and His Interlocutors,* ed. Arnold Davidson, trans. Daniel W. Smith [Chicago: University of Chicago Press, 1997], 183–92, here 184).

[42] Deleuze, *Foucault,* 72.

machines do not necessitate, cause, or even determine that particular forms organize the assemblages substantializing them. It was not panopticism, for example, that made prison, barracks, and school, as well as penal law, training, and education, the particular forms of content and of expression that organized the assemblages that substantialized it. As indicated, Deleuze and Guattari's claim that assemblages "substantialize" (or "effectuate") abstract machines means that assemblages themselves perform the division of non-finalized matters and functions into substances of and forms of content and expression (e.g., 71, 73, 100). As a result, the assemblages that concretize abstract machines bear responsibility for the particular shapes they themselves take. Deleuze and Guattari were less than clear, however, about exactly how this works, about why the assemblages that effectuate abstract machines boast the particular forms they do.

Indeed, Deleuze and Guattari offered no general account on this issue. I do not think, moreover, that they would have averred that no general account exists and that explanations of why assemblages possess particular forms lie in the details of empirical history. This tack would only make it harder to grasp why a given assemblage's form should be analyzed as an effectuation of an abstract machine that organizes the stratum on which it exists. Perhaps Deleuze and Guattari believed there are no adequate general *or* particular answers to questions of this sort, and that it just happens that the assemblages that realize a given diagram in a social field take particular forms. What is clear is that the abstract machine grounds these forms (they "derive" from it [68]), without requiring that just these forms substantialize it. What fills the gap, however, is not obvious. I return to this issue in Chapter 4.

Recall that a context is a set of distinct phenomena with powers of determination over the entities immersed in it and that a context is a contexture when it is composed of entities of different sorts from those of which it is the context. Abstract machines form a contexture in which assemblages exist. These assemblages, to begin with, are "immersed" in these machines in the sense of being actualizations of them. The machines, furthermore, are distinct beings. They are not linguistic formula or universals nominalistically construed. Nor are they objective universals or actual entities in addition to the assemblages effectuating them. Rather, they are "virtual-Real" entities, abstract singular beings (100), which are substantialized in multiple "collective" assemblages. Abstract machines, finally, also possess powers of determination vis-à-vis assemblages. These powers are not causal, but concern the movement from virtuality to actuality: Assemblages, as actualizations of virtual diagrams, are held by and to these diagrams. They are held *by* diagrams in the sense that an actualization is necessarily beholden to that which it actualizes. To exist, in other words, an assemblage is obliged to be an actualization of a particular schema. Assemblages are also held *to* abstract machines because they must be one of the machine's possible substantializations. Deleuze and Guattari wrote that abstract machines contain possibilities, or potentialities (99). They are "plateaus of variation" (511). In this regard, an abstract machine's power of determination is the delimitation of a space of possible assemblages. (This, in turn, specifies another manner in which assemblages are immersed in them.) This form of determination has a temporal aspect because transformations of assemblages in a given social field are bound to the possible actualizations of the abstract machine reigning there. It should be added that assemblages and abstract machines presuppose each other. Just as there are no assemblages without the machines they effectuate, so, too, machines do not exist without assemblages that substantialize them (100).

In Chapter 4, I contest the well-formedness of fields of possibility and the value of citing them in accounts of historical change. At the same time, I am not sure what to think about the propositions that assemblages are held by abstract machines and are contexturalized in them simply by being their actualizations. My investigative eyes have become accustomed to seeing history as a maze of contingent series, which converge, coalesce, dissolve, and bifurcate on the basis of their constituent events and movements. As a result, I find the idea that social life is broken into blocks that effectuate abstract schemas fantastic. I have also grown suspicious of "virtual" structures that allegedly configure sociality without being contained in some causal or governing factor or mechanism at work in social life. Examples of virtual structures that are so embedded are (1) Lévi-Strauss's matrixlike social structures, which are supposedly rooted in the biochemical operations of the brain; and (2) the rule-resource sets and families of homologous oppositions that, according to Giddens and Bourdieu, respectively, structure human practices by being embedded in actors' practical senses or consciousnesses. (These sets and families resemble grammatical rules conceived of as nonconscious principles governing linguistic understanding.) Regardless of one's ultimate judgment about the cogency of these particular virtual structures, their embedment in causal or governing mechanisms that are directly present in social life pre-empts criticisms based on philosophical worries about how virtual phenomena can bind actual ones.

Deleuze and Guattari did not embed abstract machines in any phenomenon, structure, or mechanism in social life.[43] Hence, why and how concrete assemblages realize virtual diagrams remains mysterious. In the end, consequently, it is woefully unclear why an assemblage, qua effectuation of a given abstract machine, assumes such and such forms and not others. Perhaps Deleuze and Guattari would have said that this issue charts the limits of sociohistorical intelligibility. This response can, however, be turned around: If this issue is irresolvable, there is no reason to think that social affairs occur under the aegis of virtual Matter-Function diagrams—especially because no means of negotiating the virtuality-actuality interface has been described. As indicated, however, I return to this issue in Chapter 4, where the full powerlessness of abstract structures to govern social reality is plumbed.

How, then, according to my account, do practices—as opposed to abstract machines—contexturalize social orders? The key to this contexturalization lies in the fact that actions presuppose practices. I defended this thesis in detail in my previous book and sketch only the essential points here. The argument revolves around the issue of what it is, by virtue of which a doing or saying constitutes a particular action. I contend that, as matter of general principle, a doing or a saying constitutes an act of X-ing on the background of (1) the circumstances in which it is performed (e.g., the immediate and wider situation, the actor's previous and future actions, his or her mental conditions) and (2) the understandings of X-ing, Y-ing, Z-ing, and so on that are alive in the actor's world.[44] As outlined, furthermore, practices are composed of doings and sayings that are linked, inter alia, by action understandings they express. The understandings of action through which doings and sayings are linked in practices encompass the understandings of action against the background of which doings and sayings constitute specific actions. A doing or saying constitutes an X-ing, consequently, against the background of an understanding of X-ing that is carried in some practice. The action, as a result, presupposes the practice concerned. Indeed, it is a moment of the practice.

Two dimensions of arrangements are examined here: relations and meaning/identity. Extrapolating the following considerations to positionality is obvious.

[43] Nor do they follow Althusser in postulating a new form of causality ("structural causality") through which abstract structures govern concrete events. See Louis Althusser, "Marx's Immense Theoretical Revolution," in Louis Althusser and Etienne Balibar, *Reading Capital*, trans. Ben Brewster (London: New Left Books, 1970), 182–93.

[44] On the basis of the discussion in the previous section, the reader might have thought that a doing or saying constitutes a given action by virtue of expressing elements of a practice's organization. True enough: The present argument is designed to show precisely this.

Consider, first, the relations that hold among components of an arrangement. Causal relations, recall, often work via human action: actions that intervene in the world and make things happen, actions that lead to further actions, and actions that respond either to other actions or to something about humans, nonhumans, and their arrangement. Because these actions presuppose practices, the causal relations that work through them do so too. People are also responsible for numerous causal relations among nonhuman components of a social arrangement, for instance, those causal relations that they intentionally or nonintentionally set up in and through their activity. As a result, many, in fact, most intra-arrangement causal relations presuppose or depend on practices. Because, finally, what participants in a given practice do reflects the organization of the practice, to say that actions and causal relations presuppose and depend on practices is to say, among other things, that they occur under the aegis of the practices' organizations. In these ways, actions and causal relations are contexturalized in practices.

For example, all the rearranging of Shakers, machines, herbs, and horse that was effected by the activities of pressing, steeping, labeling, storing, and caring for transpired in a fabric of medicinal herb production practices-interlaced-with-dispersed practices of questioning, describing, ordering, and so on. Those causal relations that embraced workers' reactions to one another's actions or to changes in the world that these actions brought about likewise transpired in this fabric, exemplifying its organization. Indeed, elaborate, at times regular and at times irregular causal chains were established under the aegis of this practice meshwork. Even workers' reactions to such occasional occurrences as breakdowns in machines, rotting herbs, inclement weather, frozen pipes, and delays in bottle returns instantiated the organizations of the practices involved. Any variety of the causal relations, finally, that transpired between parts of the machines, the horse and the machines, the herbs and the machines, and the machines themselves were set up in human activity and, thus, similarly contexturalized.

As these examples substantiate, furthermore, this fabric of practices was also the *site* where the above actions transpired. These actions did not just reflect the organization of the medicinal herb production practices. They transpired *as* components of these practices: That is to say, they were *moments* of the temporally unfolding streams of activity that were these practices. In fact, they were the actions they were *only* as part of these streams. The production practices were also, consequently, the site where causal relations between constituent actions transpired.

To the extent, moreover, that spatial relations are either the intended products or unintended byproducts of human activity, they, too, are beholden to practice organizations and established in the fabric of practices. It follows that most of the spatial relations that characterize social arrangements are established under the aegis of practices, including, for example, the physical and activity-place layouts of the laboratory, vacuum pan, printing, and drying rooms in the extract house; the locations that workers occupied in these spaces when busy in these rooms with the equipment; and the positions of the roots, herbs, and liquids that were therewith handled and altered. Intentional relations likewise stand under the aegis of practice organization, though explaining this fully would divert the current discussion substantially. The essential point is that not just the teleoaffective structure (cf. footnote 22 above), but also the organization of a practice generally, can be described as an array of normativized (enjoined and acceptable) actions and mental conditions. Intentional relations, accordingly, are beholden to the organizations of practices when the mental conditions by virtue of which they obtain are components of those organizations. As Hollister carried on herbal production practices, for example, all the obligatory and acceptable desires, beliefs, understandings, and intentions that he possessed about—and that were expressed in his actions toward—the herbs, equipment, co-workers, and horse were components of the organization of these practices: His normativized mental relatedness to the entities arranged in the herb industry was largely established in this integrative practice. Furthermore, because mental conditions (like actions) are components of practice organization, the production practices were also the *site* where this mental directedness transpired. Mental relatedness was not just beholden to, but also an integral part of, the chief integrative practice that transpired at the herb, extract, and dairy houses.

The final relation among the components of an arrangement is prefiguration, or enablement/constraint. Instead of pursuing a tedious discussion about how such relations are established in practices, I simply offer two considerations that testify to this contexturalization. The first consideration is obvious but important. How artifacts (or the parts thereof) enable and constrain one another's actions depends not just on their physical properties, but also on the organization that human activity imposes on them. Artifacts are typically components of arrangements that are extensively set up in human activity. As a result, they enable and constrain one another *as* organized in particular ways, and these relations of enablement and constraint are beholden to the practices of which the organizing activities concerned are moments. In particular, they are beholden to functions or uses that devolve from the tasks, projects, and ends that organize the practice.

The second consideration builds on an observation of Giddens's, that how something enables and constrains a person's activities depends on her or his wants,[45] more broadly (it can be generalized), on her or his mental conditions. Giddens notes, for example, that the truth in Marx's claim that workers in capitalist societies must sell their labor to employers is that doing this is their only option given their desire to survive. This observation discloses that how arrangements of people, artifacts, organisms, and things enable and constrain people's actions depends on the latter's mental conditions. Because, therefore, normativized mentality is part of the organization of practices, how arrangements prefigure actions partly depends on the practices people carry on. In ways such as these, I submit, relations of enablement and constraint are established in the fabric of practices.

A second dimension of social orders is meanings and identities. Like relations among an arrangement's components, the meanings and identities of these components are contexturalized in practices. To establish this point, I enumerate examples from the previous chapter.

Artifacts, as discussed, have multiple meanings. Both their chief and ancillary meanings derive primarily from action. What the hydraulic press, for example, principally was lay in its function, that is to say, in what was to be done with it; and what was to be done with it—pressing herbs—was a component of herb department practices. The identical point holds for all artifacts that are use-objects (*Zeug*, in Heidegger's language).[46] Many of an artifact's collateral meanings exhibit a similar dependence on practices and their organizations. For example, the hydraulic press's meanings as something run by horse power and something in need of periodic repair rested on the teleoaffective structure of the production practices, together with actions performed and connections set up in them. Whether, moreover, its meaning as something obstructing the view of the meeting between the elder and trustee Fowler rested on such matters depends on whether the would-be witness's interest in the meeting concerned herb production or something else (for example, disciplinary actions). Similarly, some of the meanings of the horse and the rats qua

---

[45] Giddens, *The Constitution of Society,* 177; cf. 309.

[46] Martin Heidegger, *Being and Time,* trans. John Macquarrie and Edward Robinson (Oxford: Blackwell, 1962), sections 15–18.

components of the arrangements of the herb industry (e.g., powerer of the press, something needing reshoeing, nuisances, and causes of water backups) were either contained in or derivative from (e.g., the rats' meanings) the actions, causal connections, and teleoaffective structure of the production practices. Other of these entities' meanings (e.g., something to be cleaned up after and, once again, nuisances) derived from the organization of further practices, such as those of hygiene.

The identities of the Shakers participating in the herb practices also depended on the production practices and their organization. Hollister both was and understood himself to be extractor, experimenter, repairman, wild herb picker, and builder, for instance, insofar as he participated in these practices and carried out those of their ends, projects, and tasks that were articulated about—and the pursuit of which helped qualify him as possessing—these identities. His identities as writer of theological texts, recorder of testimonials, elder, worshiper, and dancer similarly derived from his participation in specific Shaker practices, for instance, those of reflection, documentation, authority, and worship. Finally, he acquired his identity as brother, member of the Center Family, and Shaker by virtue of participating in a range of practices. It should be clear, furthermore, that the meanings of the people, artifacts, and organisms that composed the arrangements at the herb, extract, and dairy houses both inter-related and hung together as an array. Even the meanings of the herbs and roots, at both their natural and artifactual stages, were part of this net. While they were still natural entities, for instance, their meanings both as things to be searched for and as belladonna, cicuta, cramp bark, and so on were relative to social practices, for instance, those of herbal production, folk medicine, and botanical classification. (What they were independently of all social arrangements is not at issue here.) As they became increasingly artifactual, furthermore, their meanings derived more decidedly from the herb production practices and their organization.

Practices are not just the context, but also the site where the meanings of arranged entities are instituted. This observation illustrates the more general point that practices are a site where considerable world intelligibility (the meanings of entities) is articulated. Indeed, any practice sustains a web of intelligibility in the sense that entities that enter its purview therewith receive meanings that derive from the practice's activities and organization. More specifically, entities of the following categories possess meanings *as* part of some practice or other: (1) those that perform the practice's actions; (2) those that are employed in or are the objects of these actions; (3) those that are the objects of the mental conditions encompassed in the practice's organization; (4) those whose causal, spatial, or prefigurational relations with other entities are intentionally set up in the practice's actions (i.e., setting up the relation is what makes sense to some participant[s] to do). Of course, not all the meanings that entities of these categories enjoy occur as part of practices. Practices are not, for example, the site of those meanings that reflect states of affairs that are not intentionally set up in the practice (e.g., the press as too heavy for the floor supporting it, the pipes as overly prone to freezing). Practices still, however, form the context of these meanings to the extent that the latter are byproducts of the practice's actions.

In sum, social orders are largely established in practices. The relations among, meanings of, and, hence, positions of, the components of social orders are beholden, above all, to the doings and sayings that compose practices, in conjunction with practice organizations. The arrangements of people, artifacts, organisms, and things that help form the site of the social are laid down primarily in the interweaving and inter-related nexuses of activity that entities of the first of these sorts carry on. Whether this is all there is to the establishment of orders is an issue for the upcoming section and Chapter 4. It can be further concluded that practices are the site where much social order transpires. Many, though not all, of the meanings/identities and causal as well as intentional relations that orders exhibit occur *as* components of the fabric of practices.

In the previous chapter, I wrote that the demarcation of arrangements rests on interests and purposes. I also claimed that distributions of relations compose constellations, regions, and densities, which investigating demarcators should acknowledge. The fact that practices establish orders places additional—and exacting—constraints on this relativity. Practices establish *particular* arrangements. These arrangements are definite packages of entities, relations, meanings, and positions, whose integrity derives from the organizations of practices. As documented, for example, the medicinal herb production practices, together with the dispersed practices coursing through them, established definite arrangements of Shakers, artifacts, organisms, and things. To acquire definite contours, consequently, the arrangements that practices establish do not await the action or judgment of demarcators. Of course, practices do not establish all the relations that hold among either components of a given arrangement or entities in different arrangements. The horse was responsible for some of the relations it maintained with entities in the herb house (e.g., its oats), just as severe thunderstorms led herb industry workers to worry about their sisters and brothers in the woods gathering herbs. These extra relations give texture to the site of the social beyond the particular constellations set up in practices; and this excess leaves room for legitimately interest-relative demarcations of arrangements that diverge from the definite orders established in practices. Similarly interest relative is the discretion attending (1) how arrangements can be simplified for the purposes of representation and analysis (as in the herb industry and day trading examples in this book) and (2) how the even more far-reaching complexes formed by interconnected arrangements can be divided into regions for the same purposes. Nonetheless, the arrangements established in practices are a feature of social life—beyond the distribution of relations—which demarcators must respect if they are to demarcate propitiously.

To conclude this section, I reinforce the significance of practices as contextures by considering an aspect of Deleuze and Guattari's account hitherto neglected. In *A Thousand Plateaus,* Deleuze and Guattari claimed that every social assemblage, in addition to being composed of regimes of power and of enunciation, is strung between two poles. The first pole, called the "molecular," is the inter-related movement of its components (persons, artifacts, and statements). The second pole, called the "molar," is a rigid segmentation of the assemblage's components (41).[47] The contrast between the two poles is one between the agitation of numerous entities-in-movement (flows, quanta) and the partitioning of these entities via rigid determinations (segments, lines), otherwise called "centralization," "unification," and "integration" (41, 216). Among the examples Deleuze and Guattari offered of rigid segmentation are dwelling/getting around/working/playing; the functional division of rooms in a house, factory, or administrative building; the departmental division of the state; and social classes (e.g., 208, 213, 214). The corresponding molecular organizations are collections of nexused actions; layouts of and connections among walls, doors, ceilings, use objects, and activities; an immensely complicated maze composed of components from different assemblages; and masses of people. Assemblages, accordingly, are centralized, totalized, and hierarchical plenums of people-, artifacts-, and statements-in-motion.

---

[47] Strictly speaking, regimes of power and regimes of enunciation each possess molecular and molar dimensions (41). For the sake of simplicity, I overlook this in the following and treat these as dimensions of configurations that conjoin contents and expressions.

Deleuze and Guattari explained that the molecular and the molar are not two distinct realities. They are, instead, two systems of reference that apply to one and the same constellations of contents and expressions (217). As two faces, or dimensions, of one and the same thing, they are inseparable. Just as there is no plenum of transactions and motions without a partitioning of them into units, lines, and segments, so, too, there are no units, lines, and segments without a plenum that they organize. The molecular and molar, furthermore, interact. Particular actions and passions can elude molar segmentation and either alter the molar segments that ply an assemblage or act as condensation points around which new assemblages boasting new molar organizations coalesce and grow (see Chapter 4). At the same time, the molar regularly intervenes into the molecular where it arrests and channels movement. What is done and said in a house, for example, can upset the functional division of rooms and lead to a new functional setup; conversely, the functional division can be redesigned, leading to a rearrangement of people, activities, and statements. It should be noted that the extensiveness of the molar varies among assemblages. Assemblages lie on a spectrum between two extremes: totally rigidified arrangements, in which every entity conforms to molar organization, and totally protean arrangements, in which no entity conforms to any molar regimentation whatsoever (337). Totalitarian states tend toward the former pole (223), whereas certain gangs, bands, and nomadic groups tend toward the latter (358).[48]

According to Deleuze and Guattari, the molar organizes the molecular by way of "centers of power." These centers are charged with the maintenance of the molar organization of an assemblage, thus with the enforcement of the rigid segments composing this organization. They fulfill this charge by

[48] For reasons that cannot be explored here, Deleuze and Guattari's division of molecular from molar must be distinguished from all familiar versions of the micro/macro distinction. Examples are (1) the local/global distinction (where both local and global are understood as specific phenomena, say, city or region on the one side and all human society or the full worldwide reach of some particular system such as capitalism on the other—see Peter J. Taylor, *Political Geography: World Economy, Nation-State and Locality* (London: Longman, 1985); (2) Durkheim's distinction between individual facts and social facts, that is to say, between individuals' thoughts, feelings, actions, and group ways of thinking, feeling, and acting (*The Rules of Sociological Method,* trans. Sarah A. Solovay and John H. Mueller [New York: Free Press, 1938], chap. 1, and intro. to 2d ed.); and (3) any of the many construals of micro/macro as a distinction of size or scale, that is, smaller/bigger or fewer/more. Nor, furthermore, is molecular versus molar the same as lived (or surrounding) reality versus encompassing reality of a different sort. An example of the latter micro/macro relation is face-to-face interaction versus large-scale, patterned features of societies such as organizations and institutions (see, for example, Derek Layder, *Understanding Social Theory* [London and Thousand Oaks, Calif.: Sage, 1994], chap. 1).

"converting" molecular transactions into segments, "channeling" the incessant activities of people, artifacts, and statements into rigidified form (225). They accomplish this, in turn, by way of their own "micrological texture," their own molecular composition, which plugs them into the molecular realm. It is through interchanges between their own molecular composition and wider expanses of molecular transactions that power centers mold actions (and passions) in conformity with rigid segmentation and maintain them in this form. They succeed, of course, only so well at this task; every power center suffers a "zone of impotence" (226), where the attempt to channel transactions into rigid organization and to hold them there fails.[49]

Consider how these ideas might apply to the Shaker herb block operations in New Lebanon. The molecular texture of these operations embraced arrangements of (1) Shaker workers who pressed herbs, printed labels, and hoisted green herbs and roots to the second floor; (2) the variety of presses, tins, drying sheets, hoists, and power mechanisms involved; (3) the horse tirelessly walking around the power mechanism in the basement, along with the rats gumming up the works; and (4) the herbs and roots to which so much attention was devoted. The molar organization of these arrangements included the functional division of rooms, the division and sexual division of labor, and directional sequences of tasks (e.g., hoisting, drying, storage, conveyance downstairs, pressing, storage, packaging, labeling, distribution). What, however, maintained this organization? For Deleuze and Guattari, the question would be, What are the power centers at work?

As far as I can see, two primary power centers were present, namely, the forepersons (one male and one female) who oversaw the operations. Somewhat contrarily to Deleuze and Guattari's claims, however, these forepersons did not have to do much to maintain molar organization. They determined in a general fashion what would be pressed or packaged and who would do what when, but these decisions had more to do with the specifics of molecular action and

[49] I wrote above that Deleuze and Guattari did not embed abstract machines in any factor or mechanism at work in social life. It might be thought that power centers are such a factor and that they promise an answer to the issue of how concrete assemblages realize virtual diagrams. Deleuze and Guattari shrunk, however, from inscribing diagrams in these centers: "Segments, then, are themselves governed by an abstract machine. But what power centers govern are the assemblages that effectuate that abstract machine, in other words, that continuously adapt variations in mass and flow to the segments of the rigid line" (A Thousand Plateaus, 226). This formulation leaves it just as mysterious as before how segments are governed by an abstract machine. It furnishes no answer to the question, Just why does an assemblage qua effectuation of a given abstract machine assume—and its power centers impose—such and such forms and not others?

rarely touched or sought—or even needed to attempt—to uphold molar organization. The reason that the forepersons did not have to attend to this task
was that, in the herb industry, the molecular did not, for the most part, flee
the molar. For example, defiance of and quarrels with the forepersons rarely
occurred. (When they did, further power centers, i.e., elders, eldresses, and
ministers, invariably reestablished order.) Furthermore, the fact that power
centers act sparingly is not a peculiarity of Shaker life. It is, instead, a pervasive feature of human existence. The infrequency of power center intervention
suggests that arrangements are not preserved by power centers alone and that
something, consequently, is missing from Deleuze and Guattari's account.

The missing piece of the puzzle is the organization of practices, in the case
at hand, the organization of the herb medicine production practices. It was the
repeated expression of the same understandings, the repeated observance of
the same rules, the repeated inspiration or orientation through the same general understandings, and the repeated carrying out of teleoaffective hierarchies
falling within the practice's teleoaffective structure that preserved—and slowly
transformed—the arrangements in question. In social sites at any time and
place, the organizations of practices are primarily responsible for the typically
extensive continuity in orders found there. If it is asked, in turn, What is
responsible for the fact that humans act repetitively in these manners? The
answer is threefold: They are schooled to do so as they mature; they hold one
another to acting so once mature; and that these facts themselves hold and that
people otherwise just do act in this second-order repetitive manner is at bottom simply the human way of life.[50]

4. AGENTIAL HUMANISM I

As stated in Chapter 1, orders are arrangements of substances, whereas practices
are the organized activities that substances of one type carry out. I indicated
that the point of picking out these activities and honoring them with a general

---

[50] This answer builds on Wittgenstein's observation that what underlies a variety of features of
language-games, including the following of rules, is the brute "natural" fact that people just do
continue in certain ways in certain situations. See, for example, Ludwig Wittgenstein, *Zettel,* ed.
G. E. M. Anscombe and G. H. von Wright, trans. G. E. M. Anscombe (Berkeley and Los Angeles:
University of California Press, 1967), section 355. For an articulation of this intuition in a Heideggerian vein, see John Haugeland, "Heidegger on Being a Person," *Nous* 16(1982): 15–26. My formulation leaves open whether and how the human "form of life" is to be explained.

name was twofold: to facilitate more careful investigation of the relations between activities and arrangements and to emphasize the significance of organized activity bundles for the character of human existence.[51] The present section deepens my exploration of these themes.

Practices are intrinsically connected to and interwoven with objects (i.e., substances). The differentiation of practices from orders is not, therefore, a division into distinct ontological regions. Rather, it is an analytic distinction between components of a single mesh. The inherent and intimate yoke between practices and orders assumes many forms, only the most obvious of which is that humans carry out practices.

Many names of actions explicitly refer to objects. Examples are "hoisting herbs to the drying rooms," "reshoeing the horse," "steeping the herbs," and "cleaning up the rat droppings." Other names of actions implicitly refer to objects, for example, "pressing," "storing," "hoisting," "steeping," and "extracting." What these linguistic facts indicate is that action is not a self-contained and self-sufficient impulse that moves through the world only contingently making contact with it. Rather, it is primarily a dealing with the orders of entities that are always already there for a person through experience and previous action. Because action is inherently a coping with the world, its identity is tied to the world. Names of actions merely differ about whether the tie is explicit or unexpressed. Human activity thus implicates a world amid and with which it proceeds.

An important facet of this implication is that many actions require objects for their performance. It is difficult, for instance, to reshoe a horse without a shoe and a hammer or some equivalent blunt object. Similarly, it is difficult to press something without a press. A second important facet of this implication is that many actions are directed at objects. Reshoeing requires, in addition, a horse, just as pressing additionally requires something that is pressed. Similarly, asking Long to come over and help lift the evaporating pan requires there to be a Long, even if he has left the room, left the Shakers, or left the world. Of course, the opposite side of these inherent connections of action to the world is that what entities are is tied to action.

---

[51] Margolis offers a third possible rationale: to uphold a rigorous distinction between reference and predication. Although I suspect he would say I have granted practices too much existence (referential reality), I do not pursue the issue here. For his analysis of reference and predication, see Joseph Margolis, *Historied Thought, Constructed World: A Conceptual Primer for the Turn of the Millennium* (Berkeley and Los Angeles: University of California Press, 1995), chap. 3.

Actions and objects are locked, not just constitutively, but also in a variety of contingent but nonetheless tight ways. I mentioned above that practices, over time, take on new projects and tasks. The advent of novel activities often occurs coordinately with or in response to the development and incorporation of new objects, for instance, new machines or materials with which to work. An example of such an object is the vacuum pan, a device with which to reduce extracts, whose introduction required that old tasks (preparation, reduction, cleaning, repairing, etc.) be carried out in new doings and sayings. In this case, doings and sayings became part of herb production practices as a result of the installation of new equipment. Because, furthermore, this equipment was developed (it seems probable) in these same practices, this example also illustrates the processional reciprocal determination of practices and orders. By contrast, the switch in the 1830s to producing medicinal herbs in block form instead of loosely piled in containers required not just new doings and sayings, but new projects and tasks as well. Examples are pressing the herbs, collecting herb blocks from the auxiliary machine that received them as they came off the press, and storing the blocks into the machine in the storeroom that preserved their form until the further new tasks of papering and labeling the blocks could be carried out. These projects and tasks arrived to some extent as a package. They were also bound up with the new machinery and materials and required physical and activity-space reorganizations of the herb house. In ways such as this, new activities and orders coordinate and can be introduced en masse. Another aspect of the coordination between activities and objects is that the presence of objects both stabilizes and regularizes doings and sayings, as well as projects and tasks.[52] That in the herb and extract houses the workers repeatedly carried out the same doings and sayings, which constituted the same tasks of pressing, storing, hoisting, steeping, and the like, is tied to the presence in these buildings of the presses, tins, cupboards, hoists, and kettles used in the herb production practices.

Objects and orders not just are coordinate with, but also exert a causal impact on activities and practices. Both the introduction of the vacuum pan and the phenomenon of "machinelike" stabilization illustrate this fact, though they even more clearly evince the coordination of orders and practices. Whenever, more generally, something breaks, breaks down, or acts contrary to expectations, and people react to this situation, nonhumans exert a causal

---

[52] Harry Collins calls such activity "machine-like"; Harry Collins, *Artificial Experts: Social Knowledge and Intelligent Machines* (Cambridge, Mass.: MIT Press, 1990).

effect on activities: They make activity happen by leading to it, by drawing activity—though not necessarily specific actions (see Chapter 1)—out of people. When the rats got into the drainage pipes leading from the basement and clogged them with garbage, workers reacted by cleaning out the drains. When the coal piled up against the iron shield of the boiler caught fire, Hollister and the others put it out. When leaks sprang in the pipes of the kettles, Hollister drove plugs into the holes. In all these cases, objects caused activity. The effects of nonhuman agency are even clearer vis-à-vis machine performance and the execution of extract experiments. The gumming up of the presses by the resin that pressed herbs released, the foaming up of the belladonna when it was overheated, and the butternut liquor running back into the boiler and damaging the extract were all events that the combined action of artifacts and things made happen. Insofar, moreover, as Long and Hollister reacted to these events, material agency changed the course of activity. It bore on, not just which of a practice's activities participants performed, but also, as both extract experimentation and George Whiting's ceaseless efforts to design a new press at the Shaker village at Harvard, Massachusetts, suggest, the introduction of new activities, the abandonment of extant ones, and thus the future course and direction of activity. In short, human activity is closely bound, constitutively and causally, to the objects amid which it courses.

One current of thought that has been pushing this message on social theory is the "posthumanist" wing of science studies.[53] This wing opposes the once dominant social constructivist Edinburgh-type sociology of scientific knowledge, which reasserts a conceptual and ontological dominance of the social over the material reminiscent of philosophical idealism. These posthumanist analyses (1) release the how, and sometimes also the what, of material entities from the sway of social activity, cognition, and interest; (2) endow material entities with powers of determination that either render these entities as potent as social phenomena or make materiality and sociality codetermining; and in some cases (3) hold some third phenomenon responsible for the properties, capacities, and even being of both humans and material entities. One suite of this posthumanist wing is Latour's and Callon's actor-network theory. A

---

[53] Another is the "sociocultural theory of mediated action," which argues that the fundamental unit of sociocultural study is an indissoluble complex of active agents and cultural tools. See, for example, James V. Wertsch, Pablo del Río, and Amelia Alvarez, eds., *Sociocultural Studies of Mind* (Cambridge: Cambridge University Press, 1995); James V. Wertsch, *Mind as Action* (New York: Oxford University Press, 1998).

further office is Pickering's theory of the mangle. Pickering argues that human agency and material agency (the doings of artifacts and things) are equally, and symmetrically, emergent from the contingent, happenstance course of events to which both contribute.[54] Vis-à-vis human agency, this means that actions, intentions, projects, and ends are both tied to and altered in response to the contingent flow of events that results from the intertwining and conjunction of human doings with material ones. Actions, intentions, and ends are never, therefore, stable. Because, moreover, the future is not just unforeseeable, but also not yet determined, just what these actions, intentions, and ends turn out to have been remains perpetually open. Symmetrically, material agency both contributes to and alters along with the happenstance course of events, to which humans also contribute. As a result, neither human nor nonhuman agency can claim priority in the determination of the future—both are equally "mangled" (i.e., circumstantially transformed) as events proceed.

Rouse goes a step further. Pickering is still willing to use the expression "practices" to designate human activities. Rouse uses the term to denote meaningful configurations of the world that embrace actions together with the material settings in which they occur, thereby signaling a more radical attempt to undermine human exceptionalness.[55] (In principle, moreover, the actions involved can be those of humans or nonhumans.) Practices are "the field within which both the determinations of objects and the doings and respondings of agents emerge as intelligible."[56] This gambit, he argues, overcomes any remaining humanist division between a human "inside" and a nonhuman, material "outside." Of course, Rouse's analysis does not deny human activity a significant presence in practices. It portrays activity, however, as a response to the solicitations of a meaningful world and not as the determinant and origin of that meaningfulness. Actors are always enveloped in an already meaningful world to which they respond, and whose meaningfulness is the product of past states of the world to which actors had responded and thereby reconfigured.

---

[54] Pickering, *The Mangle of Practice,* chap. 1.

[55] Rouse, *Engaging Science,* chap. 5.

[56] Ibid., 149. Compare his earlier treatment of practices in Joseph Rouse, *Knowledge and Power: Toward a Political Philosophy of Science* (Ithaca: Cornell University Press, 1987), 58–67, 159–62. See also Donna Haraway, "Situated Knowledges: The Science Question in Feminism and the Privilege of Partial Perspectives," *Feminist Studies* 14, 3 (1988): 575–99, here 595. For the same idea in the context of the philosophy of physics, see Karen Barad, "Meeting the Universe Halfway: Realism and Social Constructivism Without Contradiction," in *Feminism, Science, and the Philosophy of Science,* ed. Lynn Hankinson Nelson and Jack Nelson (Dordrecht: Kluwer, 1996), 161–94.

Because the intelligibility of activities and objects alike, as well as the intelligibility of the very distinction between them, is beholden to an ontologically prior relational complex, this account grants neither human activity nor objects ultimate constitutive and causal primacy in practices. Indeed, these formulations of Rouse's position in the language of "activity" and "objects" already, so to speak, come too late: What agency is and what is and is not an agent are themselves constituted in the progress of practices.

Pickering and Rouse join actor-network theory in emphasizing the mutual determination, dependence, and—in Rouse alone—shared ontological derivativeness of human activities and material entities. Pickering and actor-network theorists also explicitly claim that most traditions in social theory have ignored this interwovenness. Incidentally, I do not think that it is accidental that this charge emanates from science and technology studies. In science and heavily technologized arenas of social life, objects and machines are the focus of considerable thought and activity. Perhaps, consequently, it is here most palpable that social relations, joint activities, and coexistence generally are mediated by, and tied to, material objects. In any event, the intimate weave of activity and objects clearly does not exist in these arenas alone, but instead characterizes the full extent of the social realm, however that realm is demarcated. What is more, there is truth to the charge that, historically, sociological theory has slighted this weave and largely theorized as if the social was composed of facts, events, and formations pertaining solely to humans, their activities and relations, and constellations of these. I write "sociological theory" because it seems to me that this cannot be asserted of economic theory, and especially not of anthropological theory, where commodities, resources, and fixed capital, on the one hand, and implements and material contexts of life processes, on the other, have never escaped theoretical attention and analysis. Even in sociology, moreover, many writers working in the penumbra of phenomenology have explicitly incorporated the social presence and role of material objects into their theories.[57] Furthermore, the Hegelian tradition at large, on the basis of the concept of objective spirit, has even recognized the constitutive and causal roles of objects as *necessary*.[58] Still, too many theoretical accounts in sociology

---

[57] See, for example, Peter Berger and Thomas Luckmann, *The Social Construction of Reality* (Garden City, N.Y.: Doubleday, 1966); also Harold Garfinkel, *Studies in Ethnomethodology* (Englewood Cliffs, N.J.: Prentice-Hall, 1967).

[58] Examples are Karl Marx, *Economic and Political Manuscripts of 1844* (Moscow: Progress Publishers, 1959); Wilhelm Dilthey, *Gesammelte Schriften,* vol. 7: "Der Aufbau der geschichtlichen Welt" (Leipzig, B. G. Teubner, 1927).

and, in addition, humanistic social theory give scant official recognition to the contextualization of human activity in configurations of substances. A good example is the absence of any mention of nonhuman entities in the vast majority of contributions to a recent collection on social ontology.[59]

It is plausible to hold, furthermore, that explicit consideration of the objectual context of practices underwrites more clairvoyant analyses of human coexistence. An example is Karin Knorr-Cetina's notion of object-centered sociality.[60] Knorr-Cetina sets her discussion off against current sociological analyses that espy in the contemporary Western world a variety of "post-social" developments, such as the retreat of social policies and the welfare state, a weakening of "socialist" thinking in the face of ascendant liberal (in the European sense) ideas, and the loosening of large-scale administrative and corporate structures. She contends that these developments, far from being "post-social," are instead simply transformations of the social. According to her diagnosis, furthermore, new social configurations are prominently marked by "knowledge cultures" and what she calls "object-centered socialities." The latter are forms of sociality centrally governed by or focused on objects—forms of life embracing, among other things, traditions and collectives centered on objects, personal ties to objects, and object-created emotional worlds. Knorr-Cetina further holds that the forms of object-centered sociality that are of ever increasing significance in the contemporary world revolve around objects of scientific investigation. These forms of coexistence are found, paradigmatically, in scientific laboratories, scientific disciplines, and expert systems.

Such theoretical developments, which promote material or nonhuman objects as a pivotal social theoretical theme, are grounded in the recognition that activity and objects are intimately intertwined. I want now to raise some cautionary notes about taking this recognition too far. In particular, I want to defend what Rouse might call a "residual humanism." Let me begin by following up on object-centered socialities.

Saying that sociality is centered on material or nonhuman objects is much stronger than saying it is to tied to and mediated by them. Indeed, social arenas vary in the extent to which the forms of sociality found there are centered on, and not just tied to and mediated by, objects. Object-centeredness

---

[59] John D. Greenwood, *The Mark of the Social: Discovery or Invention?* (Lanham, Md.: Rowman & Littlefield, 1997).

[60] For example, Karin Knorr-Cetina, "Sociality with Objects: Social Relations in Postsocial Knowledge Societies," *Theory, Culture, and Society* 14, 4 (1997): 1–30.

is particularly prominent in scientific laboratories, expert systems, technology enterprises, and even scientific disciplines, for all these social formations are "defined" in some sense by reference to objects. Notice, however, that greater colonization by science and technology does not entail that an arena's forms of sociality are more object centered. A good example is those modern forms of non-face-to-face interaction that, although inherently mediated by technological devices, are at best only occasionally centered on them (e.g., e-mail communication).[61] This state of affairs implies, contrary to Knorr-Cetina's intent, that the domain of what she calls "knowledge society"—arenas of social existence where processes of knowledge formation and application define sociality—is not coextensive with the realm of object-centered socialities. In turn, this variance shows that knowledge and technology themselves are not responsible for the centering of sociality on objects. What, then, is?

The medicinal herb industry at New Lebanon clearly fell into the domain of "knowledge society." It relied on advanced technology, applied the latest scientific knowledge, and in the 1850s was as up-to-date as any pharmaceutical outfit in the United States. The objects that most strongly qualified as objectual axes around which sociality revolved there were, of course, the herbs and roots. Not only were they objects of a great deal of attention and activity, but the fates awaiting them were reference points that partitioned the medicinal production practices. In many ways, consequently, sociality at the herb and extract houses did center on them. At least, it did so in a way that it did not center on the machinery used there, which was at best the center of more limited and occasional forms of coexistence that arose when machines were repaired, maintained, moved around, jointly operated, and discussed. It was not, however, these things and artifacts, or for that matter the projects and tasks of the production practices, that were ultimately responsible for these entities serving however they did as centering axes of coexistence among medicinal herb workers. Rather, it was the ends that all this activity subtended. It was because the Shakers sought both to make profit and to meet demand that the herbs and roots received so much attention, that the machines were repaired and discussed, and that in the herb and extract houses Shaker coexistence centered around these objects.

The same point holds for scientific laboratories and disciplines. Forms of coexistence among scientists center on epistemic objects because the end of

---

[61] Another good example is day trading (see Chapter 3), which is inseparable from computer networks but only occasionally focused on them.

understanding this or that portion or component of the world centrally organizes the practices of science. Similarly, what underlies the fact that advanced
technology and information products are centering axes of sociality in technology firms and expert systems are the overall ends pursued in those firms and
systems, namely, the development of technology and the design-application of
informational products. In saying this of science, incidentally, I do not imply
that the goals of specific scientific research programs are stable, that is to say,
that such goals survive the shocks of the unexpected or perdure through the
"exploratory and groping"[62] process of scientific experimentation. I am saying
only that a general telos pervades scientific practices, a telos that specifically
orients scientific activity only when it is further articulated in the form of more
specific research goals.[63] This point, moreover, is not affected by the existence
in scientific endeavor of either other overall ends that substitute for that of
understanding some portion of the world (e.g., intervening into society or into
the human genome) or more personal ends such as mastery, fame, and power.
In any event, sociality is centered on objects to whatever extent it is because
of the general ends of the practices through which it transpires. That objects
play this role is due to the practices concerned, not something that objects
force on humans.

This point is a feature of what seems to me the properly chastened humanism of a third allegedly "posthumanist" analysis of science, that of Hans-Jörg
Rheinberger. According to Rheinberger, experimental science (molecular biology, in particular) is a field composed of heterogeneous assemblages called
"experimental systems." Each such system is a local, singular, and temporally
limited assemblage of such items as skills, social relations, machines and instru-
mentation, concepts and theories, and objects investigated. Whereas Pickering
stresses that histories of science and technology disclose a mangling of these
items that is not under the control of any of them, Rheinberger shows that
the experimental field is a mesh of drifting, fusing, and bifurcating systems.
Experimental systems are also purely contingent complexes, as evidenced by

---

[62] Michael Hagner and Hans-Jörg Rheinberger, "Experimental Systems, Objects of Investigation, and
Spaces of Representation," in *Experimental Essays—Versuche zum Experiment,* ed. Michael Heidelberger and Friedrich Steinle (Baden-Baden: Nomos Verlagsgesellschaft, 1998), 355–73, here 358.

[63] In this regard, Rheinberger is correct that "there is no overarching telos ... at which the movement
of research could come to a rest" (Hans-Jörg Rheinberger, *Toward a History of Epistemic Things:
Synthesizing Proteins in the Test Tube* [Stanford: Stanford University Press, 1997], 107). This is not
because, as he sometimes seems to imply, there is no overarching telos in science, but instead because
the nature of the telos is such that its pursuit is never complete.

the ways that elements break away, new elements enter, and the systems metamorphose in the course of research, merging with and separating from other
temporally transmogrifying systems.

In one sense, Rheinberger—like Pickering and Rouse—displaces humans
from the center of the action. To begin with, humans and nonhumans are not
segregated into separate domains, but combined in a single one (experimental systems). Not only, consequently, is human activity just one component
of such systems, but experimental systems also exhibit a form of "differential
reproduction" that is not under human control: No one controls how the items
that compose systems mix and break off or how systems evolve. Following
Derrida, moreover, Rheinberger treats experimental systems as significational-
material "spaces of representation." Scientific objects are traces in such spaces,
and experimental as well as theoretical knowledges are inscriptions in them.
Scientific knowledge, accordingly, is neither the possession of human minds nor
the product of human cognition alone. In a sense, it is a feature of the system.

Still, such systems are not kin to Rouse's prehumanized and preobjectified
fields of relation, in which intelligible agents and actions as well as intelligible
objects and configurations thereof coalesce. An experimental system is, profoundly, a human affair. Experimental systems, Rheinberger writes, are "epistemic practices that constitute a particular kind of material culture." They are
"systems of manipulation designed to give unknown answers to questions that
the experimenters themselves are not yet able clearly to ask," "[the] material
formations, or dispositions, of epistemic practice within which a scientist or
group of scientists generate the epistemic products that they characterize as the
'results' of their craft."[64]. In such a system, the activities are those of humans;
the machines are ones they build; the concepts, theories, and skills are ones
they develop; and the spaces of representation do not exist independently of
human signification and the products of human activity. Experimental systems
happen to and with humans, their activities, skills, cognition, and products
thereof. As Rheinberger's own account shows, furthermore, in tension with his
claim that scientific strategies are not directed by stable goals,[65] nothing would
occur if humans did not seek to understand the material world (or to pursue
fame or to intervene in human life, etc.). Indeed, continuity in this end marks
experimental systems. Rheinberger writes that a system ceases to be productive

[64] Rheinberger, *Toward a History of Epistemic Things*, 19, 28, and 135, respectively.
[65] See Hans-Jörg Rheinberger, "From Microsomes to Ribosomes: 'Strategies' of "Representation,"
Journal of the History of Biology 28 (1995): 49–89.

once it no longer constantly produces differences, that is to say, unprecedented events and pristine techniques, concepts, and objects of investigation. In the absence of the end of grasping the world, the production of differences would not count as a mark of enduring fruitfulness and would hold no (or quite different) significance for scientists.

Despite his best efforts, furthermore, Rouse's analysis of practices exhibits its own residual humanism. This is expressed in his use of terms that designate paradigmatically human phenomena to characterize allegedly prehumanized (and preobjectified) practices. He begins cleanly with a characterization of practices as temporally extended events and processes. Soon thereafter, he resolves these events and processes into doings and actions, which need not be those of humans. He then argues that the patterns of actions that constitute practices are sustained only through normativity. Now, normativity is not a human phenomenon alone. Its home, however, is human existence; and what it amounts to there is that by reference to which the normativity of other species is comprehended. Rouse seems, in fact, to agree. Drawing on what he himself calls "humanist" accounts of normativity, he writes that "an event counts as correct or deviant practice on the basis of how those recognized as practitioners respond to it," as to an action performed by a practitioner they understand to be capable of acting in accordance with norms.[66] It is evident that the behavior of some animals satisfies this description. It is also clear, however, that specifications such as this of the conditions under which something enjoys normative status are articulations of what normativity amounts to in human life.

As noted, Rouse characterizes practices as "the field within which the determinations of objects and the doings and respondings of agents emerge as intelligible." He also describes practices as "the relational complex of embodied agents in meaningfully configured settings for possible action."[67] I applaud Rouse's idea that activity-setting complexes are wholes through which actions and objects are to be understood. The concept of a social site comprising practices and orders expresses a similar intuition. I second, further, the end that Rouse believes this idea serves, namely, avoiding any previous distinction between "autonomous social and/or natural 'worlds'" (see Chapter 3). His repeated use of such terms as "intelligibility" and "meaningful" betrays once

---

[66] Rouse, *Engaging Science,* 139–40.
[67] Ibid., 150.

again, however, that he cannot avoid characterizing this relational whole as paradigmatically a *human* affair. For instance, to speak of settings as meaningful is to characterize entities in a way they are, first, for humans. I affirm that objects and doings are intelligible and meaningful for animals too. Talk of meaning and intelligibility receives its sense within human life, however, and it is extended to animals only to the extent that they are similar to us, that they are incorporated into our orders and practices, and that empirical research reveals details about their lives that support the judgment that how the world is for us is also how it is for them.[68] A truly "posthumanist" approach would characterize the prior site or complex in which "subjects and objects" emerge in a vocabulary that does not find its meaning and first home in descriptions of "subjects" (i.e., people). I take it that Heidegger's late use of the concepts of mortals, divinities, earth, and sky (the "fourfold") to characterize the clearing of being (to which Rouse's prior complex bears great similarity) represents such an attempt.[69]

The residual humanism propounded in the current work has two components. The first is this chapter's defense of the special constitutional, causal, and prefigurational significance of human activity in both human life in general and social existence in particular. The second is Chapter 4's vindication of the unique richness characteristic of human agency. The end implicit in the first component, namely, understanding human life and social existence, might also be a primordial humanist fixation. In any event, the present account of the causal, constitutional, and prefigurational significance of human activity does not entail (1) erecting a metaphysical divide between humans and nonhumans (see also Chapter 4), (2) carving out an "inside" to human life or practice over against the "outside" material world,[70] or (3) recognizing a prior division between "autonomous" human/social and natural worlds (see Chapter 3). As discussed, activity is inherently entwined with objects. Moreover, objects (including organisms) exert causal and prefigurational effects on activity. In short, human activity proceeds amid entities that mold it and to which it is constitutionally bound. Hence, just as practices form a contexture in which

[68] The inspiration for this formulation is Ludwig Wittgenstein, *Philosophical Investigations,* 3d ed., trans. G. E. M. Anscombe (New York: Macmillan, 1958), sections 281, 284.
[69] See, for example, Martin Heidegger, "The Thing," and "Building, Dwelling, Thinking," in *Poetry, Language, and Thought,* ed. Albert Hofstadter (New York: Harper and Row, 1971), 163–86 and 143–62. On this topic, see Jacques Derrida, "The Ends of Man," in his *Margins of Philosophy,* trans. Alan Bass (Chicago: University of Chicago Press, 1982), 109–36.
[70] Rouse, *Engaging Science,* 59.

arrangements exist, orders compose a contexture in which practices transpire. Indeed, this co-contexturalization is one aspect of the claim that the social site is a mesh of practices and orders (see Chapter 3). Human coexistence is not simply a matter of people carrying on organized activities, but also one of their acting in a world of inter-related artifacts, organisms, things, and people through which their fates as humans are coupled together.

Still, activities and objects are not equals here. The character of social existence is, in the end, much more the responsibility of practices than of orders. In the first place, as discussed in the previous section, practices are largely responsible (directly or indirectly) for the meanings of both actions and objects. This holds not just of the orders that are set up in or through their constituent actions, but also of all those objects and events such as tornadoes, earthquakes, solar flares, and viruses that intrude into social life and disrupt or even destroy practices, orders, and coexistence. Objects lack the capacity to institute meaning.

Practices and orders also enable and constrain one another. What artifacts, organisms, things, and people qua components of arrangements do is enabled and constrained by other components and features of the arrangements into which human activity inserts them (what holds of them independently of arrangements is not at issue). Conversely, these entities enable and constrain the activities humans perform, including what humans do with them. Even amid, however, such apparent symmetry, activities hold the edge. For as also discussed in the previous section, the enabling and constraining effects of objects and arrangements on activities are relative to actors' ends, projects, hopes, fears, and so on. Objects, if you will, make a contribution, but the nature of that contribution depends on us.

Even in the realm of causality, activity holds the upper hand. To see why, consider for the moment experimental science. In this enterprise, the attempt to grasp the nature of the real leads to the construction of experimental setups through which humans hope to infer how things work outside the setups by way of grasping the contributions things make to what happens in or via these constructions. In the present context, what is relevant about these setups is that things contribute to what happens in and through them because humans have set matters up that way. This means that activity and its ends circumscribe the relevance of material causality for the cooperative disciplinary venture of experimental science. Even more overtly, whenever humans build machines that something other than human effort powers or use living organisms and things for their purposes, the causal contribution to and significance of these entities (and arrangements thereof) for human coexistence is either set up by or otherwise relative to human practices (actions, ends, projects). Objects and their arrangements do bear on human activity, cause its reorganization, and thereby shape the forms of coexistence that transpire through practices. Humans do alter their purposes, projects, and arrangements in response to breakdowns and setbacks that befall or arise from artifacts, organisms, things, people, and heterogeneous assemblages of them. These phenomena, however, confirm the overall point—for reorganizations and alterations are undertaken with an eye to the ends that ground the teleological structuring of practices. Events also can, of course, so befall arranged entities, or be so caused by them, that humans forsake existing ends and embrace new ones. The reactive institution of new high-level ends is, however, a rare and momentous event.

Today, the entities and arrangements thereof through which human coexistence transpires are mostly, though not entirely, set up or otherwise established in social practices under the aegis of these practices' organizations. The orders through which coexistence transpires do extend beyond established ones, but over history human coexistence has been increasingly confined in set-up orders, and nothing indicates that this development will abate in the future. As a result, practices, and the arrangements they establish, largely mediate the causal relevance of materiality for social life. The issue, notice, is not one of control or impact, of whether humans or objects are causally more imposing. In this regard, objects are not just equal, but often superior to humans. Solar flares, earthquakes, tornadoes, viruses, and poisonous snakes all intervene into social life, where they lead to alterations in extant practices and forms of coexistence as well as destroy practices, orders, and socialities. The annihilative potency of these phenomena can overpower human activity and whatever defenses it sets in place. Such events, however, are poor justification for a posthumanism worth its name. And even here, as indicated, humans remain the masters in one regard, however trite to some and redemptory for others, namely, in the significance these events hold for them.[71]

It might be objected that the priority of activity over objects is predetermined by my choice of subject matter, namely, *social* life. This is wrong in one way and true in another. Human coexistence is not eo ipso a realm in

[71] In this I agree with Sartre, though not with his contention that each individual has absolute power to attribute significance; cf. Jean-Paul Sartre, *Being and Nothingness,* trans. Hazel Barnes (New York: Pocket Books, 1966).

which human activity enjoys constitutional, prefigurational, and causal primacy. Things could have been otherwise. One can imagine all sorts of scenarios, according to which, say, extraterrestrials script human existence and help people to a life of sweet idleness. What is true about this objection is that, given the *actual* character of human life, choosing to analyze social existence *is* demarcating a subject matter in which human activity is central. This fact, however, does not critique, but instead reaffirms the analysis, namely, that the world is such that human activity takes the lead in the mesh of practices and orders where human coexistence takes place.

To illustrate the above contentions, I now consider an example that Pickering spells out with the aim of demonstrating their contrary, that is, the nonpriority of human action. Taken from the history of technology, this example, he asseverates, evinces how the contingent course of events "mangles" the social.

In the early 1960s, the General Electric Corporation introduced numerically controlled machine tools (N/C) into its plant in Lynn, Massachusetts. Before this event, metalworking factories had contained arrays of "lathes and milling machines in a corporate machine shop, [which were] operated by wage labor within a classic Taylorite disciplinary apparatus of specified social roles and relations."[72] Management's decision to introduce N/C equipment responded to perceived underperformance in the plant's operations; the decision was reached in the hope that computers could run the operations and the human factor could be reduced to the role of button pushers. Management also decided to lower the pay of labor because lower levels of skills would now be required. Contrary to management expectations, however, production rates dropped, and the quality of the finished parts declined after the changes were implemented. The union also protested the pay decrease on the grounds that because workers, again contrary to management expectations, had to supervise the machinery and make sure it ran correctly, higher skills and, in addition, greater tension and fatigue were now demanded of workers. Pickering characterizes the production slump, quality decline, and labor protest as "resistances" to management plans that "emerged" in practice, that is to say, that just happened to result from the contingent, unforeseeable course of events. Management subsequently reacted to (in Pickering's words "accommodated") these resistances with a variety of tactics that only led to a major strike in 1965, which ended when pay was restored to earlier levels. Production rates and parts

[72] Pickering, *The Mangle of Practice*, 159; the episode is described in Chapter 5, Section 1.

quality remained problematic, however, and management's new accommodation to these continuing resistances was a series of traditional Taylorite measures (such as bribing operators), which in turn led to a breakdown in relations both among workers and between workers and supervisors.

In response to this new emergent development, management responded with the so-called Pilot Program, which completely restructured labor organization. Among other things, the program allocated various traditional management functions to operators, allowed workers to perform multiple functions, and eliminated foremen. The restructuring was also open-ended in that management intended to let it develop on its own accord in the hope that through this process the company could learn how best to utilize the N/C equipment. Once the Pilot Program was implemented, workers seized the initiative, carrying out diverse tasks, developing new ones, suggesting operational reorganizations, designing more flexible schedules, and so on. After participants in the program were granted even more freedom for self-organization, new "resistances" appeared at the interface between the Lynn plant and the rest of General Electric, and in 1975 the program was ended and the plant reorganized along prevailing Taylorite lines.

I agree with Pickering when he writes that the resistances and accommodations documented in this narrative were temporally emergent in the sense of contingently determined, that is to say, that nothing predetermined the course of events and that things at various points along the way could have turned out differently. (Whether no one could have foreseen what happened is a different matter.) Pickering tells the story, however, to draw the "posthumanist" lesson that the episode "cannot be understood in purely social (human) terms," adding that the transformations of the social organization of production at the Lynn plant cannot be "reduced" to management goals. Rather, "the material form and performance of the N/C machines have to be seen as constitutive of the trajectory of emergence of work discipline."[73] As evidence for this conclusion, Pickering adduces the facts that (1) resistance could occur only once the machines were actually in place; (2) the forms of self-organization developed by the workers in the Pilot Program were tied to the performances of the machines; (3); negotiations that took place between workers and programmers presupposed the relevance of programmers to shop floor operations, and for this relevance installation of the N/C machines was required; and (4) the

[73] Ibid., 166–67.

development of worker self-organization in coordination with the machines' performance was a learning process whose results management fed back into the new Taylorite regime it installed in 1975. All this shows, he writes, that "the center of gravity of the story" lies not in human agency, but instead at the intersection of human and material agency.[74]

The performance and material form of the N/C equipment clearly helped determine the sequences of events composing this episode. In any realm of social life, people respond to what artifacts, organisms, and things do, and in this story the objects to which management and workers responded were, above all, the N/C equipment. However, the equipment was there in the first place to be responded to because of the practices of management. What is more, the fact that the equipment was something to which management and workers responded reflected the practices they carried out. How they did respond, moreover, depended on the significance of the machinery's performances and breakdowns as this devolved from the organization of these practices. Hence, the fact that machinery co-determined the course of events is ultimately based on the humans involved carrying on certain practices. The issue is not, in the present instance, how "mangled" practices might be through events that material agency co-determined, that is to say, how much ends, projects, and activities might change in response to these events (however interesting this fact might be and however much certain schools of social theory might neglect it). Rather, the point is that the very facts that material entities could do this and that these events occurred at all are attributable to and matters of human activity—attributable to and a matter of what people were up to in their practices. No one required management to start things down this path, and nothing required either management or labor at any point along the way to respond to new developments. They did, however, because from beginning to end the whole episode rotated around what people sought and pursued.

Pickering, consequently, does not help his case in writing that the story's "center of gravity" lay at the machine-human interface. Whatever significance this interface has for the story and for the actual evolution of events derives from what the humans in the story-episode were up to. Human activity was, in this sense, the center of gravity of the story, as it is throughout social life, though Pickering is certainly correct that the story is equally one about human and material agency.

---

[74] Ibid., 167–68.

Before shifting gears, let me mention one last priority of practice over objects. I noted that different practices could be carried on amid the arrangements at the herb and extract houses. This fact evinces that connections between practices and orders are contingent. Although at any moment orders can determine that particular practices are carried out, other activities could always have been performed. No matter how specialized or exotic equipment, organisms, and things might be, and no matter how tied their development or use might be to particular activities and how attuned, coordinately, such activities might be to them, any order is a site where multiple practices can take place. Which practices occur, moreover, is in the hands of the humans involved. Conversely and similarly, practices can determine orders, and it is always the case that an order different from the one actually established could have been the one laid down. In this case, however, which order is established is not up to the objects. Once again, it is the province of humans. Of course, once established, orders can rearrange themselves (for instance, in breakdowns) and be changed by objects and events that do not stand under the aegis of practices. As I have been acknowledging, nonhuman agency is a distinct facet of the social site. Such alterations occur subsequently, however, to the establishment of orders. Objects can also resist human attempts to establish orders, but in the present context this is a rearguard action that only limits what humans can do. The asymmetry remains. The contingency of the connections between practices and orders lies in human hands: The indeterminacy of the emerging and future mesh of practices and orders arises from the indeterminacy of forthcoming human activity (see Chapter 4).

THE SITE OF THE SOCIAL

Social life transpires through human activity and is caught up in orders of people, artifacts, organisms, and things. As such, it is not just immersed in a mesh of practices and orders, but also exists only as so entangled. The mesh of practices and orders is the *site* where social life takes place. The current chapter elucidates and substantiates this analysis of social being and also places it in a wider horizon of social ontologies. Conceiving the social site as an overall phenomenon also raises issues about its relation to a different panoramic phenomenon called "nature."

These issues parallel those once pressed under the label "society and nature" and pertain to the distinction between and the distinctiveness of, as well as the character of and the relations between, the social site and nature. I begin with a step back to survey ontological approaches to social life.

1. A TALE OF TWO ONTOLOGIES

Many readers of this text are familiar with both the topic of social ontology and the two major categories of such ontologies, individualism and socialism. It will prove useful for ensuing discussions, however, to review this material in my own way before turning to the third, less familiar category, that of site ontologies.

Social ontology is the study of the nature, constitution, and basic structures of social life. Its origins as a discernible concern date to the first half of the nineteenth century, above all in the work of G. W. F. Hegel and J. S. Mill. Of course, intellectual interest in "the social" existed from the eighteenth century back through Greek philosophy, though not under this label."[1] During the nineteenth century, moreover, the scope of scientific notions of the social steadily expanded, so that by the end of this century, as exemplified in the work of Herbert Spencer and Emile Durkheim, it included all domains of human interaction or coexistence. During the same period, the expression "society" coordinately became a term of art for the sum-total of relations among, or of collective states of affairs embracing, a large, perhaps unified group of people. "Individual and society" therewith became a social theoretical, and not just a political philosophical, issue. Raymond Williams noted that the path that led to the term "society" designating large-scale units was opened much earlier than these scholarly developments.[2] The earliest uses of "society" in the English language from the fourteenth to the mid-sixteenth century equated it with fellowship and companionship (in line with the meaning of its

[1] In ancient Greece, for example, the experience of the organization of the Greek *ethnos* as a set of *poli* undergirded a theoretical reflection about the nature of the polis that, without too much distortion, can be characterized as "social analysis"—or even more suggestively, with the idea of wholes in the background, as "theory of society." See Plato, *The Republic*, books 2–4 and 10; Aristotle, *The Politics*, books 1–2 and 7. In this context one might also mention the traditional "nomos-physis" debate about the nature of value and social norms, which began with the Sophists in the fifth century B.C.

[2] See the entry for "Society" in Raymond Williams, *Keywords: A Vocabulary of Culture and Society* (Oxford: Oxford University Press, 1976), 243–47.

Latin root, *socius*). The more general and inclusive sense of the term began developing in the middle of the sixteenth century, and Williams placed the "decisive transition" to the more general sense in the work of late eighteenth-century political economy.

During the nineteenth century, moreover, and even more strongly in the twentieth, "social" and "society" came to designate not just all or the sum-total of interactions, relationships, and collective states of affairs befalling some group of people, but also a state of being. This development was marked by, among other things, the ascension of the term "socialization" and the advent of the idea that "the social" is a dimension of human existence or a realm of human life. This development was also a context in which the idea of a social site became possible. By the beginning of the twenty-first century, consequently, "social" and "society" have come to possess a double role: "[A]s our most general term for the body of institutions and relationships with which a relatively large group of people live; and as our most abstract term for the condition in which such institutions and relationships are formed."[3]

The aforementioned formula "individual and society" articulates a dichotomy around which opposed ontological positions have gathered since the origins of social ontology in the first half of the nineteenth century. As noted in the previous chapter, individualisms maintain that social reality is a labyrinth of individuals and seek to analyze social affairs in these terms. According to such ontologies, any social phenomenon, including a family, a government, an economic system, a religion, and an interaction on the street, is a constellation of (inter-related) individuals. (Recall from Chapter 2 that this formulation covers the thesis that social phenomena are instituted by the actions and mental states of individuals.) What, moreover, has come to be known as "methodological individualism" avers, programmatically, that any social event or phenomenon—a stock market crash, a war, a governmental structure, social anomie—can and should be explained by reference to "individuals": their states of mind, their actions, their situations, and maybe also their relations.[4]

It is important to stress that, although ontological and explanatory individualisms are usually embraced as a package, only an elective affinity, strictly speaking, exists between them. For instance, it can be maintained without

[3] Raymond Williams, *Keywords*, 243.
[4] A clear statement is found in J. W. N. Watkins, "Ideal Types and Historical Explanation," in *Readings in the Philosophy of Science*, ed. Herbert Feigl and May Brodbeck (New York: Appleton-Century-Crofts, 1953), 723–44.

contradiction (although I am not aware of an example) that all social phenomena are to be explained by reference to configurations of individuals, even
though at least some social phenomena are irreducible to such configurations.
Various theorists have maintained, moreover, that although social formations
are in some sense nothing but configurations of individuals, these configurations cannot be explained solely by reference to properties of individuals (and
their relations), but only either through these properties in conjunction with
social phenomena or through principles that apply to the configurations as
wholes.[5] Indeed, positions that are characterized as "anti-individualist" sometimes combine the latter thesis with ontologically individualist-sounding analyses. An example is the proposition that societies or domains thereof are systems
of individual action that can be explained only through principles that apply
to the systems as wholes. Further muddying the proper delimitation of individualism is disagreement in the individualist camp about the identity of the
material with which analyses and explanations of social formations are to be
formulated. Not only do theorists disagree about whether the "stratum of the
individual" includes individuals alone or individuals together with relations
among them, but unsettledness reigns about, first, the role of artifacts (organisms and things are not considered) and, second, the range of admissible
"action-governing" factors. What, for instance, is the ontological status of a
rule that governs action? Is it an "individualist" phenomenon? Some individualists answer in the affirmative; certain of their opponents answer negatively.

Nonindividualisms contest the reduction of social formations, and/or the
explanation of them, by reference solely to individualist phenomena. I resist
calling this family of views, as it is sometimes denoted, "wholism," because not
all the irreducible social phenomena that positions opposed to ontological
individualism endorse are wholes.[6] A good example is Durkheim's social facts,
which are group ways of thinking, feeling, or acting that both are external to
and possess powers of coercion over individuals. Durkheim's account reveals
some of the conundrums bedeviling discussions of this topic. As is discussed
below, in defending the sui generis nature of social facts, Durkheim might

[5] For the first option, see, for instance, Steven Lukes, "Methodological Individualism Revisited,"
British Journal of Sociology 19 (1968): 119–29. Lukes's argument turns on an issue broached below,
the proper specification of the "reducing stratum" of individualism. For another example, see May
Brodbeck, "Methodological Individualisms: Definition and Reduction," *Philosophy of Science* 25
(1958): 1–22. Proponents of the second option are cited in note 8 below.

[6] See L. J. Goldstein, "Two Theses of Methodological Individualism," *British Journal for the Philosophy
of Science* 9 (1958): 1–11.

simply have been opposing facts about sets of (inter-related) individuals to facts about individuals as individuals. If this is the case, Durkheim, despite serving as a prominent standard bearer for nonindividualist ontology, was an ontological individualist in the general sense of that term employed in the previous paragraph.

Many alleged ontological nonindividualisms turn out to be ontological individualisms in exactly this way, their "opposition" to individualism thus being a stand against too narrow a construal of the stratum of the individual.[7] This situation renders it perilous also to employ the term "collectivist" to designate the nonindividualist camp, because this term aligns social phenomena with collections of individuals. It is important to reiterate, however, that many ambiguous ontological individualisms adopt nonindividualist accounts of explanation. Indeed, "nonindividualism" is often taken to be a thesis about explanation alone. Durkheim provides an example if he was in fact an ontological individualist because, as discussed in Chapter 1, he claimed that social facts are to be explained, in part, by the useful results they provide for society as a whole. Most so-called wholisms maintain something similar. Parsons's early systems theory, for example, analyzed society as a total self-subsistent system of actions of individuals. At the same time, it explained the operation of societies wholistically: Societies as wholes are governed by imperatives to maintain equilibrium and to adapt to external changes, and they fulfill these principles through their subsystems' contributions to realizing them.[8]

A true ontological nonindividualism contends, by contrast, that social facts, events, or formations of some sort are distinct, though not independent, from facts about, events befalling, or collections of inter-related individuals. Perhaps the best name for this front, despite the unwanted political connotations, is "socialism." Durkheim's analysis of social facts is standardly taken to be an archetypal form of socialism. Another historically important faction includes those wholisms that analyze particular social phenomena, above all societies, as wholes that (1) possess an existence distinct from that of any particular

[7] This holds of many theorists who invoke rules or norms and call themselves, with regard to rule following or norm observance, something other than "individualist," say, "collectivist" or "Durkheimian." Interactionists of many sorts exemplify this derangement of names. This ambiguity does not, in my opinion, mark the work of the father of interactionism, G. H. Mead, whom I classify as a socialist. This is not the place, however, to analyze his position.

[8] Talcott Parsons and Edward A. Shils, "Values, Motives, and Systems of Action," in *Toward a General Theory of Action*, ed. Talcott Parsons and Edward Shils (Cambridge, Mass.: Harvard University Press, 1951), 47–243, esp. chap. 4, "The Social System."

collection of individuals in them and (2) enjoy a nature that transcends the properties of any such collection. (These theories also hold that the principles that govern wholes are distinct from those applying to such collections.) Paradigmatic of such wholisms are late nineteenth-century theories that treat society as if it were an organism.[9] Two other prominent forms are later functionalisms (and neofunctionalisms) that ascribe(d) such phenomena as ends, purposes, and emotions to whole societies; and those systems theories that analyze systems of action, especially societies, with the help of a comprehensive theory of systems that elucidates properties of systems in general.[10] A third socialist coterie includes all structuralisms and institutional analyses that hold that structures or institutions are both distinct from and determinative of individuals. Structuralisms of this ilk typically operate with hypostatized versions of Lévi-Strauss's opposition-based matrices of transformational possibilities[11] and claim that abstract structures are arrays of nonspatial-temporal factors that govern human activities. As becomes clearer in the following chapter, Deleuze and Guattari offered an account of this sort. According to the institutional analyses I have in mind, institutions are schemes of interlocked roles that determine individuals' actions and interactions, even though they cannot in principle be the property of any particular set of individuals. One mark of such structuralisms and institutional analyses is that they describe individuals as occupying "slots" or "positions" in the structures and institutions that condition, constrain, or form activities.[12]

I have already noted that the elective affinity and possible divergence that characterize ontological and explanatory individualism also hold for ontological and explanatory socialism. The situation is even more complicated in the socialist case, however, because socialism is not always as totalitarian as

---

[9] For example, Herbert Spencer, *Principles of Sociology* I (London: William & Norgate, 1882), passim pt. 2 and chap. 2.

[10] Vis-à-vis functionalism, see, for example, Bronislav Malinowski, *Crime and Custom in Savage Society* (London: Paul, Trench, Trubner, 1926). Vis-à-vis systems theory, see Talcott Parsons, *Societies: Evolutionary and Comparative Perspectives* (Englewood Cliffs, N.J.: Prentice-Hall, 1966), chap. 2; Niklas Luhmann, *Soziale Systeme: Grundriß einer allgemeinen Theorie* (Frankfurt am Main: Suhrkamp, 1984).

[11] Claude Lévi-Strauss, *Structuralist Anthropology*, trans. Claire Jacobson and Brooke Grundfest Schoepf (New York: Basic Books, 1963). A neostructural example is Foucault's notions of epistemes and discourses; cf. respectively, Michel Foucault, *The Order of Things: An Archaeology of the Human Sciences* (London: Tavistock, 1970); Michel Foucault, *The Archaeology of Knowledge*, trans. A. M. Sheridan-Smith (New York: Harper and Row, 1972).

[12] For example, Louis Althusser, *For Marx*, trans. Ben Brewster (London: Allen Lane, 1969); Roy Bhaskar, *The Possibility of Naturalism* (Atlantic Highlands, N.J.: Humanities Press, 1979), chap. 2.

individualism. What I mean is that ontological socialism sometimes concedes the cogency of individualist analyses of certain social phenomena, for example, interactions, insisting only on the irreducibility of those social formations to which it ascribes powers of determination over individuals (e.g., social facts, societies, structures, and institutions). In the end, I believe, both this reluctance simply to deny individualism—even in the face of individualist gainsayings of the hard reality of all social phenomena—and the pervasiveness of the combination of ontological individualism and explanatory socialism reflect the fact that individualist phenomena are experiential entities.[13]

On these two venerable and indefatigable ontological paths of thinking, the general question "What is the nature and constitution of social life?" is transformed into different sets of more specific issues. For individualism, the two paramount such questions are "What is a social action?" and "What is a social phenomenon?" The first question reflects the ubiquitous individualist stress on human activity as both constitutional factor and causal force in social life. The first chapter of Weber's *Economy and Society* presents the paragon and most widely cited exemplar of this approach to social existence. Aiming to provide a survey of the basic concepts of sociology, this chapter begins with a definition of sociology as the interpretive-causal study of social action. It then defines social action as a particular type of action: A social action is an action that is related to the behavior of others, in the actor's understanding of it, and thereby oriented in its course.[14] This specification, in turn, grounds Weber's stipulation that a social relation exists when a plurality of individuals are mutually oriented toward one another in their actions (or when there exists the chance that they will act so oriented). These two definitions together underpin a typology of social action and a delineation of collective orders, as well as analyses of such then sociological stocks in trade as struggle, associations, unions, communization (*Vergemeinschaftung*), and societization (*Vergesellschaftung*). To the question "What is the nature of the social?" the Weberian perspective

---

[13] Individualists have sometimes used this fact to argue that social formations are constructions and not realities. Most socialists counter not by denying this fact, but by disputing the inferences based on it. Compare F. A. Hayek, *The Counterrevolution in Science: Studies on the Abuse of Reason* (Glencoe: Free Press, 1952), chap. 6, with Bhaskar, *The Possibility of Naturalism*, chap. 2. Of course, some socialists instead reply that social formations construct experience. See, for example, Georgi Lukacs, *The Destruction of Reason*, trans. Peter Palmer (London: Merlin, 1980).

[14] Cf. Max Weber, *Basic Concepts of Sociology*, trans. H. P. Secher (Secaucus: Citadel, 1972), 29. The reader of this translation is best advised to check the original routinely: Max Weber, *Soziologische Grundbegriffe* (Tübingen: J. C. B. Mohr, 1984), 19.

replies, "It is the realm of social action and of the organization and configurations of such action."

This style of answer remains rife today. To take one example, in his contribution to a recent anthology that canvasses different positions on the "mark" of the social (and as the most recent of the rare collections on social ontology is copiously cited in the following), Paul Secord treats this question of the mark of the social—from square one—as an issue about the nature of social action. After surveying how several contemporary social science subdisciplines analyze social action, he proposes that an action is social when it is socially constituted; that is to say, when it instantiates a "representation" of action that members of society or of some subgroup in it recognize (a representation of an action is a specification of what it is). Near the end of the article, Secord writes that the "social world . . . is . . . constructed out of human interactions taking place in a setting that is organized."[15] The social, therefore, is the realm of a particular sort of social action (interaction).

The second form that the question of the nature and constitution of social life assumes in individualist hands is "What is a social phenomenon?" As noted, individualist answers to this question analyze social phenomena as constellations of individuals. A continually recurring variant of this answer contends that the central or paradigm type of social phenomenon is the group, where a group is a collection of individuals that share something(s) in common, above all, a mental condition that has the group as its object (e.g., a feeling of allegiance or belonging, an understanding that the individuals concerned form a group).[16] This approach transforms the question of the nature of social life into one about the character of collectives, that is to say, associated individuals. Of all forms of individualism, this approach most strongly lives off intuitions grounded in the Latin root and historically early meanings

---

[15] Paul Secord, "The Mark of the Social in the Social Sciences," in John D. Greenwood, ed., *The Mark of the Social: Discovery or Invention?* (Lanham, Md.: Rowman & Littlefield, 1997), 59–80, here 75.

[16] Examples include Georg Simmel, "How Is Society Possible?" in *Philosophy of the Social Sciences,* ed. Maurice Natanson (New York: Random House, 1953), 73–92; Gerda Walther, "Zur Ontologie der sozialen Gemeinschaft," *Jahrbuch für Philosophie und phänomenologische Forschung* 6 (1923): 1–158; and more recently Margaret Gilbert, *On Social Facts* (Princeton: Princeton University Press, 1989). See also Margaret Gilbert, "Concerning Sociality: The Plural Subject as Paradigm," in Greenwood, *The Mark of the Social,* 17–36. For Gilbert, the paradigm social phenomenon is something she calls "plural subject phenomena." These are formations that are held together by virtue of people jointly committing, as a body, to perform some action, to hold some belief, and/or to uphold certain values, and so on.

of the English word "social" (companionship and fellowship). Correlatively, this brand of individualism most slights the more general and abstract senses of the term that are documented by Williams and that have proliferated in social theory during the past century and a half.

Individualist analyses of social phenomena as constellations of individuals need not highlight the subset of constellations made up of groups. Indeed, many configurations of individuals do not exhibit the phenomenon of "we-ness" that is incarnated in groups.[17] In microeconomics, for instance, economic formations even as broad as entire economies are analyzed as associations of rational, utility-maximizing or utility-satisfying individuals held together by such relationships as buying and selling and decision and command. Many of these associations (e.g., markets and corporations) neither amount to groups nor encompass individuals who are oriented toward the association in a common way. In his contribution to the Greenwood-edited volume, *The Mark of the Social,* for instance, Scott Gordon analyzes societies, or "social complexes," as associations of individuals that subtend the achievement of ends that individuals cannot attain on their own.[18] The processes through which such associations come about are exchange, custom, convention, hierarchical decision and command, and enforcement. This analysis extends a tradition, coeval with the one that group individualists perpetuate, according to which organization around goals (as opposed to personal orientation toward something like group values, projects, or goals) is constitutive of either the paradigmatic social phenomenon or such phenomena in general. Gordon goes on to declare that the "macrosociological system" is an elaborate network, or ensemble, of these complexes.[19] This formulation illustrates the contention, propagated in this breed of individualism, that the social is a web of associations of individuals.

For socialists, on the other hand, the question "What is the nature or constitution of the social?" looks different. It is not, for instance, transformed into the question "What is a social phenomenon?" Those socialists who concede the wisdom of individualist (ontological) analyses of particular social phenomena do not seek overall answers to questions of this latter form, which can

---

[17] Note that I am not denying the phenomenon of "we-ness" (groups), only the adequacy of defining the category of social phenomena by reference to it. This phenomenon is, certainly, an important feature of social life. It is not, however, analyzed in the following.

[18] Scott Gordon, "How Many Kinds of Things Are There in the World? The Ontological Status of Societies," in Greenwood, *The Mark of the Social,* 81–104.

[19] Gordon, "How Many Kinds of Things Are There in the World? The Ontological Status of Societies," in Greenwood, *The Mark of the Social,* 94.

compete with individualists' all-inclusive accounts. For them, the constitution of social is instead an issue about the nature of those social entities that are distinct from all particular constellations of unified, organized, and/or inter-related individualist phenomena. Accordingly, their ontological analyses aim to secure the distinctiveness of such entities as against such constellations and to explain how these entities determine the latter. Thus, for Durkheim the issue was, What is a social fact? and his answer distinguished such facts from facts about individuals on the basis of externality to and causal powers over individuals. For structuralists, the question was "What is social structure?" and the theories of such authors as Lévi-Strauss, Althusser, Roland Barthes, and the Foucault of *The Order of Things* all identified a stratum or dimension of struc-turing that was distinct from, while also formative of, actions, interactions, statements, beliefs, and artifacts. For wholists, finally, the central question has always been "What is a society?" Their analyses have repeatedly probed the nature of such wholes and the principles that govern them. As mentioned, for instance, socialist wholists contend that societies are more than any sum of the inter-related individuals in them, and that these wholes are governed by dynamic principles that do not apply directly to the actions of individuals, but instead either establish conditions and constraints to which these actions are beholden or determine these actions through the structuring of institutions, practices, and subsystems.

The following section examines a third ontological path, that of site ontol-ogy. The remainder of the current section offers brief arguments against the individualist and socialist approaches. Despite differences among individualist analyses, the basic ontological thesis of individualism is relatively straight-forward. As a result, the challenge to individualism presented below contests a wide variety of individualist ontologies. Socialism, by contrast, has no single basic ontological thesis. About all socialist ontologies agree on is that the social encompasses something in addition to the stuff into which individualism seeks to resolve social phenomena—they have very different conceptions of this residuum. Curiously enough, however, these conceptions often commit the same mistake: that of reification. By "reification," I mean treating abstract or nominalist entities as distinct, substantial realities. Given, however, the diver-gence among socialist conceptions of what resists individualist reduction, this allegation can be shown only case by case. I propose to illustrate this charge through Durkheim's social facts, in part because Durkheim's position, as in-dicated, was paradigmatic for much twenty-century socialism. Analysis of a second example, exemplifying key ontological principles of a second prominent twentieth-century socialism, structuralism, is concluded in the following chapter (Deleuze and Guattari's theory of social assemblages).

One historically pervasive challenge to individualism questions the integrity of its reduction base, that is to say, whether the individualist matters in/of which social phenomena allegedly consist themselves presuppose something that cannot be understood as just more individualist stuff. Maurice Mandelbaum developed a famous argument to this effect in his article "Societal Facts."[20] Here is a different argument.

In virtue of what is it the case that among the things someone is intentionally doing on a given occasion is A-ing? For instance, in virtue of what is it the case that among the things that Hollister is intentionally doing when waving his hand is calling his assistant hither? In light of the discussion of action in the previous chapter, this issue can be rephrased as, In virtue of what does performing a doing or saying B in conditions C amount to the performance of action A?[21]

Many individualist analyses reply that B amounts to A in virtue of the actor's desires, beliefs, and intentions. It might be said, for instance, that Hollister wanted to A (or wanted to carry out project P, the execution of which involved A-ing). Hollister, furthermore, must have had certain pertinent beliefs, for instance, that the circumstances were appropriate for A-ing or that carrying out project P required A-ing. The desires, beliefs, and intentions involved might also be conceived of as joining to cause A (or its performance). All told, that Hollister's waving constitutes a call for his assistant to come hither depends on his possessing certain mental states and on these states determining the action.

Of course, that Hollister's waving is calling might also have something to do with the circumstances in which it occurs. Maybe the trustee told him to call the assistant hither, and Hollister typically obeyed the trustee. Maybe the assistant called Hollister hither, and Hollister, always the disciplinarian, responded by calling the assistant hither. Individualism can accommodate these cases. This is not so clear, however, when that to which someone responds is not another's

---

[20] Maurice Mandelbaum, "Societal Facts," *British Journal of Sociology* 6 (1955): 305–17.

[21] Notice that I am not addressing the general nature of what Goldman calls "level generation" (Alvin Goldman, *A Theory of Human Action* [Princeton: Princeton University Press, 1979], chap. 2). I am asking only about, so to speak, the first level of generation: the first intentional action constituted by a given doing or saying. What further actions that action, in turn, might constitute is not at issue, although some considerations in the text bear on these further generations.

action, but a social state of affairs, say, a declaration of civil war (reported, for example, by a messenger). In such a case, the actor does not respond (though he or she could have) to the messenger's act of reporting. He or she responds, instead, to a social state of affairs: the declaration of war. Further argument is needed to demonstrate that this state of affairs is nothing but the actions of specific individuals. Accordingly, the institution of actions might not be amendable to individualism when the performance of doings and sayings constitutes an action that responds to a social state of affairs.

What, however, *enables* a wave to be a call? After all, it is not the case that Hollister, by virtue of his desires and beliefs, can perform whatever action he pleases by performing this or that doing or saying. Only certain actions can intelligibly be carried out through the performance of particular doings and sayings, and which these are is not typically up to the actors involved (cases of explicit conventions offer exceptions). What if, furthermore, Hollister lived in a social world where the only action waving could amount to is calling? In such a world, mental states, actions, and circumstances would not be immediately pertinent to his waving amounting to a calling. Considerations such as these indicate that, even if individualist analyses marshaling beliefs, desires, and intentions capture part of the institutional story, something is missing, namely, that which is responsible for the facts (1) that only certain actions, A (1)–(n), are intelligibly constituted by a given doing or saying, B, and (2) that different doings and sayings, B (1)–(n), can amount to the same action, A. This further factor is an essential part of the *complete* story about why the performance of B constitutes the performance of A.

As indicated in the previous chapter, the further factor is the understanding of A that is carried in the practices the actor carries on.[22] Waving can amount to calling only in a practice in which doings and sayings are understood to constitute callings, and waving, in particular, is intelligible as such. Apart from such an understanding and practice, waving *cannot* amount to calling (explicit agreements aside). The relevant understanding is carried in a practice that the actors concerned (Hollister and his assistant) and not others carry on, because it is an understanding that informs the course of their activities.

This account of the further factor contravenes individualism because such

---

[22] Elsewhere I have argued against the idea that this further factor is a norm or rule of intelligibility. See Theodore R. Schatzki, *Social Practices: A Wittgensteinian Approach to Human Activity and the Social* (New York: Cambridge University Press, 1996), chap. 2. Brief comments are offered below on a third alternative, namely, beliefs about what amounts to what in given circumstances.

understandings cannot be construed as possessions of specific people. Rather, they are something carried in the practices that people perform. This is because action understandings, as a matter of fact (though not necessarily of necessity), are established, acquired, sustained, and transformed through the actions that compose these practices. They cannot, therefore, be disengaged from the practices. The intelligibility of waving amounting to calling hither is, in other words, an affair (or a feature) of a practice: of the open-ended array of actions that constitute the dispersed practice of calling hither. Of course, Hollister and his assistant, in participating in this practice, each have an understanding of calling hither. Their understandings are versions, however, of that understanding of calling hither that is carried in the practice. This understanding, furthermore, is distinct from participants' versions: It is a feature of the practice and cannot be fractured into the participants' sometimes divergent versions. In Charles Taylor's phrase, action understandings (like the practices carrying them) are "out there" in public space, accessible in principle to anyone.[23] Individuals come to have understandings of action by becoming attuned to these public understandings. Note that belief is a poor concept for capturing this complicated situation. It is not the case (1) that actors collectively—and perhaps independently—believe that B-ing is intelligible as A-ing, or (2) that some practice carries the belief that B-ing is intelligible as A-ing and actors believe this (or something approximating it). B(1) ... (n) *are* intelligible as A's. This understanding, moreover, is out there in the practice, carried in the ways people act and react to one another, regardless of whatever beliefs they might have about A, B (1) ... (n), and circumstances.

In sum, the performance of doing or saying B amounts to the execution of action A only given a public, practice-borne understanding that A's can be performed via B's. Hence, one key category of individualist stuff, action, presupposes something nonindividualist, namely, practices and the understandings they carry.[24]

Durkheim famously contended that social facts, which he also called collective representations, are a unique order of facts distinct from facts about

---

[23] Charles Taylor, "Interpretation and the Sciences of Man," reprinted in his *Philosophy and the Human Sciences: Philosophical Papers* 2 (Cambridge: Cambridge University Press, 1985), 15–57.

[24] I cannot develop the point here, but I believe, as Tyler Burge has stressed, that a second category of individualist stuff, namely, mental conditions such as belief and desire, likewise depends on practices and the understandings practices carry. What constitutes not just a call, but also believing that one has been called, depends on practices and understandings. See, for instance, Tyler Burge, "Individualism and the Mark of the Social," *Midwest Studies in Philosophy* 4 (1979): 73–121.

individuals.[25] Facts about individuals are, above all, psychological facts about individuals separately. More specifically, Durkheim claimed that social facts are ways of thinking, feeling, or acting that have two features distinguishing them from facts about individuals: their externality to and their exercise of coercive power over individuals. A language, for instance, is not contained in individual actions and states of mind. To say such and such, moreover, a person must utter certain words and not others.

Durkheim was unclear whether social facts are external to individuals taken one by one or external to all pertinent individuals as a collection. Many of his phrases and examples suggest the former. If his position is to distinguish itself from individualism, however, he had to affirm the latter. The clearest indication that he did this is his thesis that the substratum of a social fact is a group: The ways of thinking, feeling, and acting labeled "social facts" are features of groups of individuals. Groups, moreover, are not just collections of individuals, as in individualist conceptions of them. Durkheim drew his position into the orbit of wholism by suggesting that a group of individuals is a totality distinct from the sum of individuals in it. Accordingly, social facts are properties of something that is distinct from collections of individuals. In this sense, these facts are "external" to such collections. In defending, consequently, the sui generis nature of social facts, Durkheim opposed facts about groups of individuals to sums of facts about individuals.

An ambiguity remains, however. Did Durkheim think that a social fact is distinct from a sum of facts about individuals separately or a sum of facts about individuals and their relations? He spoke of social facts arising from the "synthesis" and "association" of individuals. He also indicated that a group is a totality "formed by the union" of individuals.[26] It is plausible that such a totality might be distinct from the collection of individuals composing it. Such a totality cannot, however, be distinct from the complex of inter-related individuals involved: A group cannot be anything different or apart from the complex involved, that is to say, from a specific (possibly open) set of individuals in their relationships to one another. If, then, groups are the substrata of social facts, social facts are properties of complexes of inter-related individuals. As such, it is not obvious that social facts are distinct from collections of facts about individuals and their relations. In any event, in defending the distinctive

---

[25] Emile Durkheim, *The Rules of Sociological Method,* trans. Sarah A. Solovay and John H. Mueller (New York: Free Press, 1964), chap. 1 and intro. to 2d ed.

[26] Durkheim, *The Rules of Sociological Method,* xlvii.

nature of social facts, Durkheim opposed facts about inter-related individuals to sums of facts about separate individuals.

It is misleading, consequently, to speak of the sui generis nature of social facts. Facts about inter-related individuals are distinct from sums of facts about individuals, but facts about group, or complex, A are also distinct from those about group, or complex, B. It is hard to know whether facts about inter-related individuals are more or less distinct from facts about individuals than is one collection of facts about inter-related individuals from another such collection. Once the individual-social opposition becomes one between sums and groups of individuals, that is to say, between individuals aggregated and inter-related, the distinction loses its clear categorical character.

As I have been portraying matters, the externality mark of the distinctiveness of social facts is a byproduct of the specification of the substratum of that set of facts (social facts) whose distinctiveness from another set is at issue. There remains the causal criterion. If social facts are facts about groups, is the coercive power of such facts something other than the coercive power that group individuals exert over one another? Durkheim needed to answer this question affirmatively to maintain the distinctiveness of social facts. No forthright demonstration is to be found, however, in his text. His examples concern the coercive power of social facts over a particular individual (referred to as "I"). They are compatible, therefore, with the coercive power of social facts being nothing but the coercive power of group individuals over one another.

My diagnosis of the situation is as follows. Durkheim sought to delimit the domain of the social. Moreover, he wanted this domain to be distinct from that of the psychological, because only so would sociology have its own subject matter different from those of psychology and biology. Accordingly, he isolated a category of facts that boast certain properties distinguishing them from psychological facts and called these facts "social facts." Problems arose when he felt himself called on to specify the substratum of these facts; that is to say, when he felt obliged to specify of what configurations or dimension of the stuff, which all contrahents agree the world contains, these facts are properties. His specification of this substratum merges—rightly, in my opinion—the social and the individual: Groups are complexes of inter-related individuals, hence something partly constituted by the psychological. This specification, consequently, also reveals the dubiousness of the initial presumption that the social is distinct from the psychological. This result undermines, however, the distinctive character of the social. It shows that social facts are nominalist entities and that the clear distinctiveness of the social can be upheld only so long as these facts are treated as a distinct level of reality; that is to say, only so long as they are reified. Once a substratum is provided for them, and their reification is correspondingly canceled, the distinctiveness of the social disappears.

2. THE SOCIAL SITE

In recent theoretical decades, a new ontological path has opened up alongside individualism and socialism. I call this path "site ontology." Recall that something occurs in a site when it is inherently a part of a context in which it occurs. Site ontologies either locate the social in or identify it with some site. Their doing this has partly to do with their particular notions of the social. It also arises from their sense of embedding immersion, in conjunction with the continuity of being between the social and what contextualizes it as these theories conceive of these. I emphasize that the ontologies I assign to the site category neither call themselves thus, nor articulate the idea of site ontology, nor argue explicitly for a specific account of sites, nor even acknowledge kinship with their site brethren. The idea of site ontology, like the categorization of particular ontologies as exemplars, is mine.

Site ontologies are set off from individualist and socialist ones through their recognition of sites.[27] Although ontologies of the individualist and socialist sorts acknowledge that social phenomena and events transpire in contexts, none of the contexts involved are sites. I indicated in Chapter 2 that essentially all individualisms recognize contexts of the type I call "textures." Such ontologies conceptualize social reality as, ultimately, one huge maze of organized individuals; and this total fabric is a comprehensive and omnipresent texture in which any particular collection or configuration of individuals exists. (The set of all configurations of individuals likewise forms a texture.) The most rigorous individualisms recognize no contexts but strict textures. Weber's occasionalism, for instance, reduces the social organization of individuals to the chance that individuals will perform particular social actions. For Gilbert, moreover, only

---

[27] The historical prominence of individualism justifies dividing social ontologies into two categories: individualist and nonindividualist. Site ontologies, like the ones I label "socialist," belong to the latter category. So catalogued, site ontologies are not a categorical novelty, but instead simply a new nonindividualist approach. I have chosen to demarcate site ontologies from the ones the text calls "socialist" to emphasize that the notion of a site has no pendent in either individualist or hitherto prominent nonindividualist ontologies.

those interactions and relations that are part of group ("plural subject") phenomena count as "proper" social interactions and relations. Many individualists, however, above all when focusing on the condition of "the individual," invoke what might be called "pseudocontextures." A pseudocontexture is an organized configuration of individuals that is labeled a social phenomenon and contrasted with individualist phenomena. It makes an appearance when, for instance, a theorist writes that individual action proceeds in the context of both overtly individualist phenomena and configurations of individuals that the theorist refers to with expressions for social formations. In the previous section, for instance, I explained that Secord characterizes the social world as interactions taking place in organized settings. The phenomena that he claims organize settings fall into two categories: those that are overtly individualist in character, for example, "the history of previous interactions ... and the relationships among the actors"; and those, the proper analysis of which has pitted individualists against socialists, for instance, "society and its social institutions."[28] According to individualists, of course, social formations of the latter sorts (as Secord argues) are configurations of individuals: Pseudocontextures are, strictly speaking, nominalistically simplified elaborate textures.

None of the textures that individualism recognizes are sites. The identity of something that exists in a site is tied inherently to the site involved. Among the different concretizations this proposition can take is a thesis of the current work, that the identity of an action is intrinsically wedded to a practice, that is to say, an organized nexus of actions (see Chapter 2). Individualism, by contrast, does not argue that the identities of the basic stuff of social life—actions and mental conditions—are inherently tied to the actions and mental states of other people. What actions a person performs and which mental conditions she is in might be related to the properties of other people, but the connection is contingent (and typically causal). Actions, furthermore, do form arrays, but their identities as actions do not derive from these arrays (e.g., from something that governs arrayed actions in common). Individualism contends that arrays of action are simply collections, and that the only thing governing arrayed actions in common is the conjunction of the relevant, only contingently identical or interwoven properties of individuals. Individualism likewise ties relationships among individuals to the individuals related, though this stratagem, it is important to emphasize, does not preclude different sets of individuals from

[28] Secord, "The Mark of the Social in the Social Sciences," in Greenwood, *The Mark of the Social,* 75.

maintaining "the same" relationship. In Hayek's words, "If the social structure can remain the same although different individuals succeed each other at particular points, this is not because the individuals which succeed one another are completely identical, but because they succeed each other in particular relations, in particular attitudes they take towards other people, and as the objects of particular views held by other people about them."[29] For individualists, consequently, actions, interactions, and relations do not occur *as* part of textures. Configurations of action are, instead, either mere byproducts or contingent, enforced resultants of these actions, interactions, and relations. All these aspects of individualism, be it noted, are facets of its nominalism.

Socialisms, by contrast, emphatically recognize contexts of the sort I called "contexture." These contextures are composed of those components or dimensions of social life that are not amendable to individualist analysis. These structures, institutions, societies, and social facts qualify as contextures because, as discussed, they "surround" and determine individuals (e.g., the actions they perform and the relationships they maintain), sometimes causally and sometimes via enablement and constraint. Although socialist contextures differ greatly from the texture(s) of individuals that individualism promotes, they do not amount to sites. The burden of these socialisms has always been to defend a difference in being between individualist stuff and some distinct, irreducible component of the social. As a result, individualist phenomena such as actions cannot be intrinsically *part of* these societies, social facts, abstract structures, or institutions. They may be inseparable from these phenomena, but the latter do not constitute a site where they occur.

Most site ontologies are inspired by Heidegger's *Being and Time.* They make a space, that is, an opening or pervasive medium of some sort, central to the nature or constitution of the social. Their reliance on spaces makes palpable why these ontologies are of the site variety: Spaces qua openings or mediums are preeminently qualified to be something where, and as part of which, events occur and entities exist. Most site ontologists, be it noted, are also practice theorists. This convergence of sites and practices reflects the Heideggerian provenance of their ontologies and, in addition, the influence Wittgenstein exerted on them. Of course, the sense of embedded located-ness articulated in the notion of space is not unique to this Heideggerian line of thought. The Hegelian tradition has always stressed the inherent insertion of the individual

[29] Hayek, *The Counter Revolution in Science,* 34.

into society as a whole;[30] and ontological socialisms generally view individuals as contexturalized in social phenomena. What is new is Heidegger's intuition of a space of being and intelligibility in which entities are.

According to Heideggerian site ontologies, the social is either such a clearing of being and intelligibility or inherently tied to one. This approach contravenes individualism in holding that actions, groups, and constellations of individuals exist *in* the social. It diverges from socialism in working with contexts (sites) that are alien to socialist ontologies. It also diverges from wholism in maintaining that there are no principles that govern the social realm as a whole. It is worth remarking that the fact that being and intelligibility can become prominent in *social* ontologies reflects Heidegger's conviction that the clearing is a human affair even though it does not find its source in individual minds.

In Chapter 1, I described Laclau and Mouffe's concept of discourse, of arrays of inter-relatedly and systematically meaningful actions, things, and words (positions). The authors write that part of what forms the exterior of any given discourse is other discourses, other constellations of systematically related positions.[31] They also claim that the sum-total of discourses that exists at any given moment or *durée* subsides in something called the "field of discursivity." This field is an inexhaustible openness, or potential, of articulability that overflows the totality of articulations contained in the sum of discourses at any time and thereby undercuts the ostensible stability of any given extant discourse.[32] Laclau and Mouffe waver somewhat in their specification of the social. Sometimes they describe the social as the sum-total of discourses; at other times this epithet seems to be conferred on the field of discursivity.[33] This difference corresponds to two different social ontologies. Qua sum-total of discourses, the social is a plenum that subsides in a metaphysical space. Qua openness of discursivity, it is a clearing in which discourses exist. Despite this

---

[30] The Hegelian tradition continues today to converge with the Heideggerian path. For a recent example, see Joseph Margolis's account of societies as discursive spaces in "The Meaning of 'Social,'" in Greenwood, *The Mark of the Social*, 183–98.

[31] Ernesto Laclau and Chantal Mouffe, *Hegemony and Socialist Strategy: Towards a Radical Democratic Politics* (London: Verso, 1985), 135.

[32] The resemblance of this field to Derrida's supplement is confirmed in their characterization of it as a "surplus of meaning"; Laclau and Mouffe, *Hegemony and Socialist Strategy*, 111.

[33] In a later text, Laclau seizes the first of these options in identifying the social as "sedimented forms of 'objectivity,'" that is to say, as extant, taken for granted inter-relatedly articulated positions. See Ernesto Laclau, "New Reflections on the Revolution of Our Time," in his *New Reflections on the Revolution of Our Time* (London: Verso, 1990), 3–85, here 35.

uncertainty, Laclau and Mouffe meld the social with a space of discursivity in which actions, people, objects, and words are inter-relatedly meaningful.

Laclau and Mouffe maintain that the social either is a space or subsists in one. A second raft of Heideggerian site ontologies analyzes the social as nexuses of practices that *carry* spaces of intelligibility. According to Charles Taylor, for instance, social reality is practices.[34] The actions, moreover, out of which a given practice is composed are tied to the language used in the practice. Together, past actions and uses of language (along with desires, feelings, and emotions) articulate a "semantic space" that envelopes everything that henceforth composes or is encountered in the practice. Practices, consequently, open fields of meaning in terms of which they themselves proceed; and the individuals who carry on practices, as well as the relations they maintain in doing so, are embedded in the fields of meaning that the practices they carry on open and sustain. For Taylor, consequently, practices form the site where humans live and relate.

Much the same picture is found in Spinosa, Flores, and Dreyfus. Spinosa, Flores, and Dreyfus define a world—also called a "disclosure space"—as any organized set of practices that produces a relatively self-contained web of meanings.[35] Each such world contains a specific range of activities that are undertaken for particular purposes (themselves tied to the identities of actors), and whose performance involves the use of a specific array of equipment. In addition to being organized through this array of uses, activities, purposes, and identities (Heidegger's *Verweisungsganze*), a world exhibits an embracing style that, in determining how things matter to people, coordinates its activities (Heidegger's *Befindlichkeit*). Worlds, furthermore, can occur in broader worlds whose shared practices they presuppose; a family "subworld," for example, can occur in the more extensive world of a given "culture." Consequently, people primarily exist, and their relations largely transpire, in particular worlds, meaning that who they are, what they do, and how they relate is beholden to the organizations and styles (i.e., the webs of meaning) involved. Human coexistence is inherently embedded in hierarchically (i.e., presuppositionally) organized sets of practices that produce multiple, relatively self-contained webs of meaning.

[34] Taylor, "Interpretation and the Sciences of Man," 33–34.
[35] Charles Spinosa, Fernando Flores, and Hubert Dreyfus, *Disclosing New Worlds: Entrepreneurship, Democratic Action, and the Cultivation of Solidarity* (Cambridge, Mass.: MIT Press, 1997), chap. 1; cf. Charles Spinosa and Hubert Dreyfus, "Two Kinds of Anti-Essentialism and Their Consequences," *Critical Inquiry* 22 (summer 1996): 735–63.

Bourdieu's neo-Heideggerian site ontology similarly highlights spaces that combine activity and meaning. Central to Bourdieu's account is the notion of a field. A field is a bounded realm of activity, for instance, agriculture, cooking, education, intellectual work, marriage, politics, and celebration. These bounded realms closely resemble the domains of activity widely recognized in sociological and anthropological theory. They differ because what happens in a given field is governed by a habitus (battery of practical senses) that (1) is acquired by people in growing up under the objective conditions characteristic of the field; (2) generates actions that perpetuate the practices and conditions found in the field; and (3) bestows meanings on actions, events, and arrangements that people encounter there. What is more, the actions that habitus produces, like the meanings it fashions, are those and only those that are possible given, or compatible with, the field's objective conditions. Certain stakes, finally, are at issue in a given field's activities; and actors draw on particular capitals (cultural, symbolic, material) in pursuing those stakes. In sum, a field comprises stakes, capitals, objective conditions, and a space of actual and possible activities and meanings.[36] Bourdieu also contends that the different fields in which a given people lives are organized homologously, and that these fields thereby compose a whole that resembles in scope what traditionally has been labeled a "society." These wholes of homologous fields open overall spaces of activity and meaning. For Bourdieu, therefore, the social is a practice-field compound that funds homologous activity-meaning spaces.

Below I sketch my own account of the social site and criticize the rival analyses just summarized. Before doing this, it is important to point out that, although sites possess "fieldlike" qualities, they should not be assimilated to any of the fields that are used in social analysis. To substantiate the difference between sites and fields, consider the following four field concepts that are pervasive and crucial to social ontology.

One such concept is that of a clearing. A clearing (*die Lichtung, das Offene*) is an opening in which entities (*das Seiendes*) are, a space in which "things can show up," to use Dreyfus's phrase.[37] The significance of this concept for

[36] See Pierre Bourdieu, *Outline of a Theory of Practice*, trans. Richard Nice (Cambridge: Cambridge University Press, 1976); Pierre Bourdieu, *The Logic of Practice*, trans. Richard Nice (Stanford: Stanford University Press, 1990).

[37] Martin Heidegger, *Being and Time*, trans. John Macquarrie and Edward Robinson (Oxford: Blackwell, 1962), section 28; Hubert Dreyfus, *Being-in-the-World: A Commentary on Heidegger's Being and Time, Division i* (Cambridge, Mass.: MIT Press, 1991).

contemporary social ontology has already been suggested.[38] The guises in which it has been rearticulated in twentieth-century thought more generally are legion. One prominent example is Derrida's notion of textuality. A further notable instance in social thought is Hannah Arendt's notion of the public as an open space where people are visible to one another amid a world of things in common. This open space is the realm of human reality, intimate thoughts, passions, and feeling leading by contrast only "an uncertain, shadowy existence" in the "twilight" of private subjective experience.[39]

Closely related to the notion of a clearing is a second type of field, fields of possibility. Examples are fields of possible actions, possible causal determinations, possible representations, or possible ways to be. Although some interpretations treat Heidegger's clearing as such a field, I want to separate the notion of a field of possibility from that of a clearing. Neither Arendt's public nor Laclau and Mouffe's field of discursivity is a field of possibility. The public, for instance, is at best the site (in the second sense of the term) where human beings live out their possibilities, whereas the field of discursivity is a content-less potential of ever further intelligibility. In any event, the notion of a field of possibility is rampant in social thought where it by and large assumes the form of fields of possible action. To quote one already-cited example, Bourdieu writes: "In short, being the product of a particular class of objective regularities, the *habitus* tends to generate all the 'reasonable,' 'common-sense,' behaviors (and only these) which are possible within the limits of these regularities."[40] Fields of possible action are discussed further in Chapter 4.

A third type of field is plenums. A plenum is a finite plenitude of particular, usually inter-related phenomena. To say that it is a "finite plenitude" is to say that a field of this sort is exhaustively described by the specific phenomena

---

[38] The clearing has no being (the "ontological difference"). It itself, consequently, cannot be a site. The conceptions of intelligibility spaces that Heidegger's notion of the clearing has inspired are, instead, key components of a series of site ontologies.

[39] Hannah Arendt, *The Human Condition* (Chicago: University of Chicago Press, 1958), 50–51. For a discussion relating the public to Heidegger's clearing, see Seyla Benhabib, *The Reluctant Modernism of Hannah Arendt* (Thousand Oaks, Calif.: Sage, 1996). Various commentators, incidentally, have interpreted the Foucault of both *The Order of Things/ The Archaeology of Knowledge* and *Discipline and Punish* as working with a notion of clearing. For two very different interpretations to this effect, see Hubert Dreyfus, "On the Ordering of Things: Being and Power in Heidegger and Foucault," in *Michel Foucault: Philosopher,* ed. Timothy Armstrong (London: Routledge, 1992), 80–94; Gilles Deleuze, *Foucault,* trans. and ed. Séan Hand (Minneapolis: University of Minnesota Press, 1988), 56–60. Deleuze writes that the prison form is a "first light" that institutes, or "makes visible," the visibilities of its contents (i.e., their ontological determinations).

[40] Bourdieu, *The Logic of Practice,* 55.

composing it. A similar idea is captured in Deleuze and Guattari's notion of a rhizome: A rhizome is a multiplicity that has no dimensions over and beyond its lines, which fully fill, or occupy, its dimensions by constituting them.[41] Sometimes, as with a field of poppies, the components of a plenum are of a single type. Usually, however, plenums embrace heterogeneous phenomena. An example is the networks of actor-network theory, which embrace people, artifacts, organisms, and things. A plenum's elements are also usually inter-related (sociotechnical networks again offer an example). I note that some theorists contrast analyses of specific social domains as mere aggregates of entities with analyses of these domains as plenums of inter-related entities. Examples are those individualists who analyze social phenomena as aggregated, as opposed to inter-related, individuals. In my terminology, both aggregates of entities and plenitudes of inter-related phenomena are subtypes of the same general category, plenums. Note that a field of possibility is not a plenum because it lacks finitude (see Chapter 4). A plenum is always a fullness of actualities.

A fourth type of field is bounded realms. Bounded realms are fields whose contents are defined by principles, rules, constraints, ends, functions, or underlying generating factors. As just explained, the boundaries of a plenum are defined particularistically, that is to say, by the plenum's actual contents: Something belongs to the plenum if and only if it is one of its actual contents. The limits of a bounded realm, by contrast, do not coincide with its actual extent. A field of this sort also encompasses phenomena that can or might fulfill, follow, observe, realize, or be generated by the phenomena that govern it. In addition, therefore, to embracing a finite set of past and present phenomena, a bounded realm is open-ended.

Exemplifying this fourth type of field are most social theoretical concepts of domains of activity. Recent prominent examples of such concepts, whose theoretical importance commenced with the discovery of markets in eighteenth-century political economy, are systems of action à la Parsons and his followers, Goffman's interaction order, and Bourdieu's fields.[42] In addition to encompassing a finite set of actual actions, a domain of any of these sorts embraces

---

[41] Gilles Deleuze and Félix Guattari, *A Thousand Plateaus: Capitalism and Schizophrenia,* trans. Brian Massumi (Minneapolis: University of Minnesota Press, 1987), plateau 1.

[42] For example, Parsons and Shils, "Values, Motives, and Systems of Action," chap. 4; Erving Goffman, "Presidential Address: The Interaction Order," *American Sociological Review* 48 (1983): 1–17; Bourdieu, *The Logic of Practice.*

further actions that can or might occur in it because they satisfy its governing principles, constraints, ends, or factors (cf. the previous Bourdieu quotation on possible actions). It is worth remarking that the contemporary prevalence of these conceptions coordinates with the ascendance, noted in Chapter 1, of the pair "enablement and constraint." Underlying these conceptions is one or both of two intuitions: that which actions are possible at any moment (or *durée*) in a given realm rests partly on the history of actions performed there up to that moment; and that the actions that do occur there at any time are restricted to a range of possibilities. The union of these two intuitions yields the progression, actuality establishes possibilities, which delimit the succeeding actuality, which (re)establishes possibilities, which delimit the following actuality, which (re)establishes possibilities, . . . that some contemporary theorists impute to the flow of social affairs.

A site is a creature of a different sort from a clearing, a space of possibility, a plenum, or a bounded domain. A site is a context, some or all of whose inhabitants are inherently part of it. This definition leaves completely open whether, and in what way, a given site is composed of fields. As it is, site ontologies typically employ field concepts. Laclau and Mouffe, for instance, conceptualize the social as a plenum of discourses coalescing in a clearing qua web of intelligibility (i.e., discursivity). Spinosa, Flores, and Dreyfus join Taylor in construing the social realm as a plenum of practices that carries clearings qua webs of intelligibility (webs of meaning and semantic spaces). Bourdieu treats the social as homologous bounded realms (i.e., fields), each encompassing a bounded realm of activity and meaning. Regardless of the extent, however, to which site ontologies employ field concepts, there is no inherent connection between sites and fields.[43]

My formal definition of the social site as the context (if any) as part of which the social inherently transpires is neutral vis-à-vis different definitions of the social and different accounts of its constitutional contexts. In Chapter 1, however, I noted that I have elsewhere urged that "social" be interpreted as pertaining to human coexistence. The social site, consequently, can be defined

---

[43] Indeed, many individualist and socialist ontologies also work with one or more of these field concepts. Although individualisms eschew notions like clearings and bounded realms, plenums and fields of possibility are plentiful among them. Both inter-related individuals and configurations of such individuals constitute plenums, whereas social action in general à la Weber composes a region of being à la Husserl (a fifth sort of field). Some socialist theories, too, countenance fields. Examples are all accounts that contend that social facts, societies, structures, or institutions open spaces of possible action and relation.

more specifically as the site specific to human coexistence: the context, or wider expanse of phenomena, in and as part of which humans coexist. The qualifier "specific" indicates that the object of concern is that particular context that is the site of human coexistence and of nothing else. The biosphere, the site of life on earth, is not, for example, what is intended.

This definition upholds the individualist intuition that social affairs have to do with individuals: Human coexistence is a state of affairs that pertains to people. This is the case, moreover, because a human life is always the life of an individual person. (Group and collective lives consist in individual lives linked in particular contexts.) As discussed, however, individualism stops here: Social affairs are *nothing but* constellations of inter-related individuals. That individuals exist and relate only in a site of a certain general sort goes unrecognized in its analyses.

The social site is the site of human coexistence. As also indicated in Chapter 1, human coexistence, in turn, is the "hanging together" of human lives. With this expression, I mean how lives inter-relate in and through the dimensions that compose them individually. By "a human life," furthermore, I mean the mental conditions that a person is in together with the actions he or she performs. More precisely, a human life is a developing manifold of mental conditions and actions (1) that is attributable to the person whose bodily doings and sayings express and constitute them; (2) whose component mental conditions determine practical intelligibility (cf. Chapter 2, Section 2); and (3) whose component actions take place in linked settings. Lives hang together, then, through practical intelligibility, mentality, activity, and settings.

The best way to clarify this analysis is to enumerate and illustrate important ways that lives hang together in these four dimensions. I call these ways "forms of coexistence" (or "forms of sociality"). Lives hang together, first, through the interpersonal structuring of mentality and practical intelligibility. Such structuring has two chief modalities: commonality and orchestration. Commonality exists when the same understanding, rule, end, project, or emotion is expressed in different people's actions or when the same action makes sense to different people to perform. This phenomenon requires no illustration. Orchestration exists when different understandings, rules, ends, projects, and emotions are nonindependently expressed in different people's actions (or when different actions nonindependently make sense to different people to perform). An example would be Hollister starting maceration because Long was distilling or Hollister expressing his chagrin to an elder because Long was mercilessly pursuing the accumulation of profit. A completely different way that two lives hang together is for one person—her or his actions, mental conditions, situation—to be the object of another's actions or conditions. This latter form of coexistence is a subtype of a relation that holds between entities in arrangements, namely, intentional relations.

A number of forms of coexistence transpire in the domain of settings. Lives hang together, for instance, when people find themselves simultaneously in the same setting and also when some event in that setting ushers in a new situation for each of them (as an overflowing evaporation pan in the corner did for Long and Hollister as they worked in the laboratory). Lives can also hang together through the physical and activity-space setup of the artifacts, organisms, things, and people in a setting. This held of Long and Hollister, for example, whenever they were in the laboratory together carrying on medicinal herb production practices. Another way lives hang together in a single setting is through people nonindependently performing different actions at different times in one place. An example would be Hollister setting the belladonna to steep in the kettle in the morning and Long checking on it in the afternoon (while Hollister was out with the sisters and boys looking for wild herbs).

Lives hang together not just in and through single settings, but also across multiple ones. Above all, three types of phenomena are responsible for this coexistence: nonindependent situation-initiating entities, intersetting arrangements, and physical connections. An example of the first is the ringing of the Center Family's bell signaling lunchtime, whereupon James Vail (the record keeper) went into the basement to tell the person working the noisy hydraulic press that it was time to eat. Here, the life of the presser and those of the other family members hang together through the bell ringing and the telling, which nonindependently initiate new situations for them. A good example of an intersetting setup is the arrangements of artifacts, things, and organisms across rooms and different floors that composed the power systems in the extract and herb houses. Finally, examples of the physical connections I have in mind—continuous physical structures, avenues of access, and technological communication connections—are the walkways between the Center Family's buildings, the doors in the extract and herb houses, and the telephone lines connected later in the century to the trustee's house. (The sound waves that the striking of the bell generated count, too.)

The final form of coexistence I mention here is chains of action. As noted in passing in Chapter I, a chain of action is a series of actions, each member of which is a response either to the immediately preceding member or to an event or change that the immediately preceding member brought about in the world. Like the coexistence that transpires through intentionality, such chains form a subtype of a sort of relation that links entities in arrangements, namely, causal relations. I believe it is obvious that lives hang together through such chains. Indeed, more or less all contemporaneous human lives in the modern world are related, however indirectly, through this avenue.

In sum, lives hang together through intentional relations, chains of action, and the interpersonal structuring of mentality and practical intelligibility, as well as through layouts of, events occurring in, and connections among the components of material settings. Although this brief overview does not exhaust the forms of sociality, it should give the reader a sense of what I mean by "human coexistence." Notice that meaning is interwoven into these socialities. Intentionality, actions, and both the significance and relevance of features of settings for human life are tied to the meanings entities have for people.

At the beginning of the chapter, I announced that the site of human co-existence is a mesh of practices and orders. It is probably patent, to begin with, that some human coexistence occurs not just in the context, but inherently as part of arrangements. As just noted, for instance, several forms of coexistence are at once relations that link entities in arrangements: The particular forms of coexistence involved are nothing other than those causal, spatial, and inten-tional arrangement relations whose relata are humans. Other forms of coexis-tence often work through further arrangement-composing relations, one or both of whose relata are nonhumans. Examples are two herb workers simulta-neously observing the horse for signs of inferior shoeing and the lives of the horse tender and the hydraulic press operator being linked through the power system. Hence, much human coexistence transpires *as* arrangements of people, artifacts, organisms, and things. A significant dimension of any arrangement is the human coexistence it ipso facto embraces.

Human coexistence does not take place solely as a dimension of arrange-ments. Those forms of coexistence, however, that are not features of arrange-ments are, instead, aspects of practices. At the herb and extract houses, for instance, commonalities in and orchestrations of normativized (enjoined and accepted) (1) mental conditions, (2) intentional relatedness, (3) reactions to events in settings, and (4) nonindependent actions in the same settings at dif-ferent times were all components of the medicinal herb production practices. Most of the chains of action circulating there similarly comprised actions that were components of those practices. What is more, whenever the actions that workers performed, the teleoaffectivities that governed their activities, and their intentional relations to one another contravened the normative strictures of the production practices, the actions, teleoaffectivities, and relations involved were almost invariably aspects of *other* practices that the workers were carrying out in the herb or extract houses. When Hollister, for instance, thought to himself that Long's dogged pursuit of profit was nothing short of sacrilegious, he was—unintentionally—for the moment taking up religious practices. When Long tainted the quassia just before apostatizing in 1860, he was engaged in a practice like revenge or sabotage in which such actions were acceptable (he went to work for a nearby competing pharmaceutical company). When Hollister examined the quassia to check its quality, the chain of actions linking his life to Long's embraced acts from different practices (those of herb production and of revenge or sabotage). The only form of coexistence that can occur outside the mesh of *all* practices and orders is intentional relatedness, especially thoughts about others. Practically all intentional inter-relatedness, however, is part of this mesh. All in all, human existence happens *as part of* practice-arrangement meshes.

The previous chapter argued that practices establish orders. Those features of orders in which human coexistence consists are established, for the most part, through human activity. Shaker medicinal herb practices, for instance, did not simply contain the intentional relations, action chains, and meanings/identities of humans and nonhumans through which the lives of the herb workers hung together. They also were directly or indirectly responsible for most of the *further* arrangement-composing relations through which these lives were linked: physical connections among entities at the herb and extract houses (in the same and different rooms), spatial setups of and across these rooms, and communication connections linking those arrangements (and the production practices) to other Shaker orders (and practices). Human coexistence transpires as part of a mesh of order-establishing practices and mostly set-up orders.

Connected to the arrangements at the herb and extract houses were the orders both at the other buildings and on the wider grounds of the Center Family compound. The practices family members carried out likewise composed a net of which the herb production practices were but one component. Coexistence among family members thus occurred as part of a wider mesh of orders and practices at the compound. This mesh, in turn, was linked to the broader complex of orders and practices that both composed the village of

New Lebanon and was the overall site of coexistence among the village's inhabitants; and this complex itself linked up with the even wider horizon of practices and orders falling away on all sides of the village's boundaries, which taken together formed the site where the village's inhabitants coexisted with outsiders. As this centrifugal movement suggests, the overall site where contemporaneous social life transpires is one immense mesh of practices and orders. It is an immense plenum of interconnected plenums (orders) linked to innumerable interweaving bounded realms (practices). Incidentally, the spaces that this plenum institutes are spaces of prefigured, and not of possible, actions. As is explained in the following chapter, the futural openness of social life is best analyzed not through the notion of possibilities, but instead through the characterization of action paths by indefinitely many such modalities as easier and harder, longer and shorter, and prescribed and proscribed.

This analysis of the social site must be distinguished from the site ontologies discussed above. As described, Laclau and Mouffe construe the social as a plenum of discourses that subsists in a clearing of discursivity. The site they thereby circumscribe is this complex of discourses-in-the-field of discursivity, as part of which any articulation of meaning, and any inter-related delimitation of a totality of actions, persons, objects, and words, occurs. Conspicuously absent from this specification of the social as complexes of inter-relatedly meaningful positions are movement and change. Laclau and Mouffe are not unaware of these. They claim that discourses are instituted in activity that, arising from extant discourses, dislocates their articulations of intelligibility and establishes new determinations. In arguing so (and thereby assigning movement and change to the political),[44] Laclau and Mouffe divide activity into two classes: that great mass of ordinary actions that occupy places alongside objects and words in static orders and those rare efforts that decisively dislocate and rearticulate. This duality of relative stability and dramatic upheaval infelicitously dichotomizes human activity into two categories: component of arrangements and determining force. It thereby overlooks, first, that one and the same nexus of organized activity both maintains and establishes/alters orders; and, as a result, second, that the social occurs (in part) as this nexus. Their account fails, furthermore, to acknowledge that orders can contribute to their own evolution.

[44] "[T]he problem of the political is the problem of the institution of the social" (Laclau and Mouffe, *Hegemony and Socialist Strategy: Towards a Radical Democratic Politics,* 153; cf. Laclau, "New Reflections on the Revolution of Our Time," 61).

Taylor, by contrast, contends that social reality is a plenum of practices that carries clearings of intelligibility. This thesis implies that social affairs transpire in and as intelligibility-articulating practices. Practices, accordingly, constitute the site of the social. This picture rehabilitates what Laclau and Mouffe lost through dichotomization, namely, that social affairs inherently take place as a nexus of organized activity. It loses something, however, that Laclau and Mouffe emphasize, viz., that these affairs also transpire through arrangements of enti-ties: The semantic spaces that are carried in practices embrace actions, words, and mental conditions, but not also objects. Of course, nothing in Taylor's picture proscribes the incorporation of objects. Still, his focus on practices effectively disconnects social phenomena from organized materialities, which help constitute social phenomena and contribute to their evolution.

In depicting the social world as homologous bounded realms of activity and meaning, Bourdieu's theory, too, emphasizes the constitutive and causal omnipresence of human activity. His account of the social even more closely approximates my own than does Taylor's, for it both acknowledges social orders qua layouts of settings and locales and highlights the significance of activity amid those layouts for the inculcation of habitus. For Bourdieu, more fully stated, the site of social life is an array of homologous bounded realms of activity, meaning, and arrangement. This conception nevertheless diverges from the present one in significant ways. To begin with, Bourdieu ties orders and activities into tight, self-propagating packages. Thereby lost are the facts that practices in different bounded realms ("integrative practices," in my lan-guage) interweave, that what I call "dispersed practices" cut through multifar-ious realms, and that arrangements are connected laterally across realms both dependent on and independent of the practices in those realms. What is more, Bourdieu collapses the organization of practices into the structure of habitus. Elsewhere I have discussed at length the significant differences that therewith distance his account of practice organization from my own.[45] Finally, Bourdieu's picture of homologous bounded realms imputes to the overall site of the social large-scale integrated units whose scope resembles that enjoyed by societies in most wholist conceptions of these. I do not believe that the mesh of practices and orders is organized into large-scale united parcels. Foucault and those work-ing under his tutelage are right that practices and orders form a convoluted,

---

[45] See Theodore R. Schatzki, "Practices and Actions: A Wittgensteinian Critique of Bourdieu and Giddens," *Philosophy of the Social Sciences* 27, 3 (1997): 283–308.

shifting, and variegated mass,[46] and that whatever large-scale formations characterize this mass are both tangent to the great unities that the theoretical tradition countenances (e.g., society or state) and held together by principles that
do not unify their components.[47] The current book can be viewed, in part, as
an attempt to ground these theses in a thorough account of the social site.

Spinosa, Flores, and Dreyfus do not address questions of social ontology.
Because, however, their notion of worlds as meaning-disclosing, arrangement-
encompassing practice plenums resembles my notion of practice-order complexes, it is worth articulating several differences between them. First, a minor
point: Spinosa, Flores, and Dreyfus acknowledge that, in situations of breakdown and unfamiliarity, people encounter entities as something other than
"equipment" (Heidegger's *Zeug*). The arrangements that help compose worlds,
however, are pure equipment totalities. This rendering lamentably underplays
the variegated composition and significance of arrangements for social existence. It also reflects an overly tight packaging of practices and objects, which
minimizes the significance of orders.

Indeed, I am skeptical that the mesh of practices and orders is broken up
into worlds exhibiting unified styles. Consider, first, styles: A style is a way
of being, a manner of carrying on, that, in establishing how things matter to
people, coordinates all the actions in a given world. Examples are the "relative
passivity and sensitivity to harmony" of Japanese actions, the "calm, all-too-
happy-to-please" style of driving in the American Midwest, and the "aggressive
energy of a laissez-faire system in which everyone strives to express his or her
own desires," which characterizes American economic and political worlds.[48]
I concur that styles—and these ones in particular—exist. I doubt, however,
that they are parceled out one per world. Both the world of a "culture" and the
smaller subworlds in it can accommodate multiple styles. The same style,
moreover, can traverse worlds. Aggressive and calmer manners of driving, like
the passive harmonizing and the active self-assertive styles of conducting
business, commix in different proportions in Japanese and American worlds

[46] See, for instance, Michel Foucault, "Nietzsche, Genealogy, History," in *The Foucault Reader,* ed. Paul
Rabinow (New York: Pantheon, 1984), 76–100; the essays in Andrew Barry, Thomas Osborne, and
Niklas Rose, eds., *Foucault and Political Reason: Liberalism, Neo-Liberalism and Rationalities of
Government* (London: UCL Press, 1996).
[47] For a fine illustration of this theme, see Michel Foucault, "Politics and the Study of Discourse," in
The Foucault Effect: Studies in Governmentality, ed. Graham Burchell, Colin Gordon, and Peter
Miller (Chicago: University of Chicago Press, 1991), 53–72.
[48] Spinosa, Flores, and Dreyfus, *Disclosing New Worlds,* 19–21.

(and, for present purposes, it does not matter whether the mixing arose through migration). Practical organizations and styles relate contingently and in various combinations.

The picture of a multiplicity of worlds, moreover, is a bit too chunky. Dreyfus, Flores, and Spinosa write that worlds connect and that smaller ones are ordered in broader ones. Nonetheless, because each world is composed of a particular equipmental totality plus set of practices, it enjoys greater discreteness than do interweavings of practices and orders in my hands. Practices and orders do, of course, bundle. An example is the bundle constituting the New Lebanon medicinal herb business, which is composed of arrangements at the herb and extract houses in connection with the medicinal herb production practices. As I pointed out, however, the orders at the herb and extract houses were the site (in the second sense) where various practices were carried on. The herb practices were also shot through with dispersed ones. So practices and orders are not just contingently but also incompletely and precariously packaged into bundles. Indeed, the very notion of a "mesh" of practices and orders is meant to suggest that activities and arrangements form a great evolving horizontal web of interweaving practices amid interconnected orders. Whatever consolidations of practices and orders occur in this mesh are contingent, regularly disrupted, and always perforated by the moving rhizomes of dispersed practices that lace through the social site.

I close this section by saying a few more words about the horizontal structure of this intricate, contingent, and shifting site. As illustrated in the following section, practices and orders are entwined with each other and with others of their own kind in varyingly tight or loose multilayered webs. The particular shapes that appear in this web are an empirical and contingent matter. Among these are fragile and metamorphosing bundles of practices and orders (such as the medicinal herb business); larger nets containing multiple, closely knit, and overlapping bundles as knots (such as Shaker life at New Lebanon); spatially scattered confederations of linked and imbricated bundles or nets (such as, respectively, the pharmaceutical industry in the United States in the mid-nineteenth century and life at all Shaker villages taken together); regions of relatively unconnected practices crisscrossing amid particular orders (as in public squares); wandering dispersed practices running through these agglomerations and regions; and particular integrative practices that take place amid different orders scattered through sociohistorical time-space (for example, the practices of the Olympic Games). These bundles, nets, confederations, regions, and dispersed and scattered practices are linked together as one gigantic, intricate, and evolving mesh of practices and orders. At its fullest reach, moreover, this web is coextensive with sociohistorical space-time.

As is also illustrated shortly, nothing about the topology just offered reflects peculiarities of Shaker life. It is equally feasible to catalogue the practice-order shapes that characterize social sites at other historical moments or in other geographical arenas. It is an open question, moreover, what shapes would supplement those mentioned in the previous paragraph in a detailed typology based on careful consideration of the historical record and the contemporary world.

Despite its evident complexity, the social site is held together by the same sinews that were identified in the previous chapter as holding practices and orders together with each other and with others of their own genre. Practices, to begin with, overlap through common organizational elements (rules, ends, projects). For example, practices both at New Lebanon and across different Shaker villages overlapped through the observance of the same rules, just as industrial practices again both at New Lebanon and throughout different villages overlapped through the common pursuit of profit. Organizational orchestration plays a role in joining practices, too, as the division of labor both in and among Shaker families and villages suggests. Practices also overlap by virtue of doings and sayings belonging to multiple practices. Shaker repair and herb production practices overlapped, for instance, whenever the equipment at the herb and extract houses was repaired. Similarly, when Shaker workers who were busy drying, pressing, and making extractions asked one another questions, explained what they were doing, or described the weather outside, dispersed practices cut through the herb production ones. Causal chains are a further avenue through which practices are joined. Shaker practices of eating, discipline, worship, herb production, and broom making were interlaced via action chains that embraced actions from two or more of them. For instance, the Center Family's various industrial practices were causally linked through the consumption in one practice of the products of others; meetings among the trustees, deacons, and forepersons; and excursions by participants in one practice to use the equipment utilized in others (as when apple cider was pressed in the herb presses). Finally, practices (and orders, too) are linked through intentional relations, as when people think, believe, and feel something about another practice, order, or component thereof. In ways such as this, practices are stitched together into one overall but variegated and modulatingly dense web.

As for the connections that practices maintain with orders, I want to offer one observation beyond my earlier remarks. A practice is not linked just to the specific orders it establishes. It is also linked to those entities and arrangements that lie exterior—but still connected—to the orders it establishes and that are used, acted toward, or mentally related to in its constituent activities. The herb practices, for instance, were linked in these ways to both the orders at the sawmill where the boards used in the cupboards, desks, and shelves at the herb and extract houses were produced, and the arrangements in the woods where the wild herbs and roots were gathered.

Like practices, orders are interconnected. In some cases, the connections are set up (e.g., the walkways between the Center Family's buildings). In other cases, orders are connected outside practices through causal, spatial, and pre-figurational relations among their components. The rats, for example, which were occasional nuisances in the herb and extract buildings, inhabited a sub-terranean ecosystem that was linked to both the orders at these buildings and natural orders embracing other organisms and things. These natural links were not established in Shaker practices (though they did not occur independently of these practices and the orders established therein). Indeed, the fact that the rats inserted themselves into arrangements at different buildings illustrates how relations that are not set up in practices can link orders that are so established (and the practices establishing them). Shaker orders were also perva-sively linked to natural orders through relations of space and of enablement and constraint. Examples are spatial propinquity and distance, as well as that reciprocal enablement and constraint between humans and nature illustrated in the fact that the dam the Shakers constructed to create a basin for washing herbs was built in the stream and not in the adjacent field. Interlinked in this way, Shaker and natural orders were also co-susceptible to events such as frost, lightning, and drought. Finally, practices and orders constrain and enable each another. At any given moment, for instance, only so much coal was on hand at New Lebanon, and at moments of low supply the blacksmith's claim con-strained what was available for herb medicine production, and vice versa. Sim-ilarly, the layouts of the extract and herb buildings enabled and constrained the production activities there, just as the total layout of the Center Family's compound prefigured the frequent expansions of the herb production arrange-ments. I return to these forms of prefiguration in the following chapter.

Through such phenomena as these, practices and orders form an immense, shifting, and transmogrifying mesh in which they overlap, interweave, cohere, conflict, diverge, scatter, and enable as well as constrain each other. Such is the nature of the social site.

3. CYBER STOCK MARKET

The current section introduces the second empirical phenomenon through which my account of the social site is developed, illustrated, and corroborated: day trading on the National Association of Security Dealers Automated Quotation (Nasdaq) system. I should reiterate the division of labor between this example and the Shaker one. The New Lebanon medicinal herb industry has been used up to this point to substantialize a sequence of theoretical propositions about arrangements, practices, and the social site. The point of this cumulative use of a single example was to provide greater substance, clarity, and palpability to the theoretical claims. Day trading is presently described to substantialize the totality of these claims in a summary fashion. The point of re-illustrating these propositions as a package through a second single example is to provide a greater overview sense of how the theoretical edifice works out concretely. Further development of my account of the constitution of the social commences in the following section, using the two examples in tandem. On the assumption that many readers are unfamiliar with the Nasdaq market, I first describe it before turning to day trading.[49]

A stock market is an arena where stocks are bought and sold. Many people picture such an arena as an actual location, a specific arrangement, where traders scurry among stations buying and selling stocks for customers. Such a stock market (e.g., the New York Stock Exchange) is called an "auction market." In such a market, transactions in a given stock occur primarily through a single trader known as the specialist. The specialist's job is to match buy and sell orders that traders bring to him at his station or, as is more likely today, that brokers electronically send to him. However he or she receives them, the specialist effects trades by matching orders.

---

[49] My description of the Nasdaq market has been compiled from the following sources: Carol Vincent, "Do We Need a Stock Exchange?" *Fortune,* 22 November 999, 251ff.; Bob Baird and Craig McBurney, *Electronic Day Trading to Win* (New York: John Wiley & Sons, 1999); Marc Friedfertig and George West, *Electronic Day Traders' Secrets: Learn from the Best of the Best Day Traders* (New York: McGraw-Hill, 1999); David S. Nassar, *How to Get Started in Electronic Day Trading* (New York: McGraw-Hill, 1999); and Jennifer Basye Sander and Peter J. Sander, *Day Trading like a Pro* (New York: Alpha Books, 1999).

The Nasdaq market is an example of a second type of stock market: the negotiated or over-the-counter market. At its most basic, a negotiated market involves purchasing and selling stock (or anything else) through direct negotiation between purchaser and seller or their representatives. Such a market has no fixed location where buying and selling transpire. These practices can take place wherever and however stocks and money can be exchanged. Since the opening of the computerized Nasdaq market in 1971, stock transactions on negotiated markets have increasingly occurred over computer networks. Unlike an auction market, which has a definite trading floor, a negotiated market has as many trading floors as there are places where exchanges occur. The Nasdaq market, in particular, embraces as many "trading floors" as there are computer terminals plugged into its automated quotation system. In negotiated markets, furthermore, there are no specialists. No single individual matches orders to buy and sell a given stock. Trading instead occurs, as noted, through direct exchange between buyers and sellers or their representatives. In the Nasdaq market, these representatives are called "market makers." Market makers usually work for large securities firms and number in the thousands. In the Nasdaq market, consequently, trading practices transpire at sundry locations containing one or more computer terminals; and they are not just mediated by, but are inseparable from cybertechnic arrangements.

In the Nasdaq market, orders to buy or sell a given stock are placed with one of the stock's market makers. Makers execute a buy order either by selling the customer stock from their own inventory or buying shares from another maker and selling them to the customer. Conversely, they execute a sell order by buying stock from the customer and either adding it to inventory or selling it to another maker. Makers trade among themselves by way of entering orders, and "hitting" orders entered, into the electronic quotation system—a sort of electronic bulletin board—to which they all have access.[50] In each stock for which they are registered, moreover, makers are required to maintain a "two-sided market." This means that they must post orders to buy so and so many shares of stock X at such and such a price ("bids") as well as orders to sell so and so many shares of X at such and such a price ("offers"). Market makers' orders for a given stock are displayed in the electronic quotation system in order of attractiveness, with the highest bid displayed at the top of the bid list on the screen and the lowest offer at the top of the offer list. Collectively, the

---

[50] Until 1997, there were actually two such bulletin boards, a complication that can be ignored for present purposes.

best bid and offer are called the "insight quote," or "inside market." This display system is designed to enable would-be buyers and sellers of a given stock quickly to ascertain, and to buy or sell at, the best available price. The available prices, however, are set by the market makers; and makers have interests, for example, making a profit, which differ from those of their clients (the investors), for example, getting the best price. Accordingly, makers set bid and offer prices that often work to their own advantage.

Suppose you, an individual investor, want to purchase stock X at the current inside price.[51] You send the order to your broker. Your broker, in turn, sends the order to either (a) a market maker in the broker's firm or (b) a market maker in a firm with which your broker's firm has an "order-flow" agreement to send orders for stock X. In either case, the market maker, call him A, fills the order either by selling you shares of X from his inventory at his current offer price (which is always higher than the current inside bid price) or, in case he does not own enough shares or his current offer price is lower than the price he paid for the shares, by purchasing stock X from another market maker and then selling it to you—at a price higher than what he just paid: A maker's offer price for a given stock is always higher than his bid price for it. (The difference is called the "spread.") However the trade is effected, you receive your stock, and the maker pockets the spread.

Market makers set bid and ask prices partly in response to the orders they receive. Their prices also reflect judgments about where stock prices are headed. Like individual investors, market makers review charts and analyses of company performance. They also watch the Tape (the continuous, in recent years real-time register of sales volumes and prices) and have knowledge of impending changes in their own firm's ratings of stocks. If, in their estimation, a stock is headed higher, meaning that they anticipate an influx of buy orders, they want to purchase the stock ("accumulate a position") forthwith so as to sell it later at the higher price that the order influx brings about. Conversely, if they believe a stock is headed lower, meaning they anticipate an influx of sell orders, they want to sell inventoried stock presently so that they can buy it back when the price is lower.

Market makers can play shenanigans with prices to maximize gain. If a maker receives a buy order from a broker who has an agreement to send orders the maker's way, nothing stops the maker from filling that order from inventory

---

[51] This is a so-called market order. Limit orders, which are orders to purchase/sell stock at, or not above/below, a given price, are a different sort.

at a price higher than his advertised offer price, thus in effect raising his price. Only a little less avariciously, nothing forces a maker to fill an order immediately. If, for example, you place an order to buy X, and the maker thinks that the price of X is going to rise, he might wait to see whether he can fill your order from inventory at a higher price. If, moreover, no one is trading X, and the maker's current offer price is lower than the price at which he bought the shares he can sell, he can simply let the order go unexecuted.

Market makers can earn considerable profits through skillful price determination, post facto quote changes, adroit timing, and order-flow agreements with brokerages. Until the 1990s, market makers also had exclusive access to two key pieces of information (among others): the Tape and other market makers' current bid and ask prices. These advantages made the Nasdaq market something of an inside business, with which individual investors interacted at their peril.

The first major reform of the Nasdaq system came in 1985 with the introduction of the Small Order Execution System (SOES). SOES gave individual investors greater access to the market by increasing the likelihood that their orders were rapidly executed. It achieved this by giving market makers the technological capability of executing (market) orders of 1,000 shares or less automatically. When an order is entered into SOES, it is routed to the market maker at the inside quote. That maker can then execute the order automatically. Moreover, he is likely to do so, for executing it does not interfere with his attending to larger trades that require negotiation with other makers and promise larger earnings. Because SOES executes orders at the current inside quote, investors are also protected from some of the price shenanigans described above. SOES thus made it considerably more likely that investors could sell or buy when they wanted at better prices.

The "Black Monday" market crash of 19 October 1987 led to further reforms in June 1988. One change made rapid execution of SOES orders mandatory. Another required market makers to honor the price quotes they had in effect when orders were placed. These reforms led to a new form of trading, SOES trading, which is the forerunner of today's day trading. Market makers suddenly began to receive small orders that they had to fill at advertised prices. Unaccustomed to this situation, they began to be taken by SOES traders who, among other things, hit outdated (often only by seconds) inside maker prices in stocks whose order structures were rapidly changing. Speed and volatility suddenly became factors as they never had before. In the ensuing turmoil, the small community of so-called (by market makers) SOES bandits made relatively easy money.

In addition to the above stratagems, market makers could maximize spreads by (1) hiding limit orders that were priced better than the price at which they wanted to trade,[52] and (2) waiting until the market closed to report large transactions so that no one else could act on them. In January 1997, a set of momentous order-handling reforms targeted these and other such tactics. One reform eliminated the option of keeping customer limit orders in-house (see [1] above) by requiring market makers to (a) execute them immediately, (b) post them on Nasdaq, or (c) send them to an electronic communications network (see below) where everyone logged on could see them. By ensuring that the best orders were known to all, this reform guaranteed that buyers and sellers of Nasdaq stocks received the genuinely best prices available, not just whatever prices the market makers gave them. More fundamentally, this reform meant that investors were now able to trade with one another through the intermediary of the market makers, instead of trading with market makers who mediated between buyers and sellers by trading among themselves. Vis-à-vis (2), market makers were now required to report all trades immediately to the Nasdaq Tape. The Tape, furthermore, was no longer the exclusive preserve of the makers: Anyone, in principle, could have access to it. Given the proper software and feeds, individual investors could now pull up on their computer screens most of the information that market makers saw. This second set of changes greatly leveled an advantage that market makers had continued to enjoy over individual investors after previous reforms, namely, access to information.[53]

There was one further reform. Quotes from Instinet—a separate computer system in which makers communicated the prices at which they were willing to buy from and sell to one another independent of client orders—were now included in Nasdaq's comprehensive trading board. This change led to the proliferation of electronic communications networks (ECNs) similar to Instinet but open to investors generally. In such networks, individuals and not just makers can post as well as hit bids and offers. What is more, the best prices

---

[52] Suppose that you place an order to purchase stock X with market maker A. Suppose, further, that A is displaying a sell price of Z even though he has just received an order to sell X at Z−1/8. If he keeps the order secret, he can sell you X at the higher, advertised price of Z and avoid filling your buy order through the sell order of his other customer.

[53] It did not, however, completely level it because, inter alia, orders of greater than 10,000 shares or of greater than $250,000 in value still do not need to be displayed—and these so-called block orders, although rare, can have a dramatic effect on prices.

currently available in each ECN are displayed on Nasdaq's electronic board. Together with the reforms discussed in the previous paragraph, this final change meant that individuals could now trade directly with one another, without having to use market makers even as intermediaries.

The military excepted, it is fair to say that stock markets moved more quickly into cyberspace than did any other relatively large confederation of practice-order bundles. Since 1971, new regulations and technologies (computer networks, informational display software, and the Internet) have provided Nasdaq investors continually greater access to information and efficient order execution, thereby allowing them to participate in the market in hitherto unavailable ways. This development spawned the present-day phenomenon of day trading, an outgrowth of earlier SOES banditry. Day traders seek to outmaneuver market makers by taking advantage of stock price volatility. They make money by moving more quickly than the makers whose activity they shadow. The practice's frenetically cascading activity and occasional heady profits have created something approaching a "wild-west-atmosphere"[54] of cybernetic individualistic capitalism.

Peeled to its core, day trading is the pursuit of extremely short-term profit through rapid selling and buying of stock, often over a period of minutes or even tens of seconds. It involves making split-second judgments about the direction and speed of change in a stock's price and entering or exiting the market faster than anyone else to make money off these changes. Because nascent or intensifying price movement is key to day trading activity, day traders deal primarily with stocks having great volatility, typically technology issues. The practice is called *day* trading because traders typically liquidate their positions (i.e., sell their shares) by the end of the trading day. Overnight, their accounts carry cash alone. As of summer 2000, there were approximately five thousand full-time day traders and an unknown but much larger number of part-time ones.[55]

Several overall ends are pursued in day trading. One is making money, including as much money as possible. This is not, however, the only end.

---

[54] Burton Malkiel, "Day Trading and Its Dangers," *The Wall Street Journal*, 3 August 1999, p. A22.

[55] Day trading must be distinguished from the practice of investing through online brokerage firms such as E*Trade, Ameritrade, and Charles Schwab & Sons. Online investing is the same in principle as other forms of investing through a broker. The differences are that communication between broker and investor occurs over the Internet and that the brokerage offers a panoply of services on its investment website. Day traders enter and exit the market directly, thus not through the intermediary of a broker.

Another is success, or winning. Day trading is a high pressure, often frenzied, and at times pandemonically unfolding pursuit in which repeated gains or losses can be exceedingly satisfying or painful. Instant gratification is the name of the game.[56] Succeeding, winning at the quest, is very much an end that most taking up the practice pursue. This pursuit connects with a third overall end, enhancing the sense of self-worth. In the words of one successful day trader, "There are self-esteem goals. If I make winning trades, I am a good and worthy person. People will love me. If I lose, I am no good. Nobody will love me. That, I think, goes on a lot."[57]

In pursuit of profit, success, and self-esteem, day traders implement a wide variety of acceptable and enjoined projects and tasks. Two overall points should be made about the practice's teleoaffective structure. The first is that, in contrast to the slow evolution of the Shaker herbal medicinal practices, new acceptable or enjoined activities can quickly appear and sometimes displace existing ones. This rapidity reflects the keen competition sustained in trading practices. The second point, again contrasting with the Shaker example, is that traders constantly gravitate away from prescribed projects and tasks to ones that, though acceptable, bring them to or over the brink of financial ruin. Estimates vary, but at best a small proportion of day traders make money. This gravitation reflects, in my opinion, the fear and greed that inhabit the teleoaffective structure of the practice.

The following are a few of the most prevalent projects, tasks, and actions implemented in day trading: keeping track of the Standard and Poors Futures Index (as a barometer of overall market direction); watching activity in specific stocks (anywhere from 10 to 500); knowing these stocks' historical patterns of high and low prices; watching the activity of market makers in those stocks; anticipating changes in market action; selling a stock short (borrowing and selling it immediately in anticipation of a price decline); going long in a stock (buying in anticipation of a price rise); gradually building a position (purchasing small volumes of stock at intervals); taking, or booking, profits (selling shares in a stock that has appreciated in value without holding out for a higher price); keeping a diary (to figure out and learn from one's mistakes; there is

---

[56] This means that day traders tend to be younger investors in their twenties. For discussion, see Diane Rochon, "Different Strokes for Different Folks," *Futures* 28 (1999): 10–11. The pressure and potentially high stakes of day trading have also made it attractive to students. See Lee Clifford, "The Semester of Living Dangerously," *SmartMoney* 9, 5, 2000, 144–52.

[57] Words of Tom Hendrickson, reported in Friedfertig and West, *Electronic Day Traders' Secrets*, 148.

also software for this purpose); discussing strategy with other day traders; sharing information and successes with them; observing their activity; crafting a game plan that specifies overall strategy or initial moves at market opening; attending a trading seminar that is offered online or through the day trading firm at which one has an account; and consulting Internet chat boards for information.

Examples of the doings and sayings that traders carry out in performing these projects, tasks, and actions are looking at charts on a computer screen; watching color patterns on the screen;[58] scanning the screen while keeping an eye on a particular graphic; looking up information in the newspaper; typing on the keyboard; hitting the short sell button; pointing and dragging the mouse; uttering words to compatriots; blurting out words at the screen; watching fellow traders; writing in notebooks; sitting at tables and listening; and getting up from the workstation and walking away.

The practical understandings alive in day trading practices reflect the above compilation of activity. Linking the practice's doings and sayings are understandings of such actions as selling short, watching price swings, accessing price histories, checking the futures index, and keeping a diary. These understandings consist, primarily, of knowing how to carry out such actions. They also consist of both knowing how to recognize these actions (as performed, say, by traders at adjacent workstations) and knowing how to prompt and respond to them. The practice is held together, further, by such motor-cognitive skills as knowing how to type and knowing how to scan the screen, and by such perceptual-cognitive skills as knowing how to read trading software graphics and knowing how to recognize other traders' strategies on the basis of graphical displays.

One decisive, widely enjoined but often unimplemented, day-trading project is maintaining discipline. A task often prescribed in pursuit of this project is setting specific levels of gains and losses at which trading ceases for the day. Performing this task amounts, in effect, to giving oneself rules. Another task that traders—especially those with repeated recent losses—frequently carry out for the sake of discipline is booking profits. Considering this task in greater detail prepares for upcoming discussions.

Suppose that the current inside market maker quote for stock X is 10 (bid)

---

[58] Day trading software uses colors to mark supply (offers) and demand (bids) in chosen stocks. This enables day traders immediately to grasp changes in supply and demand (and, thus, in stock prices), simply by noting color changes on the screen. A good explanation of this is found in Nassar, *How to Get Started in Electronic Day Trading*, chap. 5.

× 10½ (offer). Believing that the price of X is about to rise, a day trader might post a bid of 10⅛. Anyone wanting to sell X now hits the day trader's bid instead of the market maker's. Suppose the anticipated influx of buy orders materializes. The inside price will rise. Suppose the inside quote minutes later is 10⅜ × 10⅞. To book profits, the day trader now posts a sell order of 10¹³⁄₁₆. Anyone wanting to buy the stock now hits the day trader's offer. As this scenario illustrates, a day trader can earn smallish profits by quickly posting orders at prices inside current quotes. Nothing, in principle, prevents a market maker from proceeding in this manner. Market makers, however, respect the long term perspectives of their clients (pension funds, mutual funds, brokerages, and individual investors). Accordingly, they wait for profits larger than those that day traders book.[59]

Suppose the price of X continues to rise. The day trader might repeat the above maneuver. As long as prices are in motion, the day trader can profit by moving inside the market quote. Day traders profit most, consequently, when stock prices are most volatile. As prices rise or fall, they enter/exit and exit/enter the market repeatedly, time and again making off with small profits.[60] The absolute prices do not matter. The trader who anticipates market movement best and is quickest on the keyboard comes off best.

Three sorts of rules enter day trading. Rules that traders impose on themselves compose the first type. These can take the form of targets, maximum gains or losses, elaborate game plans, directives (posted at one's workstation) to control emotions or to maintain control, and adages such as "Get out of a trade when you can, not when you have to."[61] Which such rules individual day traders follow is a personal and often labile matter. The second class of rules

---

[59] Things are more complicated in reality. Market makers do not just execute customers' orders, but also trade their own accounts, frequently carrying on day trading-like activities when doing the latter. For a good description, see Greg Ip, "Nasdaq Market Maker, Seeing All the Orders, Becomes Canny Trader," *The Wall Street Journal*, 55, 45, 3 March 2000, pp. A1, A8.

[60] There is considerable professional controversy about the extent to which day trading is responsible for market movement and for the increased volatility the Nasdaq market has experienced since 1998. Representatives of day traders typically deny responsibility, whereas representatives of market makers typically assert it. For a vivid illustration of this disagreement, see the congressional testimony offered by trade representatives and university professors in U.S. Congress, House Subcommittee on Finance and Hazardous Materials, "The Impact and Effectiveness of the Small Order Execution System," *Hearings Before the Subcommittee on Finance and Hazardous Materials*, 105th Cong., 3 August 1998, serial no. 105-3. Voices in the media seem generally to agree that day trading neither moves markets nor increases volatility.

[61] For discussion, see Friedfertig and West, *Electronic Day Traders' Secrets*, interview with Eric Fromm, 89–106.

embraces regulations that day trading firms impose on traders. These include minimum deposits required to open accounts, commissions that must be paid on trades, and requirements that traders frequently trade. The third type of rule, finally, is regulations mandated by the dealers' trade association, the National Association of Security Dealers (NASD). These are often designed to defend market makers against day traders. As of summer 2001, the U.S. government had not directly regulated day trading.

Finally, the general understandings imbuing the Shaker herbal medicine industry were religious conviction and a sense of community. Although some sense of community pervades day trading practices at day trading firms (see below), religious conviction is largely absent. Taking its place is a sense of the wonder and goodness of the free pursuit of individual gain. Day traders tend to be fierce individualists. They revel in the opportunity that day trading provides to pursue gain in a manner primarily under their control. Indeed, day traders are their own masters to an extent much greater than in other capitalist practices. The practice, therefore, proves intoxicating for many. The result is delicious satisfaction accompanying accumulating gain as well as hollow despondence accompanying mounting loss.[62] (Many have exhausted their retirement savings or college loans.) Perhaps it is not surprising that many day traders are recent immigrants to the United States.[63]

Amid what orders are the ends of day trading pursued, its rules observed or ignored, and its projects, tasks, rapid doings, and intermittent sayings carried out? Day traders work in two principal venues: at home and at branch offices of day trading firms. In either locale, they are likely to sit at a workstation whose most prominent feature is a computer monitor. Day trading can in fact take place wherever there is a computer terminal that is outfitted with the proper software and linked to a day trading firm (by phone, modem, or satellite connection): a hotel room, the back of a limousine, an airplane cabin. (All day traders must open an account at a day trading firm, which, in exchange for commissions, provides training, seminars, loans, perhaps a workstation, and the feeds and software—and thus the technological connection with Nasdaq and the ECNs—necessary for engaging in the practice.) Given that a terminal and an information link are all that is required, it is not surprising that, unlike the Shaker practice of herbal medicine production, which could occur only

---

[62] On this, see Rebecca Buckman and Ruth Simon, "Day Trading Can Breed Perilous Illusions," *The Wall Street Journal*, 2 August 1999, pp. C1, C16.

[63] See John Helyar, "The New American Dream?" *Money*, April 2000, 128.

amid a fairly elaborate order, the practice of day trading is carried out at divers highly scattered locations.

The day trading firm branch office, in addition to the offices, meeting rooms, supply closets, and bathrooms that any elaborate organizational order boasts, includes one or more trading rooms. These trading rooms contain rows of workstations separated by partitions or placed on long desks; each station contains a computer terminal that supports high-performance feeds and is outfitted with trading software; and at each sits a trader, among other things, observing the screen, typing on the keyboard, and shouting out tips. The feeds and software supply real-time information about the Tape, Nasdaq market trends, current bids and offers for chosen stocks, price and volume changes in those stocks over selected time frames, and so on.[64] Television sets on the ceiling, often many in number, are continuously tuned to a business-news-information network like CNBC. The room might also contain a table where seminars or training sessions occur. The branch managers have offices off or adjacent to the trading room. To give some sense of the numbers involved, Tradescape.com, one of the largest day-trading firms, in February 2000 served approximately 2,500 day traders and maintained trading rooms in ten cities. Its New York branch office housed 400 traders squeezed together in trading rooms spread over four floors in two buildings.[65]

The arrangements at a day trading branch office undergird a dimension of day trading broached above: the sociality of day trading. People working at home have practically no social life qua day traders: They might only talk on the phone with a broker or manager of their day trading firm. Considerable sociality, by contrast, transpires in day trading rooms.[66] Day traders are always talking to one another, giving one another tips, alerting one another to opportunities, shouting out successes that others might want to emulate, consoling colleagues who have suffered extensive losses, telling jokes to relieve tension, and so on. Novice traders often spend considerable time observing, learning from, and receiving guidance from veterans, and technical support personnel

---

[64] For a detailed and informative analysis of the trading screen, see Baird and McBurney, *Electronic Day Trading to Win,* chap. 6. For a consumer-oriented comparison of day trading software packages, which concisely describes their information, technique, and connectivity dimensions, see James T. Holter, "Day-Trading Software Shootout," *Futures* 28 (1999): 30–34.

[65] For more details, see Nelson D. Schwartz, "Meet the New Market Makers," *Fortune,* 21 February 2000, 90ff.

[66] In this context, it is worth mentioning that most women day traders work at home and that most traders in trading rooms are men.

are always available. Traders also interact at seminars and workshops and exchange analyses and ideas on firm-sponsored chat rooms. All this reveals that participants in the practice of day trading enjoy identities in addition to day trader, including ally, colleague, teacher, and learner. The practice-order bundle that is day trading is also the site where both the above interactions and the other forms of coexistence characteristic of day trading transpire.

Although substantial camaraderie joins day traders at individual day trading branch offices, considerable competition reigns among traders generally.[67] Because, as mentioned, day traders tend to invest in technology issues, many watch the same stocks. They see the same orders, peruse the same graphics, watch the same Tape, and keep tabs on the same indexes. When anything happens, they know about it simultaneously. Because traders also often use the same strategies, those who follow the same stock tend to react similarly to events and new information pertaining to it. Order deluges are the frequent result. Consider the strategy called "playing relative strength and weakness." According to this strategy, a stock that performs relatively weakly/strongly in an up/down overall market is (1) one to sell/buy or (2) the first to dump/acquire when the overall market turns down/up. Suppose that the market had been moving up, then suddenly turns down, and a big market maker posts a large sell order for a stock that had been a weak performer. Ten (or more) day traders might more or less simultaneously hit their sell buttons, trying to beat the maker's offer and get out of the stock before the price drops (further). Given this competition among day traders, the fortunes of any given trader depends on his or her ability to recognize such trends, to make split-second decisions, and to post orders as quickly as possible. It also pays to have the fastest access to real-time information that is technologically possible.[68]

Intensifying the need for quick information and nimble minds and hands is the fact that day traders trade on the basis of the current day's trends and not on the basis of the economic strengths and weaknesses of the companies traded. Day traders usually abjure reading business publications, expert evaluations, and company financial reports. They believe it is best not to have opinions about where the overall market and particular stocks are headed. Indeed, one guide waxes that "the beauty of . . . day trading is that the day trader really

---

[67] Market makers also compete with and try to outsmart one another, a fact left undiscussed in my above description of market making.

[68] For discussion, see Mike Mosser and Carla Cavaletti, "Technology Opens the Door to Day-Trading," *Futures* 28 (1999): 26–28.

needs no information about a company at all to be a successful trader. One may never even have heard of the company you are buying and selling, much less know what the company does. You certainly aren't concerned about its long-term prospects or what the quarterly earning report will be, except how this information affects the stock on the very day you are looking at it."[69] This behavior contrasts with that of the "position trader," who in pursuit of long-term profit attends to past performance and future prospects—real economic value—and holds onto the stock of strong or promising firms. Day trading, in other words, is further removed from real economic activity than traditional stock trading already is. The end of outmaneuvering the competition through hit-and-run tactics geared to very short-term trends and profits has supplanted consideration of economic fundamentals or even long-term market stability.[70]

Day trading is a practice-order bundle. The practice involved embraces a range of ends, rules, and activities that are densely executed at approximately one hundred elaborate arrangements (day trading firms) and more thinly implemented at a greater number of scattered and variable simpler orders (at homes, airports, etc.). The orders involved are also technologically connected with further electronic arrangements (the computer networks of day trading firms and of the Nasdaq and ECN systems). The two practice-order complexes with which day trading primarily engages are day trading firms and professional market making. As I now elucidate, the practice of day trading overlaps and coheres with those of day trading firms, whereas it competitively intersects with the practice of professional market making.

The overall day trading firm industry is a confederation of nets of practice-order bundles. In this industry confederation, each day trading firm is a net of practice-order bundles, and each of its branch offices is such a bundle. Each office bundle, to begin with, embraces arrangements that encompass rooms, technological arrays, employees, and potted plants and that are linked both to one another and to the Nasdaq and ECN computer systems. Amid these arrangements, different practices are carried out, for example, those of marketing, law, planning, accounting, technical operations, education, and support. These practices are interwoven: Actions performed in different practices form

[69] Baird and McBurney, *Electronic Day Trading to Win*, 15. For discussion, see Matthew Schifrin, "Free Enterprise Comes to Wall Street," *Forbes* 161, 7, 6 April 1998, 114–19.

[70] For worries about what this portends for the power of regulators or anyone else to control future markets, see Gene I. Rochlin, *Trapped in the Net: The Unanticipated Consequences of Computerization* (Princeton: Princeton University Press, 1997), chap. 5.

chains; different practices' actions are performed at the same places in the arrangements of the branch office; the practices share organizational structure (for instance, making the firm profitable); given doings and sayings belong to more than one practice (as when a trader is tendered legal advice); and actions in one practice are the intentional object of participants in others (as when a lawyer ponders a manager's activity). The practice-order bundles that compose the different branch offices of a given firm are themselves similarly interconnected via action chains, technological arrays, common practice organization, and joint actions (such as workshops for technicians from the different offices). Because of these connections, the overall day trading firm is a net of practice-order bundles, and the entire industry is a confederation of such nets.

The practice-order bundle that is day trading both overlaps and interacts with the nets of bundles that are day trading firms. To say that two practice-order complexes overlap is to say that elements of practices and orders are common to both. Day trading and day trading firms primarily overlap in embracing activities that occur amid the same orders. To say that two complexes interact is to say that there exist action chains that contain actions from both. Action chains that link day trading and day trading firms encompass, among many other actions, imposing rules on traders; offering technical support and investment training; lending on margin; offering traders psychological counseling; and encouraging traders to borrow money from one another. Many of these chains are mediated by elaborate technological arrangements, as when trading activity incurs commissions, which are automatically deducted from traders' accounts; when technicians install new informational feeds; or when the activity of a trader at one firm comes to the attention of a manager at another. When practices interact so as to sustain one another, they can be said to cohere. When the interaction is not mutually sustaining, the practices conflict. Day trading practices tend to cohere with those of day trading firms.

The interaction between day trading and professional market making, by contrast, is conflictual. The interweaving of market making with the big securities firms that employ market makers resembles—topologically—the interweaving of day trading with day trading firms. The former weave, however, is tighter. Although market making, like day trading, is carried on in multiple locations, the locations are always office suites of securities firms. Through the firm's technological setup, these suites are plugged into the same Nasdaq and ECN systems to which day traders are connected via the computer systems of day trading firms. Accessing much the same information and enjoying comparably rapid order execution, day traders and the market makers whose activity they shadow perpetually duel. Further underlying this clash are three key differences between market making and day trading: (1) The practice of market making contains a project absent from day trading, namely, executing clients' orders; (2) makers have exclusive knowledge of their customers' orders, including the large institutional orders that have the greatest impact on the market; and (3) because these customers have long horizons, market making is as oriented to long-term profitability as day trading is to short-term gain. The second difference, incidentally, is considerable. As of 2 March 2000, for example, Knight/Trimark, the largest market maker firm, executed 21 percent of the Nasdaq dealers' daily trading volume. Because of this, the firm had far more knowledge then anyone else about the directions certain stocks were likely to go in the immediate future.

By virtue of their large institutional orders, market makers are the primary actors in the market. Day traders are reactors who make money by recognizing market makers' intentions and pre-empting what makers do to carry them out. If a market maker, for example, needs to buy stock X, the day trader tries to do so first. Suppose a maker who has a large buy order for X posts an inside bid for part of the order and keeps reposting it as people hit him. The day trader who recognizes what is occurring bids slightly higher than the maker's current inside bid. Sellers then hit the day trader's, not the maker's, offer. Because the maker must fill the order, he or she still wants to purchase the stock. So the day trader either turns around and sells it to the maker at a higher price, thus booking a smallish profit, or waits a few minutes for the price to rise even higher.

Because day traders try to identify makers' intentions, many market makers use tricks to disguise their plans. The maker in the previous example, seeing that day traders are repeatedly outbidding him and fearful that this front running will drive the price too high, might suddenly post a *sell* order at the current inside sell price. This stratagem is designed to confuse the day traders vexing him. Unsure of the maker's intentions, the day traders will likely cease bidding the price up. The price might even come down. Then, suddenly, the maker will again reverse gears, posting a buy order at the inside bid and buying stock before the day traders can react. Needless to say, there are many strategies of this sort ("headfakes," "jiggles and wiggles," "fading the trend"), various ways of recognizing and counteracting them, and thus numerous trajectories the intraday price of X can take. The fact that offers can be posted on

ECNs also leads to price discrepancies between Nasdaq and the ECNs and among the ECNs, which market makers and day traders alike can exploit.[71] Market makers can even evade day trading completely by "unofficially" trading among themselves at mutually agreeable prices before market opening.[72]

All in all, however, market makers have suffered under the competition with day traders. The 1997 handling rules that allowed day traders to post orders better than the inside quote reduced spreads and thereby cut market maker profits.[73] Makers also have overhead costs that day traders are spared. The result has been a decrease in the number of market makers and a corresponding increase in the percentages of total trading volume that particular market maker firms control.

Competition has been a prominent feature of social life throughout human history. As the above discussion shows, even the most modern cybernetic competition transpires as part of a nexus of practices and arrangements: The metamorphosing competition between day traders and market makers occurs both as and through connections between two practice-order bundles. This competition is a contest (1) that consists in numerous chains of action (and reaction), whose moments are carried on amid firm and home arrangements; (2) whose constituent chains are mediated by a vast electronic system, itself composed of interlocking electronic systems (those of day trading firms, securities firms, brokerages, Nasdaq, ECNs, and regulators);[74] (3) in which the contrahents pursue the ends, projects, and activities of day trading and market maker practices amid the scattered arrangements at firms or at home; and (4) in which the

---

[71] The fragmentation of over-the-counter trading into the Nasdaq and various ECN markets has spawned various calls and proposals to unite these markets into a single electronic one. Arthur Levitt, the SEC chairperson, issued such a call early in fall 1999. See the accounts by Gretchen Morgenson, "S.E.C. Chief Wants One Site for Posting All Stock Prices," and Floyd Norris, "A New Market, Disturbingly Fragmented," *The New York Times*, 24 September 1999, pp. A1, C8 and C1, C8. See also Robert A. Kanter, "Day Traders: How They Help Markets Work Better," *Barron's*, 27 September 1999; "American Financial Regulation—Cui Bono?" *The Economist*, 4 March 2000, 76.

[72] I cannot discuss this here, but market makers also compete among themselves, a fact that helps lower spreads. For discussion, see Sunil Wahal, "Entry, Exit, Market Makers, and the Bid-Ask Spread," *Review of Financial Studies* 10, 3 (1997): 871–901.

[73] Day traders were willing to make odd sixteenths offers, which market makers were not. For discussion of an earlier phase of this suspicious phenomenon, see William Christie and Paul H. Schultz, "Why Nasdaq Market Makers Avoid Odd-Eighth Quotes," *Journal of Finance* 49 (1994): 1813–40.

[74] For some sense of the almost inscrutable complexity of these systems, see the description of the computer system operated by the discount online broker Charles Schwab & Sons, in Matt Richtel, "Keeping E-Commerce on Line: As Internet Traffic Surges, So Do Technical Problems," *The New York Times*, 21 June 1999, pp. C1, C6.

execution of projects and the realization, or lack thereof, of ends—thus, the determination of winners and losers—are tied essentially to the electronic transmission, storage, and posting of information. All in all, the nexus that is composed of the bundles that are day trading and market making is the site where this competitive human coexistence transpires. Together with the nets of practice-order bundles that compose day trading and securities firms, this nexus is likewise the site where all other types of coexistence characteristic of day trading and market making occur.

The Nasdaq day trading–market-making nexus is just part of the overall contemporary negotiated trading scene. Other actors and arenas include institutional investors, Internet brokerages, NASD, the Electronic Traders Association, the Securities and Exchange Commission, markets in other parts of the world, and markets in futures and other derivatives. As I hope the above detailed description substantializes, negotiated trading in toto is one giant nexus of confederations of nets of practice-order bundles. Moreover, just as the competition between day traders and money makers transpires as part of a confederation of net-ed bundles, all the ways in which individuals in and across the above social phenomena coexist transpire through and as part of the practices and orders that compose and link these institutions. This immense nexus is the site where the sociality of negotiated trading occurs. Of course, this overall nexus connects with further large-scale nexuses such as governments, central banks, industries, and international trading, eventually forming the entirety of contemporary "late," "disorganized," or "postfordist" capitalism. Imagining ever-wider practice-order expanses eventually tops off at the total site of the social: the total nexus of practices and orders amid and through which contemporary human coexistence transpires.

In its ontological fundamentals, social life has not changed since the Shakers produced herbal medicine—indeed, it has not changed in this regard since social life commenced. Human coexistence always transpires as part of a nexus of practices and arrangements. What, together, the two examples illustrate is that the shapes taken by practice-order bundles, nets, and confederations are geohistorically variable. The Shaker medicinal herb industry at New Lebanon was a singular and tightly knit bundle, and the overall Shaker medicinal herb industry was a bundle consisting of practices that occurred, with relatively little variation, amid five principal orders. The New Lebanon community, meanwhile, was a net of overlapping, cohering, and occasionally competing practice-order bundles (the different families and industries), while

Shaker life in general was a linked confederation of such nets. Day trading, by contrast, is a bundle whose practice is carried on amid diverse arrangements. This bundle closely coheres with the approximately one hundred practice-order nets that constitute day trading firms. It also conflicts with the practice-order bundle that is market making, which in turn coheres with the nets of bundles that are securities firms. All in all, the site of day trading is a confederation of cohering, conflicting, and overlapping bundles and nets connected via an elaborate artifactual order, something considerably more topologically complex than the Shaker medicinal herb industry.

4. SOCIAL SITE VERSUS NATURE?

Oppositions between society (or culture) and nature are an enduring feature of social thought. The one typically the world of humans and their artifacts, the other typically the realm of organisms and things, the alleged peerlessness of human being and creation has underpinned a family of rigid separations between the two domains. Interminglings and overlaps of the two allegedly distinct worlds have, in turn, served as fodder for theoretical disquisitions challenging their segregation. The question mark in the section heading signals skepticism that "society-nature" marks a substantial division. My arguments in this section do not join, however, a recent spate of analyses that challenge the cogency of the distinction between the social and the natural. Upholding a rough and ready analytic line between social entities and natural ones, they instead contest the proposition that these entities compose distinct substantial worlds.[75] It is important to emphasize the limits of the current discussion. I am trying neither to fathom the full nature of either artifacts or nature nor to explore the varied, controversial, or symbolic relations that theorists and peoples have attributed to society and nature. My remarks are restricted to showing that a distinction between social and natural entities does not entail a substantial division in domains.

In Chapter 2, I wrote that social orders are composed of four types of entities: people, artifacts, organisms, and things. This typology is not meant to be an unassailable, immutable, or mutually exclusive classification of either the entities that are or those that enter social life. It claims only to be a useful,

---

[75] For a contestation of this proposition based on commonalities between humans and animals, see Stephen Horigan, *Nature and Culture in Western Discourses* (London: Routledge, 1988).

experientially based sorting of the entities significant to humans through which their lives hang together. Nor does it pretend to be either the only sensible or the "natural" taxonomy of significant coexistence-mediating beings. It is simply an effective and adequately comprehensive parsing of the entities amid and through which people inter-relatedly live. I do not presume, furthermore, that such a taxonomy is written in stone.

I defined "people," for instance, as members of the biological species *Homo sapiens* to whom actions, mental conditions, self-consciousness, gender, and identity (self-understanding) are ascribed. One day we humans might decide to apply the concept of person (or something like it) to entities other than members of this species and to honor these beings with some or all of the basic rights and duties accorded human persons. Thinking machines, extraterrestrials, and certain higher primates, above all bonobos, are the leading candidates today. We have not, however, reached that moment yet. It remains the case that the above phenomena, as a package, are ascribable to members of our own species alone. At present, consequently, there is no reason to alter the category. In any event, it does not affect the substance of my arguments if what falls under the category "person" changes in the future or, more generally, if the categories of entity that constitute social life need someday to be adjusted in the face of developments to come.

The division of life into persons and living organisms, moreover, is neither exclusive nor fixed. Persons, of course, are living organisms. What warrants the dual categories is the experienced, unavoidably reckoned-with rich and multidimensional distinctiveness of humans as opposed to other living creatures. Animals and plants might—and do—boast various combinations of the ways of being that humans possess, perhaps in diluted form. Although as far as we know today none of them fully possesses all human modalities, just how and how much such creatures as bonobos and dolphins are like us is an empirical question; the results of animal research, in combination with our attempts to teach and communicate with these creatures, could eventuate in altered, perhaps finer-grained typologies. Again, however, this day has not yet arrived. It is also not amiss to acknowledge parenthetically the widely recognized obscurity of the boundaries of life.

The definition of artifacts and the ways that artifacts contrast with both things and natural entities similarly stir up a hornet's nest. I wrote that artifacts are the products of human activity. This means that they exist because of human doing. Indeed, the word "artifact" suggests this. It comes from the

Latin *art,* "art," and *factus,* "to make." Etymologically, therefore, artifacts are entities made by art. Things, furthermore, were defined as nonliving entities whose being, which I now specify as form and inner structure, does not result from human action. This definition, too, highlights human activity.

Given this emphasis on activity, I should acknowledge the long tradition in Western philosophy that analyzes artifacts not through activity, but through the absence of something thought to characterize natural entities: internal natures containing the principles of activity that govern changes in, or the developments of, entities.[76] As this formulation indicates, the issue for this tradition in analyzing artifacts is the nature of human products, as opposed to the nature of the entities that humans do not make. That artifacts are the products of human activity seems, for the most part, to be taken as obvious. Aristotle wrote, for example, that "a bedstead or a garment or the like, in the capacity which is signified by its name and *in so far as it is craft-work,* has within itself no such inherent trend towards change, though owing to the fact of its being composed of earth or stone or some mixture of substances, . . . it incidentally has."[77] This philosophical tradition thus supposes, in the main, that a necessary condition for something being an artifact is that human activity produces it. For present purposes, this necessary condition can also be taken as sufficient: An artifact is anything that human activity produces. (An artifact can even be defined as anything that would not exist but for human activity.)

Treating this necessary condition as also a sufficient one entails that no products of human activity qualify as nonartifactual.[78] In this, my definition of artifacts contrasts with the traditional Aristotelian delineation of them as entities possessing external sources of development and change. According to the traditional demarcation, such entities as cooked wheat, bread, chemically engineered polymers, prosthetically enhanced bodies, and selectively bred

---

[76] For discussion and critique, see Michael Losonsky, "The Nature of Artifacts," *Philosophy* 65 (1990): 81–88.

[77] Aristotle, *Physics,* books 1–4, rev. ed., trans. P. H. Wicksteed and F. M. Cornford (Cambridge, Mass.: Harvard University Press, 1957), 192b20–22 (emphasis added). Quoted in a different translation in Losonsky, "The Nature of Artifacts," 81.

[78] Tim Ingold has argued that artifacts are those products of human activity that result from the self-conscious attempt to realize a pre-existent idea, design, or plan. I do not examine his argument here because doing so would require considering his account of activity, which postulates a hard dichotomy between nonteleological (but intentional) actions grounded in practical know-how and teleological actions grounded in explicit, or conscious, ends, ideas, and plans. See Tim Ingold, *Evolution and Social Life* (Cambridge: Cambridge University Press, 1986), chap. 7.

organisms all count as "natural" entities.[79] The Aristotelian analysis, however, is antiquated. The capacity of humans to intervene in nature today far outstrips anything Aristotle could imagine, and this phenomenon only makes more palpable how basic human activity is, and how important it is to mark its significance in basic categories.

My definition also recognizes as artifacts not just overtly artificial constructions such as computers, machines, texts, works of art, and buildings, but in addition modifications of "nature" such as altered landscapes, cooked meat, packaged herbs, and re-engineered human bodies. I acknowledge that some ecologists and environmental philosophers dispute definitions of artifacts that entail that alterations and modifications of nature are artifactual[80] (or that do not recognize the products of animal activity as artifacts, e.g., a beaver dam). My response to critics of the first sort is to distinguish subcategories of artifact (see below). My response to disputants of the second sort is that their ecological interests diverge from my interest in understanding social life. Those who still strenuously object to the equation of artifacts with the products of human activity can simply drop the word "artifacts" and rename the category involved "products of human activity."

Latour, among others, has recently attacked categorical differentiations among entities that refer primarily to human activity. In particular, he criticizes the distinction between artifacts and natural entities (natural entities are nonartifactual organisms and things, in my terminology). He does so by pointing to a range of present-day entities that are not purely the one or the other, for example, the ozone hole, global warming, hybrid corn, frozen embryos, expert systems, digital machines, sensor-equipped robots, whales outfitted with sonar devices, and, it might be added, the Oncomouse™ about which Donna Haraway has written.[81] He calls such entities "hybrids." Hybrids are not, however, the exotic products of modern technology alone. Latour's real point is that not only have hybrids existed for centuries, but everything humans come across on earth is one (already). I understand the point as follows: With the first appearance of humans, the effects of human action began to radiate

---

[79] See Carl Mitcham, *Thinking Through Technology: The Path Between Engineering and Philosophy* (Chicago: University of Chicago Press, 1994), 172–74.

[80] See Mitcham, *Thinking Through Technology,* 328–29 nn. 23 and 24, for references pro and con this and related issues.

[81] Bruno Latour, *We Have Never Been Modern,* ed. Catherine Porter (Cambridge, Mass.: Harvard University Press, 1993), 49. For Oncomouse™, see Donna Haraway, "When Man™ Is on the Menu," in *Zone 6: Incorporations,* ed. Jonathan Crary and Sanford Kwinter (New York: Urzone, 1992), 39–43.

around the earth. Either in short order—if one believes that everything in the earth's overall ecosystem is intimately interconnected—or over time, but certainly by the beginning of written history, human activity had altered, however subtly, everything on earth, including humans themselves. This point is only more convincing if formulated more conservatively as the claim that human activity has, at least, slightly altered all the overt natural beings with which humans cope, for instance, climate, fauna, and flora.[82] One possible reaction to this evident truth is the conclusion that everything on earth related to human life (including humans) is an artifact. Latour, likewise, collapses everything into a single category. I sense that he avoids the term "artifact," however, because it highlights human activity. It thereby lends itself to analyzing the aforementioned entities as mixtures of something social/subject and something nature/object and, therewith, to affirming the modernist partitioning of beings into distinct human and natural worlds, which Latour wants to undermine. The expression "hybrids" is designed to avoid these implications.[83]

I want to resist this breakdown of categories. Arguing that the earth is populated by entities that are neither pure subjects nor pure objects and only misleadingly analyzed as a bit of each is an effective strategy if one's goal is to combat a prior division of entities into subjects and objects, humans and nature. My project, however, is to understand social life; to this end, it is reasonable to construct a straightforward experiential typology that classifies entities on the bases of their standings vis-à-vis human activity and of their significance for human coexistence. In this spirit, then, I define "natural beings" as those organisms and things whose form, inner structure, and existence have been relatively little, if at all, affected by human beings. El Niño, earthquakes, lions on the Serengeti, polar bears in Arctic climes, tubular life in continental rift zones, canopy birds in tropical rain forests, geological strata immediately below the surface of the earth, the herbs and roots that Shakers collected in the wild, and the organic fertilizer they harvested in the cow pens—all these

[82] The same sort of argument can be found in François Dagognet, *La Maîtrise du vivant* Paris: Hachette, 1988), chaps. 1–2. It also goes back at least to Marx and Engels; cf. Karl Marx and Frederick Engels, *The German Ideology* (New York: International Publishers, 1970), 63. For an argument to the effect that this comprehensive transformation has taken place only with the advent of global pollution, see Bill McKibben, *The End of Nature* (New York: Random House, 1989).
[83] See the form of argument in Latour, *We Have Never Been Modern*, 78. See also Michel Callon and Bruno Latour, "Don't Thrown the Baby Out with the Bath School! A Reply to Collins and Yearly," in *Science as Practice and Culture*, ed. Andrew Pickering (Chicago: University of Chicago Press, 1992), 343–68, here 350. Whether "hybrid" is well chosen in this regard is open to question.

entities are beings of nature, despite the fact that human activity has not left them undisturbed. Human bodies, too, are fundamentally natural phenomena, the products of gene-cellular environment processes, even though their surfaces have always been the location of human invention and their organs and construction are becoming increasingly artifactual today (via either direct intervention or the impact of the human-made environment on bodily systems). Incidentally, this delineation of the natural entails that the distinction between society and nature cannot be lined up with the one between humans and nonhumans. Humans, too, are part of nature. Not all organisms, furthermore, are natural phenomena. The herbs growing in a Shaker physics garden or in a pot in the corner of a day trading room are examples because their existence in these places results from human activity.

Under the category of artifacts, moreover, three overlapping types can be distinguished on the phenomenalistic grounds of source, relatedness to human activity, and significance for social existence. The first class embraces "fabrications." These are products of human activity for which things of nature serve as the material. Their production involves a reworking of natural entities and a disappearance of these entities in their original form. Most use objects (equipment), built architectural structures, and works of art fall into this class. Shaker and day trading examples include hoists, pens, paper, workstations, machines, the extract house, the day trading office, and the extracts and ointments that resulted from herb production activity. The second class of artifacts, "mongrels," refers to former natural phenomena, either to which humans have added something, in which they have induced some change, or which would not have existed if it were not for human activity. In each case, human activity either induces some basic alteration in or is responsible for the fundamental form, composition, or existence of the entity. Examples from Latour's list include the ozone hole, global warming, hybrid corn, and whales outfitted with sonar devices (Oncomouse™ and cyborgs, too); from the Shaker and day trading examples, the horse power system, the herbs in the garden, the pressed herb blocks, the cut stones in the cellar floor, and the potted plant in the corner. Notice that the rats qua components of Shaker orders hover on the line between natural beings and mongrels because their presence in these orders results in part from human activity. Finally, "intelligent machines" are those products of human artifice that (1) perform or take over cognitive operations previously associated with or performed by humans and/or (2) are able in some way to produce themselves (for instance, through engineering or learning).

Sensor-equipped robots and digital machines are the examples from Latour's list. Computers are the recurring such entity in the current book's examples.[84]

Thus, I shall continue to write of people, artifacts, organisms, and things and to use the expression "nature" to refer to most entities of the two latter classes. What is more significant than the precise contours of this typology, however, is the fact that it does not subtend a separation of social site and nature as two substantial domains or worlds. This is important because many attempts to gainsay "the" distinction between the social and the natural (e.g., the biological or biophysical) presume that the distinction requires that the social and the natural be so conceived.

A recent example is Tim Ingold's excellent contribution to the volume edited by Greenwood. The just-mentioned presumption is contained in his formulation of the issue the essay addresses: whether there is a "separate domain of society, beyond the limits of nature, within which properly human life is lived."[85] Ingold argues that there is no such domain. The world in which human beings "properly" live is populated by a diversity of nonhuman entities, which cannot—and the relations of humans to which cannot—be clearly divided into social and natural. What is more, these entities as much form the context for people and interpersonal relations as people and interpersonal relations form a context for them. Ingold claims that these two observations underwrite three theses: that a realm of social entities and relations cannot be rigorously demarcated from a realm of natural ones, that the world in which humans live is not a separate domain aside from nature, and that the relevant focus of analysis is the one complete world of organic life formed by these different human and nonhuman entities, together with all the relations among them. In sum, human life does not possess its own world, but instead is part of the single, more encompassing realm of evolutionary life.[86]

I agree with all these points in some form or other except the claim about the relevant focus of analysis. In formulating the idea of a site where social life

---

[84] This threefold typology should be contrasted with alternatives constructed on different grounds. Two examples are Mumford's functional-energetic typology of utensils, apparatuses, utilities, tools, and machines (expanded by Mitcham to include clothes, structures, automata, toys, objects of art/religion, and tools of doing) and Lafitte's pure energetic typology of passive, active, and reflexive (e.g., dwellings, highways, clothing; tools; car engines, computers). See Lewis Mumford, *Technics and Civilization* (New York: Harcourt Brace, 1934), 9–12; Mitcham, *Thinking Through Technology,* 182–83; Jacques Lafitte, *Réflexions sur la science des machines* (Paris: Bloud et Gay, 1932).

[85] Tim Ingold, "Life Beyond the Edge of Nature? or the Mirage of Society," in Greenwood, *The Mark of the Social,* 231–52, here 232, cf 250.

[86] See Ingold, "Life Beyond the Edge of Nature?, 244–45.

transpires, no claim is thereby made that there is something unique or distinctive about whatever qualifies as this site (other than that it and not something else is this site). This formulation simply defines an approach to a topic, to a subject matter of study, namely, social life: its forms, its location, its determinants. Once this approach is defined, questions can arise about the relations of the social site to nature. By itself, however, the idea of a social site does not determine that the relations involved are relations between two distinct realms. It leaves open such issues as what, specifically, qualifies as the social site, what nature is, whether and in what senses (if any) the social site and nature are realms at all, and the overall character of the relatedness between them. The idea of a social site is a *starting point* from which these issues can be addressed. Note that the interest in social affairs that is embodied in this idea robs Ingold's observation about the mutual contextualization of humans and nonhumans of significance (except to the extent that the character of social life depends on how humans form a context for nonhumans). It also contravenes Ingold's claim about the relevant object of analysis. What qualifies as a relevant object of study is relative to one's interests and preoccupations.

In fact, nature and the social site are not substantially distinct realms, domains, or worlds. As discussed, the arrangements that help constitute the site of the social are composed of people, artifacts, organisms, and things. This list can now be recast as people, artifacts, and nature, because organisms and things fall into one or the other of the latter two categories. Nature, consequently, is part of the arrangements that constitute the site of the social: Organisms and things of nature number among the phenomena through, around, and by reference to which human coexistence transpires. Examples are herbs and roots "in the wild," devastating frosts, solar storms that knock out communication systems, locations of streams, plots of land where the extract house and day trading offices are built, and such precursors of fabrications and mongrels as stones unearthed in quarries and oil pumped from subterranean reservoirs. Social life is interfused with nature, around which it is organized and through which it is altered, destroyed, and reestablished. Social life also transpires around, through, and by reference to a range of mongrels that, although strictly artifactual, are close enough to being natural, and for centuries have been taken to be such, as to warrant a label that acknowledges these peculiarities. Examples of the phenomena I have in mind are the forests where the Shakers searched for wild herbs and roots, which reflected human practices as much as natural processes; the terrain preserved as U.S. Federal Wilderness

Areas; and the behavior of such animals as elephants and rats, which live in proximity to humans. Such phenomena can be called "second nature": "nature" because they look and feel and are also often thought to be untouched by humans, and "second" because appearances are misleading and human activity has in fact significantly altered them.[87]

Nature is part of the social site. Consequently, social site-nature is not a substantial, but only an analytic distinction. The distinction between, on the one hand, the sinews and site of human coexistence and, on the other, the organisms and things of nature divides entities into two overlapping, interacting, and constantly metamorphosing sets whose members form changing constellations over time. In short, the natural entities that enter social life are *at one and the same time* social and natural phenomena. (In this sense, but only in this sense, does Ingold's point about division into social and natural hold.)[88]

An article by Paul Rabinow provides a fine, though inadvertent illustration of this twofoldness. According to Rabinow, Western societies today are experiencing a dissolution of the category of the social and the commencement of a new phase of "autoproduction" called "biosociality." By "the social" (or "society"), Rabinow says he means "the whole way of life of a people (hence open to empirical analysis and planned change)."[89] In fact, it is unclear whether the dissolution that is illustrated in his discussion of Robert Castel's *La Gestion des risques* is a dissolution of "peoples" and "whole ways of life" (and the identities and practices attached to these) or a wilting of the social conceived of in some narrower sense similar to Jacques Donzelot's domain of social welfare

87 This formulation emphasizes parallels between Lukacs's original use of the term "second nature" and my appropriation of it. See Georgi Lukács, *The Theory of the Novel,* trans. Anna Bostock (Cambridge, Mass.: MIT Press, 1978).

88 Steven Vogel has argued, similarly, that the entities that populate the "world we inhabit" (the human *Umwelt*) do not categorically divide into social or natural. His defense of the "social construction" of nature, however, reveals significant divergences from my account. For instance, although we agree that nature mediates social practices, he equates nature with physical entities, an equation I reject. Listing artifacts as examples of physical entities, he also points out that such entities are the product of human labor. This observation slights the many natural entities (in my sense) that mediate human coexistence and are found in the "world we inhabit." Even though, finally, Vogel half-heartedly concedes the existence of both nature and second nature (in my senses), instead of acknowledging the contribution they make to social existence he relativizes them to social context by declaring that "the 'natural environment' is never *encountered* independently of social context" (emphasis added). See Steven Vogel, *Against Nature: The Concept of Nature in Critical Theory* (Albany: State University of New York Press, 1996), chap. 2, section 1, quotation 38.

89 Paul Rabinow, "Artificiality and Enlightenment: From Sociobiology to Biosociality," in *Zone 6: Incorporations,* 234–52, here 242.

concern and policy.[90] In any event, what is important to the present discussion is Rabinow's description of biosociality as "the formation of new group and individual identities and practices arising out of … new truths,"[91] which advances in biomedical-genetic diagnostic and investigative techniques have made available. An example of the group and individual identities he has in mind are, respectively, possessing a particular gene and being the son of an alcoholic sickle-cell father. According to Rabinow, then, modern Western societies are undergoing a change in the character of both individual and group identities and practices: As new ones defined by biological and medical facts emerge, those tied to peoples, social environments, and collective lives retreat.

In my terms, the emergence of these new identities and practices does not amount to a dissolution of something called "the social"[92] in favor of an ascendant something called "biosociality." Rather, it represents a transformation in social life and its site, in particular, (1) the advent of new forms of coexistence that transpire through and around biological entities and are partially articulated via new identities, and (2) the coordinate emergence of new orders and practices that encompass and focus on these entities and identities. This two-fold development results, moreover, from the new practices and orders of biomedical genetics, in conjunction with the knowledge therein generated. With the advent of these new practices, orders, identities, and knowledges, natural

---

[90] In his well-known book, *The Policing of Families,* Donzelot shows that a particular notion and realm of the social arose during the nineteenth century in connection with state policies and interests (Jacques Donzelot, *The Policing of Families,* trans. Robert Hurley [London: Hutchinson, 1979]). The notion involved is that employed in the expression "social welfare" and the realm coordinate with this notion embraces, roughly, the objects of social welfare policy, for instance, poverty, immigrants, housing, and hygiene. The social whose origin and consolidation Donzelot documents counts as a *specific* region of people's "whole ways of life." For more recent discussion of this realm, see the essays in D. Rueschemeyer and T. Skocpol, eds., *States, Social Knowledge, and the Origins of Modern Social Policies* (Princeton: Princeton University Press, 1996).

[91] Paul Rabinow, "Artificiality and Enlightenment: From Sociobiology to Biosociality," in *Zone 6: Incorporations,* 234–52, here 242.

[92] Jean Baudrillard offers a different version of this dissolution. Equating the social with the realm of civil society that, on his analysis, is disappearing in contemporary Western societies, Baudrillard pithily announces the "end of the social." Raymond Williams argued that the gathering strength of society as a general and abstract notion did roughly coincide with the eighteenth-century discovery in theory of what later came to be called "civil society." Even, however, if Baudrillard is right about the fate of civil society, and this is hardly clear, its demise cannot amount to the end of the social as this is understood in social ontology (unless one subscribes to the idea that what something is shows forth most clearly at its historical emergence). See Jean Baudrillard, *In the Shadow of the Silent Majorities, or the End of the Social and Other Essays,* trans. Paul Foss, Paul Patton, and John Johnston (New York: Semiotext(e), 1983); idem, *For a Critique of the Political Economy of the Sign,* trans. Charles Levin (Saint Louis: Telos Press, 1981).

entities, in particular, certain biological entities of which people are composed, come to play an enhanced role in the forms of sociality found in Western countries. That is to say, natural beings assume new significance in the groups people form, the themes on which they collectively focus, the orders and causal chains through which their lives hang together, and their understandings of themselves and one another. (Certain biological beings also thereby become more susceptible to transformation into mongrels and fabrications.) The term "biosociality" captures well the spread of forms of coexistence in which bio-genetic phenomena play crucial roles. As this example shows, moreover, which and how natural phenomena enter social life changes—and ebbs and flows—over geohistorical space-time.

The intersection-overlap of the social and the natural reveals the inade-quacy of conceptualizing the social as a unique, distinct level of reality. An example of such a conception is the social as a distinct level of organization beyond biological and physical organization (e.g., Scott Gordon in his con-tribution to the volume edited by Greenwood). The organizations of social formations are clearly distinct in type from the organizations of organisms and mechanisms. This is, however, an easy difference. It leaves open, among other things, how distinct human coexistence is from the social life of animals or extraterrestrials. As indicated, how far animal life shares dimensions of human life is a multifaceted empirical matter of animal behavior, capacities, anatomy, neurophysiology, and the similarities of these to our own. Similarly, the extent to which animals share a social existence that overlaps with our own depends on the empirical facts just cited together with further facts about the organi-zation of their activities, the nature of their interactions, their forms of com-munication, and the arrangements of entities they set up and are part of. It is an open question, consequently, whether the social site is sui generis over against the organization of the collective lives of other species. Incidentally, this version of the social as a distinct level of reality presumes—as do almost all such conceptions, including Durkheim's conception of the social as a dis-tinctive set of facts beyond psychological facts—that the relation of society to other pertinent domains is vertical, the social always emerging above the physical, biological, or psychological. In fact, society and nature are linked horizontally, that is to say, they overlap and interact (see next chapter).

I close this chapter by considering a position that, instead of portraying nature and society either as disparate worlds or as interactively locked, con-siders both to be products of a third thing. According to the actor-network theory of Latour and Callon, nature and society are effects of networks. Indeed, networks produce different natures and societies at different times and places. These societies and natures exert, moreover, no return effect on the networks causing them. They are responsible for neither the formation nor the dissolution of networks.

Actor-network's avowedly relativist or better "relational " approach to nature presumes (1) that networks never, including during the modern technoscientific era, enjoy access to a pre-existent nature, and (2) that there is no nature "out there" to which networks lack access. Nature is, instead, something produced. Latour describes its production in modern societies as follows.[93] Laboratory scientists first isolate entities that are initially defined purely by what they do, for instance, what they do to other things (e.g., chemical substances) in specific situations (e.g., being mixed together). Over time, routine citation and use transform these so-called actants into things, where a thing is not purely something that does this or that, but rather a subsistent entity one of whose properties is the performance of those activities. If, finally, things successfully resist scientists' attempts to discredit them, they become reality, that is to say, nature. In the modern world, in other words, nature is the outcome of scientific research and controversy. A similar, less instrumented story can supposedly be told about premodern networks.

The same argument applies to society. Just as nature is the outcome of scientific investigation and disputation, so, too, is society the outcome of social scientific research and controversy.[94] A definite or stable society exists, as a result, only if social scientists agree, or continue to agree, on a particular specification of its general and particular components. The persistence of unresolved disputes about and contending perspectives on the social, however, entails that it is constantly changing and partially indeterminate. This argument, moreover, can be broadened. What society is lies in the adjudicative province not of social science alone, but of actors more generally. What society is is what actors generally accept it as being after struggles over different definitions of the social and its components are resolved.[95]

According to actor-network theory, society is a product of networks in a

---

[93] Bruno Latour, *Science in Action: How to Follow Scientists and Engineers in Society* (Cambridge, Mass.: Harvard University Press, 1987), chap. 2, pt. 2, pt. B.

[94] Latour, *Science in Action*, 254–57.

[95] Bruno Latour, "The Powers of Association," in *Power, Action, and Belief: A New Sociology of Knowledge?* ed. John Law (London: Routledge, 1986), 264–80, here 270–73.

second way. This approach, contrary to its professed agnosticism, regularly works with an individualist conception of the social as the realm of relations among individuals: Society is ordered individuals. Because, furthermore, one dimension of a network is the alignment and coordination of its component humans, any network embraces a state of society. Society, so understood, is an effect of networks because the alignment of individuals is a function of the establishment of networks; and a "stable" society exists only when networks persist. I might add that not just nature and society individually, but the very distinction between them is an effect of scientific work, in this case, of a set-tled partitioning of academic disciplines into the natural and social sciences.

The intended targets of these arguments are threefold: scientific realists who seek to explain experimental results, the closure of scientific arguments, and the succession of theories by reference to a fixed nature "out there"; social constructivists who propose to explain these same matters by reference to fixed social phenomena "out there"; and social scientists who intend to explain what goes on among people by reference to phenomena that are something other than relations among individuals or relations between individuals and artifacts. These arguments also strike, however, against any position such as my own that makes pronouncements about the nature of physical phenomena or social affairs before the conclusion of ontological and explanatory disputes in the physical or social sciences. In the words of Callon and Law, "It is widely accepted in the microsociology of science that the investigator should not make use of assumptions about the character of the natural world if he/she wishes to explain the outcome of controversies. The principle of generalized agnosticism has the effect of extending this injunction to the social dimensions of disputes and asks the investigator not to make assumptions about the char-acter of society or economy."[96] By contrast, what, according to actor-network theory, need not await the conclusion of these scientific controversies are anal-yses of the components and character of networks, as well as investigations of the intranetwork transactions responsible for their maintenance, extension, and dissolution. For instance, in *Science in Action,* Latour steadfastly presumes that the technoscientific networks he examines are composed of entities of four types: humans, instruments, inscriptions, and visual displays. Similarly, Callon

[96] Michel Callon and John Law, "On the Construction of Sociotechnical Networks: Content and Con-text Revisited," in *Knowledge and Society: Studies in the Sociology of Science Past and Present,* eds. Lowell Hargens, Robert Alun Jones, and Andrew Pickering (Greenwich, Conn.: JAI Press, 1989), 57–83, here 77.

regularly asserts that technoeconomic networks are composed of such and such elements, for instance, literary inscriptions, technical artifacts, human beings, and money.[97] As far as I know, neither author ever clarifies why he advocates a particular typology before the resolution of scientific controversy. My suspicions are that these catalogues escape scientific disputation because their entries are overt objects of experience, and that actor-network theory thus commences from a position of naive realism about at least some clear-cut experiential objects.[98] Hence, the apparent reason why the reality, substantiality, and independence of the entities to which actor-network theory ascribes the above reality "effects" is simply presumed, whereas nature and society are said to be effected, is that these entities, unlike the phenomena of nature and society, are objects of experience.

The present section argued that it is sensible to identify, among the objects of experience, a subclass of them that are natural phenomena. If some natural entities are objects of experience, then at least part of nature (i.e., its experiential component) is just as "not produced" as network components are. Actor-network theory's argument for the production of nature is thus incomplete: It can apply only to *nonovert* natural entities. A counter-reply to the effect that my demarcation of this subclass is a product of the networks to which I belong (so that, once again, nature is the product of networks) applies equally well to actor-network's conceptions of network components. Hence, the issue whether and how nature is produced cannot be settled by such metalevel considerations. Individual proposals must be debated on their own merits.

Furthermore, actor-network's stance vis-à-vis social phenomena is self-contradictory. The theory itself maintains an asymmetric relation to the natural and social sciences. Grant for the moment that society and nature await the consensual judgment of social and natural science. Although no one would say that actor-network theory is a piece of natural science, it does count, to a large extent, as social science. Despite its claim that networks traverse and thereby make ontological and disciplinary boundaries problematic, its detailed accounts of the entanglements of science, technology, money, human activities, and social relations definitely look like social inquiry. This holds all the

[97] For instance, Michel Callon, "Techno-Economic Networks and Irreversibility," in *A Sociology of Monsters: Essays on Power, Technology, and Domination,* ed. John Law (London: Routledge, 1991), 131–61, here 135.

[98] This suspicion seems to be confirmed in Callon and Latour, "Don't Throw Out the Baby with the Bath School! A Reply to Collins and Yearly," 351.

more of those texts that explore the weave of technology and society.[99] In addition, the theory does not counsel jettisoning the term "sociology," but instead redefining it as the study of networks.[100] It follows that the actor-network notions of a network and of society as ordered individuals are party to the ontological controversies that rage among students of social life. If, therefore, social science produces society, actor-network theory should heed the admonitions it directs at social scientists who explain relations among people through broader social phenomena, namely, first, do not presume you know what social reality is; second, defend your ideas on this topic; and third, do not explain anything by reference to your preferred social phenomena until your arguments have ended all disputes. If actor-network theory respects this injunction, however, it must suspend the claim that networks produce society—for it must first convince everyone to accept the reality of networks, the unreality of social phenomena, and the proposition that society is that dimension of networks consisting of arrangements of individuals.

To do this, however, actor-network theory must enter the general argumentative terrain trod in the current chapter and engage the traditional and ongoing debates addressed there. If it takes this path, however, it can no longer critique the present analysis—whatever its faults—on the grounds that it has drawn its conclusions prematurely. Perhaps, therefore, actor-network theory is better advised simply to withdraw the admonition and to enter the fray.

---

[99] To cite just two examples, Michel Callon, "Society in the Making: The Study of Technology as a Tool for Sociological Analysis," in *The Social Construction of Technological Systems: New Directions in the Sociology and History of Technology,* ed. Wiebe E. Bijker, Thomas Hughes, and Trevor Pinch (Cambridge, Mass.: MIT Press, 1987), 83–103; Bruno Latour, "Where Are the Missing Masses? The Sociology of a Few Mundane Artifacts," in *Shaping Technology/Building Society: Studies in Sociotechnical Change,* ed. Wiebe E. Bijker and John Law (Cambridge, Mass.: MIT Press, 1992), 225–58.

[100] See, for example, Latour, "The Powers of Association" (an article about society), 277; Callon, "Society in the Making: The Study of Technology as a Tool for Sociological Analysis," 99.

BECOMING AND CHANGE

Movement and change have filled the previous chapters, more or less explicitly whenever causality was at issue and relatively unmarked in all the substantive discussions of orders, practices, and the social site. Their omnipresence reflects the fact that agency is the central motor of a constant becoming that sweeps the social site. Agency, that is to say, is that through which the mesh of practices and orders is continuously taking place and frequently mutating. Accordingly, an account of the social site is inherently one of ceaseless movement and incessant rearrangement and reorganization, even if it is not explicitly developed as such. The agency involved, moreover, is that of nonhumans in addition to humans. The doings of humans and nonhumans combine to make the social site the scene of continuously metamorphosing orders and perpetually performed, and often evolving, activities. The current chapter charts dimensions of this tumult of becoming. Sections 1 and 2 examine, respectively, agency and the prefiguration of agency, how the social site channels forthcoming actions much as a gravitational field bends light. Section 3 charts the endless becoming that pervades this site. Section 4 then substantializes the horizontal relations between social site and nature through a conception of social history as a natural history.

1. AGENCY (AGENTIAL HUMANISM II)

"Agency" is a word in which social and humanistic theorists have much invested. Its significance reflects the equation of agency with free will, which marks much of Western intellectual history, as well as the consignment of both phenomena to humans, which was cemented in Descartes's mechanistic understanding of animals. It is against this backdrop, for instance, that discussions of agency in twentieth-century social thought focused, above all, on the nature, conditions, and scope of intentional individual or group action; that analyses of agency in post–World War II analytic philosophy have almost exclusively examined the character and possibility of intentional human activity; and that contemporary feminists argue that, in modern Western discourses, agency has been attributed primarily to men. Of late, however, this confinement of agency to humans has begun to unravel, in part through updated understandings of animals, which undermine metaphysical divides between humans and our cousins in the animal kingdom; in part through a variety of theoretical critiques of the givenness, basalness, and authority of the individual human subject over action and meaning-significance; and in part through theoretical developments that stress the contribution of entities other than ourselves to the character of human worlds. What implications each of these developments holds for theorizing agency is a disputed matter. Because these developments have occurred, however, it is no longer possible to *presume* that agency is intentional human action. The intellectual terrain today demands a defense of any such constricted conception, as well as a sensitivity to both the contentiousness of erstwhile humanist divides and the once self-mastering subject's widely heralded loss of sovereignty.

All I mean by "agency" in the following, consequently, is doing. I no longer, moreover, restrict the expression "doing" to bodily human doings. Such a rendering can be common ground to humanists and posthumanists alike. Posthumanists can be satisfied because it acknowledges that nonhumans do things as much as humans do.[1] Humanists can concede, without prejudice, that the notion of doing is central to their equations of agency with intentional human conduct or with the choosing and carrying out of actions. Indeed, in the present context, the word "agency" can be defined without artifice as doing. To say that Y is attributable to the agency of X is to say that X either did Y or did something that determined Y. If Y is an action, the agent is whatever performed it; if Y is an articulation of intelligibility, the agent is whatever articulated it (a practice, a person, a text); and if Y is a change in the world, such as a computer's change of location or the breaking of the herb house's windows, the agent is whatever directly brought it about, for example, a trader or a mighty hailstorm. (The storm occurred on 28 June 1830 at New Lebanon. In addition to breaking six thousand panes of glass, it leveled fields and gardens.)

By "doings," moreover, I mean a type of occurrence in the continuous flow of events that befalls humans, organisms, artifacts, and things, singly or collectively. Doings are a subset of the general category of events. Whereas events are units of occurrence, doings are incidences of accomplishment or carrying out. Doings implicate entities that, first, accomplish or carry them out and, second, thereby commence or continue chains of events in the world. The doers so implicated, moreover, are either the entities that the doing-events befall or other entities connected to these. In short, doings are events that are assigned to humans, organisms, artifacts, and things qua perpetrators. As indicated, the events involved are ones that happen either to their perpetrators or to entities connected to their perpetrators. Events that cannot be so assigned are not doings.[2] Notice that this delineation of doings employs responsibility,

---

[1] See, for instance, Donna Haraway, "The Promise of Monsters: A Regenerative Politics for Inappropriate/d Others," in *Cultural Studies: A Reader,* ed. Lawrence Grossberg et al. (New York: Routledge, 1992), 295–337, here 297–98 and nn. I should make explicit that in the following I use the expressions "agent" and "actor" interchangeably.

[2] Nietzsche argued that doings do not entail a doer: "There is no 'being' behind doing, effecting, becoming; 'the doer' is merely a fiction added to the deed—the deed is everything" (Friedrich Nietzsche, *On the Genealogy of Morals,* trans. Walter Kaufmann [New York: Vintage, 1969], 45). His two examples are human activity and lightning. In both cases, the gainsaid "doer" is, formally, a

not intentionality, as is standard in analytic philosophy of action, to mark this subclass of events.[3]

The different types of agency are the different types of doing that entities exhibit. The social site, accordingly, is populated with actors of various types. As becomes evident below, however, two types of doing, or agency, are of overwhelming significance to social life: a causal type and a performance type. To do something causally is to make (or, along with other entities, to help make) something happen. In the social site, making something happen consists in bringing about or leading to some feature of orders and/or practices (cf. Chapter 1). Examples are intervening in and modifying an arrangement and bringing about an action by occasioning it. Nonhumans and humans alike do things causally. The second type of agency is performing an action. As discussed in Chapter 2, performing an action is carrying out bodily doings and sayings that, in the circumstances, amount to performing it (omissions are analyzed slightly differently). Performing an action is also, at once, carrying on the practice of which it is a part. Many human doings instantiate this sort of agency. The extent to which nonhumans can be accorded it is an open question.

The current section is not an in-depth examination of the multifaceted nature of agency. Its principal goal is to vindicate the integrity and unique richness of human agency; that is to say, the integrity and unique richness of the avenue through which humans contribute to the becoming of the social site. The present discussion thus continues the defense of agential humanism initiated in the contention of Chapter 2: that human activity holds special

---

substantial entity that lies behind phenomenal events. Vis-à-vis human activity, the illusory doer is a substantial self, subject, or ego. In the case of lightning, there is no obvious candidate, and Nietzsche remarks that the doer just doubles the deed. His comments leave open the possibility, however, that what carries out the doings associated with such entities as humans, organisms, artifacts, and things are these entities themselves—the possibility, for example, that human beings, as opposed to egos or subjects, perform human doings. (For a different, but convergent expression of the parallel idea concerning reason, see John McDowell, *Mind and World* [Cambridge, Mass.: Harvard University Press, 1994], lecture 6.) Nietzsche is right that there is no "doer" associated with lightning. This is just another way of saying, however, that lightning is not a doing. On the application of Nietzsche's comments to gender, see Judith Butler, *Gender Trouble: Feminism and the Subversion of Identity* (New York: Routledge, 1990), 20–25. Butler's critique of a gendered subject conceived of in terms of the "inherited discourse of the metaphysics of substance" opposes only the traditional "noumenal" genre of gendered doer.

[3] Making my definition more precise would nonetheless require paying attention to the issue of proper causal chains, which has exercised these philosophies. For example, Donald Davidson, "Agency" and "Intending," in his *Essays on Actions and Events* (Oxford: Oxford University Press, 1980), 43–62 and 83–102.

causal, prefigurational, and constitutive significance for human life in general and social existence specifically. From the beginning, however, it must be stressed that the unique richness of human agency is neither necessary nor metaphysically significant. It is contingent in a double sense: It is a feature of the world as things happen to be *and* as far as we know how things happen to be.

I suspect that many readers will find trivial the theses that human agency is intact, that it is the most complex form of agency, and that it holds special determining significance for social existence. Not only, however, are these theses far from trivial in the eyes of contemporary theorists such as those discussed in the present section, but many such theorists claim that one or another of them is false. My defense of agential humanism is thus, to a large extent, directed toward these thinkers. What is more, the truth of these theses, in particular the ones concerning integrity and significance, is the condition of politics. If the goal of creating a better—more humane, just, and hospitable—world is to make sense, these theses must be true.

Adding poignancy to this defense of agential humanism is the fact that it, together with what might be called "value humanism," is all that is left of theoretical humanism today. As mentioned in the preface, value humanism is the thesis that humans, as opposed to God, being, the order of the cosmos, or the structure of reason, are responsible for political-ethical values.[4] Three other historically prominent theoretical forms of humanism are indefensible in the contemporary world: psychological humanism, or the belief that humans are the masters of both their psyches and the phenomena of meaning and intentionality; epistemological humanism, or the proposition that the human mind or subject is the exclusive place of knowledge; and definitional humanism, or the thesis that the being of humanity is such that human life essentially contrasts with or differs absolutely from animality or animal life. Defending what many take to be simple intellectual common sense is, thus, a stand in favor of one of the remaining strands of what Immanuel Kant called the "Copernican revolution."

Foucault once warned against the "blackmail" of the Enlightenment, its insistence that one be either for or against it.[5] Similarly, one must guard against

[4] Blumenberg called the gradual development of this self-conception in the modern era the "self-assertion" of humanity. See Hans Blumenberg, *The Legitimacy of the Modern Age,* trans. Robert Wallace (Cambridge, Mass.: MIT Press, 1983).
[5] Michel Foucault, "What Is Enlightenment," in *The Foucault Reader,* ed. Paul Rabinow (New York: Pantheon, 1984), 32–50, here 43.

a certain blackmail of some posthumanisms, namely, that one is either a head-in-the-sand humanist or an up-to-date posthumanist. Latour and Callon promulgate a subtle and affable variant of this blackmail in writing: "The choice is simple: either we alternate between two absurdities [pure human world versus pure thing world—unenlightened humanism] or we redistribute actantial roles [attribute the properties of entities belonging to either world to entities of the other—clairvoyant posthumanism]."[6] I believe there is room between these alternatives.

DISCOURSE MULTIPLICITY

Section 1 examines two types of arguments that their proponents believe undercut all vestiges of agential humanism. One discursive and the other constitutional-embedding, these arguments bring considerations of multiplicity to bear on both the integrity of human agency and the claim that humans alone are capable of the most complex and multidimensional agency known. The first line of argument, which is paradigmatically found in actor-network theory and follows Foucault's dispersion of the subject into multiple discourse positions, cleaves the occurrence and nature of agency to the multiplicity of attributions thereof. The second line of argument, again presaged in Foucault's treatment of the subject, analyzes human agents themselves as multiplicities.

The discourse multiplicity approach to agency take its lead from Foucault's conception of subject positions. Above all in *The Archaeology of Knowledge*, Foucault countered the once dominant idea that subjects are the source of discourse by dispersing them among subject positions carried in discourses. As mentioned in Chapter 1, examples of these positions are perceptual ones such as observer and listener and information-network ones such as teacher and questioner. A subject is "dispersed" among such positions in that a multitude of positions replaces its erstwhile self-sameness. Part of the import of the notion of a subject position is that the discourses carrying them specify what is entailed in occupying them. When someone, for instance, occupies the position "author" that is found in certain modern discourses, the fact that the name of the author performs a classificatory function vis-à-vis texts and that to be the author of a text is to own it, to have a "deep motive" for producing it, or

---

[6] Michel Callon and Bruno Latour, "Don't Thrown the Baby Out with the Bath School! A Reply to Collins and Yearly," in *Science as Practice and Culture*, ed. Andrew Pickering (Chicago: University of Chicago Press, 1992), 343–68, here 356.

to be the source of the expression manifested in it—these matters are specified by the discourses concerned and do not result from anything a particular author is or does.[7]

Foucault's analysis in the *Archaeology of Knowledge* is widely taken to epitomize contemporary "decenterings" or "fragmentations" of the subject. Because it enjoys this status, and because Foucault is often said to have become increasingly humanist in his subsequent writings, it is worth pointing out that *The Archaeology* does not impugn the integrity of human agency. That Foucault "fragmented" the subject is indisputable: "Thus conceived, discourse is not the majestically unfolding manifestation of a thinking, knowing, speaking subject, but ... a totality, in which the dispersion of the subject and his discontinuity with himself may be determined."[8] It turns out, however, that the subject who is discursively dispersed is an acting person. Indeed, action is central to subject-hood in *The Archaeology*. Confirmation of its importance is found, inter alia, in the fact that throughout the book, without adequate explication, Foucault calls discourses "discursive practices." Only on pages 208–9 does the reason for this language become clear: A discourse's statements are things people do, that is to say, actions. A statement is (1) something (2) said, the said component remaining the action of a human being however much it tends in that text toward the status of an event. As a result, the rules that govern a discourse's dispersed objects, concepts, positions, and so on are, in fact, rules that govern discursive activity, although they are "not so much limitations imposed on the initiative of subjects as the field in which that initiation is articulated, ... rules that it puts into operation, ... relations that provide it with a support.... [Mine] is an attempt to reveal discursive practices in their complexity and density; to show that to speak is to do something."[9]

Subjects are actors. Discourse positions are the diverse statuses they assume in one of their capacities as actors: that of being *discoursers,* that is to say, speakers, writers, listeners, observers, and reasoners. Not only does this thesis leave human agency intact, but no one would claim that this is all there is to being an actor. As Foucault's subsequent writings detail, people are also performers of nondiscursive actions, as well as bodily creatures possessing and

[7] Michel Foucault, "What Is an Author?" in *The Foucault Reader,* ed. Paul Rabinow, trans. Josué V. Harari (New York: Pantheon, 1984), 101–20.
[8] Michel Foucault, *The Archaeology of Knowledge,* trans. A. M. Sheridan-Smith (New York: Harper & Row, 1976), 55.
[9] Foucault, *The Archaeology of Knowledge,* 209; cf. 200.

possessed by physiology, anatomy, sensations, and pleasures. It is true that these later writings, like *The Archeology,* on subject positions, analyze body and nondiscursive activity as socially molded phenomena. Still, Foucault never denied that the social constituted "subject" is an intentional, acting person. Attention to this only became more elaborate in later work.

Various writers who appropriate *The Archaeology*'s notion of subject positions and, at the same time, acknowledge nondiscursive actions press nondiscursive activity, like its discursive kin, into the fragmented template of subject positions.[10] These theorists often continue to associate subject positions with something they call "discourse," although they can do so only by expanding the notion of discourse so that it absorbs what Foucault called the "nondiscursive." For these theorists, the subject positions that encompass both nondiscursive and discursive activity are scripts or bundles of norms (whose specificity and malleability vary depending on the theorist considered). As far as I can see, these theories do not so much fragment the subject and undermine the integrity of its agency as emphasize the social formation and multiple centering foci of agency.

Actor-network theory applies discursive dispersion to agency. It treats actor as a discursive status, though not one that discoursers occupy but one that is discursively attributed to entities. According to this theory, the weightiest feature of a network is the division of its components into actors and intermediaries, where actors are defined as entities that do something and intermediaries as entities that actors circulate in the world. Latour, for example, analyzes actors as actants, where an actant is, roughly, anything said (in a story) to do something. Anything that, as narrated, has effects, brings about something, affects this or that, or makes a difference in some way counts as an actor. More picturesquely, Latour defines an actor as a stabilized "list of answers to trials [of strength]": a stabilized concatenation of performances, occurring in different agonistic states of affairs (each embracing multiple actions), which is attached to a name and thereby attributed to a substance.[11]

---

[10] For example, Judith Butler, *Bodies That Matter* (New York: Routledge, 1993).

[11] Bruno Latour, "Technology Is Society Made Durable," in *A Sociology of Monsters: Essays on Power, Technology, and Domination,* ed. John Law (London: Routledge, 1991), 103–31, here 122. In later essays, Latour argues that the notion of an actor is inadvisable for social theory. What he argues against, however, is the idea that an actor is a fixed point of origin (e.g., a subject) for a transportation of force that modifies the world. He does not challenge his own notion of an actor. See Latour, "On Intersubjectivity," *Mind, Culture, and Activity* 3, 4 (1996): 228–45; idem, "Do Scientific Objects Have a History: Pasteur and Whitehead in a Bath of Lactic Acid," *Common Knowledge* 5, (1996):

Callon writes that an actor is anything able to associate texts, humans, non-humans, and money in a network.[12] People obviously qualify. When at work, for instance, a day trader ties together fellow traders, tips, pads of paper, computers, computer software, managers, market makers, profits, and the day trading room. The computers, too, associate entities by running software, providing information, drawing technicians into the trading room (by crashing), making an accountant miscalculate profits (the system has crashed and caused an uproar), and leading traders to attend to specific transactions. According to Callon, who or what the agents are in a network is a matter of who or what is credited with associating entities. As a result, who or what is associator (actor) or associated in a network is relative to who describes the network, the circumstances in and purposes for which descriptions are essayed, and the discursive conventions observed when describing.

According to actor-network theory, consequently, the division of network components into actors and intermediaries is not an inherent property of the network. Rather, it is an effect of the imputations that network components make of these statuses to one another. For instance, the herb block presser might have treated the press as an unruly associate and the herbs as placid recipients of their fate, whereas the label printer observing him treated the press as a passive instrument in the hands of its operator and the herbs, which kept falling out of the machine, as refractory agitators. Because what qualifies as an agent or nonagent depends on imputations (as do the types of agents that those qualifying as agents are), "display[ing]" a sociotechnical network is "defining trajectories by actants' association and substitution, [and] defining actants by all the trajectories in which they enter, by following translations and, finally, by varying the observer's point of view" (i.e., assuming the perspectives of the different actants).[13] The analyst must canvas different perspectives because describing a sociotechnical network, detailing what it is, requires re-presenting it from all points of view at work in it.

Moreover, for John Law, an actor-network theorist working under Foucault's impress, such imputations are organized in the form of discourses. This entails

---

76–91. Not only does Latour continue to speak affirmatively of actions and actors, but the "action" of an event, which he claims is more propitious for social thought than the action of an actor, is, more or less, an occurrence of one of the "agonistic states of affairs" mentioned in the text.

[12] Michel Callon, "Techno-Economic Networks and Irreversibility," in Law, *A Sociology of Monsters*, 131–61, here 140.

[13] Latour, "Technology Is Society Made Durable," 129.

that what qualifies as an agent derives from discourses. Whereas in some discourses, for example, events result from indomitable structural forces, in others even the same events arise from the efforts of individuals or the struggles of collectives. In Law's words, "it is possible to impute several *modes of ordering* to the talk and actions of managers. And I'm saying that people are written into them in varying degree.... So I am saying that agents are effects which are generated by such modes of ordering. The subject has been decentred."[14]

According to actor-network theory, an actor is any entity that is said to do something. Accordingly, this extension of agency beyond humans amounts to the observation that doing is attributed to entities of many sorts. However, despite its predilection for multiplicity, actor-network theory toys with distinctions in what *types* of doing are appropriately attributed to different entities.

Compare, for instance, attributions of agency to a person, the herb house horse, and a geomagnetic storm. When one says of Hollister that he did something, say, macerated the belladonna, more than likely one is saying that he did so intentionally, that is to say, aimed at the result brought about. Many of the actions Hollister intentionally performed were also deliberately carried out or as a result of planning.[15] In many cases, finally, when he did something unintentionally (e.g., exhausted his assistant), his doing so was a product of things he did intentionally and maybe also as a result of planning (e.g., relentlessly trying to complete the maceration and evaporation before the Sabbath). By contrast, when the horse is said to have done something (e.g., eat its oats, rear up at the sight of the rats), it is only sometimes said to have done so intentionally. (Today, of course, we mean this considerably more often when attributing doings to, say, dogs, bonobos, and dolphins.) Horses usually act without intention, and nothing they do is done either deliberately or as a result of planning. Saying of the geomagnetic storm, finally, that it shut down an electronic communications network does not entail intentionality, let alone deliberation and planning. It implies only that a solar phenomenon had certain physical effects. Agency in this case is physical causality and nothing more. If doubts linger about the significance of these differences, consider the very

[14] John Law, *Organizing Modernity* (Oxford: Blackwell, 1994), 74. Actor-network theory here links up with broader "poststructural" ways of thinking that construe agency as a subject (or discourse) position that is carried by, attributed in, and dependent for its character on discourses. See, for example, Bronwyn Davies, "The Concept of Agency: A Feminist Poststructuralist Analysis," *Social Analysis* 31 (1991): 42–53.

[15] For a discussion of different ways of doing something, see John Austin, "Three Ways of Spilling Ink," in his *Philosophical Papers,* 2d ed. (Oxford: Oxford University Press, 1970), 272–87.

different measures that are taken against marauding Shakers, animals, and geomagnetic storms, or the very different techniques that must be employed to "enroll" these different entities into networks.

These points, I assume, are obvious. Yet, actor-network theorists insist on ascribing a paradigmatically human type of do-ing, intentional agency, to a wider variety of nonhuman entities than is customarily the practice. At one point in his well-known article about the scallops of Saint Brieuc Bay, for instance, Callon describes them as "dissidents."[16] A trio of scientists had concluded that scallop larvae would anchor themselves to collectors immersed in the bay. Many larvae, however, failed to do so, thereby "betraying" their "enrollment" into networks of scientists, fishermen, local politicians, tides, and parasites as previously "negotiated" with the scientists. Descriptions such as this, however jarring, raise a familiar and important issue: To which nonhuman entities is intentionality *correctly* ascribed? Today we know that animals boast varying degrees of intentionality and that machines might soon qualify as intentional beings. But scallops?

Actor-network theorists nowhere argue that certain entities hitherto denied purpose and will, for example, scallops and geomagnetic storms, have been wronged. Without offering arguments germane to particular cases, they simply extend a way of talking that is paradigmatically applied to human beings to creatures immensely different from the paradigm case. (My complaint, note, is not that actor-network theory anthropomorphizes or that anthropomorphisms are illicit.) As justification, Callon and Latour claim that expansive extension of the language of intentionality is required to overcome an absolutist distinction between "the language of things in themselves" and "the language of scientists among themselves," that is to say, a hard and fast division between nonhumans and humans.[17] Indeed, they do not really mean, they write, to grant intentionality to things. The point of extending the language is methodological—to force recognition of the interminglings of humans and nonhumans and the contributions of nonhumans to the networks of which humans are elements.[18] Latour and Callon add that they are trying only to

---

[16] Michel Callon, "Some Elements of a Sociology of Translation: Domestication of the Scallops and the Fisherman of St. Brieuc Bay," in *Power, Action, and Belief*, ed. John Law (London: Routledge, 1986), 196–233, here 219–20.

[17] Callon and Latour, "Don't Thrown the Baby Out with the Bath School! A Reply to Collins and Yearly," 354.

[18] For defenses of Callon and Latour along this line, see, for instance, Susan Leigh Star, "Power, Technologies, and the Phenomenology of Conventions: On Being Allergic to Onions," in Law,

develop a "symmetric metalanguage" for the description of humans and non-humans and cannot be held responsible if no "unbiased" vocabulary currently exists.[19]

An unbiased, symmetrical vocabulary does exist, however: the language of doing, applicable without prejudice to humans and nonhumans alike. If, more-over, the issue is one of recognizing the contributions of nonhumans to human existence, in particular to social life, the vocabulary of doing is sufficient. There is no need to add to this common vocabulary further terms that apply paradigmatically to humans. Doing this is likely, in fact, to undercut the goal of sorting out the contributions of different entities. Using a vocabulary that connotes human ways of being obfuscates the overwhelming likelihood that entities act in categorically different ways, that is to say, that the natures of their doings and contributions vary—and getting these different contributions right requires differential application of terms, indeed, probably some of the very differences leveled by Latour and Callon's overly thick symmetrical meta-language. In addition, justifying the extension to nonhumans of terms para-digmatically applied to humans on the grounds that doing this overcomes absolutist distinctions between humans and nonhumans ignores the fact that any such distinction is already blurred in extant practices, for instance, by the widespread attribution of intentionality to chimpanzees, dolphins, dogs, and even the herb house horse. Attributing intentionality to scallops, in particular, and to nonhumans, in general, is unnecessary for the purpose of counteracting theories that consign intentionality to humans alone.

In short, it is one thing to say on linguistic or other grounds that scallops, bonobos, humans, geomagnetic storms, and computer networks are all agents, that is to say, doers. It is quite another to attribute intentionality to them. Cer-tain distinctions among entities must be respected, and not every word used for humans should be applied to nonhumans indiscriminately (or at all).[20]

A Sociology of Monsters, 26–56, here 43; John Law and Wiebe E. Bijker, "Postscript; Technology, Sta-bility, and Social Theory," in *Shaping Technology/Building Society: Studies in Sociotechnical Change*, ed. Wiebe E. Bijker and John Law (Cambridge, Mass.: MIT Press, 1992), 290–307, here 291. On the other hand, see Latour's cagey remarks in "Where Are the Missing Masses? The Sociology of a Few Mundane Artifacts," in *Shaping Technology/Building Society: Studies in Sociotechnical Change*, ed. Wiebe Bijker and John Law, 225–58, here 235–36; also Law's more categorical claims in "Notes on the Theory of the Actor-Network: Ordering, Strategy, and Heterogeneity," *Systems Practice* 5, 4 (1992): 379–93, here 383.

[19] Callon and Latour, "Don't Thrown the Baby Out with the Bath School!," 354.

[20] See ibid., 353.

To approach this point from a slightly different angle, consider Steve Woolgar's attempt to defend the attribution of activity and mentality to machines. In response to the objection that such talk is metaphorical, Woolgar remarks that the interesting question is what entitles us to attribute intentionality to humans in the first place.[21] The answer is that nothing "entitles" us. What I wrote about normativity in Chapter 2 applies equally to intentionality: The language of mentality is today, paradigmatically, a discourse about human beings, whose extension to nonhumans is an empirical question reflecting, among other things, the degrees to which the activities and compositions of these entities resemble those of humans. The more creatures approximate us, the easier and more comprehensive the attribution to them of actions and mental conditions. Incidentally, these claims imply that the differences I am highlighting between humans and nonhumans vis-à-vis intentionality are *not* a priori cleavages. They reflect (1) analyses of the human form of life that theoreticians find themselves already carrying on once they attain the sophistication to do analysis, and (2) observed differences between the character of that form of life and the lives of other species. In any event, even though conceptions of human kinship to other entities vary during sociohistorical spacetime, and even though "primitive" peoples attributed intentionality to a wider variety of phenomena than modern Westerners do, Woolgar, in the contemporary scientific context in which he writes, illegitimately shifts the burden of proof. Detractors of actor-network's profligacy need not defend the applicability of the language of mind/action to humans—it is already ubiquitously applied to them, and it is here that it acquires its meaning. Rather, actor-network theory must argue for the extension of this language to nonhumans on a case-by-case basis; it is not enough that this extension contravenes misguided absolutist ontological divides and calls attention to nonhuman doings.

Actor-network theory's proliferation of agency does not subvert the unique richness of the intentional, deliberate, planning, and self-conscious agency humans enjoy. Attributing agency to animals, machines, storms, and social phenomena such as day trading firms only, at best, corrects a misguided humanism that proclaims people the sole agents. What does challenge the unique richness of human agency is the possibility that entities other than humans are the same type of actor as humans. Perhaps dolphins or bonobos act intentionally, deliberately, and on the basis of plans. Maybe machines will

[21] Steve Woolgar, "Configuring the User: The Case of Usability Trials," in *A Sociology of Monsters,* ed. John Law, 57–99, here 91.

one day soon confront and confound us with such behavior. Maybe some day prosthetic and implant technology will produce exotic human-machine hybrids who display it. Perhaps one day we will be contacted by extraterrestrials who have been acting so all along. Modesty precludes definitively adjudicating whether humans alone possess the self-conscious, intentional, deliberative, and planning agency they display. At the same time, we must not overlook that, as far as we know today, humans alone, and not even all of them, possess it fully.

Before turning to a second line of posthumanist argument, I want to pursue the above general point about differences further. Latour and Callon claim that humans and nonhumans alike *impute* the statuses of actor and nonactor (intermediate) to other network components. Humans accomplish this through speaking, acting, and building. Artifacts accomplish this variously. About texts, for instance, Callon writes:

> The choice of journal, of language and of title—these are the methods by which an article seeks to define and build an interested audience. . . . Here, then, is the start of a network. But that network extends into references and citations. These rework the cited texts, insert them into new relationships, and identify and link new actors together. Words, ideas, concepts, and the phrases that organize them thus describe a whole population of human and non-human entities.[22]

(By "describe," Callon primarily means imposing and imputing the statuses of actor and nonactor on and to the population involved.) A text must also "create a reader with the skills needed to mobilise, consolidate, or transform the network described in the paper."[23] Technical artifacts, moreover, "describe" networks through the programs of action they embody. An artifact's program of action is the set of actions that it prescribes to or imposes on humans and other entities if they are to figure in a network with it.[24] A computer, for example, prescribes an elaborate set of actions whenever a day trader seeks to use it to trade. With the assistance of the trader, software, and electricity, the computer also imposes the doings of printing and signaling an empty paper tray on the attached printer. The computer sometimes translates entities as

---

[22] Callon, "Techno-Economic Networks and Irreversibility," 135.
[23] Ibid., 140.
[24] For extensive discussion, see Latour, "Where Are the Missing Masses? The Sociology of a Few Mundane Artifacts."

nonactors, too. An example is when it strains a trader's eyesight and brings about a headache.

The translations that texts and technical artifacts effect are clearly, for the most part, the responsibility of humans. The particular network that a text describes is directly attributable to the human writing the text, whereas the text's creation of a reader is part and parcel of the role of texts in human life. Similarly, artifacts possess programs of action because the humans who create them or put them to new uses give them such programs. That artifacts translate other entities is, thus, itself the product of human activity. (This holds also of the latest text-writing computers.) Consequently, the fact that artifacts translate does not imply that artifacts do something (translation) in the same ways humans do.[25] For reasons discussed in Chapter 2 and not to be rehearsed here, the only nonhumans that translate independently of humans are those entities and events such as rats, lightening, and geomagnetic storms that causally assail people, orders, and practices in ways humans have not set up. Of course, such entities and events effect translations through physical processes, as when the computer translates a trader as something to make headachy. These processes are neither "imputations" nor "prescriptions," the operations through which, say Latour and Callon, entities of all sorts translate others. Humans can impute and prescribe the statuses of actors and nonactors (and in this might already or in the future be joined by animals and thinking machines). Artifacts, however, carry out translations that are intentionally or accidentally built into their design and otherwise effect them through physical causality. At a metalevel, furthermore, the fact that computers, rats, and storms enjoy the status of actor qua translator is a matter of how we humans have decided to describe the situation. I affirm the propriety of attributing agency to nonhumans. These attributions, however, must respect differences. In this case, different modes of "translation" must be acknowledged and *our* imputations of these modes sorted out.

COMPOSITIONAL-EMBEDDING MULTIPLICITY

Posthumanist thinking does not simply fracture agency into diverse occurrences of doing. Some versions also treat agents as heterogeneous compositions, thereby

---

[25] *Pace* Callon and Latour, who seem to think that building a speed bump and thereby bestowing a program of action on an object subverts some boundary between humans and nonhumans. See Callon and Latour, "Don't Thrown the Baby Out with the Bath School!," 361.

threatening human agency with instability, disunity, and fragmentation into the doings of other agents. For Deleuze and Guattari, for example, an entity (a person, artifact, thing, social formation, etc.) is a multiplicity of molecular assemblages.[26] It is a molar phenomenon that arises from the segmental organization of these assemblages. A human being, for instance, is a multitude of physiological, neurological, genetic, hormonal, cognitive, and conative assemblages, a molar phenomenon that arises from the organization of these assemblages. Its identity, personality, and self-consciousness, similarly, are molar properties that arise from these assemblages' organization. A person, consequently, is an integral organized assemblage of molecular multiplicities. "It will be noted that names ... function as common nouns ensuring the unification of an aggregate they subsume. The proper name can be nothing more than an extreme case of the common noun, containing its already domesticated multiplicity within itself and linking it to a being or object posited as unique."[27]

Deleuze and Guattari never focused on agency per se. Given their definitions of latitude and longitude as (roughly) the particle aggregates that belong to a body and the affects (in Spinoza's sense) of which that body is capable,[28] it makes sense to treat the agency of a human being, like his or her identity, self-consciousness, and personality, as a molar phenomenon. It follows that the stability and unity of human agency rest on the precarious organization of microassemblages, the ordering of a "city" of molecular "desiring machines." (According to Deleuze and Guattari, because the molecular realm that composes human beings is the home of desire, its components are "originally" structured as a manifold of desiring machines.) Agency, however, is a property not just of humans, but also of the molecular desiring machines whose combined action gives rise to human agency. Indeed, agency is not just something that people share with their constituent assemblages (and with other entities more broadly). It is also a property of the assemblages that humans form with other entities. A day trading firm, for instance, is a net of practice-order bundles that does things (e.g., makes profits, lobbies Congress). As with the agency of individual humans, moreover, its agency rests on the combined doings of

[26] The following description is based partly on Gilles Deleuze and Félix Guattari, *A Thousand Plateaus*, trans. Brian Massumi (Minneapolis: University of Minnesota Press, 1978), plateaus 2 and 9. I have also incorporated ideas from the first volume of *Capitalism and Schizophrenia* because this work considers the constitution of individual persons in greater detail. See Gilles Deleuze and Félix Guattari, *Anti-Oedipus*, trans. Robert Hurley, Mark Seem, and Helen R. Lane (Minneapolis: University of Minnesota Press, 1983), part 4, chap. 2.

[27] Deleuze and Guattari, *A Thousand Plateaus*, 27.

[28] Ibid., 256, 260.

its component actors (e.g., traders, managers, computers, computer networks, and branch offices).[29]

Similarly, actor-network theorists treat entities as networks to which, as in Deleuze and Guattari, unity is ascribed. A human being, for instance, is a network of neurons, muscles, memories, skills, preferences, and hormones taken as a unit. An actor, moreover, is any network to which both unity and doing are ascribed: Taking X to be an actor is apprehending the network that X is as a unit and crediting that unit with doing. "[A]n agent is a spokesperson, a figurehead, or a more or less opaque 'black box' which stands for, conceals, defines, holds in place, mobilizes, and draws on, a set of juxtaposed bits and pieces."[30] Latour, recall, defines actors as the substances to which stabilized concatenations of action are ascribed. It now turns out that the "substances" involved are, in fact, networks taken as units. Law offers a variation of this theme when he writes that any network sufficiently stable to generate power effects is an actor.[31]

Consider the practice-order bundle that is the day trading branch office. This complex of traders, managers, technicians, rooms, computers, computer network, power system, potted plants, and day trading, managerial, repair, and other practices converts electricity, computer graphics, trader savvy, and money into (1) commissions that subsidize expansion of the firm, (2) greater visibility or notoriety for the branch office in the firm, and (3) waste products such as used paper, burnt-out wiring, and carbon dioxide. If such actions as making commissions, projecting an image, and producing waste are grouped together, the actor that performs them, that is to say, the substance to which they are attached, is the practice-order bundle (the branch office). More precisely, the actor that performs these actions is this bundle treated as a unit. If, by contrast, such actions as scanning a computer screen and keeping a diary, or such doings as straining a trader's eyes and crashing, are grouped together, the actors involved are the traders or computers, respectively. These agents, too, are networks taken as units. For Latour and Callon, consequently, an ascription of agency, as in Deleuze and Guattari, is an instantaneous apprehension of multiplicity. By considering different congeries of action, moreover, agency can be seated in any component of a network, as well as in the network as a whole.

[29] On this, see Haraway, "The Promise of Monsters: A Regenerative Politics for Inappropriate/d Others," 332, n. 14.

[30] Law, *Organizing Modernity*, 101.

[31] Law, "Power, Discretion, and Strategy," in Law, *A Sociology of Monsters*, 165–91. The relevant effects are stockpiles of, degrees of discretion about, and the particular circumstantial character of both "power-to" and "power-over."

Observers of networks are not the only entities that can treat networks as units. Each entity in a network is itself a multiplicity that other network components view as a unit. For instance, a trader, a computer, a firm memorandum, and the office are each a multiplicity that is taken to be a single entity by fellow traders, managers, Securities and Exchange Commission (SEC) regulators, and the trader him- or herself. Only on such occasions as breakdown, error, deliberate scrutiny, or change in interest do components of the multiplicities involved come to attention and thereby become network components in their own right. According, therefore, to actor-network theory, the heterogeneous materials that compose networks are themselves networks of entities.

Agents are not just networks. They are also "effects" of networks. An entity cannot do anything without the support of the arrangement composing it: organs, physiological systems, understandings, and desires in the case of a day trader; computer network, employees, electricity, and so on in the case of a day trading office. Indeed, something's activity is generated by the network composing it. Agency is *also* dependent, however, on the wider network(s) in which agents are embedded: computers, workstations, fellow traders, managers, and market makers in the trader's case; other branch offices, the overall firm, the market-making industry, the Nasdaq market, and subsoil geologies in the case of the office. Hence, the networks of which agency is a unity-effect come in two flavors: compositional and embedding.[32] And the components of networks of both sorts are themselves (potential) agents that are generated by the further networks whose unities they are.

One further proposition resulting from the analysis of agents as networks-assemblages should be noted. It is eminently plausible that the type of actor something is is tied to the arrangements composing it. Both Callon and Law suggest, however, that embedding networks likewise play a role in determining the sorts of actors humans are. Imagine a network whose human components largely, first, share definitions of people, things, and situations and, second, observe the same rules in attributing agency and identity (and in blackboxing generally). In such a network, Callon claims, humans are actors who possess precise objectives and instruments, perfect but limited information, few choices,

---

[32] Harré refers to these as "endo-" and "exocollectives," respectively (Rom Harré, *Social Being*, 2d ed. [Oxford: Blackwell, 1993], 43–44). Attention should also be drawn to Simondon's analysis of technological artifacts as entities that both consist in elements and take up positions in ensembles (of artifacts and practices). See Gilbert Simondon, *Du mode d'existence des objets techniques,* 3d ed. (Paris: Aubier, 1989). Simondon's work in the 1950s appears to form a background against which both Latour and Deleuze and Guattari develop their ideas.

and no disagreements. When, contrastingly, definitions and rules diverge, people are actors who strategize, negotiate, and pursue revisable projects and varied aims. Intermediate cases between these extremes compel the application of other conceptual armatures to human activity, for instance, those of procedural rationality or game theory. For Callon and Law, consequently, "there is no theory or model of the actor, even in the plural. The actor has variable geometry and is indissociable from the networks that define it and that it, along with others, helps to define."[33] This means, I believe, that which properties beyond doing characterize a person (or anything else) qua agent depends on the networks in which it is such.

Much that is contained in these accounts of fractured agency is unproblematic. Agents, to begin with, *are* arrangements to which action is ascribed. Human beings, for instance, are molar aggregates of microassemblages, networks of organs, systems, and understandings, to which unity and doing are ascribed. Agency, moreover, *is* a unity-effect generated by these networks. Just as human consciousness depends (presumably) on brain operations, people's intentional, deliberate, and planned doings arise from the intermeshed operations of multiple bodily systems. Agency, furthermore, clearly rests on embedding networks. What, for instance, any human can do depends on the networks of people, organisms, artifacts, and things that populate the social site around her or him. Components of compositional and embedding networks, finally, are themselves (potential) agents, which the further networks that they themselves are generate: Horses, computers, herbs, bodily systems, and resin all do things, thereby qualify as agents, and on closer inspection turn out to be arrangements of entities, the components of which are likewise agents. In short, when compositional and embedding arrangements are treated as, respectively, the causal material composition of agents and the causal conditions of agency, they are relatively uncontroversial (or at least nonexotic).

The thinkers discussed here write, however, as if their conceptions of constitutive and embedding multiplicities constituted deep truths that subvert human agency.[34] Much of the fanfare attending the "discovery" that people are assemblages or networks arises from the thesis that human agents both depend

---

[33] Callon, "Techno-Economic Networks and Irreversibility," 154; cf. Law, "Notes on the Theory of the Actor-Network: Ordering, Strategy, and Heterogeneity," 283–84.

[34] Another, more recent example is Timothy Luke, "Social Theory and Environmentalism: Defining Nature/ Society in the 21st Century," paper presented to the inaugural meeting of the International Social Theory Consortium, 11 May 2000, University of Kentucky, Lexington. I do not know whether Luke would still today argue that these multiplicities subvert human agency.

on and are composed of nonhuman and "subhuman" entities that are actors as much as they are. As discussed, however, the thesis that these other-than-human entities are actors as much as humans are holds only at a high level of abstraction, namely, where they all qualify as doers. Once the thinness of the claimed equivalence is appreciated, initially provocative formulations become more familiar. For instance, the proposition that human agents are, and are effects of, networks of further agents resolves into such claims as that (1) human actors are composed of active physical subsystems that maintain causal relations among themselves and with the environment outside the skin, and (2) what people are capable of doing depends in part on the people, organisms, things, and artifacts around them. These claims do not debunk human agency. Rather, they scientifically conceptualize its character and provenance. Like the neurophysiological explanations of human activity familiar since at least the end of the eighteenth century, they challenge the integrity of human agency only on unnecessarily reductive or deterministic readings. Hence, the realization that human actors are assemblages-networks does not undermine human agency. Indeed, this realization should disconcert only those thinkers who, taking the humanist subject to be the ethereal free agent of Western lore, metaphysically distance will and its motivational context from material (and social) reality. Of course, the first obituaries of this agent appeared long ago. Consequently, insofar as contemporary posthumanists target this agent, they, like too many others today, simply re-sound its death knell in the face of dwindling efforts to save it.[35]

In their haste to level humans and nonhumans, the above writers also neglect to sort out significant differences between compositional and embedding arrangements. For example, the location of the agency that networks effect depends on the type of arrangement involved. Qua effect of compositional networks, agency is attributed to networks themselves as units; qua effect of embedding arrangements, it is ascribed to components thereof. Arrangements of these two sorts also maintain different functional relations to activity.

---

[35] Sartre may be the last great defender of metaphysical freedom. He denied that human agents are any more their compositional networks than they are their embedding ones on the grounds that nothing worldly can constitute the subject. See Jean-Paul Sartre, *Being and Nothingness*, trans. Hazel E. Barnes (New York: Pocket Books, 1966). In later works, of course, Sartre tried to square free action with sociohistorical contextualization. See the concise presentation in idem, *Search for a Method*, trans. Hazel E. Barnes (New York: Vintage, 1968).

Of a compositional arrangement, it makes sense to say that an agent is both an arrangement and an effect thereof. An actor is its compositional network because anything is that of which it is composed. An agent is also an effect of its compositional arrangement because its capacity to act as a single entity depends on the co-operation of its components. An actor is not, however, its embedding arrangements: A trader is not his computer, workstation, fellow traders, and managers, just as the day trading office is not the firm, the market-making industry, and the Nasdaq market. Furthermore, embedding networks, unlike compositional ones, do not generate (bring about) the agency of the entities they embed. The arrangements that embed the trader and the office do not generate their doings. Traders can act without their computers and fellows, just as the office can carry on in the absence of other offices (though it cannot in the absence of the Nasdaq market).

Agency is an "effect" of embedding arrangements in at least four other ways. First, agency *requires* certain general types of embedding networks, paradigmatically, arrangements of physical things, because without them there would not exist anything to act on, and the arrangements that compose agents could not function or survive. As discussed in Chapter 2, moreover, components of embedding arrangements can *lead to,* that is to say, occasion, human action. This second "effecting," unlike the first, is causal. Embedding networks can, third, *prefigure* agency (they are not alone here). Without their computers, for example, it is difficult for traders to follow market activity, though it is still easy for them to bemoan the repair delays. Similarly, with its computer network repeatedly down, the trading office has difficulty keeping its accounts, though it is still easy for it to lobby firm headquarters for additional technicians. Finally, embedding networks effect agency, fourth, whenever people in these networks *impute* agency.

The further thesis of actor-network theory, that networks determine the character of agency, overextends its insights. As described, Callon and Law maintain that which features other than intentional doing mark human agency depends on the character of embedding networks. Whereas in some networks actors must be credited with precise objectives, perfect but limited information, and few choices, in others they must be imputed strategy, negotiation, and varied aims. Variations of this sort do not entail, however, that the nature of human agency is variable and, as Callon and Law also claim, that a "model" or "theory" of the actor is impossible. Neither precise or varied objectives, nor perfect or imperfect information, nor few or many choices are constants of different models of activity. Rather, they are different values of three particular variables of a single, broadly speaking, rational-choice model of activity. The presence and absence of strategy and negotiation, moreover, result from the specific values these parameters assume in sets of individuals in particular interactional circumstances. Variability in these matters implies neither that what a human actor is varies across networks nor that a single model of agency is utopian.

I do not mean, thereby, to endorse rational-choice theory. Indeed, this approach neglects various aspects and types of human agency. These blemishes arise, however, from the patently reconstructive character of the model, in conjunction with the simplification of reality that it shares with all models. Its inadequacy does not confirm the alleged dependence of the character of human agency on embedding contexts. At the same time, as noted, differences among the agencies of humans, dolphins, scallops, herbs, computers, day trading firms, and geomagnetic storms *are* presumably tied to the different arrangements that compose these entities.

In sum, posthumanist analyses do not undermine either the integrity or the contingent uniqueness and richness of human agency. Like other developments that have shaken the hitherto-reigning equation of agency with human agency, they simply indicate that a cautious humanism alone is viable today. This is a humanism cognizant, among other things, that nonhumans are agents, that humans are multiplicities whose agency rises therefrom, and that humans may not be the sole creatures in the cosmos capable of self-conscious, intentional, deliberate, planning activity.

2. THE PREFIGURATION OF AGENCY

The future is made in the ceaseless advance of human and nonhuman agency. This advance is not, however, a leap into an empty, unfurrowed, isotropic space that receives motion in any direction. Agency does not invent the future wholesale from its own resources. Instead, it arcs through a variegated and folded landscape of variously qualified paths: Agency makes the future within an extant mesh of practices and orders that prefigures what it does—and thereby what it makes—by qualifying paths before it. Indeed, the incessant advance of agency is the endless happening of the social site, from which nascent agency "starts" in the twin senses of originating (taking place) at and being formed as the doing it is.

The following analysis of prefiguration focuses on human action alone. The discussion has implications for nonhuman agencies to the extent that they approach ours (thus for the agencies of thinking machines and "higher" organisms), but what these implications are await developments in knowledge, technology, and animal research. In the case, moreover, of fabrications, mongrels, and most beings of nature, prefiguration is, above all, the channeling of the physical causality that laces through the social site. An analysis of this phenomenon must take into account the operations of physical systems, the activities of organisms, and the efforts and constructions of humans. Although this is a fascinating area of inquiry, it is left untrodden in the current work. The prominence and unique richness of human agency warrant examining it alone.

The prefiguration of human agency is often approached through the notions of constraint and possibility, in particular, fields of possibility. The intuition behind the notion of constraint is that, although an actor self-propellingly follows an action trajectory of her or his own determination, the state of the world forces her or him to take particular twists and turns and to leave off particular routes. Giddens nicely characterizes the "structural" version of this intuition as follows: "The range of 'free action' which agents have is restricted, as it were, by external forces. . . . The structural properties of social systems, in other words, are like the walls of a room from which an individual cannot escape but inside which he or she is able to move around at whim."[36] The likening of constraints to obdurate features of the world, with which actors must cope, is widespread. Peter Galison offers a more recent version in describing constraints as "obstacles" and depicting scientists as navigating amid heterogeneous sets of technological, cognitive, procedural, economic, and engineering obstacles.[37] These obstacles, it might be added, are not fixed features of the scientific world, but instead come and go and conjoin in different combinations for different researchers.

The intuition behind the notions of possibility and fields of possibility qua aspects of prefiguration is that what people can do is limited. Not everything is possible. The dichotomy possible-not possible thereby marks a fundamental feature of the landscape of paths: the distinction between those actions that might be carried out and those that cannot. The idea that some actions are

[36] Anthony Giddens, *The Constitution of Society* (Berkeley and Los Angeles: University of California Press, 1984), 174.

[37] Peter L. Galison, "Context and Constraints," in *Scientific Practice: Theories and Stories of Doing Physics,* ed. Jed Z. Buchwald (Chicago: University of Chicago Press, 1995), 13–41.

open and others are not, that is to say, the idea that not every path is passable, in turn undergirds the notion of a field of possibility that includes all, and only, the navigable paths. Every possible course of action is an element of this field, while every impossible one falls outside it. Agency, accordingly, is limited to the first set.

The notions of constraint and field of possibility can and often do go hand in glove. For example, the action of the world's features that force free agents to twist and turn in particular ways and to forsake particular trajectories might be conceived of as the delimitation of a field of possibility. Or the phenomena credited with the delimitation of such fields might be called "constraints." On lines of thinking such as these, constraints exclude certain paths, thereby forcing actors to forgo them and to pursue alternatives that, falling into the range of the possible, stand at their disposal. Constraints operate, accordingly, through the determination of impossibility and the corresponding delimitation of possibility; that is to say, through the *exclusion* of certain actions and the concomitant leaving of others open. The walls of a room, for instance, exclude physical movement in certain directions at certain places. While precluding those motions, the walls leave others not excluded. They thereby delimit a range of physical motions open to agents within them. According to this sort of conception, consequently, the prefiguration of agency is a restriction, or limitation, of paths that the phenomena populating the social site effect. Constraints, be it noted, restrict in particular regards. Walls, for instance, make certain movements and, in addition, certain perceptions, communications, and games physically impossible. They do not, however, determine what is logically or conceptually impossible. Many theorists, furthermore, advocate a practical analogue to physical impossibility, namely, unfeasibility. A course of action is practically impossible when it is unfeasible. For these theorists, phenomena constrain not just by excluding certain actions as physically impossible, but also by excluding some actions as practically impossible. Giddens, for example, writes that structural constraint is the placing of limits on the "feasible options" open to agents.[38] Because feasible options are sometimes called "opportunities," structural constraint can also be described as the limitation of opportunity.

The negative action of constraints is fundamental. Any phenomenon warranting the label "constraint" must restrict something or other. This determination leaves open, however, at least two issues: whether the phenomena that

---

[38] Giddens, *The Constitution of Society*, 174, 177.

constrain also positively prefigure activity, and whether prefiguration is best approached thorough the notions of exclusion and the delimitation of possibilities. Before considering these issues, I want first to examine a position that denies all constraint qua exclusion in social life.

Pickering criticizes accounts that depict changes in human activity and culture as constrained. His argument is as elegant as it is simple. Recall that, for Pickering, scientific culture is composed of such phenomena as theories, facts, machines, instruments, skills, practices, and social relations, and that by "mangling" he means the transformation of items of these sorts through the contingent, happenstance course of events. Pickering avers that, in principle, any component of culture is susceptible to mangling *at any moment*. This thesis does not entail that every component of culture is changing all the time, only that no component is ever immune to change. It also entails, or so Pickering claims, that nothing constrains the development of scientific culture: Any phenomenon that allegedly constrains this development is subject to possible mangling at any moment, and something cannot constrain a development if it itself is susceptible at any moment to transformation as part of that development, that is to say, through the agencies responsible for that development.[39] Something that certain agencies can transform or eliminate at any moment cannot really *exclude* particular trajectories of those agencies. Its power to exclude is canceled, if you will, by its own inescapable susceptibility to change. Seeming constraints are simply phenomena that have not changed as a matter of happenstance.

Chapter 2 considered Pickering's account of a historical episode centered on the introduction of numerically controlled machine tools at a General Electric plant in Lynn, Massachusetts. As reported, he depicts the course of events as a series of contingent resistances and accommodations that the interweaving of human and material agency brought about. He also critiques the analysis of these events that is offered in the book from which he takes the example. According to the author of that book, David Noble, the course of events, or at least key moments of it, was determined by the enduring interests of management and labor. For instance, management's interest in controlling labor was responsible for its termination of the Pilot Program: Because this interest set limits to the changes in labor organization that management could tolerate,

[39] Andrew Pickering, *The Mangle of Practice: Time, Agency, & Science* (Chicago: University of Chicago Press, 1995), 206–7.

when the development of the program, together with its effects on the remainder of the corporation, reached those limits, management canceled it.[40] In my language: Management ended the program because its interest in control excluded particular paths, namely, allowing things to go on under their own steam, permitting the continuation of the trajectories that management and labor had taken until then.[41] As explained, Pickering believes that for something to act as a constraint, that is to say, to limit paths of action, it must be immune from change brought about by the agents it limits. He charges Noble, consequently, with supposing this about interests and adds that, as a matter of fact, despite Noble's asseverations, the interests of management (and labor) were altered over the course of the overall episode.

I do not know whether Pickering is correct that any element of culture, in my language, any component of the mesh of practices and orders, is susceptible to change at any moment. As a student of Nietzsche and Foucault, I affirm that all aspects of human culture are malleable. This form of mutability is weaker than the one Pickering advocates, for it maintains simply that nothing is immune to change over time, not that anything can change at any moment. My criticism of Pickering's argument does not, however, target this metaphysical thesis. Even if Pickering is granted such malleability, the notion of constraint is still conceptually sound.

Something constrains if it excludes courses of action. For something to achieve this, it is not necessary that it be immune to change from the actors whose activity it supposedly constrains. It is enough if, so long as it does exist, it bears on activity thus. I add, for reasons that become apparent later, that a similar point holds of prefiguration in general: To prefigure activity, it is not necessary that something be immune from change by the actors whose activity it prefigures. Pickering, simply put, pitches the notion of a constraint too high. For him, a "constraint" is something that constrains indomitably, something whose power to exclude is immune to the progress of events. This is revealed in those passages in which he compares constraints to the hard, impenetrable

---

[40] David F. Noble, *Forces of Production: A Social History of Industrial Automation* (Oxford: Oxford University Press, 1986), 318. Cited in Pickering, *The Mangle of Practice: Time, Agency, & Science*, 173.

[41] As often as interests are conceived of as setting limits to people's activity (or to people's tolerance), they are conceptualized as impelling people to act when things are a certain way. I do not, however, examine whether whatever limits interests set qualify as constraints. Pickering claims that the limits Noble invokes are constraints, so I describe the example accordingly. See Pickering, *The Mangle of Practice*, 174; for Pickering's acknowledgment of differences between interest and constraint models of agency, see 63–67.

walls of a prison, labels "Durkheimian" any position that depicts human activity and the development of technology as constrained, alleges that constraints control practices "from without," and characterizes constraints as "nonemergent" phenomena.[42] In his conception, a phenomenon is a constraint when it is an unmovable barrier that limits culture.

Constraints, however, can be conceived of as less potent. Something can contingently, in conjunction with other phenomena, and for as long as it exists, occlude certain ways of proceeding, including ways through which it itself might be changed by the agents whose activity it restricts. Even something that might, at any moment, change or disappear can determine thus—and prefigure more generally—so long as it has not changed or vanished. Construing constraint less indomitably also entails reinterpreting the meaning of "exclusion." To exclude ways of proceeding is not to render them absolutely impossible. To exclude is simply to make it the case that certain courses of action cannot be pursued at this moment in this particular configuration of phenomena. Phenomena that constrain in this weaker sense do not "control" what happens, let alone from "without."

Pickering claims, further, that it is vacuous to appeal to constraints if their "contours" cannot be specified in advance.[43] His worry is that if this cannot be done the citation of constraints does no work. Redolent of the legendary dormitive powers of opium beloved to Molière's physicians, the specification of what constraints exclude would be parasitical on whatever just happened to occur. However things turned out at any moment could be glossed as the reaching of "a limit," whose content would therewith be relativized to whatever happened to take place. Because, for example, the General Electric management ended the Pilot Program when tensions arose between the Lynn plant and the rest of the corporation, the occurrence of these tensions can be construed as the limits to management's tolerance of the program. The same, however, could have been said about any event, following which the Pilot Program was terminated. A constraint whose content varies in lockstep with the contingent outcome of events is no constraint worth the name.

I agree that citing constraints is idle if some specification of what is excluded cannot be offered independently of what happens. I am skeptical that it must be possible to formulate this specification before events, for this requirement would bar historians from adducing constraints for reasons having

---

[42] Pickering, *The Mangle of Practice*, 65–67, 174, 205.
[43] Ibid., 175.

nothing to do, pro or con, with the differences that theorists claim constraints make to activity. It is clearly too strong, however, to require that the contours of a constraint be completely specifiable. The reasons for this, as discussed shortly, are twofold: (1) Because something excludes actions only in conjunction with other phenomena, it is impossible to assign the exclusion of specific courses of action to specific restricting phenomena; and (2) the possibilities that a configuration of phenomena delimits are indefinitely complex. In any event, it is always possible to specify, independently of the actual course of events, a non-negligible number of actions that can or cannot be performed given a particular constellation of phenomena. Citing constraints is not, therefore, idle.

Until this point, I have been examining the exclusionary import of constraining phenomena. It is important to keep in mind that something that excludes also enables. No one has emphasized this point more than Giddens. The effect of what he calls "structures" on actions is the exclusion of certain courses of action as impossible together with the opening up of others as possible (structures are sets of rules and resources).[44] The rules that govern the movement of pawns in chess illustrate his point (although they are not examples of what he means by "rules"): At the same time that the rules forbid a variety of moves, they enable others, for instance, moving a pawn one empty square forward and taking another piece diagonally. Similarly, a wall closes off taking certain paths on foot at the same time that it opens up playing a game of bombardment, and a thick police cordon closes off handing the petition to the governor at the same time that it opens up charging the police line and thereby staging a media spectacle. This point holds for all phenomena that constrain human activity, including physical objects, human and nonhuman activity, arrangements of entities, and the organizations of practices.

Some theorists have been so impressed with the fact that actions can be opened up as possible that they have analyzed prefiguration simply as the enablement of activity. For these theorists, the social site channels agency by making courses of actions possible. According to this line of analysis, a free agent's space of activity is determined not by barriers that delimit it by *excluding* certain actions, but instead by enablers that create this space by *making* actions *available*. Think, for instance, of how the possession of a skill makes actions available without directly excluding any (it is the lack of a skill that directly excludes).

---

[44] Giddens, *The Constitution of Society,* 173–74.

Deleuze and Guattari's account of social assemblages exemplifies the conception of prefiguration as enablement alone. An important component of their account, which went unmentioned in Chapter 2, is the notion of a social field. The term appears often in *A Thousand Plateaus*. The closest the authors came to explicating what it means, however, is in writing "the social field considered as a stratum."[45] Elsewhere, Deleuze more or less directly equated a social field with a society (*société*),[46] though again he left unexplicated what either a field or a society is.[47] In these works, as well as in *A Thousand Plateaus*, a social field appears to be a plane, or open expanse, on which social assemblages—reciprocally presupposing regimes of power and of enunciation—exist. My earlier discussion of Deleuze and Guattari's account of social assemblages left two questions hanging: How do abstract machines govern the segments that power centers impose on people, artifacts, and things? and Why does an assemblage qua effectuation of a given abstract machine assume—and its power centers impose—such and such forms and not others? Abstract machines ground these forms, I explained, without requiring that any particular ones be imposed.

In *A Thousand Plateaus*, Deleuze and Guattari wrote that abstract machines contain possibilities or potentialities.[48] Indeed, they play a "piloting" role in history:

> Defined diagrammatically in this way, an abstract machine is neither an infrastructure that is determining in the last instance nor a transcendental Idea that is determining in the supreme instance. Rather, it plays a piloting role. The diagrammatic or abstract machine does not function to represent, even something real, but rather constructs a real that is yet to come, a new type of reality. Thus when it constitutes points of creation or potentiality it does not stand outside history, but is instead always "prior to" history. (142)

---

[45] Deleuze and Guattari, *A Thousand Plateaus*, 66.

[46] Gilles Deleuze, "Desire and Pleasure," in *Foucault and His Interlocutors*, ed. Arnold I. Davidson, trans. Daniel W. Smith (Chicago: University of Chicago Press, 1997), 183–92, 187; idem, *Foucault*, ed. and trans. Seán Hand (Minneapolis: University of Minnesota Press, 1988), 34; cf. Gilles Deleuze and Claire Parnet, *Dialogues*, ed. Hugh Tomlinson and Barbara Habberjam (New York: Columbia University Press, 1987), 135.

[47] The term "social field" is even more prominent in Deleuze and Guattari, *Anti-Oedipus: Capitalism and Schizophrenia*, pts. 3 and 4. Although once again it goes unexplicated, it seems roughly equivalent to "the social," that is, to "surrounding-immersing arrays of social things, flows, and arrangements" (which surround, primarily, individuals and families).

[48] Deleuze and Guattari, *A Thousand Plateaus*, 99. Further references are contained in the text.

Elsewhere, Deleuze wrote: "The diagram acts as a non-unifying immanent cause that is coextensive with the whole social field: the abstract machine is like the cause of the concrete assemblages that execute its relations."[49] An abstract machine acts as an "immanent cause" that "constructs a real that is yet to come" by drawing the cutting edges of deterritorialization through which assemblages dissolve, coalesce, and transmogrify into other assemblages. Deterritorialization is discussed in the next section. All that needs to be said about it here is that it is the process through which assemblages dissolve, coalesce, and metamorphose into successors. The present point is that abstract machines govern this process. As a result, they are responsible for both the evolution of and changeover in the assemblages that populate given social fields. As Deleuze and Guattari put it in *A Thousand Plateaus*, the "piloting role" of abstract machines is that of drawing becomings (510; cf. 144, 223, 333).[50]

My understanding of this thesis is as follows. An abstract machine is a virtual matter-function tensor, a sort of plan. All the assemblages in a given field actualize-*cum*-effectualize this plan. This plan is more abstract, however, than the assemblages that effectuate it, which entails that there are always more possible actualizations of it than all the assemblages that have effectualized it up to any given moment. "The abstract machine ... draws lines of continuous variation, while the concrete assemblage treats variables and organizes their highly diverse relations as a function of those lines" (100; Deleuze and Guattari were here speaking about language). This gap between abstract-virtual and concrete marks out possible changes in a social field. For change in such a field occurs through the dissolution, coalescence, and transmogrification of assemblages. And differences among the possible effectualizations of the diagram that governs the field constitute the possible lines of de- and reterritorialization along which assemblages can either coalesce or arise from the transmogrification of previous ones. It is in this sense that abstract machines "draw" the lines of deterritorialization to which assemblages are subject: "[A] machine is like a set of cutting edges that insert themselves into the assemblage undergoing deterritorialization, and draw variations and mutations of it" (333).

An abstract machine governs a social field through the possible effectualizations of its diagram. This thesis does not, however, resolve the two issues remaining from Chapter 2: why assemblages take the particular forms they do, that is to say, why they are composed of just these pairs of regimes of power

[49] Deleuze, *Foucault*, 37.
[50] See also ibid., 35.

and enunciation; and how abstract machines govern the segments that power centers impose. At most, the enabling power of abstract machines establishes that *any* assemblage in a given field (and any segment that power centers impose there) is an effectualization of the machine governing that field because it comes about through processes of de- and reterritorialization drawn by that machine. Note that this explanation seems to entail, *pace* what I wrote in Chapter 2, that Deleuze and Guattari could—without breaking the link between assemblages and machines—refer the following question to contingent empirical history: Why these particular forms and segments? *Which* possible effectualizations of an abstract machine occur is a contingent matter dependent on the specifics of time and place.

This resolution comes, however, at several prices. One is the parceling of social life into multiple distinct fields, each governed by a different machine. I touched on this general issue in the previous chapter and only indirectly rejoin it here. A second deficit is the very thesis that abstract-virtual entities govern concrete phenomena; that is to say, the thesis that concrete phenomena effectualize abstract machines and, as a result, are held to the machines' possible actualizations.

What is problematic about this thesis is best clarified by returning to the general idea that the prefiguration of action is a delimitation of fields of possibility (via constraint and enablement). As discussed, constraints exert a restrictive effect on agency. Restriction, moreover, prominently takes the form of the exclusion of certain courses of action. This form of restriction usually fails to illuminate what *actually* happens. By itself, the fact that various paths are impossible casts no light on why particular paths are taken: It indicates only that certain actions are not going to occur. The exclusion of activities makes a difference to social life only when people are aware that certain courses are impossible and act on this basis. Similarly, saying that phenomena that exclude paths also open others by itself says nothing about why particular courses of action are pursued—it indicates only that certain paths can be taken. If, consequently, prefiguration has a more than a minimal bearing on actuality, it must consist of more than the exclusion and enablement of activity. Conceiving of prefiguration as the delimitation of fields of possibility is the thinnest analysis possible.

This conclusion is reinforced by two features of fields of possibility: endlessness and indefiniteness. Consider, first, physically possible actions. The actions that it is physically possible for someone to perform are always endless.

For more courses of action are always physically possible for someone than those contained in any finite specification of them. As for practically possible actions, the actions that are feasible for someone to perform are often endless and always indefinite. Endlessness holds, once again, on those many occasions when more actions are feasible than are contained in finite specifications of them. (Lack of imagination often obstructs appreciation of this fact.) Indefiniteness reflects the fact that feasibility depends on states of the world: what others do, a person's knowledge and skills, and physical states of affairs. More specifically, indefiniteness follows from the facts that (1) other people's actions are indeterminate until they act; (2) it is not always definite whether a course of action is, in fact, feasible given specific phenomena of the above sorts; and (3) what unprecedented and innovative doings such phenomena make feasible are undefined until these doings occur. In addition, recall Giddens's observation that feasible options are relative to people's beliefs, desires, goals, fears, and so on (cf. Chapter 1). This fact implies—contrary, incidentally, to Giddens's intentions—that a person never faces a small, highly restricted field of feasible options, but instead always confronts a *plenum* of such fields that is as indefinitely diverse as are the combinations of mental conditions that might determine the practical intelligibility governing his or her action. Because, therefore, fields of feasible action are endless and indefinite, their contours indicate little about actuality, about which of their endless and ill-defined contents actually occurs. It is not illuminating, consequently, to hold that present social life prefigures future activity through fields of possibility.

Let us now return to Deleuze and Guattari. In a way, they accepted the conclusion just drawn. As discussed, what the fact that an abstract machine governs a field implies about concrete matters there is simply that the field's assemblages effectualize the machine and are bound, thereby, to its possible actualizations. (These assemblages also arise through transmogrifications that these possible actualizations define.) Which, however, of the endless and indeterminate possibilities is effectualized at given times and places depends on the twists and turns of contingent history. Hence, the fact that the abstract machine admits of possibilities says little about what, specifically, happens. Unfortunately for Deleuze and Guattari, this result undercuts the idea that abstract machines govern concrete social life.

Recall the example from Foucault with which Deleuze and Guattari substantialized their theses. In this example, the social field and its governing abstract machine are Western societies in the late eighteenth and nineteenth centuries and the panoptic diagram (to impose a particular taste or behavior on a mul-tiplicity of individuals). According to Deleuze and Guattari, this diagram admitted an array of possible actualizations, and which actually materialized can be referred to the twists and turns of European history during this time. Why, however, were the assemblages that arose during these centuries in the geographical region called "Europe" required to effectualize a particular dia-gram, the panoptic one? More generally, why are the twists and turns of con-crete history tied down to the possible effectualizations of given machines? How does an abstract machine manage to govern social affairs? How did the panoptic diagram, for example, manage to govern the assemblages that arose in late eighteenth- and nineteenth-century Europe?

No answers to these questions are found in Deleuze and Guattari. Abstract machines are supposed to determine concrete history by delimiting possible assemblages and transmogrifications. What the authors did not explain, how-ever, is just why the assemblages and transmogrifications that occur in a given swath of geohistory are tied to the possibilities drawn by one abstract machine *as opposed to any other*. Why one abstract machine, instead of another, governs events at a given time and place is simply mysterious. Deleuze and Guattari might have replied that a given assemblage *just is* part of a given field, that it just is governed by a given machine. That is to say, they might have claimed that a given machine *just does* reign in a given swath of geohistory. This reply, however, manifests the bankruptcy of the thesis that abstract machines govern concrete history. An abstract machine might admit an array of possible actual-izations, but there is no way of making assemblages materialize that machine's array instead of those of any other. Assemblages *just do or do not* effectualize a given machine; a machine just does or does not govern. As a result, abstract machines play no determining role in history. What they really do is define a set of possibilities, actualizations of which *qualify* the assemblages concerned as effectualizations of that machine. Assemblages, furthermore, do not effec-tuate a given machine because of anything attributable to the machine. It is simply happenstance if they do so. The fate of social life, in other words, is entirely and without remainder a matter of the contingent twists and turns of concrete history.

Foucault's own explanation of why social assemblages in late eighteenth- and nineteenth-century Europe were organized around the panoptic principle cites nothing more than these twists and turns. In *Discipline and Punish,* Foucault described panopticism as a project, as something that humans pursued and effected (though not, of course, under the label "panopticism"). Of Bentham's Panopticon, for instance, he wrote that it served as a "general model of functioning that has given rise, even in our own time, to so many variations, projected or realized."[51] The "mechanism of power" of which this building was an idealized "diagram" was an arrangement of things that solved the problem of how to impose a task or behavior on a multiplicity of individuals. It was the general *principle* of a new way of ordering social life that solved certain quandaries about power.[52] Because this solution, epitomized in the panoptic building, was extraordinarily attractive and widely applicable, it came to stamp the programs that reformers, politicians, planners, and administrators developed and sought to impose in diverse sectors of social life. According to Foucault, therefore, panopticism came to govern modern Western societies because it was adopted by individuals and groups who actively molded social affairs in line with it. It "governed," moreover, in the sense of being widely implemented. Panopticism did not govern through its possible actualizations.

The panoptic "diagram" was a principle, an arrangement that humans concocted. That it came to govern certain constellations in the social site was, like all other facts about social life,[53] a contingent result of concrete events. Because, moreover, this principle governed only insofar as it was successfully imposed, not all the social site of modern European societies was subject(ed) to its reign. Hence, the panoptic diagram was not an abstract matter-function tensor that governed an entire social field per the requirement that concrete assemblages effectualize it. More generally—it can be concluded—the endless becoming of social affairs does not stand under the tutelage of abstract-virtual, possibility-delimiting structures. Concrete goings on *and nothing else* determine what happens in history. The abstract forces at work in history are simply the ideas, plans, models, and principles drawn up in human thought and activity.

Two overall conclusions about prefiguration have been defended to this point. First, to analyze prefiguration as the delimitation of possibility is to reduce its bearing on the actual course of events to a minimum. A thicker and more variegated notion of prefiguration is in order. Second, prefiguration is not the work of abstract-virtual entities. It is, instead, a product of the actual

---

[51] Michel Foucault, *Discipline and Punish: The Birth of the Prison,* trans. Alan Sheridan (New York: Vintage, 1979), 205.

[52] Foucault, *Discipline and Punish,* 205–9.

[53] See Michel Foucault, "Nietzsche, Genealogy, and History," in *The Foucault Reader,* ed. Paul Rabinow (New York: Pantheon, 1984), 76–100.

concrete state of the social site. My arguments, incidentally, strike at two central pillars of all structuralist accounts of social life: the idea that abstract structures govern social affairs and the idea that they do so by delimiting fields of possibility. I should be clear, furthermore, that I do not contend that the notion of possibility should be discarded in this context. The world does exclude certain courses of action as impossible. The inconfutable example is the exclusion of actions as physically impossible. Torsten Hägerstrand has nicely captured this type of exclusion in his notions of packing and coupling constraints—respectively, the limits materiality imposes on how many humans can be physically present at a given place and time and the limits that the phenomena of distance and materiality place on physically possible face-to-face interactions.[54] It is also conceptually sound to speak of the exclusion of actions as practically impossible, that is to say, unfeasible. Unlike its physical cousin, however, this form of exclusion is relatively uncommon.

Among the phenomena that appeared to constrain courses of action in the medicinal herb industry were the number of workers available at any moment, the demand for medicines, the state of the weather, and the occasional financial mismanagement or skullduggery of trustees. During unusually wet springs, for instance, the Shakers could not work in and weed the gardens as much as they would have liked. Nothing physically prevented them from going outside to work in the rain, but given the dangers of getting sick, ruining boots and clothing, trampling new seedlings, and simply doing a bad job, the bad weather meant that they just were not going to go out and weed as much as was ideal. Similarly, the availability of hands might be thought to have constrained the foreperson's ability to run the business. The Shakers were known to fill orders for medicines as soon as they were received. At times when stocks were low or multiple orders arrived in bunches, the availability of workers occluded the possibility of filling the orders promptly and fulfilling customers' expectations. (There was constant effort, accordingly, to maintain stocks.) Of course, filling the orders expeditiously was not physically impossible. Additional workers, beyond those already transferred, could have been pulled from the other businesses and reassigned to the medicinal herb one. Doing that, however, would have involved training even more new hands, idling the operations of the other industries, annoying the forepersons of those industries,

[54] Torsten Hägerstrand, "Space, Time, and Human Conditions," in *Dynamic Allocation of Urban Space*, ed. A. Karlqvist, L. Lundqvist, and F. Snickars (Lexington, Mass.: Lexington Books, 1975), 3–14.

and failing to satisfy those industries' customers. For these reasons, workers simply were not going to be transferred, and the business simply was not going to fill orders promptly. (Notice how, in both cases, something prefigures activity only in conjunction with other phenomena, including ends, desires, and beliefs.)

In the previous chapter, I described how asymmetries in technology and information access at one time prevented individual investors from competing equally with market makers. Advances in technology and new regulations about information partially leveled these asymmetries and led to the appearance of day trading. Even today, however, among the phenomena that appear to constrain courses of action in day trading are a lack of access to certain pieces of information (e.g., large institutional orders to which market makers are exclusively privy) and slow electronic connections. Lack of information definitely affects how traders proceed. It prevents them from bidding up or down before the first signs of price movement. Nothing, of course, physically prevents traders from doing this: They can enter whatever orders they want into the system. Doing so runs the risk, however, that their decisions will be regularly thwarted by subsequent market maker-driven movement (arising from institutional orders). Day traders, consequently, are not going to act before the makers do. They remain reactors. Similarly, traders' fortunes are tied to their abilities to track and to react to particular patterns of buy and sell orders. If traders lacks fast electronic connections, they cannot receive information as quickly as other traders and makers do. Their decisions, as a result, are based on outdated information. Because they also cannot enter their orders into the queue as fast as they would like, market conditions might have changed dramatically by the time the orders are executed.

Putting aside the second day-trading example for the moment, in none of the first three examples was the activity described physically excluded. The first is a case in which a way of acting was ill-advised and potentially ruinous, the second one in which a course of action was disruptive and attended by injurious side effects, and the third one in which a way of proceeding was risky and likely disastrous. In none of these cases, moreover, were actions excluded because they were unfeasible. Going out in the rain was not unfeasible; it was ill-advised and potentially ruinous. Reassigning more workers was not an unfeasible option; it was simply *less* feasible than other ways of proceeding. "Proactively," as opposed to reactively, trading is not unfeasible, but simply stupid. No case, therefore, involved exclusion, either of the physically or the practically impossible. None, consequently, can be described as an instance of constraint, at least when constraint is construed as the exclusion of actions (as physically or practically impossible). Relatively few actions, in fact, are ever excluded as practically impossible—almost all courses of action labeled "unfeasible" are simply less feasible than alternatives. The encumbrance of actions takes forms different from practical impossibility.

The second day-trading example might seem to be a matter of physical possibility and impossibility. Lack of the proper electronic links eliminates—as a matter of physics and engineering—certain courses of action. Possessing or not possessing the links, however, is often, if not usually, a matter of money. Consequently, expeditious information reception and order execution are not so much physically as practically impossible. In reality, however, expeditious trading is not unfeasible for someone who lacks the funds to install the fastest links. Rather, inexpeditious trading is easier, less time consuming, and maybe also simply more feasible than alternative courses of action such as borrowing money from a family member, taking out a loan, and robbing a bank. Expeditious trading is not, consequently, excluded.

I draw three lessons from these examples. First, the state of the social site qualifies courses of action in a variety of ways, not just in those ways captured in constraint qua exclusion (feasible or unfeasible, physically possible or impossible). Examples of these further qualifications are ill-advised, potentially ruinous, disruptive, taxing, and more or less feasible. As a result, prefiguration is, second, only to a small extent a matter of exclusion. Third and once again, constraint and enablement qua the delimitation of physical and practical possibility illuminate precious little of what actually occurs in social life. The overall conclusion of the above arguments is that prefiguration should not be analyzed through the notions of enablement, constraint, and fields of possible action. It cannot, therefore, be adequately grasped through either Bourdieu's structuring structures (habitus), Giddens's rule-resource structures, or Foucault's "capillaries" of power. The prefiguring effect of all these phenomena is the delimitation of possible actions.

For the purposes of understanding prefiguration, I suggest that attention be instead directed to the multitudinous ways that the mesh of practices and orders makes courses of action easier, harder, simpler, more complicated, shorter, longer, ill-advised, promising of ruin, promising of gain, disruptive, facilitating, obligatory or proscribed, acceptable or unacceptable, more or less relevant, riskier or safer, more or less feasible, more or less likely to induce ridicule or approbation—as well as physically impossible or possible and feasible or unfeasible. In metaphorical phenomenological terms: The mesh of practices and orders does not simply clear some paths and obliterate others. Rather, it figures them as more distinct or fuzzy, more threatening or welcoming, more unsurveyable or straightforward, more cognitively dissonant or soothing, smoother or more jagged, more disagreeable or appealing, and so on. Bad weather, worker availability, lack of access to information, and slow electronic connections did not and do not constrain what is done in medicinal herb production or day trading. Rather, they make certain courses of action difficult, ill-advised, circuitous, disruptive, and not very feasible. A prefiguration of actions in modalities of these latter sorts bears considerably more directly on what people do than does a prefiguration of action as merely possible or impossible. It reveals, more perspicuously, the pertinence of these actions to the actors involved. That is to say, that a course of action is, say, simpler, obligatory, and disruptive provides a much thicker sense—than does its simply being feasible—of how the world channels activity, of how existing social affairs bear on incipient action. I see no reason, moreover, to limit the number of dimensions that prefiguration can assume.

The prefiguration of agency is the joint effect of practices and orders. This means that courses of action are easier or harder, simpler or more complicated, safer or riskier, obligatory or proscribed, and so on because of the practices people carry on and the orders amid which they do so. Accordingly, various more specific phenomena, including features of individual actors, prefigure what people do: the ends people pursue and those called for or acceptably pursued in their practices; the projects and tasks they carry out, as well as those enjoined or acceptably exercised for particular ends; rules, understandings, emotions, and past actions; artifacts, organisms, and things; arrangements of these entities along with humans; chains of action and intentional relations; and practice-order bundles, nets, and confederations. Such phenomena, in indefinitely myriad combinations, prefigure agency and channel what people do. Because at any moment of their waking lives human beings are carrying on practices amid both arrangements of entities and people who are carrying on the same and different practices, humans are fated to exist in a prefigured landscape of multidimensionally qualified paths

Contrary to his own stated position, Foucault half-moved away from a conception of prefiguration as the dispensation of possibility toward a conception of it as a more variegated phenomenon. As noted, he defined power as the way that actions modify others by structuring people's fields of possible action.

Foucault also, however, described the exercise of power as follows: "[I]t incites, it induces, it seduces, it makes easier or more difficult; in the extreme it constrains or forbids absolutely."[55] Power, he added, is a matter of "guiding" conduct. The fact, however, that these latter pronouncements are surrounded by formulations that highlight possibilities indicates that Foucault did not fully appreciate the change of view he was formulating.[56] More recently, Law and Bijker have made the shift. Conceptualizing structure as a set of heterogeneous relations, they write that

> structure and the actors within it represent a ... geography of [prefiguration]. Thus, some relations are much easier to create and maintain than others.... Others are expensive, awkward, and time consuming. Structure, then, is something like a system of transport. The network of paths, tracks, railway, and airlines mean that it is easy to get from some places to others.... On the other hand, other locations are far removed from one another. Maintaining links between them is time consuming, tedious, expensive, or downright impossible.[57]

Galison's discussion of constraints also points in this direction, though he neither makes nor pursues the point. His term "obstacles" suggests that constraints are resistances or requirements that guide and restrict behavior because of the effort that has to be made to overcome or meet them. As a result, they prefigure activity by qualifying paths in such ways as easier or harder and more straightforward or circuitous.

My delineation of prefiguration resembles the conception of social structure as arrays of costs and benefits, which is prevalent in contemporary American sociology.[58] That social life bears on forthcoming activity by qualifying paths

---

[55] Michel Foucault, "The Subject and Power," afterward to *Michel Foucault: Beyond Structuralism and Hermeneutics,* ed. Hubert L. Dreyfus and Paul Rabinow, 2d ed. (Chicago: University of Chicago Press, 1983), 208–26, here 220.

[56] Treating power as the way that actions modify others by structuring fields of possible actions does not deny that power is productive, that is to say, that it creates people who are specific kinds of people and who do certain things. Forming people with particular abilities, attitudes, and propensities is one way their fields of possible action can be structured, one way actions can modify other actions by structuring such fields. The productive dimension of power is not something in addition to its possibility-delimiting dimension, but one form the latter takes.

[57] Law and Bijker, "Postscript: Technology, Stability, and Social Theory," 300.

[58] For examples, see Rosabeth Kanter, *Men and Women of the Corporation* (New York: Basic Books, 1977); William J. Wilson, *The Truly Disadvantaged: The Inner City, the Underclass, and Public Policy* (Chicago: University of Chicago Press, 1987).

of action as easier or harder, longer or shorter, obligatory or proscribed, and so on converges with how social affairs, according to some sociologists, bear on actors' choices by attaching costs and benefits to courses of action. Only at the extreme, moreover, do costs exclude actions as practically impossible. My account of prefiguration nonetheless diverges from this sociological one, for at least two reasons. First, the qualifications of which I speak are not automatically costs or benefits. Whether the ease or the difficulty of a course of action is a benefit or a cost is a contingent matter that varies across individuals and contexts. Second, costs and benefits, in particular, costs and benefits as the form in which social life qualifies courses of action, are features of that reconstructive model of human activity called "rational-choice theory." The qualifier "reconstructive" reflects the fact that, whereas courses of action always possess costs and benefits for investigators who use the model, in ongoing social life such courses possess costs and benefits only for actors who calculatingly choose among them. That is to say, the action path qualifications of which I write count as costs and benefits only for someone who chooses calculatingly. This is not the place to address and criticize this pervasive model of human activity. Although my clarification of "reconstructive" suggests that human agency takes the form of calculating choice only on particular occasions, the implications of this fact for the cogency and value of the model are multiple.

I should, however, point out the following. Rational-choice models contain algorithms with which rational actors calculate what to do and social scientists predict behavior, on the basis of costs and benefits. Prima facie similarly, because prefigured paths are qualified in ways that reveal their pertinence to people's lives, they count as likely, unlikely, more or less likely, predictable, unpredictable, thinkable, and unthinkable. Given, however, the variety of types of pertinence that qualify paths, no algorithm can translate the position of a path in the n-dimensional space of import into its location on the scale of probability. No rule, for example, exists to the effect that a shorter but harder path is more likely to be taken than a longer but easier one, or that a safer but proscribed path is more likely to be pursued than a more dangerous, acceptable one. The vast number of types of qualifications indicates the hopelessness of any attempt to rank paths probabilistically on the basis of such rules.

Prefiguring the herb activities at New Lebanon were not just the bad weather and worker availability discussed above, but a variety of features of the social site there, including the organization of the medicinal herb practices, connections between these practices and others, the arrangements at the herb and extract houses, and events befalling these arrangements. To give just one example: Given the arrangements in the laboratory, the tasks embraced in the project of extraction, the jobs of other workers, the agencies of herbs, water, and fire, the desire to supervise the wild herb outing scheduled for that afternoon, the fact that the trustee Fowler had asked Long to accompany him to town that morning, and Long's fear of the consequences of refusing this request, the easiest way for Hollister to get the day's extraction going was to set the belladonna steeping in the morning and to leave it there to await Long's supervision in the afternoon while Hollister was in the woods. This was a risky, but relatively straightforward path; it was acceptable but not obligatory; and it was not the only path available to commence the day's extraction, let alone the only feasible path for Hollister that morning. He could, for instance, have pursued the harder, safer, and equally acceptable path of talking Long into staying. (He also could have helped the carpenter build shelves, etc.) It was, in any case, the course he took.

But why? With this question, we reach a decisive issue: In an environment of actions differentially qualified as easier, harder, longer, shorter, riskier, safer, pretty feasible, proscribed, and so on, what determines the path a person actually takes? Many thinkers believe that a person is "determined" to perform, or "steered" toward, an action by her or his desires, beliefs, hopes, fears, preferences, expectations, and the like. Before discussing the specific sense in which this is true, it is necessary to set aside an important but misleading conception of the work of mentality. It cannot generally be the case that mental conditions, *as opposed to the qualifications of paths,* steer people toward one or another particular path. At least in most cases, these conditions are *already* implicated in the qualifications of paths. In Chapter 1 (and again in the present section), I seconded Giddens's claim that which actions something renders feasible or unfeasible depend on features of individuals, for instance, their desires and ends. This point holds to varying degrees of the other modes of prefiguration. Which paths are easier and harder, for instance, depend on a person's skills, desires, hopes, and beliefs, just as which courses are riskier or safer depend on her or his beliefs, fears, and criteria of risk, and which are normatively prescribed or acceptable depend on his or her identity and powers of persuasion (cf. the discussion in Chapter 2 of the contents of teleoaffective structures). An individual does not, so to speak, stand self-contained over against a landscape of qualified paths. Rather, she or he is present, or implicated, in the contours and textures of the landscape. Consequently, in most cases it cannot be that desires and ends, as opposed to the qualifications of paths, were responsible for the person's acting as she or he did. The action of the one is the action of the other. Moreover, insofar as mental conditions are implicated in the qualifications of paths, it is not possible to *explain* why someone performed one action as opposed to another by citing mental conditions. All that desires and ends can elucidate is that the easier, riskier, and longer path was taken because it was easier, riskier, or longer. They cannot explain why it, instead of the safer but more difficult and shorter route, was pursued.

Jon Elster expresses a sentiment widespread in social thought when he claims that human activity is the product of two "filtering devices." "The first is defined by the set of structural constraints which cuts down the set of abstractly possible courses of action and reduces it to the vastly smaller subset of feasible actions.... The second filtering process is the mechanism that singles out which members of the feasible set shall be realized."[59] The sentence following these indicates that the second filter is mental: "Rational-choice theories assert that this mechanism is the deliberate and intentional choice for the purpose of maximizing some objective function." As just suggested, however, this division of the determination of feasible actions into two (moreover, "successive") moments is illusory. "Structural" constraints do not reduce the set of abstractly possible actions independent of whatever properties of individuals are thought to single out particular actions from the subset that allegedly results from the action of these constraints. Rather, features of individuals and of "structure" (read: the social site) together, and only together, multidimensionally qualify a manifold of paths. The prefiguration of action cannot be segregated into two distinct contributions, one social and one emanating from individuals (taken singly). Elster also, notice, assumes that an actor faces a single set of feasible actions, which is relatively small and presumably well defined.

Perhaps, however, not all of a person's psyche is implicated in the qualifications of courses of action. Perhaps, at any moment, at least some of a person's desires, ends, hopes, fears, preferences, and the like do not help qualify paths and are able as a result to settle what she or he does. It is not merely the case, however, that the determining power of mental conditions is often identical with that of the qualifications of paths (and thus with the social site's prefiguration of agency). More profoundly: A person's desires, fears, and so on can never ordain his or her activity. One reason for this is that it can never be

---

[59] Jon Elster, *Ulysses and the Sirens: Studies in Rationality and Irrationality,* rev. ed. (Cambridge: Cambridge University Press, 1984), 113.

excluded, and it sometimes comes to pass, that a person suddenly starts acting out of desires, fears, and expectations that she or he had not expressed until then. A reply to this thesis that parallels my counter to Pickering's critique of mutable constraining phenomena is inapposite. I am not claiming that mental conditions cannot settle what someone does because at any moment she or he might no longer be in any such condition. Rather, I am averring that the possession of given conditions never guarantees that these conditions—and not new ones—determine what she or he does. A person, furthermore, always has *multiple* conditions of these sorts. And it is never settled prior to action which ones will have determined what she or he does. Before the action, in other words, it is indeterminate which particular conditions will have determined what a person does. It might be added that additional evidence for the inability of mind to ordain action is the common (epistemological) experience of surprise at the actions of those with whom one is familiar.

Alternatively, one might claim that a person possesses a set of "final values" that somehow ranks types of qualifications and thereby hierarchizes the courses of action that these qualifications characterize. The first argument just made against mental conditions applies in principle to such values: Even if a person at one moment possesses a set of final values, nothing guarantees that she or he might not at any moment begin to perform actions that express an alternative set. Admittedly, people's final values change considerably more slowly than do their mental conditions. This argument, consequently, carries little weight. Just as people possess multiple conditions of any mental sort, however, they also often possess conflicting (sets of) final values. Whenever this is so, it can never be settled before action which set will have specified the ranking of action courses that determined what someone did.

It is a good question, moreover, whether final values of this sort exist. To begin with, the "values" a person possesses are just as likely to characterize action paths directly as to rank types of qualifications. The values of just and unjust, for example, are more likely to characterize paths than types. To the extent that values figure paths, values simply add more types of qualifications— valuations—to the myriad other qualifications that exist anyway. Moreover, raw preference might in theory be able to hierarchize types of qualifications. It seems to me an empirical fact, however, that people do not have many categorical preferences for one sort of qualification over another (e.g., unconditionally preferring easier to harder or riskier paths). Finally, it oversimplifies human existence to suppose that the wealth of types of qualifications can be compared and ranked through some common standard, that is to say, some common value (e.g., utility, such that the adjudication of activity reduces to the calculation of expected utility). In any event, even if it is possible to hierarchize types of qualifications, nothing guarantees that a person will pursue the highest ranked course of action.

For human activity is fundamentally indeterminate. *Nothing* determines *ante eventum* what a person—acting in a world that prefigures paths differentially—does. Until a person acts, it remains open just what he or she will have done. No matter how strongly his or her ends, desires, hopes, preferences, and the like "point toward," or even "single out," a given path of action, nothing guarantees that it or any other particular action is performed.[60] I wrote in Chapter 2 that people do what makes sense to them to do, that is to say, the action that is signified to them as the one to perform. The present thesis is that nothing prior to action settles what is going to have made sense to someone to do. Just as it remains open until a person acts what she or he will have done, so, too, it remains open until she or he acts what will have been signified as the thing to do. This fact does not imply that action is *undetermined.* It entails only that what determines action itself remains *indeterminate* until action occurs— only then will what will have determined agency have done so. The indeterminacy, at any moment, of what a person does next is compatible with the determination of whatever she or he does do. The determination of action, in other words, is a past or future perfect tense phenomenon. Because Hollister took the easier but riskier path, one locates the determination of his action in those mental conditions of his that favored ease. If, by contrast, he had taken the safer but more difficult path of talking Long into staying, one would locate the determination of action in the conditions favoring this path. Until action occurs, however, one does and cannot know where to locate it.

Theoretical recognition of the indeterminacy of action is a relatively recent phenomenon. It was first conceptually fixed in the life philosophical thesis that life leads the way before any of its forms and structures. For such thinkers as Dilthey, Nietzsche, Georg Simmel, and Oswald Spengler, life is a self-propagating and continuously advancing stream that both constantly outstrips

---

[60] The point is sometimes made in discussions of weakness of will that nothing guarantees that a person performs even an action for which everything speaks and from which nothing dissuades. The present thesis takes the point a step further: All of a person's mental conditions at a given moment cannot settle how she or he acts. Harré expresses a similar idea in writing that an intention to perform an act, in conjunction with the rules and conventions about how that act is to be performed, is neither sufficient nor necessary for action to occur; Harré, *Social Being,* 99. On weakness of will, see, for example, Donald Davidson, "How Is Weakness of Will Possible?" in his *Essays on Actions and Events* (New York: Oxford University Press, 1980), 21–42.

the structures and forms it has assumed up to any point and incessantly begets new forms and structures beyond which it thereupon moves. In the words of Simmel: "Life is more than life and more life."[61] Thinkers after life philosophy abandoned the latter's focus on life, together with its idea that life, as a self-energizing and groundless pulse, is the fundamental metaphysical event. Many prominent successors, however, have perpetuated life philosophical intuitions in according action much of the grandeur, and a number of properties, that life philosophers had attributed to life. In later hands, for example, the priority of life over structure and form becomes the thesis that action runs ahead of all conceptual and determining instances and structures. This thesis, in turn, entails, among other propositions, that action determines the instances and structures that allegedly determine it. Such an intuition has cropped up in Heidegger's early conceptions of thrownness and of the priority of involved practical dealing over reflection and theory; in Wittgenstein's account of rule following and in his conviction that action underlies language, thought, and reason; in H.-G. Gadamer's notion of continuous concept formation; in Derrida's and Judith Butler's notions of the performative citation of norms; and in what I am calling the "indeterminacy" of action.[62]

All the prefiguration in the world cannot sew up agency before it occurs. The endless becoming of social life effected in human action transpires in a social site that qualifies paths in numerous ways of import for action. Nothing, however, presettles or binds the direction that the progress of social affairs takes.

3. ENDLESS BECOMING

The social site, like any slice of reality, is home to continuous occurrences. Agency is the central motor of that steady current. Through the doings of

[61] Georg Simmel, *Lebensanschauung, vier metaphysische Kapitel* (Munich and Leipzig: Dunker and Humblot, 1918). According to my colleague Dan Breazeale, Fichte was the first to articulate this conception of human life.

[62] See Martin Heidegger, *Being and Time,* trans. John Macquarrie and Edward Robinson (Oxford: Blackwell, 1978), for example, sections 13, 16, 21, 29, 38; Ludwig Wittgenstein, *Philosophical Investigations,* trans. G. E. M. Anscombe (New York: Macmillan, 1958), sections 143–242; idem, *On Certainty,* trans. Denis Paul and G. E. M. Anscombe (Oxford: Blackwell, 1977), pars. 110, 204, 475; H.-G. Gadamer, *Truth and Method,* 2d rev. ed., trans. Joel Weinsheimer and Donald G. Marshall (New York: Crossroad, 1989), pt. 3, chap. 2, section c; Jacques Derrida, "The Force of Law: The 'Mystical Foundation of Authority,'" *Cardozo Law Review* 11, 5–6 (1990); Butler, *Bodies That Matter,* chap. 7; idem, *Excitable Speech* (New York: Routledge, 1997), chap. 4.

humans and nonhumans, practices are carried out and engage with orders, arrangements take form and channel practices, and the mesh they compose incessantly modulates. This ground-level movement is close kin to the molecular motion that Deleuze and Guattari ascribed to assemblages (see Chapter 2). Both are incessant stirrings pertaining to the entities of which arrangements are composed. Whereas Deleuze and Guattari, however, conceived of this movement as flows and quanta, I conceptualize it as a wave of doing. Agency is the chief dynamo of social becoming.

Constant doing must not be equated with change. Many human and nonhuman doings alike maintain the practice-order mesh as part of which they occur. Maintenance, accordingly, is not the absence of activity, but instead the occurrence of activity that perpetuates practices and reorders arrangements, minimally. Change, by contrast, comes about with activity that alters practices and orders more robustly.

The current section charts prominent forms assumed by the constant ground-level stirring that pervades the social site. Change enters its purview in two guises: as mutations that some doings themselves are and as alterations that various doings instigate in individual or interlinked practices and orders. Most existing theoretical accounts of sociohistorical change do not, admittedly, focus on practices and orders per se. Many theorize such phenomena as individual and collective action or institutional or systemic change, whereas others theorize transformations in specific large-scale social formations such as economies, governments, historical eras, gender relations, and technological systems. I do not relate my remarks on the developing practice-order mesh to changes in such phenomena or formations. Individual and collective action, like institutional change and transformations of the above social formations, should, in my opinion, be understood by reference to practice-order bundles. Upcoming examples provide some illustration of this thesis. Defending it in detail, however, would require lengthening the present book considerably with analyses of such topics as "we-ness" (groups), unintentional consequences of action, and the constitution of social formations.[63]

---

[63] One exception to my generalization about theories of social change not focusing on practices and orders is a slew of Darwinian, or selectionist, accounts. See, for example, Harré, *Social Being,* chap. 9; R. C. O. Matthews, "Darwinism and Economic Change," in *Economic Theory and Hicksian Themes,* ed. D. A. Collard et al. (Oxford: Oxford University Press, 1984), 91–117; and W. G. Runciman, *A Treatise on Social Theory,* vol. 2: *Substantive Social Theory* (Cambridge: Cambridge University Press, 1989). I do not confront these theories, though my account touches on Runciman's and Harré's ideas below.

The current section, moreover, does not amount to a general theory of change. The only general proposition about change that it advocates is that change comes about through agency. The following remarks, consequently, do not claim to identify all forms and mechanisms of development in the social site (i.e., all dynamic forms and mechanisms of practices, orders, and complexes thereof). My discussion likewise neither aims for systemicity nor seeks to fashion the forms and mechanisms it considers into a template that can be used either to order or to account for particular changes. It simply documents key shapes and ways of sociohistorical change, drawing on Shaker and day trading practices, orders, and complexes to illustrate them. At best, my discussion indicates the matters that can and should be documented in more detailed accounts of social change.

My account also, finally, does not address issues about either the nature of social explanation or the character and cogency of general explanatory theories of sociohistorical change. The only general thesis about explanation advanced in this chapter is that explaining change is a matter of charting the agency that constitutes and/or brings it about. I do not address the many epistemological and methodological issues that bear on the activities of uncovering, reporting, and charting agency. I do not, accordingly, defend the claim, which I nonetheless hold, that explanation is a matter of achieving sufficiently detailed surveyable descriptions of practices, orders, and complexes thereof.[64] The sorts of general explanatory theories I have in mind, furthermore, are those that propose principles or templates that apply to either societies as wholes, entire sectors of social life, or general types of social formations. What mechanisms, templates, and principles such theories should propose, for what these mechanisms, templates, and principles are good, whether they can ever be more than simplifying models of the complex movements and processes swirling in the social site, and whether this fact delegitimates them—all these questions are set aside here.

These remarks can be concretized by relating the following account to two theories that make practices central to social evolutionary processes. For W. G. Runciman, practices are "functionally defined units of reciprocal action informed by the mutually recognized intentions and beliefs of designated persons about the [respective power they possess] by virtue of their roles."[65] He

---

[64] For a version of this thesis in the philosophy of history, see Walsh's claim that explaining historical phenomena is a matter of giving finer-grained descriptions (W. H. Walsh, *An Introduction to the Philosophy of History* [London: Hutchinson, 1951]).

[65] Runciman, *A Treatise on Social Theory*, vol. 2: *Substantive Social Theory*, 41.

argues that practices so defined are the objects for which social evolution selects. This means, for him, that practices are the phenomena whose survival, spread, and demise are determined by social selection processes. Practices are selected, moreover, because of the advantages (or disadvantages) they bring to the groups of people ("systacts") who occupy the roles they carry, in the general competition for economic, ideological, and coercive power that occurs among humans. This implies that, according to Runciman, practices come and go on the basis of the advantages and disadvantages they bring these groups in their struggles with one another. For Rom Harré, on the other hand, practices are sequences of human doings and sayings (in my sense). They are generated by cognitive capacities and, in turn, constitute practical and expressive acts (in the way that, on my account, doings and sayings constitute actions). Likening practices and capacities to the vehicles and replicators theorized in Richard Dawkins's theory of evolution,[66] Harré stakes two claims. The first is that social evolution selects for the cognitive resources that give rise to practices. The second is that successfully replicating resources are selected for because the practices they generate are "adaptable" to social context (the selection conditions).[67] This means that cognitive resources come and go on the basis of the suitability, or unsuitability, of the practices they generate in the social environments in which these practices operate.

Runciman remarks that his theory says nothing about the mutation and combination processes that throw up the practices for which social evolution selects: "the social theorist can and must treat the emergence of variants as random—that is, ... not as uncaused and therefore inexplicable, but as independently caused and therefore explicable only at a different level."[68] Such a remark befits a sociological historian who focuses on broader social events and developments. Harré concurs that a theory of social evolution cannot explain changed capacities, which are at once new objects of selection. Because he is a social psychologist, however, he adds that investigators need not rest content with noting the existence of "personal fluctuations and innovations." They can also offer theories of mutational processes. The theory Harré proposes is that mutations in capacities (and, thereby, practices) sometimes occur because of tensions that arise from mismatches in people's positions in practical and expressive activities.[69]

---

[66] Richard Dawkins, *The Selfish Gene* (Oxford: Clarendon Press, 1976).
[67] Harré, *Social Being*, chap. 9.
[68] Runciman, *A Treatise on Social Theory*, vol. 2: *Substantive Social Theory*, 42.
[69] Harré, *Social Being*, 225–26, 246.

The mutation and combination of what Runciman and Harré call "practices" fall squarely in the domain of the incessant human (and nonhuman) doings that pervade the social site. These doings often maintain extant practices, orders, and practice-order complexes. As the current section documents, however, this perpetual swell can also reorder arrangements and both alter and underlie the emergence of practices and complexes. It harbors, furthermore, a dimension of unintended metamorphosis. The rush of doing thus constitutes and effects what Runciman and Harré call the "mutation" and "recombination" of practices. I believe that the forms and mechanisms of this movement are the stuff of social change in general. As indicated, however, I do not explore such issues as (1) how explanations of large-scale social phenomena are to be framed in terms of these forms and mechanisms and (2) whether there exist further templates and principles—such as selection—that *systematically* explain why practices, complexes, sectors, or sociohistorical formations develop as they do.

ORDERS

My map of endless becoming begins with the constant reordering of arrangements. All orders, to varying degrees, are reordered through actions performed by their components. The very physical movement of humans as they act, for instance, alters the spatial dimensions of the orders of which they are part. As a day trader, for example, works on the keyboard and interacts with fellow traders in the trading room, the spatial orders there metamorphose accordingly. More consequentially, arrangements are reordered through continual intervention into, and continual assumption of intentional directedness toward, them and their components. The trader's unremitting observation of market activity involves diverse tasks, varied graphics, varying doings and sayings, and multiple combinations of computers, pens, beepers, and other artifacts. In keeping tab on his or her stocks, he or she uses, transforms, and transports these graphics, machines, and materials variously, typically reinforcing, but sometimes altering, the causal, spatial, intentional, and prefiguration relations of the branch office arrangements.

The nonhuman components of orders also make significant contributions to the constant becoming that engulfs orders. At the office, for example, computers, computer networks, printers, pens, televisions, and beepers are continually doing things that maintain the arrangements there. They also sometimes act in ways that lead to alterations in these arrangements. Computer systems, for example, often crash and require adjustment, repair, replacement, and occasional transport. Because, furthermore, wiring can overheat and water can leak through roofs and into basements, wiring must be redone, roofs repaired, and the physical environment around the office so refashioned that rainfall flows away from the foundations. Termites and fires also can so rearrange things that humans have to respond. Arrangements, consequently, are continuously maintained and continually altered by the doings of their components.

Chapter 2 argued that orders are established in social practices. It should be apparent that the continual reordering of arrangements also occurs largely under the aegis of practices and their organization. All the actions that day traders perform when watching stock activity, selling or buying, keeping a diary, and discussing strategy are part of day trading (and various dispersed) practices; just as all the actions that technicians and workers carry out when dealing with computer networks, wiring, roofs, and foundations are moments of various sorts of repair (and dispersed) practices. Likewise, as discussed, the inexorable contribution of nonhumans to the perpetuation and alteration of arrangements is subject, to varying degrees, to practice-based determination. In particular, almost all those doings of the nonhuman components of office arrangements that maintain orders there occur under the aegis of practice organizations. Hence, the constant reordering that marks the social site transpires in the contexture of practices.

It follows that purely nominalist accounts of social arrangements are insufficient. As discussed, for example, Latour and Callon contend that the only phenomena relevant to the perpetuation and alteration of networks are transactions among their components, for instance, the doings detailed above. The only context in which these doings occur, moreover, is the texture of networks. All the contextures that social theorists claim these doings occur in are, in fact, aver Latour and Callon, nothing but nominalist effects of these networks. They are not, therefore, really contextures. Examples of such alleged contextures are power, society, capital, classes, ranks, hierarchies, professions, institutions, organizations, authority, roles, and culture.[70] Power, to take one example, is something people possess by virtue of the networks of which they are part, in particular, by virtue of how others connected to them act.[71] The possession of power is, thus, an effect of others' actions. It itself cannot determine these actions. Power, as a result, is not a contexture in which these actions occur. In

---

[70] This list is taken from Bruno Latour, "The Powers of Association," in *Power, Action, Belief: A New Sociology of Knowledge?* 264–80, here 276–77.

[71] Latour, "The Powers of Association," 264–66.

ways such as this, the phenomena that theorists claim form the contexture of networks are actually themselves effects of the doings of network components, which alone also account for the establishment, maintenance, and dissolution of networks.

This argument does not apply to practices. Indeed, practices are—and must be—absent from Latour's list of erstwhile contexturalist phenomena that are effects of what they supposedly determine. The human doings that (partially) account for the maintenance and progress of networks occur only as elements of the organized nexuses of activity that I call "practices." The reshuffling of orders, consequently, is contexturalized in practices.

Deleuze and Guattari offered a contextural depiction of the becoming inherent to assemblages that, with certain (albeit significant) modifications, can be carried over to arrangements as I conceive of these. Deleuze and Guattari focused on something they call "deterritorialization." Deterritorialization is the encompassing, and even continuous, metamorphosis through which assemblages evolve into other assemblages. All assemblages are subject to this process.[72] As Deleuze and Guattari wrote in *A Thousand Plateaus,* moreover, each *durée* of such a process is a "block of becoming," in which the humans, artifacts, and configurations thereof that make up an assemblage so reorganize that the assemblage that is becoming enters the "zone of proximity" of the assemblage that it is becoming (272–73). Strictly speaking, however, there is no "this" assemblage that becomes "that" assemblage in a block of becoming. Such a block is, instead, a continuous reorganizing of entities, on which a demarcation into starting and ending assemblage is imposed.[73] A block of becoming is the coexistence of the asymmetric movements of entities that are converging to form a new assemblage that is already metamorphosing into a new one through the continuing, divergent or convergent movements of these and further entities (cf. 293). At times, furthermore, something's motion catapults it completely away from the interweaving entities amid which it had previously moved. Exitings of this sort are usually accompanied by corresponding reterritorializations,

[72] Indeed, "a society, a social field, does not contradict itself, but what is primary is that it takes flight; it first of all flees in every direction" (Deleuze, "Desire and Pleasure," 187). See Deleuze and Guattari, *A Thousand Plateaus,* 90, 220, 398.

[73] "What is real is the becoming itself, the block of becoming, not the supposedly fixed terms through which it supposedly passes.... This is the point to clarify: that a becoming lacks a subject distinct from itself; but also that it has no term, since its term in turn exists only as taken up in another becoming of which it is the subject, and which coexists, forms a block, with the first" (Deleuze and Guattari, *A Thousand Plateaus,* 238).

in which departed entities either join extant formations, compose new assemblages together with other deterritorialized entities, or act as condensation seeds around which new assemblages grow. Deterritorializations of this more radical sort also often lead to the dissolution of the assemblages from which things have fled.

This conceptual apparatus provides a superlative depiction of the incessant rearranging that occurs in the social site. It captures how arrangements at the extract house or a day trading office, like those of the herbal medicine business and a day trading firm, like those of the complexes that make up the day trading and market-making industries, slowly metamorphose over time through the actions of their components. A range of historical events also fits the more radical sort of deterritorialization. When the chemist Long apostatized in 1860, for example, he deterritorialized away from the arrangements of the medicinal herb business and the Center Family more generally and reterritorialized on the assemblages of the Tilden Company, a competing pharmaceutical firm located across the Lebanon Valley. Of course, the notion of deterritorializing becoming cannot stand just as Deleuze and Guattari presented it. To begin with, the superstructure of abstract machines and social fields must, as discussed, be dropped. Moreover, the "asymmetric movements" of which becomings consist must be treated as the trajectories and effects of human and nonhuman agency. Human agency must also be understood as something contained in practices (i.e., as the performance of doings and sayings that constitute the actions that compose practices). All this implies, finally, that becoming must be conceived of as largely occurring under the aegis of the practice organizations.

PRACTICES

Practice organizations are not static. The understandings, rules, and teleoaffective structures that organize integrative practices frequently change. So, too, do the doings and sayings that constitute these practices. These two processes can be called "reorganization" and "recomposition." I reiterate that the constant flow of human and nonhuman doings, in addition to altering practices, maintains them. Human activity maintains a practice when it carries out bodily doings and sayings that (1) already constitute the practice and (2) express extant elements of the practice's organization. Clearly, much human activity accomplishes this. Activity can also, however, recompose and reorganize practices.

In the medicinal herb business, for instance, the following projects and tasks were among the many added over time: pressing the herbs into blocks, evaporating in the copper vacuum pan, operating the hydraulic press, producing ointments in addition to powders and powders in addition to extracts, assigning individuals to specific stations, cultivating herbs in a garden, purchasing herbs from outside vendors, repairing engines, and keeping cats to chase away rats. These tasks and projects were introduced, moreover, in response to occurrences of different types, for example, events befalling the arrangements at the extract house, changes in the Center Family (e.g., increased need for profit), and developments outside New Lebanon (such as fluctuating wishes of physicians, new operations at other villages, and the emergence of competing "worldly" firms). They also frequently reflected the ingenuity of the workers and forepersons. Rules, likewise, changed under various circumstances—as experience with the business's operations accumulated, as technical knowledge deepened and was formulated as explicit directions, when Long and Hollister followed recipes that professors and other outside chemists newly provided them, and when directives about work were handed down from the elders or the central ministry. Ends, by contrast, evolved little. Although pursuit of maximum profit seems to have fluctuated in accordance with changes in forepersons, the ends of making profit, meeting demand, maintaining stock, and keeping the machinery functional organized the medicinal herb practices more or less throughout their career. Notice that changes in ends, projects, tasks, and rules can involve borrowing elements of other practices or creating analogues to them. (Reordering also sometimes takes this form.)

The reorganization of rules and teleoaffective structures is an occasional and largely intentional process. By contrast, both recompositions of practices and shifts in their practical understandings are continual and largely unintentional events. Shaker workers regularly carried on the herb production practices through the performance of doings and sayings that were different from those performed before. This recomposition usually coordinated with the introduction of new machinery, orders, projects, and tasks, or responded to events that befell the orders at the extract house, including rearrangements that resulted from nonhuman causal interventions. For example, shuffled doings and sayings were performed coordinately with the introduction of the hydraulic press and the vacuum pan, rearrangements of the laboratory and extract house, the implementation of the new projects and tasks mentioned in the previous paragraph, the recurrent interventions of the rats, the frequent breakdowns in

equipment, the occasional fire, and the reorderings and reorganizations consequent on these phenomena (e.g., the changed location where coal was stored
consequent on a fire that started as a result of too much coal piling up next
to the boiler). Insofar, moreover, as the specific circumstances of action constantly altered, the specific movements performed amounted to endless variations on one another (this holds for human activity generally).

In most of these cases, especially those involving subtle variations of doings
and sayings, change was an unintentional consequence of intentionally sought-
after results. The Shakers' practical understandings of the actions that composed the medicinal herb practices similarly exhibited a metamorphosis that
no one controlled or intended and that, in most cases, occurred uncognized.
For example, Hollister's and Long's understandings of maceration and distil-
lation, that is, their grasp of which doings and sayings constituted those
actions in particular circumstances, evolved with experience, with changes in
their bodies (e.g., Hollister's loss of the fingers of his left hand in 1859), and
with changes of all the aforementioned sorts in the activities in and the orders
amid which Long and Hollister macerated and distilled. Only rarely, for example, on occasions of breakdown or instruction, did these understandings come
to attention and become explicit objects of concern. Such occasions were also
moments when doings and sayings swung into view and became possible
objects of deliberate manipulation.

The doings and sayings that people perform in carrying on integrative practices continually evolve because of changing circumstances, accumulating experience, bodily peculiarities, and shifts in the orders and practices that the
actions engage or are part of. Dispersed practices are subject to the same metamorphosis. Indeed, because dispersed practices are sets of doings and sayings
linked primarily by understandings alone, they are beset by constant unintended metamorphoses. The particular doings and sayings that constitute asking a question, describing something, and ordering someone to do something
are constantly changing because of accumulating experience and, above all,
constantly changing circumstances. Dispersed practices thereby constitute
transmogrifying rhizomes, whose advance in lacing through the social site is
probably the closest thing to continuous change found there. The pervasiveness
of dispersed practices secures the ubiquity of ground-level change in social life.

The general understandings that help organize integrative practices often
exhibit the same unintended metamorphoses that doings, sayings, and practical understandings do. They chiefly become objects of attention, however,

when formulated. Explicitization often reinforces such understandings through their further development or refinement (or through reaffirmation, indifference, or resignation). It can also, however, underwrite transformations in understanding—and not just by virtue of the disputation that explicitization makes possible, but also because the very event of formulation alters the situation: What was before unspoken, not thought through, or forgotten suddenly stands open to view. In the medicinal herb practices, explicitizations of the Shaker understanding of work as consecration and of the Shaker sense of communal solidarity served principally as renewal, palliative, reminder, or cudgel. In day trading practices, explicitizations of the wonders of the free pursuit of individual gain serve principally to renew lagging spirits, to celebrate victory, or to articulate pride and a sense of belonging. In neither case was or is the result altered understandings. Two reasons for this in the Shaker case were that these two general understandings pervaded more or less all Shaker practices and were regularly articulated in different arenas, above all in contexts of worship. As noted, however, things need not work this way. Formulation can also occasion contention and change. In addition, all general understandings, including those of the Shakers and day traders, are subject to unintended metamorphosis resulting from the variation exhibited by serial formulation. Shaker practices, incidentally, also exemplify a further point, which I do not defend here: General understandings need to be maintained through at least sporadic formulation. They cannot remain unspoken or unformulated indefinitely if people's actions are to continue expressing them.

The contribution of nonhumans to the reorganization and recomposition of practices must also be borne in mind. Changes in rules and teleoaffective structure often respond to the doings and combined doings of artifacts, organisms, and things (e.g., machinery, computers, software, horse, storms, herbs, and fires). Similarly, the evolution of doings, sayings, and understandings is often keyed to the doings of entities that people use or with which they must deal (e.g., computers, machinery, rats, steam, ink). Pests, repeated breakdowns, and climatic events, among many other things, can also occasion reflection about and evolutions in general understandings. In all these cases, moreover, the entities involved can come from within or without the social site.

As indicated, alterations in rules, teleoaffective structures, and general understandings occur intermittently, whereas unintended metamorphoses of doings, sayings, and practical understandings are continual or even continuous. Ends, moreover, shift more slowly than projects and tasks do. The fact that integrative practices are complexes of elements that alter at different rates raises the issue of what unifies such practices over time. In Chapter 2, I wrote that the unity of a practice is secured by its organization: Different doings and sayings constitute a given practice when they express elements of the same collection of understandings, rules, and teleoaffective structure. Given that such collections evolve, this account of unity must be refined to accommodate the temporality of practices.

An excellent analogue of the temporal unity of practices is found in the evolution of experimental systems in science as Rheinberger describes this.[74] Experimental systems, he explains, evolve through a reshuffling of their components to which no particular component or type thereof is in principle immune. (These components include skills, instruments, techniques, theories, and objects of investigation.) What enables such a system to remain the same system over time is the piecemealness of this reshuffling: Changes in particular elements are accompanied by continuity in others. Hence, experimental systems persist through alterations across time because of the type of history they undergo, one of continual, stepwise, and accumulative change amid general continuity. Such a history does not, of course, exclude the possibility that the composition of an experimental system at one moment can differ remarkably from its composition at a different moment.

Similarly, when components of its extant practice organization change piecemeal, or when multiple mutations are accompanied by continuities in other components, a practice lives on. In saying this, incidentally, I do not mean to assimilate practices to Rheinberger's experimental systems. Not only are practices, as I conceive of them, absent from Rheinberger's account, but systems, unlike practices, encompass material arrangements. I am simply pointing out an analogy between the temporal identities of practices and experimental systems. In any event, different sayings and doings over time constitute a given practice if and only if they express elements of a slowly modulating collection of understandings, rules, and structure. The evolution of the Shaker herbal medicine practices illustrates this process. By contrast, when changes in organization are vast or wholesale, or a practice's projects and tasks are simply no longer carried out, former practices expire (regardless of the fate of their components, individually or in clusters, and whether new practices have coalesced

---

[74] Hans-Jörg Rheinberger, *Toward a History of Epistemic Things: Synthesizing Proteins in the Test Tube* (Stanford: Stanford University Press, 1997), chaps. 5 and 11.

in their place). The transition from early SOES banditry to day trading illustrates this process since regulatory and technological changes led to massive change in projects and tasks. Similar remarks apply to the unity of an order over time. Of course, the line between piecemeal and multiple on the one hand and wholesale and massive on the other is undefined. As a result, whether a practice perpetuates or dissolves (and is replaced by a successor) is sometimes a judgment call keyed, inter alia, to chosen points of comparison and the broader situation amid which the changes involved take place. The line between the continuance and dissolution of a given practice is not, consequently, fixed. Nonetheless, it is the slow processional change in their organization that secures the unity of practices over time.

The default, and also predominant, state of practices in human life is slow metamorphosis and smallish punctual change. Given a sufficiently capacious time frame, such evolution can yield practices that differ considerably from those that existed before. Of course, gradual evolution is only one process through which different practices arise. Sometimes, for example, authorities create "new" practices through the massive overhaul or replacement of existent ones. The NASD and SEC regulations that helped give rise to day trading exemplify how authorities can bring about significantly altered practices. On other occasions, a nexus of activities of sufficient inter-relatedness to be a practice condenses around an idea, a novel technique, or a technological innovation. An example is contemporary communication practices anchored in electronic innovations. Practices differing from their predecessors also arise through the appropriation of extant bundles of activity for new purposes. The medicinal herb industry at New Lebanon came about in the 1810s, for example, through the realization that the extant and relatively simple practice of growing herbs for domestic use harbored the potential for earning profit. Different practices can also ensue, finally, when climatic and natural disasters, invasions of armies or microbes, and revolution or economic collapse interrupt, or even terminate, the evolution of practices and constellations thereof. When this occurs, practices and orders are often shattered into fragments—bundles of doings and sayings and/or ends, projects, and tasks—which are differentially taken up into the practices that now occupy the people and places previously home to the disrupted or destroyed ones. The quick hit tactics of SOES bandits, for instance, were absorbed into day trading. The American Civil War, moreover, had such an effect on the herb practices at different Shaker villages. During the war, Union and Confederate soldiers repeatedly beset the villages in Kentucky, demanding and receiving material sustenance. The ensuing drain on resources decimated the minor herb industries there. Fragments of the herb practices and orders (e.g., growing herbs, drying and storing them, the use of presses, and the aim of making profit) nonetheless continued in these villages as elements in other practices, orders, and bundles. A similar fragmentation occurred in most of the northern villages, in this case because of the loss of their southern routes and markets.

PRACTICE-ORDER COMPLEXES

The foregoing discussion has already indicated that the rearrangement of orders and the reorganization and recomposition of practices are linked phenomena. As discussed in the previous chapter, practices and orders form bundles, nets, and confederations, as well as wider and looser configurations with one another and with others of their own kind. Because of this interwovenness, they are co-determined, co-determining, and interdependently evolving entities. Human and nonhuman doings also alter different components of the practice-order mesh at different moments and at differential rates. The overall perpetuation and alteration of linked practices and orders is the temporal passage of the social site.

This section describes a number of dynamic forms and mechanisms that characterize the evolving mesh of practices and orders. In contrast to the processes described in previous paragraphs, which transpire in or to individual practices and orders, the present forms and mechanisms concern the evolution of either practice-order bundles or linked practices and orders more broadly. I emphasize that the particular forms and mechanisms presented do not exhaust those that exist. As indicated, moreover, my map of them does not constitute a theory of social change. The forms and mechanisms themselves, it might be added, are not models or posits, but instead phenomena that appear here and there in the social site. All of them, moreover, are effected in or work through human and nonhuman agency.

The first form of change is contagion. Contagion is not just the rapid spread of a practice, order, or practice-order complex through social life.[75] As I use the term, contagion is the rapid spread of a practice, order, or complex because of, first, previous dissemination of information about the practice and so on and,

---

[75] See D. A. Levy and P. R. Nail, "Contagion: A Theoretical and Empirical Review and Reconceptualization," *Genetic, Social, and General Psychology Monographs* 199 (1993): 235–84.

second, its attractiveness at achieving some end (e.g., solving some problem, satisfying some desire or need). Subsequent to its introduction, for example, the activity-arrangement packet through which herbs were packaged in block form quickly disseminated among Shaker villages. Word of its innovation spread quickly, and the advantage of the new packaging over the tin form was obvious. The rapid expansion of day trading presents another example. As my definition suggests, and as recent theorists of innovation have emphasized, social contagion, unlike to some extent its medical counterpart, does not occur under its own steam. It takes place because people appropriate practices and orders that exist elsewhere. It usually consists, consequently, in people bound up in one complex taking over activities and orders found in others. Notice that social contagion results from human activity alone, however much nonhuman activity might be part of what spreads. (Of course, appropriative activity might respond to nonhuman doings, for instance, those involved in electronic break-downs, the use of animals, and climatic distress.)

Like individual practices and orders, the bundles that practices and orders form are not static. Human and nonhuman doings constantly alter their contours through reorganization, recomposition, and reordering. The particular identity over time that characterizes practices also applies to practice-order bundles. Both day trading and the medicinal herb business illustrate this fact, though the latter does so considerably better given the short time that day trading has existed. During its lifetime, the medicinal herb business suffered continual or continuous alteration in its constituent projects, tasks, doings, sayings, machines, things, and arrangements; by 1870, say, it possessed a considerably different composition than at its inception in the 1810s. Its integrity over time lies in the character of its history, one of punctuated alteration and continual metamorphosis amid continuities of organization and arrangement. That the business was carried out for years in the same buildings, and that its equipment was moved into new buildings when these were readied in 1832 and 1851, are two, though only two, important pieces of continuity by virtue of which the same packet perpetuated through time.

Continuity of ends is a further important feature of practice-order packets, which helps establish their integrity over time. As noted, the aim of making profit and maintaining adequate stock organized the medicinal herb business throughout its history. That both the Shakers and their observers could look back and speak of the history of *the* business derived in part from this continuity, along with those just mentioned in buildings and equipment and

many other, temporally overlapping ones besides. I do not claim that unchanging ends are a necessary feature of practice-order bundles, that is to say, that
their integrity over time is tied to the continuing pursuit of particular ends.
The ends of a practice can change. Still, it so happens that the ends of bundles
do not change that often, and that occasions when either they are altered or
attempts are made to modify them are often junctures when bundles bifurcate
into multiple successors or are destroyed through conflict.

Practice-order bundles, as well as nets and confederations thereof, do not
develop independently of one another. Packets, orders, and practices link, and
interdependently arise, develop, and terminate, in multifold ways. Rheinberger
describes two dynamic processes at work in ensembles of experimental systems:
"hybridization" and "bifurcation." Hybridization is the "bringing together [of
experimental systems] whose articulation, amalgamation, and blending was
not assumed to lie in the nature of the things so brought together."[76] Bifurcation is the development of "offspring" systems that usually, though not always,
remain closely linked. Both these processes have analogues in social life. The
recent joining of day trading with online investing in futures markets illustrates the first, whereas growing disparities between day trading at firms and
at home is a nascent example of the second. To these two dynamic processes,
others can be added. As discussed in the previous chapter, for example, bundles,
nets, and confederations can both cohere and conflict. Examples are, respectively, the couplings of day trading with day trading firms and of the herbal
medicinal business with the village of New Lebanon, and the interactions of
day trading with market making and of the Shaker business with its increasingly diverse competitors after the Civil War. A further dynamic category
embraces processes in which something is incorporated into a practice-order
bundle, net, or confederation. One example is the fragmentation and appropriation described in the previous section. Another, which might be called
"insemination," involves the insertion of some element of a practice or order
into a bundle, whereupon the bundle proliferates. The incorporation of Level
II screens, which display current market maker bids and offers for stocks, into
day trading illustrates this process. There also occur processes, to which the
name "poisoning" can be given, where the insertion of some component of
practice or order eventually destroys a bundle, net, or confederation. Clearly,
a great number of dynamic processes such as these can be typologized.

[76] Rheinberger, *Toward a History of Epistemic Things: Synthesizing Proteins in the Test Tube*, 136.

In this context, consider Deleuze and Guattari's notion of a line of deterritorialization or line of flight. A line of flight is the path followed by an individual, tool, organism, thing, or group thereof, through whose actions a given assemblage is unraveling and maybe also metamorphosing into a different one.[77] As indicated in the previous section, Deleuze and Guattari contended that all assemblages suffer lines of deterritorialization, along which their dissolution and the coalescence of possible successors propagate. Regardless of whether the authors are right that social life is beset with constant dissolution, they correctly observed that parts of assemblages (in my language, components of practices, orders, and complexes thereof) can spin off and join other assemblages, bind together with other ejecta to form further assemblages, or act as condensation points around which new assemblages coalesce. These ejecta can be humans, artifacts, organisms, things, ends, projects, sayings, or combinations thereof. The formation of day trading firms—and of high-tech companies generally—provides numerous examples because the emergence of these firms, as to a lesser extent their dissolution, is tied to mobile individuals: All day trading firms have been founded by individuals who fled existing Wall Street or other large financial firms. The coalescence of day trading companies was also closely tied to the development of specific projects and artifacts, which individuals invented. A good example is Jeffrey Citron and Joshua Levine's development of software that enables day traders to monitor market maker activity and to sell short by hitting a single keyboard button.[78]

Apostasy offers a particularly clear example of these processes in Shaker life. Most individuals who fled the Shakers reterritorialized on existing assemblages. As noted, for instance, Long reterritorialized on a competing medicinal herb firm across the valley after leaving. Other individuals returned to their families. A few apostates, by contrast, set up industrial operations that exploited and cannibalized Shaker recipes, reputations, and practices. A former physician at New Lebanon, D. M. Bennett, for example, gave a certain S. D. Howe the recipe allegedly used at the village to produce Sarsaparilla Syrup. This Howe set up a company in New York to manufacture the syrup, called "Dr. S. D. Howe's Shaker Compound Extract of Sarsaparilla Syrup." Another example is William Tripure, the leader of a troupe known as the "Case Family," whose traveling road show in New York, Ohio, and Massachusetts in the

---

[77] See Deleuze and Guattari, *A Thousand Plateaus*, 283.
[78] See Matthew Schifrin and Scott McCormack, "Free Enterprise Comes to Wall Street," *Forbes* 161, 7, 6 April 1998, 114–19.

late 1840s featured men and women who whirled around and carried on in outlandish manners that were advertised and presented as genuine Shaker worship dances.[79]

Two further phenomena that secure the coordinated or interdependent evolution of practices, orders, and practice-order bundles, nets, and confederations are (1) the interdependent reactions of people and groups to events and (2) media of communication. What I have in mind with the first are the ways that events can alter the situations of participants in various practices and complexes, command their attention, and induce responses from them. Examples are assassinations, economic collapses, the issuance of new regulations, and droughts. In calling forth actions from large numbers of humans (and nonhumans), such events can lead to widespread coordinated or interdependent changes in the social site.

By "media of communication," I mean events, actions (including speech acts), and physical phenomena through which information flows among people who are carrying on the same or different practices at the same or disparate orders. Examples are puffs of smoke, fiber-optic cables, the sounding of sirens, electromagnetic waves, and the series of actions and events that constitute the delivery of mail from sender to recipient. Media of this general sort often decisively mediate changes in practices, orders, and complexes thereof. Notice that media of communication of this materialist sort differ from the media of communication of systems theory. For systems theorists, a medium of communication is, roughly, an avenue over which one person's actions influence those of others. Parsons characterized these media as symbolic in character: "[They] *control* behavior in the process of interaction. They do so, however, by *symbolic* means, i.e., by presenting the actor, not with an intrinsically important object, such as a food object, but with a symbolic 'representation' of such an object."[80] The symbolic character of Parsons's five media—language, money, power, value commitment, and influence—contrasts with the material and mere information-transmission character of what I call "media of communication." So, too, does the character of Habermas's media (money, power, and language), which are media of action coordination.[81] Effecting the control

[79] The two episodes are recounted in Galen Beale and Mary Rose Boswell, *The Earth Shall Blossom: Shaker Herbs and Gardening* (Woodstock, Vt.: Countryman Press, 1991), 140, 126–27, 243, n. 33.

[80] Talcott Parsons, "Interaction," in *The International Encyclopedia of the Social Sciences*, ed. David L. Shills (New York: Macmillan, 1968), 440

[81] Jürgen Habermas, *Theory of Communicative Action*, vol. 2: *Lifeworld and System: A Critique of Functionalist Reason*, trans. Thomas McCarthy (Boston: Beacon Press, 1987), for instance, 181–85. See

and coordination of action is only one way that media of communication link practices and complexes.

Politics is a final exemplary mechanism through which practices, orders, and complexes develop coordinately or interdependently. By "politics," I mean the collective intentional management of (some sector of) the social site. Because agency is the motor of the becoming and change that pervade that site, politics can also be understood as the collective intentional management of the directions and flows of agency. Politics is collective because it is an activity that people carry out together (regardless of how much contention and conflict are involved). It is intentional because participants know that its point is management and join in to help realize this end. By "management," moreover, I mean oversight, direction, and encumberment, in outline and at a general level.[82] Politics thus amounts to government, not in the Anglo-American sense of government institutions, but in the older sense of guiding and directing human conduct.[83] Politics of this sort takes the form of specific practices that are both contingently linked to particular orders (e.g., at government buildings) and tied in various ways to nonpolitical practices and complexes. An example is SEC practices, which take place at certain locales and are linked to the varied practices of market traders, including day traders. Another is the temporal activities of the central ministry at New Lebanon. Political activities secure coordinated change in multiple practices and complexes because decisions taken in political practices alter and prefigure activities in broader swaths of the social site. Politics is clearly a central feature of social life, a key determinant of the coordinated and interdependent directions that human, and also nonhuman, activity takes. According to this definition, moreover, the familiar contemporary thesis that politics is pervasive in social life becomes the proposition that

---

also Luhmann's analysis in, for example, Niklas Luhmann, "Einführende Bemerkungen zu einer Theorie symbolisch generalisierter Kommunikationsmedien," in his *Soziologische Aufklärung* 2 (Opladen: Westdeutscher Verlag, 1975), 170–92.

[82] This specification resembles Oakeshott's early definition of politics as the tending to general arrangements: Michael Oakeshott, "Political Education," in his *Rationalism in Politics and Other Essays,* new, expanded ed. (Indianapolis: Liberty Press, 1991), 43–69, 44.

[83] For discussions of governmentality, all resting on Foucault's resurrection of the older meaning of the term, see *The Foucault Effect: Studies in Governmentality,* ed. Graham Burchell, Colin Gordon, and Peter Miller (Chicago: University of Chicago Press, 1991); Alan Hunt and Gary Wickham, *Foucault and Law: Towards a Sociology of Law as Governance* (Boulder: Pluto Press, 1994); *Foucault and Political Reason: Liberalism, Neo-Liberalism, and Rationalities of Government,* ed. Andrew Barry, Thomas Osborne, and Niklas Rose (London: UCL Press, 1996); Jon Simon, *Foucault and the Political* (London: Routledge, 1996).

practices in which people join together to oversee and direct their and others' affairs are widespread in the social site. Traders joining together to challenge the policies of day trading firms is an example of such so-called micropolitics.

The dynamic forms and mechanisms so far discussed—contagion, continuity over change, hybridization, bifurcation, fragmentation and appropriation, coherence, conflict, insemination, common events, media of communication, and politics—are features of the moving mesh of practices and orders. They are general constellations of linked human (and nonhuman) activity. They also manifest that practices, orders, and configurations do not simply interlace, but also progress interdependently. It might be noted that these interdependencies transpire through the same sinews through which practices and orders are interwoven: chains of action, intentional relations, doings and sayings that belong to multiple practices, organizational elements common to different practices, and physical, above all communication, links among orders. For example, untold chains of actions link day trading practices to those of day trading firms, market maker firms, the SEC, and so on, just as myriad chains linked the medicinal herb practices at New Lebanon to all the other practices of the Center Family. I mention this obvious fact because, although most of these links are too trivial to warrant mention in the annals of historiosocial science, any of them, given the right circumstances, could have turned out to be consequential. What is more, of each of them one never knows *ante eventum,* and often does not and cannot know *post factum,* whether it, because of a strange twist of history, actually initiated a major change or otherwise significantly contributed to the development of social affairs (cf. the so-called butterfly effect). Indeed, little imagination is required to transform particular action chains, such as herb workers making excursions to use the equipment in the buildings of other industries, into "important" historical events. The significance of fine details is a further feature of the wave of human and nonhuman doings that maintain and alter the social site.

Two final categories of changes: The first includes all those events and processes that occur to or are propagated by the organisms and things, and in particular the organisms and things of nature, which enter human coexistence. The spread of rats through various orders, not only at New Lebanon, but pervasively through the social site, is one example. Another is the variety of climatic processes that transpire in the earth's atmosphere. Processes such as these do not necessarily take place within the social site. Insofar, however, as they or their consequences impinge on this site and modify arrangements, bring about crippled or changed practices, or constitute phenomena to which people respond, they contribute to the progress of social life.

The second category of change encompasses the reorderings, reorganizations, and recompositions that result from thought and cognition. "Idealist" depictions of intellectual history as a procession of miraculous geniuses and new ideas qua uncaused causes have recently fallen on hard times. Building on ideas that date back to Marx, social history has taught that fathoming both the emergence and the character of intellectual products requires appreciating the wider intellectual and sociocultural fields in which they occur.[84] However salutary this correction might be, it is important not to swing too far in the other direction and to dissolve the thought, cognition, and inspiration of individuals into their contexts. However tied to circumstance, discipline, training, personal history, and cultural background unprecedented or innovative ideas may be, they largely emerge because of the fortunes of circumstance or because individuals make an effort to think and imagine (which is not to say that they control what, if anything, results). To be sure, new ideas are not uncaused causes, and geniuses do not invent their thoughts from whole cloth. Yet such ideas are not totally explicable through what precedes them, and geniuses, as well as lesser lights, do bring forth ideas and products that differ from the existing stock. Hence, an account of the progression of the social site that leaves out the creative contribution of individuals—working alone or in teams, in disciplines or as part of the wider scene of cultural, technical, and intellectual production—overlooks an absolutely crucial site of innovation, rearrangement, and reorganization. The contributions of Citron and Levine to the emergence of day trading was noted above. When, to take another example, Sarah Babbitt of the Harvard Shaker village was watching a weaver at her spinning wheel one day, it occurred to her that a circular saw would facilitate many cutting tasks.[85] Such a saw was promptly constructed, and circular saws soon spread to other Shaker villages because of their usefulness. Babbitt's sudden idea started a current of human and nonhuman activity that spread through the social site and reorganized, as well as rearranged, practices and orders

I do not have anything original or significant to say about insight, thought,

[84] For discussion, see Fritz Ringer, "The Intellectual Field, Intellectual History, and the Sociology of Knowledge," *Theory and Society* 19 (1990): 269–94. See also Reinhardt Koselleck, *Critique and Crisis* (Cambridge, Mass.: MIT Press, 1988).

[85] See Edward R. Horgan, *The Shaker Holy Land: A Community Portrait* (Harvard, Mass.: Harvard Common Press, 1982), 72.

and imagination in this context. My only point is that the panorama of endless becoming in the social site cannot be satisfactorily grasped if it is referred only to phenomena of the ilk of contagion, coherence, insemination, politics, rodent migration, and atmospheric disturbance. The contribution of individual thought and insight in initiating currents and redirecting extant ones must not be forgotten.

I conclude this section by discussing how the energeticalness of the social site undercuts, or better, uproots as oppositions two key dualisms through which theorists have analyzed social affairs: stability-change and continuity-discontinuity. Although several contemporary theories challenge the oppositional character that their predecessors accorded these dualisms, it might be of interest to point out how the endless movement of human and nonhuman agency also does so.

The doings and sayings that sweep the social site both maintain and alter practices, orders, and complexes thereof. These doings and sayings are subject to unintended metamorphosis. Both the maintenance and alteration of rules and teleoaffective structures, consequently, are effected through continually transmogrifying streams of activity. It follows that social life, during any given *durée,* cannot be dichotomously analyzed as either stable or changing (and not both). Whatever stability qua perpetuation of the same rules and teleoaffective orders occurs coexists with continual modulation. Teleoaffective structures and rules are also subject to intermittent and even frequent alteration. All told, then, stability and change come together in the social site. There is no question of *either* stability *or* change. The only question is how slight or prodigious the differences are over time among the doings and sayings, rules, and teleoaffective structures that compose practices. "Social stability" (or "maintenance") connotes slight alteration—for instance, the usual unintended metamorphosis plus minor changes in practice organizations plus well-behaved nonhumans. "Social change" implies substantial or larger-scale modifications in one or more of these registers. Where exactly, consequently, stability gives way to change is relative to the comparisons that an investigator has in mind, the aspects of practices highlighted, and which contexts of the activity examined he or she considers.

Largely responsible for this mixing and relativizing of stability and change is the fact that the same streams of activity constitute-effect both phenomena. As suggested in the discussion of Laclau and Mouffe in the previous chapter, it is a mistake to divide activity into two classes coordinate with the stability-change dichotomy. The question can never be whether practices, orders, and complexes are stable or changing, but only whether they are more or less stable and changing, in which registers, and in which mixes. What is more, the continual metamorphosis of activity cannot be dismissed as too trivial a phenomenon to undercut such a significant dichotomy as stability-change. Any of the slight or robust differences that appear in the flow of activity can be in principle—however rarely this turns out to be the case—the beginning of more momentous changes.[86] The above dissolution of the opposition between stability and change acknowledges this fact and encourages the search for obscure and modest beginnings in the historical record.

This dissolution yields the additional conclusion that explanations of stability and explanations of change do not form distinct epistemological categories. As indicated, I do not pursue this topic. I simply, and baldly, assert that explaining social affairs requires an apparatus that charts and accounts for the paths and orientations of activity. Because, consequently, activity effects both stability and change, the apparatus used to account for activity applies to both.[87]

The fate of continuity-discontinuity is clearly that of stability-change. Human and nonhuman activity is perpetually introducing differences (of activity, organization, ideation, materiality, and order) into the social site. The endless becoming of the social, in other words, is a *continual production of difference*. Because, therefore, discontinuity is built into the fabric of continuous activity, continuity and discontinuity cannot be posed as mutually exclusive, alternating states of social life. Rules, teleoaffective structures, and general understandings are similarly subject to intermittent and frequent modification. It follows that practices and practice-order complexes exhibit diverse mixes of continuity and discontinuity and that "continuous" or "discontinuous" practices and complexes are ones that display, respectively, slight or more momentous differences in one or more of their registers. Once again, therefore, just where continuity gives way to discontinuity is a matter of points of comparison, focuses of attention, and broader contexts. Discontinuity cannot, in any event, be stylized as a deep rent in the social site.

Foucault offered a lucid explication of this latter truth. A discontinuity, he

---

[86] Giddens argues, similarly, that replacing the synchrony-diachrony dichotomy with his notion of structuration entails that the possibility of change inheres in every moment of reproduction; cf. Anthony Giddens, *Central Problems in Social Theory: Action, Structure, and Contradiction in Social Analysis* (Berkeley and Los Angeles: University of California Press, 1979), 114, cf. chap. 6.

[87] Similarly, although he does not put things this way, Giddens's theory of structuration (of action and structure) contains the basic armature with which he explains both stability and change. See Giddens, *Central Problems in Social Theory,* chap. 2, for the package, and chap. 6 passim, for its implications for change and explanation.

declared, is a "'phenomenal' set of mutations"[88] To discern such a set is, simply, to register a problem. A discontinuity is not an unintelligible break in an "inert continuum," but a singularity in a field of crisscrossing series that embraces change as well as perpetuation. The problem that the recognition of a discontinuity sets, consequently, is how to explain a particular singularity. According to Foucault, this task should be executed through "eventalization," which involves breaking the singularity down into its component processes and relating these processes to the ongoing series of practices, techniques, discourses, and procedures that gave rise to them.[89] In such a "polyhedron of intelligibility," the so-called discontinuity becomes simply a unique complex that is brought about through the convergence and interweaving of multiple, heterogeneous series. Discontinuities, consequently, are singularities in a complex field of advancing, linking, and intersecting apparatuses. They are moments, it can be said, of significant difference, which contrast with the advancing streams bringing them about, which are series of continual and less significant differences.

What, then, of that age-old shibboleth novelty? What is the "new"? New is that which is significantly different in some regard(s) from what went before. Significance, however, is not laid into the fabric of social life as difference is (via being). As with the transitions from stability to change and from continuity to discontinuity, just where alterations of the old give way to the emergence of the new is a matter of comparison, context, and judgment. It is not an inherent feature of practices, orders, and their components. Old-new can thus be added to the other two dualisms as a dichotomy that cannot be construed as an either-or, whose terms strictly speaking designate overlapping phenomena, and which is best reinterpreted as an elastic distinction relative to context.

4. SOCIAL HISTORY AS A NATURAL HISTORY

My discussion in the previous three sections has focused on the becoming and change endemic to the social site.[90] Questions about the relation of these

---

[88] Michel Foucault, "Questions of Method," in *The Foucault Effect: Studies in Governmentality*, ed. Graham Burchell, Colin Gordon, and Peter Miller (Chicago: University of Chicago Press, 1991), 73–86, here 75. Compare the discussion of discontinuities in Foucault, *The Archaeology of Knowledge*, chap. 1.

[89] Foucault, "Questions of Method," 76–77.

[90] An earlier version of this section was incorporated into my essay, "The Social Bearing of Nature," *Inquiry* 43 (2000): 21–38.

processes to nature were largely put aside. I want now to bring nature back into the picture. Building on the discussion of the society-nature divide in the previous chapter, this concluding section sketches a conception of social history as a natural history. It thereby demonstrates one way that social life and nature can be analyzed as horizontally locked, instead of vertically ordered.

Westerners have long viewed nature as a wide expanse that extends beyond, and in all likelihood predates, humanity and the human sociality that have taken up abode in it. Such a view suggests that either (1) nature forms a backdrop against which society develops at least semiautonomously, or (2) social life, appearances perhaps notwithstanding, is in fact part of nature. Indeed, this either-or articulates the two conceptions of the relation of natural to social change that have dominated the Western imagination since the mid-nineteenth century: social change as something that spirals away from natural change and obeys principles other than those of the latter versus social change as a piece of, and ultimately subject to, the laws of natural alteration. The thesis defended in the previous chapter, that nature is part of the social site, challenges both these construals of the relation between natural and social change.

Nature is certainly, inter alia, a backdrop against which society develops: The realm of natural entities, together with whatever principles that changes in these entities obey, extends well beyond whatever part of that realm is *also* part of the social site; that is to say, whatever natural entities are something through and around which human sociality transpires. Yet, nature is *also,* as this formulation acknowledges, part of the social site. Indeed, it was an especially prominent part of this site when the latter first emerged. Moreover, the social site is a place where the fate of nature is determined, both the fate of surrounding nature, as has occurred from the dawning of human history, and that of "inner" nature, as is increasingly the case today. As a transformed sphere, nature is likewise an omnipresent component and determinant of the course of social life—something made into human fabrications (e.g., computers, extracts, and day trading offices), something transformed into mongrels (e.g., cut stones in cellar floors, horse-power system couplings, genetically altered mice, prosthetic technology), and something converted into the second nature that surrounds humans and forms a crucial dimension of the geobiosphere in which they coexist (e.g., forests, electricity, the ozone hole). Consequently, because nature is both part of the social site and transformed there, social life has never, in the course of its development, left nature behind. More specifically, nature around us is always present as more stuff to admire, explore, and transform (that is an observation about history, not my personal evaluation of nature); second nature is an omnipresent product, feature, and determinant of social life; and nature in us constantly accompanies and undergirds all developments in human life. Hence, any conception of social change that portrays it as spiraling away from natural change cannot be adequate.

The other dominant approach to the relation of social to natural change absorbs sociality (and humanity) into nature and treats it as a natural—physical, biological, or ecological—phenomenon. According to this approach, social change is part of nature. It is a process that inter-relates, and thereby forms a system, with the developments of both nonhuman life and the earth's geo-climate. Social history, accordingly, is a natural history, where natural history is defined as the development of nature. This biological-ecological conception of social change as a natural process is the dominant contemporary conception of human history as a natural history.

There is something to this general approach. Humans *are,* in part, nature. Moreover, nature in and surrounding us is part of human coexistence and the social site. Hence, natural processes and the principles governing them must somehow apply to social life. The social site, however, is a human practices-artifact-nature nexus. Consequently, its progress must be subject not to natural processes and principles alone, but to teleological and social ones as well. As mentioned, moreover, the social site is a place where nature is transformed, including that nature without which human life would be impossible. It would be odd if the development of that which is at least partly responsible for both the fate of nature and the forms of second nature were itself subject solely to the processes and principles of nature.

It is imperative, consequently, (1) that some significant distinction be maintained between social life and nature, (2) that social history be accorded distinctness and partial independence from natural change, and (3) that an amalgamation of social history and natural change be imagined that encompasses varied developmental processes and mechanisms. To uphold these theses, however, and still comprehend human history as a natural history (the presence of nature in the social site indicates that it should be so conceived in some sense), a conception of natural history different from the above dominant one is required. For reasons mentioned in the previous paragraph, it will not do, as bioecological approaches insist, to construe natural history simply as an affair of nature, such that human natural history, including the history of the social site, is the development of a particular dimension of nature. Furthermore, it behooves anyone who approaches human history from the side of social inquiry, which champions human activity as the chief determinant of social affairs, to imagine a history in which the social and the natural are entwined. One might even be tempted to reverse the polarities and treat society and nature as the major and minor players, respectively.

A propitious alternative was developed by the young Karl Marx, above all in the *1844 Manuscripts*. [91] This text swims at once in and against a German tradition—originating in Kant and continued today by certain philosophical anthropologists—which draws a hard division between nature and causality, on the one hand, and history and freedom on the other. According to Marx, natural history is the development of humankind through its entanglement with nature, that is to say, the development of humankind *as* something so entangled. In conceptualizing such a development, Marx opposed those myriad nineteenth-century schemes that elevated humans above nature and thereby separated history from nature. Marx agreed with these schemes that history is initiated by the appearance of humanity. He refused, however, to treat history as a process that spirals away from and is only contingently connected with natural processes. Instead, in history the character of what predates it, nature, and the character of that whose appearance sets it off, humankind, become mutually dependent and subsequently change in tandem. Humankind progresses through its transformation of nature, just as nature changes through its encounter with humans. History, consequently, is the development of, in Marx's words, "naturalized man" and "humanized nature." For Marx, consequently, human history is a natural history (primarily) because it embraces changes in the transformation of nature and in relations between humans and natural beings. [92]

To capture the interaction between humankind and nature that contributes to the development of each, Marx famously developed the idea of the "metabolism" of humankind with nature. I believe that, today, this idea used metaphorically offers the most promising framework through which to approach social history as a natural history. Marx is right that the development of human

[91] Marx, *Economic and Political Manuscripts of 1844*.
[92] For a parallel interpretation of Marx, see John Bellamy Foster, *Marx's Ecology: Materialism and Nature* (New York: Monthly Review Press, 2000). For a convergent conception of natural history, see Yrjö Haila and Richard Levins, *Humanity and Nature: Ecology, Science, and Society* (London: Pluto Press, 1992); in a biological context, Richard Levins and Richard Lewontin, *The Dialectical Biologist* (Cambridge, Mass.: Harvard University Press, 1985).

life should neither be reduced to a natural process nor analyzed through a hypostatized dualism of society and nature. On the one hand, human practices are social, not natural phenomena. On the other hand, not only do society and nature overlap, but hypostatizing the dualism slights the fact that fabrications and mongrels have increasingly replaced unmodified human bodies and surrounding nature as axes and mediators of human coexistence. Day trading, like the entire Nasdaq market, makes this palpable. This is not to deny either that surrounding nature remains a reservoir from which new artifacts (including second nature) constantly emerge, or that nature in us continues to sustain human existence. But practices, artifacts, and nature form an evolving complex to whose development each component makes various contributions. None of these components should be reduced to another or thought to swing free and to develop independently. The metaphor of metabolism captures the evolving, consuming, and creative order-maintaining and -dissolving tangle of processes that pervade the practice-artifact-nature complex and constitute its development.

Marx supposed that nature is passive: The activity at work in the metabolism of humankind with nature is that of humans alone. He also confined this metabolism to the domain of production. As discussed, however, artifacts and nature are also doers. Moreover, however dominant production might have been in earlier phases of human history, it is important today (and also in anticipating an increasingly artifactual future) to expand the scope of this metabolism to embrace any domain of social existence. Indeed, the metabolic process is complex and multifold, embracing:

1. The continual transformation in human practices both of nature (including the human body) into artifacts (including second nature) and of artifacts into further artifacts. Once all industrial "production" that sustained human life fell here. Today, less and less of the sustaining industrial and informational production does so. As compensation, the human body is increasingly the target of such transformation.
2. The continual transformation by artifacts both of nature into artifacts and of artifacts into further artifacts. Industrial and informational processes of this sort are increasingly prevalent today, and the possibility of their dominance has been the fodder of imagined utopias ever since the advent of factory machines in the nineteenth century.
3. The constant alteration of practices and artifacts in response to nature.

Prominent examples are many of the precautions humans take in response to biological, geological, and climatic threats.

4. The intermittent and sometimes lethal incursion of nature into the social site.

5. The constant erosion of artifacts because of nature. The physical maintenance of equipment is a remarkably costly enterprise that constitutes an impressive proportion of economic and household operations everywhere.

6. The continual alteration of practices in response to artifacts (including second nature). Every invention and transformation of the environment has had this effect. As the arrangements amid which we live become ever increasingly artifactual, the pace of such alterations hastens. Many precautions taken against ecological threats also fall into this category.

7. The determination of activity and practices by inner nature, that is to say, by the human body, and the subjection of this determination to biological selection. (This category excludes those processes in which intentional activity is neurophysiologically realized.) The most prominent sort of bodily determination of human activity is alleged genetic determinations of phenotypic behavior. Other familiar examples are the neurophysiological determination of deviant behavior and brute preference (e.g., for flavor of ice cream), the olfactory determination of sexual partner, and the establishment of activity by biological rhythms.

8. The conditioning of biological selection by developments in the social site. This is a controversial category given current disagreement about the length of time required for social changes to stabilize alterations in the human genome that underwrite new phenotypic characteristics. Finally,

9. Biochemical-physical continuity between the body and surrounding nature. This is a highly speculative category acknowledged here for the sake of completeness. The embeddedness of circadian rhythms in wider, species-nonspecific and biosphere-pervading rhythms would be an example.

These categories are disparate. They also do not capture the many ways in which humans, artifacts, and nature prefigure one another's activity. Not only, moreover, are the specific processes that fall under these categories varied. They also, most importantly (though I do not argue the point here), neither form wholes of any rigorous sort nor are subject to overarching principles that organize the changes they embrace and lend these changes and processes order or direction. Whatever patterns are discernible from the bird's-eye perspectives of general historians emerge as by-products of the rich and intricate congeries of processes that contingently join and fall apart with (and partly as) the passage of the social site. In other words, the movement of the social site is the execution of myriad smallish, contingently bundled and disconnected processes of different kinds whose outcomes are indeterminate before their occurrence, bundling, and disconnection. Their only overall "form" is the social ontology that establishes the dimensions of natural history.

In recognizing diversity, the above scheme contrasts with those coevolutionary approaches to natural history that focus exclusively on, and thereby reduce the history of human existence to, the evolution and determination of human activity or human culture (defined as ideational units).[93] These approaches slight the activity of artifacts, the transformation of nature, and the full range of processes that link practices, "ideation," artifacts, and nature. I laud these approaches for recognizing the difference, distinctness, and at least semi-autonomy of social evolution from biological evolution/genetic determination (though not necessarily from natural selection or Darwinian principles generally). As accounts of natural history, however, they are too limited. This charge applies all the more to those coevolutionary views that acknowledge a distinction between natural and social evolution only to draw the latter back into the former ontologically and explanatorily.[94] Biological selection is just one process at work in this overall movement.

Natural history is the evolution of the metabolism of humans with nature. The social site is where this metabolism transpires (in the second sense of site distinguished in Chapter 2). This is because processes of the above-enumerated sorts occur in and to the mesh of practices and arrangements that composes that site. For instance, human transformations of nature, responses to nature, and artifact maintenance all transpire as moments of industrial, housing, scientific, informational, medical, and hobby (etc.) practices. These transformations, responses, and maintenances also typically involve alterations of arrangements of humans, artifacts, organisms, and things of which the people executing them are elements. Similarly, artifactual transformations of nature into artifacts, and

[93] See, for example, Richard Boyd and Peter J. Richerson, *Culture and the Evolutionary Process* (Chicago: University of Chicago Press, 1985); William H. Durham, *Coevolution: Genes, Culture, and Human Diversity* (Stanford: Stanford University Press, 1991); Daniel Dennett, *Darwin's Dangerous Idea: Evolution and the Meanings of Life* (New York: Touchstone, 1995).

[94] See, for example, Charles J. Lumsden and Edward O. Wilson, *Genes, Minds, and Culture: The Coevolutionary Process* (Cambridge, Mass.: Harvard University Press, 1981), and so-called Darwinian anthropology more generally.

of artifacts into further artifacts, like artifactual inducements of changed human activity, typically transpire through alterations of the arrangements or practices through which people coexist. Examples of such transformations and inducements are the steaming of herbs gathered in the wild in steam chests, the use of industrial robots, and changes in herbal medicinal production practices coordinate with the introduction of new machines. Generally speaking, consequently, the social site mediates the metabolism of humankind with nature.

Do metabolic processes of types 4 and 7 fall within the social site? As discussed, nature's destruction of practices and arrangements, like the bodily determination of human activity, occurs through natural processes such as plagues and earthquakes that originate outside and can extend well beyond the social site. These natural processes are *interruptions,* however, only insofar as they affect human existence. The difference, furthermore, that they make to social life reflects the practices that the humans involved carry on. (This is utterly true, as indicated, of the meanings interruptions have for people.) Qua component of the human metabolism with nature, consequently, natural interruptions are mediated by society. This might also hold of processes of type 7. All theories, for instance, that conceptualize the genetic determination of behavior as the coding of programs that generate different behaviors in different human lives and cultures[95] concede that genetic determination is socially mediated. Neurophysiological determination of deviancy, preference, and sexual partners might similarly be subject to social molding.

It is reasonable to hypothesize, consequently, that Marx is right that the social site mediates the entire human metabolism with nature. Recall conversely, however, that nature, including now second nature, mediates much of social life. Human activity always depends on bodily neurophysiological operations, and most of what is taken for granted as human life would be impossible without the nature that has been absorbed, or *aufgehoben,* in varying degrees of effacement, into the second nature and constellations of artifacts amid which humans proceed. Social life is just as dependent on inner and ultimately surrounding nature as it itself mediates the human metabolism with nature.

These thoughts lead to a final formulation of human natural history. The shape of human activity is tied to both the human body and the character of

---

[95] See, for instance, John Tooby and Leda Cosmides, "The Psychological Foundations of Culture," in J. Barkow, L. Cosmides, and J. Tooby, eds., *The Adapted Mind: Evolutionary Psychology and the Generation of Culture* (New York: Oxford University Press, 1992), 19–136.

the evolving practices of which it is a moment. At the same time, the evolution of practices is tied to the presence and transformation of nature, second nature, and artifacts in them. Qua the study of the history of humankind as something entangled with nature, consequently, natural history addresses the presence of and transformation of inner and surrounding nature, in and in relation to human practice and its products, whose own characters are tied to an evolved social mesh of practices and orders that is itself transformed through its entanglements with these natures, artifacts, and practices.

CODA

This book has analyzed the constitution of sociality through an account of the social site, the context as part of which human coexistence inherently transpires. This site is an overall mesh of practices and orders, itself organized as a nexus of practice-order bundles, nets, and other complexes. This mesh is also carried along and altered by streams of human and nonhuman doings, though human activities enjoy primary responsibility for maintaining and transforming its forms.

My attention has focused on ontological matters. Although many of these issues—for example, the character of social order and of practices, the role of agency in the social site, the bearing of nature on social life, and the forms and mechanisms of social change—are central to social thought, my account has left many further crucial questions untouched. The book's ontology provides, however, a starting point from which some of these questions can be approached.

One battery of unaddressed issues is the epistemological questions that are the central focus of most philosophy of social science. I explained in the preface that addressing these issues would distract from the ontological concerns that are my chief interest. Although I have occasionally noted or commented on epistemological issues that immediately attend or bear on proffered ontological theses, I have assiduously avoided engaging these issues in any detail. Social ontologies, however, hold considerable consequences for the character of social investigation. I hope, for example, that my depiction of day trading gave some indication of what multiscalar description of human coexistence looks like on my account. As this depiction suggests, to describe social life and social phenomena is to detail the practice-order complexes that are at once that as part of which human coexistence occurs and that which constitutes such phenomena. An important issue that arises in this regard is how an investigator identifies the contours of specific practice-order complexes. Furthermore, I stated that my ontology implies that to explain social affairs is to chart and to account for the agencies that bring them about. Little, however, was said beyond this. Left unaddressed were also the hermeneutic implications of my ontology, that is to say, its implications for interpretation and for understanding others.

A second general task is conceptualizing specific social domains in the terms of the ontology. Although, for instance, my examples have been economic, I have not attempted to offer either a general characterization of economies or analyses of specific economies. I believe much can be learned from thinking of economies as made up of linked bundles, nets, and confederations. Little has also been said about politics in the current work, though politics is a crucial mechanism bearing on social becoming and change. As explained, politics is the intentional, collective effort to manage the overall shape of some sector of the social site. Human fortunes partly rest on success and failure at this task. Social life, in fact, is scarcely imaginable in the absence of politics, which is rendered practically necessary by such phenomena as unintentional consequences of action, people's lack of overviews of the social sites as part of which they live, the ways humans and nonhumans cut into and exit orders and practices, and the indeterminacy of action. Conceptualizing politics as a set of practices linked to sundry orders and practice-order complexes is, clearly, a portentous task.

Carrying out this task requires special attention to two phenomena. The first is collective agency, or "joint" actions, many of which are carried out by "we's," that is to say, groups. Unlike theorists of the group sort of individualism, who take we's to be the primordial, and perhaps only genuine, social phenomenon, I believe that collective agency and groups should be analyzed as all social formations should: as aspects of the mesh of practices and orders. The formation of groups and the performance of collective actions are the institution and carrying out of practice nexuses of a particular sort. The second phenomenon is power. Power has not been absent from the present account. Hierarchies, for instance, were examined in chapters 1 and 2 as features of orders and practices. Both authority and disputation, moreover, were broached and closely tied to teleoaffective normativity. I have not, however, directly addressed this phenomenon or examined accounts of power that are congenial with the present ontology.

A third set of topics concerns the mutual penetration and determination that exist between the social site and nature. I demonstrated that the social site and nature are so related and that this being the case has implications for conceptualizing human history. I have not, however, delved into the contents of human social-natural history. Writing this history in the terms of the book's ontology is a yet unexecuted and—given the state of the earth and the dominance of biological and ecological conceptions of human natural history—pressing task. To take it up is, among other things, to acknowledge the responsibility that human activity holds for the state of the contemporary social site and for the nature and second nature with which it is inescapably coupled.

LIST OF REFERENCES

Adorno, Theodor. *The Jargon of Authenticity.* Trans. Knut Tarnowski and Frederic Will. Evanston: Northwestern University Press, 1973.

Akrich, Madeleine, and Bruno Latour. "A Summary of a Convenient Vocabulary for the Semiotics of Human and Nonhuman Assemblies." In *Shaping Technology/Building Society: Studies in Sociotechnical Change,* ed. Wiebe J. Bijker and John Law, 259–64. Cambridge, Mass.: MIT Press, 1992.

Alexander, Jeffrey. *Theoretical Logic in Sociology,* vol. 1: *Positivism, Presuppositions, and Current Controversies.* Berkeley and Los Angeles: University of California Press, 1982.

———. *Twenty Lectures: Sociological Theory Since World War II.* New York: Columbia University Press, 1987.

Althusser, Louis. *For Marx.* Trans. Ben Brewster. London: Allen Lane, 1969.

———. "Marx's Immense Theoretical Revolution." In Louis Althusser and Etienne Balibar, *Reading Capital,* trans. Ben Brewster, 182–93 London: New Left Books, 1970.

Andrews, Edward Deming. *The Community Industries of the Shakers.* Albany: State University of New York Press, 1933.

———. *The People Called Shakers,* new enlarged ed. New York: Dover, 1963.

Andrews, Edward Deming, and Faith Andrews. *Work and Worship Among the Shakers.* New York: Dover, 1974.

Anon. *Account Book,* New Lebanon, 1860–62. Edward Deming Andrews Memorial Shaker Collection, Winterthur Library, Winterthur, Del., manuscript no. 839.

———. "American Financial Regulation—Cui Bono?" *The Economist,* 4 March 2000, 76.

———. *Catalogue of Medicinal Plants, Barks, Roots, Seeds, flowers, and select powders with their Therapeutic qualities and botanical names; Also, Pure Vegetable Extracts, Prepared in vacuo, Ointments, Inspissated Juices, Essential Oils, Double Distilled and Fragrant Waters, &c &c., Raised, Prepared, and put up in the most careful manner by the United Society of Shakers at New Lebanon, N.Y.,* 1851. Shaker Manuscripts, Microfiche MCA 178, Western Reserve Historical Society, Cleveland.

————. *Center Family Journal,* New Lebanon, 1848–57. Emma B. King Library, Shaker Museum and Library, Old Chatham, N.Y., manuscript no. 8831.

————. *Herb Medicine Department Records,* New Lebanon, 1869. Emma B. King Library, Shaker Museum and Library, Old Chatham, N.Y., manuscript no. 4456.

————. *Millennial Laws,* 1843. Reprinted in Edward Deming Andrews, *The People Called Shakers,* 243–89. New York: Dover, 1963.

Anscombe, G. E. M. *Intention.* Ithaca: Cornell University Press, 1957.

Arendt, Hannah. *The Human Condition.* Chicago: University of Chicago Press, 1958.

Aristotle. *Physics,* books I–IV. Rev. ed. Trans. P. H. Wicksteed and F. M. Cornford. Cambridge, Mass.: Harvard University Press, 1957.

————. *The Politics.* Trans. Ernest Barker. Oxford: Oxford University Press, 1995.

Austin, John. "Three Ways of Spilling Ink." In his *Philosophical Papers,* 2d ed., 272–87. Oxford: Oxford University Press, 1970.

Bainbridge, William Sims. "Shaker Demographics, 1940–1900: An Example of the Use of U.S. Census Enumeration Schedules." *Journal for the Scientific Study of Religion* 21 (1982): 352–65.

Baird, Bob, and Craig McBurney. *Electronic Day Trading to Win.* New York: John Wiley & Sons, 1999.

Baker, Arthur. *Shakers and Shakerism.* London: New Moral World Series, 1896.

Barad, Karen. "Meeting the Universe Halfway: Realism and Social Constructivism Without Contradiction." In *Feminism, Science, and the Philosophy of Science,* ed. Lynn Hankinson Nelson and Jack Nelson, 161–94. Dordrecht: Kluwer, 1996.

Barnes, Barry. *The Elements of Social Theory.* Princeton: Princeton University Press, 1995.

Barry, Andrew, Thomas Osborne, and Niklas Rose. *Foucault and Political Reason: Liberalism, Neo-Liberalism, and Rationalities of Government.* London: UCL Press, 1996.

Baudrillard, Jean. *For a Critique of the Political Economy of the Sign.* Trans. Charles Levin. Saint Louis: Telos Press, 1981.

————. *In the Shadow of the Silent Majorities, or the End of the Social and Other Essays.* Trans. Paul Foss, Paul Patton, and John Johnston. New York: Semiotext(e), 1983.

Beale, Galen, and Mary Rose Boswell. *The Earth Shall Blossom: Shaker Herbs and Gardening.* Woodstock, Vt.: Countryman Press, 1991.

Benhabib, Seyla. *The Reluctant Modernism of Hannah Arendt.* Thousand Oaks, Calif.: Sage, 1996.

Berger, Peter, and Thomas Luckmann. *The Social Construction of Reality.* Garden City, N.Y.: Doubleday, 1966.

Bhaskar, Roy. *The Possibility of Naturalism.* Atlantic Highlands, N.J.: Humanities Press, 1979.

Bijker, Wiebe J., and John Law, eds. *Shaping Technology/Building Society: Studies in Sociotechnical Change.* Cambridge, Mass.: MIT Press, 1992.

Blumenberg, Hans. *The Legitimacy of the Modern Age.* Trans. Robert Wallace. Cambridge, Mass.: MIT Press, 1983.

Bohman, James. *New Philosophy of Social Science.* Cambridge, Mass.: MIT Press, 1991.

Bourdieu, Pierre. *Outline of a Theory of Practice.* Trans. Richard Nice. Cambridge: Cambridge University Press, 1976.

————. *The Logic of Practice.* Trans. Richard Nice. Stanford: Stanford University Press, 1990.

Boyd, Robert, and Peter J. Richerson. *Culture and the Evolutionary Process.* Chicago: University of Chicago Press, 1985.

Brandom, Robert. "Freedom and Constraint by Norms." *American Philosophical Quarterly* 16 (1979): 187–96.

———. *Making It Explicit: Reasoning, Representing, and Discursive Commitment.* Cambridge, Mass.: Harvard University Press, 1994.

Brodbeck, May. "Methodological Individualisms: Definition and Reduction." *Philosophy of Science* 25 (1958): 1–22.

Buckman, Rebecca, and Ruth Simon. "Day Trading Can Breed Perilous Illusions." *The Wall Street Journal,* 2 August 1999, pp. C1, C16.

[Bullard], Sister Marcia. "Shaker Industries." *Good Housekeeping* 43 (1906): 33–37.

Burchell, Graham, Colin Gordon, and Peter Miller. *The Foucault Effect: Studies in Governmentality.* Chicago: University of Chicago Press, 1996.

Burge, Tyler. "Individualism and the Mark of the Mental." *Midwest Studies in Philosophy* 4 (1979): 73–121.

Butler, Judith. *Gender Trouble: Feminism and the Subversion of Identity.* New York: Routledge, 1990.

———. *Bodies That Matter: On the Discursive Limits of "Sex."* New York: Routledge, 1993.

———. *The Psychic Life of Power: Theories in Subjection.* Stanford: Stanford University Press, 1997.

Callon, Michel. "Some Elements of a Sociology of Translation: Domestication of the Scallops and the Fisherman of St Brieuc Bay." In *Power, Action, and Belief: A New Sociology of Knowledge?* ed. John Law, 196–233. London: Routledge and Kegan Paul, 1986.

———. "Society in the Making: The Study of Technology as a Tool for Sociological Analysis." In *The Social Construction of Technological Systems: New Directions in the Sociology and History of Technology,* ed. Wiebe E. Bijker, Thomas P. Hughes, and Trevor Pinch, 83–103. Cambridge, Mass.: MIT Press, 1987.

———. "Techno-economic Networks and Irreversibility." In *A Sociology of Monsters: Essays on Power, Technology, and Domination,* ed. John Law, 131–61. London: Routledge, 1991.

Callon, Michel, and Bruno Latour. "Don't Thrown the Baby Out with the Bath School!" In *Science as Practice and Culture,* ed. Andrew Pickering, 343–68. Chicago: University of Chicago Press, 1992.

Callon, Michel, and John Law. "On the Construction of Sociotechnical Networks: Content and Context Revisited." In *Knowledge and Society: Studies in the Sociology of Science Past and Present,* ed. Lowell Hargens, Robert Alun Jones, and Andrew Pickering, 57–83. Greenwich, Conn.: JAI Press, 1989.

Christie, William, and Paul H. Schultz. "Why Nasdaq Market Makers Avoid Odd-Eighth Quotes." *Journal of Finance* 49 (1994): 1813–40.

Clifford, Lee. "The Semester of Living Dangerously." *SmartMoney* 9, 5, 2000, 144–52.

Collins, Harry. *Artificial Experts: Social Knowledge and Intelligent Machines.* Cambridge, Mass.: MIT Press, 1990.

Cosgel, Metin M., Thomas J. Miceli, and John E. Murray. "Organization and Distributional Equality in a Network of Communes: The Shakers." *American Journal of Economics and Sociology* 56, 2 (April 1997): 129–44.

Dagognet, François. *La Maîtrise du vivant.* Paris: Hachette, 1988.

Danto, Arthur. "Basic Actions." *American Philosophical Quarterly* 2 (1965): 141–48.

Davidson, Donald. *"Essays on Actions and Events.* New York: Oxford University Press, 1980.

Davies, Bronwyn. "The Concept of Agency: A Feminist Poststructuralist Analysis." *Social Analysis* 30 (1991): 42–53.

Davies, Bronwyn, and Rom Harré. "Positioning: The Discursive Production of Selves." *Journal for the Theory of Social Behavior* 20, 1 (1990): 43–63.

Dawkins, Richard. *The Selfish Gene.* Oxford: Clarendon Press, 1976.

Deleuze, Gilles. *Foucault.* Trans. and ed. Seán Hand. Minneapolis: University of Minnesota Press, 1988.

——. *The Logic of Sense.* Trans. Mark Lester with Charles Stivale. New York: Columbia University Press, 1990.

——. *Negotiations * 1972–1990.* Trans. Martin Joughin. New York: Columbia University Press, 1995.

——. "Desire and Pleasure." In *Foucault and His Interlocutors,* ed. Arnold Davidson, trans. Daniel W. Smith, 183–92. Chicago: University of Chicago Press, 1997.

Deleuze, Gilles, and Félix Guattari. *Anti-Oedipus: Capitalism and Schizophrenia.* Trans. Robert Hurley, Mark Seem, and Helen R. Lane. Minneapolis: University of Minnesota Press, 1983.

——. *A Thousand Plateaus: Capitalism and Schizophrenia.* Trans. Brian Massumi. Minneapolis: University of Minnesota Press, 1987.

Deleuze, Gilles, and Claire Parnet. *Dialogues.* Trans. Hugh Tomlinson and Barbara Habberjam. New York: Columbia University Press, 1987.

Dennett, Daniel. *Darwin's Dangerous Idea: Evolution and the Meanings of Life.* New York: Touchstone, 1995.

Derrida, Jacques. *On Grammatology.* Trans. Gayatri Chakravorty Spivak. Baltimore: Johns Hopkins Press, 1974.

——. "Différance." In *Margins of Philosophy,* Alan Bass, ed., 1–21. Chicago: University of Chicago Press, 1982.

——. "The Ends of Man," In *Margins of Philosophy,* ed. Alan Bass, 109–36. Chicago: University of Chicago Press, 1982.

——. "The Force of Law." *Cardozo Law Review* 11, 5–6 (1990).

Dilthey, Wilhelm. *Gesammelte Schriften* 7. Leipzig: B. G. Teubner, 1927.

Dixon, William Hepworth. *New America* 2. New York: AMS Press, 1971.

Donzelot, Jacques. *The Policing of Families.* Trans. Robert Hurley. London: Hutchinson, 1979.

Dreyfus, Hubert. *Being-in-the-World: A Commentary on Heidegger's Being and Time, Division I.* Cambridge, Mass.: MIT Press, 1991.

——. "On the Ordering of Things: Being and Power in Heidegger and Foucault." In *Michel Foucault: Philosopher,* ed. Timothy Armstrong, 80–94. London: Routledge, 1992.

Durham, William H. *Coevolution: Genes, Culture, and Human Diversity.* Stanford: Stanford University Press, 1991.

Durkheim, Emile. *The Rules of Sociological Method.* Trans. Sarah A. Solovay and John H. Mueller. New York: Free Press, 1938.

Elster, Jon. *Ulysses and the Sirens: Studies in Rationality and Irrationality.* Rev. ed. Cambridge; Cambridge University Press, 1984.

Ely, Richard. *The Labor Movement in America.* New York: Thomas Y. Crowell & Co., 1886.

Estes, J. Worth. "The Shakers and Their Propriety Medicines." *Bulletin of Historical Medicine* 65 (1991): 162–84.

Feinberg, Joel. "Action and Responsibility." In *Philosophy in America,* ed. Max Black. London: Allen and Unwin, 1965, 134–60.

Foster, John Bellamy. *Marx's Ecology: Materialism and Nature.* New York: Monthly Review Press, 2000.

Foster, Lawrence. *Religion and Sexuality: Three American Communal Experiments of the Nineteenth Century.* New York: Oxford University Press, 1981.

Foucault, Michel. *The Order of Things: An Archaeology of the Human Sciences.* London: Tavistock, 1970.

———. *The Archaeology of Knowledge.* Trans. A. M. Sheridan-Smith. New York: Harper and Row, 1976.

———. *Discipline and Punish: The Birth of the Prison.* Trans. Alan Sheridan. New York: Vintage, 1979.

———. "The Confession of the Flesh." In *Power/Knowledge,* trans. and ed. Colin Gordon, 194–228. New York: Pantheon, 1980.

———. *The History of Sexuality,* vol. 1: *An Introduction.* Trans. Richard Hurley. New York: Vintage, 1980.

———. "The Subject and Power." Afterword to Hubert L. Dreyfus and Paul Rabinow, *Michel Foucault: Beyond Structuralism and Hermeneutics,* 2d ed., 208–28. Chicago: University of Chicago Press, 1982.

———. "Nietzsche, Genealogy, History." In *The Foucault Reader,* ed. Paul Rabinow, 76–100. New York: Pantheon, 1984.

———. "What Is an Author?" In *The Foucault Reader,* ed. Paul Rabinow, 101–20. New York: Pantheon, 1984.

———. "What Is Enlightenment?" In *The Foucault Reader,* ed. Paul Rabinow, 32–50. New York: Pantheon, 1984.

———. "Politics and the Study of Discourse." In *The Foucault Effect: Studies in Governmentality,* ed. Graham Burchell, Colin Gordon, and Peter Miller, 53–72. Chicago: University of Chicago Press, 1991.

———. "Questions of Method." In *The Foucault Effect: Studies in Governmentality,* ed. Graham Burchell, Colin Gordon, and Peter Miller, 73–86. Chicago: University of Chicago Press, 1991.

Friedfertig, Marc, and George West. *Electronic Day Traders' Secrets: Learn from the Best of the Best Day Traders.* New York: McGraw-Hill, 1999.

Gadamer, H.-J. *Truth and Method.* 2d rev. ed. Trans. Joel Weinsheimer and Donald G. Marshall. New York: Crossroad, 1989.

Galison, Peter. "Context and Constraints." In *Scientific Practice: Theories and Stories of Doing Physics,* ed. Jed Z. Buchwald, 13–41. Chicago: University of Chicago Press, 1995.

Garfinkel, Harold. *Studies in Ethnomethodology.* Englewood Cliffs, N.J.: Prentice-Hall, 1967.

Giddens, Anthony. *Central Problems in Social Theory: Action, Structure, and Contradiction in Social Analysis.* Berkeley and Los Angeles: University of California Press, 1979.

———. *The Constitution of Society.* Berkeley and Los Angeles: University of California Press, 1984.

————. "Time, Space, and Regionalization." In *Social Relations and Spatial Structures,* ed. Derek Gregory and John Urry, 265–95. London: Macmillan, 1985.

Gifford, Don, ed. *An Early View of the Shakers: Benson John Lossing and the Harper's Article of 1857.* Hanover, N.H., and London: University Press of New England, 1989.

Gilbert, Margaret. *On Social Facts.* Princeton: Princeton University Press, 1989.

————. "Concerning Sociality: The Plural Subject as Paradigm." In *The Mark of the Social: Discovery or Invention?* ed. John D. Greenwood, 17–36. Lanham, Md.: Rowman & Littlefield, 1997.

Goffman, Erving. "Presidential Address: The Interaction Order." *American Sociological Review* 48 (1983): 1–17.

Goldman, Alvin. *A Theory of Human Action.* Princeton: Princeton University Press, 1970.

Goldstein, L. J. "Two Theses of Methodological Individualism." *British Journal for the Philosophy of Science* 9 (1958): 1–11.

Gordon, Scott. "How Many Kinds of Things Are There in the World? The Ontological Status of Societies." In *The Mark of the Social: Discovery or Invention?* ed. John D. Greenwood, 81–104. Lanham, Md.: Rowman & Littlefield, 1997.

Gorovitz, Samuel. "Causal Judgements and Causal Explanations." *Journal of Philosophy* 62, 23 (2 December 1965): 695–711.

Greenwood, John D., ed. *The Mark of the Social: Discovery or Invention?* Lanham, Md.: Rowman and Littlefield, 1997.

Habermas, Jürgen. *The Theory of Communicative Action,* vol. 2: *Lifeworld and System: A Critique of Functionalist Reason.* Trans. Thomas McCarthy. Boston: Beacon Press, 1987.

————. *The Logic of Social Sciences.* Trans. Shierry Weber Nicholson and Jerry A. Stark. Cambridge, Mass.: MIT Press, 1988.

Hägerstrand, Torsten. "Space, Time, and Human Conditions." In *Dynamic Allocation of Urban Space,* ed. A. Karlqvist, L. Lundqvist, and F. Snickars, 3–14. Lexington, Mass.: Lexington Books, 1975.

Hagner, Michael, and Hans-Jörg Rheinberger. "Experimental Systems, Objects of Investigation, and Spaces of Representation." In *Experimental Essays—Versuche zum Experiment,* ed. Michael Heidelberger and Friedrich Steinle, 355–73. Baden-Baden: Nomos Verlagsgesellschaft, 1998.

Haila, Yrjö, and Richard Levins. *Humanity and Nature: Ecology, Science, and Society.* London: Pluto Press, 1992.

Haraway, Donna. "Situated Knowledges: The Science Question in Feminism and the Privilege of Partial Perspectives." *Feminist Studies* 14, 3 (1988): 575–79.

————. "When Man™ Is on the Menu." In *Zone 6: Incorporations,* ed. Jonathan Crary and Sanford Kwinter, 39–43. New York: Urzone, 1992.

————. "The Promise of Monsters: A Regenerative Politics for Inappropriate/d Others." In *Cultural Studies: A Reader,* ed. Lawrence Grossberg et al., 293–337. New York: Routledge, 1992.

Harré, Rom. *Social Being.* 2d ed. Oxford: Blackwell, 1993.

Harré, Rom, and Edward Madden. *Causal Powers.* Oxford: Blackwell, 1975.

Hart, H. L. A., and A. M. Honore. *Causation in the Law.* New York: Oxford University Press, 1959.

Haugeland, John. "Heidegger on Being a Person." *Nous* 16 (1982): 15–26.

Hayek, F. A. *The Counterrevolution in Science: Studies on the Abuse of Reason.* Glencoe: Free Press, 1952.

Heaton, John M. "Language-Games, Expression, and Desire in the Work of Deleuze." *Journal of the British Society for Phenomenology* 24, (1993): 77–87.

Heidegger, Martin. "The Thing," In *Poetry, Language, and Thought,* trans. Albert Hofstadter, 163–86. New York: Harper and Row, 1971.

———. "Building, Dwelling, Thinking." In *Poetry, Language, and Thought,* trans. Albert Hofstadter, 143–62. New York: Harper and Row, 1971.

———. *Being and Time.* Trans. John Macquarrie and Edward Robinson. Oxford: Blackwell, 1978.

Helyar, John. "The New American Dream?" *Money,* April 2000, 128.

Hill, Isaac. "The Shakers," *Farmer's Monthly Visitor,* 31 August 1840, pp. 113–18.

Hoffman, George Niles. "Mt. Lebanon Medicine Makers—The Shakers." *Pharmaceutical Era* (July 1920): 197–98, 229–31.

Hollister, Alonzo. "Reminiscences of a Soldier of the Cross." Shaker Manuscripts, Series X: B31, Western Reserve Historical Society, Cleveland.

———. *Daily Journal of Extract Business Kept by A. G. H.* New Lebanon, 1856–60. Shaker Manuscripts, Series III: B 19, Western Reserve Historical Society, Cleveland.

Hollway, Wendy. "Gender Difference and the Production of Subjectivity." In *Changing the Subject,* ed. J. Henriques et al., 227–63. London: Methuen, 1984.

Holter, James T. "Day-Trading Software Shootout." *Futures* 28 (1999): 30–34.

Homans, George. "Bringing Men Back In." *American Sociological Review* 29, 5 (December 1964): 809–18.

Horgan, Edward R. *The Shaker Holy Land: A Community Portrait.* Harvard, Mass.: Harvard Common Press, 1982.

Horigan, Stephen. *Nature and Culture in Western Discourses.* London: Routledge, 1988.

Howells, W. D. *Three Villages.* Boston: James R. Osgood & Co., 1884.

———. *The Undiscovered Country.* Boston: Houghton, Mifflin, & Co., 1888.

Hunt, Alan, and Gary Wickham. *Foucault and Law: Towards a Sociology of Law as Governance.* Boulder: Pluto Press, 1994.

Ingold, Tim. *Evolution and Social Life.* Cambridge: Cambridge University Press, 1986.

———. "Life beyond the Edge of Nature? or the Mirage of Society." In *The Mark of the Social: Discovery or Invention?* ed. David D. Greenwood, 231–52. Lanham, Md.: Rowman & Littlefield, 1997.

Ip, Greg. "Nasdaq Market Maker, Seeing All the Orders, Becomes Canny Trader." *The Wall Street Journal* 55, 45, 3 March 2000, pp. A1, A8.

Kanter, Robert. "Day Traders: How They Help Markets Work Better." *Barron's,* 27 September 1999.

Kanter, Rosabeth. *Men and Women of the Corporation.* New York: Basic Books, 1977.

Kern, Louis. *An Ordered Love.* Chapel Hill: University of North Carolina Press, 1981.

Knorr-Cetina, Karin. "Sociality with Objects: Social Relations in Postsocial Knowledge Societies." *Theory, Culture, and Society* 14 (1997): 1–30.

Koselleck, Reinhardt. *Critique and Crisis.* Cambridge, Mass.: MIT Press, 1988.

Laclau, Ernesto. *New Reflections on the Revolution of Our Time.* London: Verso, 1990.

Laclau, Ernesto, and Chantal Mouffe. *Hegemony and Socialist Strategy: Toward a Radical Democratic Politics.* London: Verso, 1985.

Lafitte, Jacques. *Réflexions sur la science des machines.* Paris: Bloud et Gay, 1932.

Latour, Bruno. "The Powers of Association." In *Power, Action, and Belief: A New Sociology of Knowledge?* ed. John Law, 264–80. London: Routledge, 1986.

———. *Science in Action: How to Follow Scientists and Engineers Through Society.* Cambridge, Mass.: Harvard University Press, 1987.

———. "Technology Is Society Made Durable." In *A Sociology of Monsters: Essays on Power, Technology, and Domination,* ed. John Law, 103–31. London: Routledge, 1991.

———. "Where Are the Missing Masses? The Sociology of a Few Mundane Artifacts." In *Shaping Technology/Building Society: Studies in Sociotechnical Change,* ed. Wiebe E. Bijker and John Law, 225–58. Cambridge, Mass.: MIT Press, 1992.

———. *We Have Never Been Modern.* Trans. Catherine Porter. Cambridge, Mass.: Harvard University Press, 1993.

———. "Do Scientific Objects Have a History? Pasteur and Whitehead in a Bath of Lactic Acid." *Common Knowledge* 5, 1 (1996): 76–91.

———. "On Intersubjectivity." *Mind, Culture, and Activity* 3, 4 (1996): 228–45.

———. "On Actor-Network Theory: A Few Clarifications." *Soziale Welt* 47, 4 (1996): 369–81.

Law, John. "Power, Discretion, and Strategy." In *A Sociology of Monsters: Essays on Power, Technology, and Domination,* ed. John Law, 165–91. London: Routledge, 1991.

———. "Notes on the Theory of the Actor-Network: Ordering, Strategy, and Heterogeneity." *Systems Practice* 5, 4 (1992): 379–93.

———. *Organizing Modernity.* Oxford: Blackwell, 1994.

Law, John, and Wiebe E. Bijker. "Postscript: Technology, Stability, and Social Theory." In *Shaping Technology/Building Society: Studies in Sociotechnical Change,* ed. Wiebe E. Bijker and John Law, 290–307. Cambridge, Mass.: MIT Press, 1992.

Layder, Derek. *Understanding Social Theory.* London and Thousand Oaks, Calif.: Sage, 1994.

Lee, Charles. "The Shakers as Pioneers in the American Herb and Drug Industry." Talk given at the American Pharmaceutical Association, 1959, Edward Deming Andrews Memorial Shaker Collection, Winterthur Library, Winterthur, Del., manuscript no. 1203.

Lévi-Strauss, Claude. *Structural Anthropology.* Trans. Claire Jacobson and Brooke Grundfest Schoepf. New York: Basic Books, 1963.

Levins, Richard, and Richard Lewontin. *The Dialectical Biologist.* Cambridge, Mass.: Harvard University Press, 1985.

Levy, D. A., and P .R. Nail. "Contagion: A Theoretical and Empirical Review and Reconceptualization." *Genetic, Social, and Social Psychology Monographs* 119 (1993): 235–84.

Lockwood, David. "Social Integration and System Integration." In *Explorations in Social Change,* ed. George K. Zollschan and W. Hirsch, 244–57. London: Routledge, 1964.

Losonsky, Michael. "The Nature of Artifacts." *Philosophy* 65 (1990): 81–88.

Lossing, Benson J. "The Shakers." *Harper's New Monthly Magazine* 15 (June–November 1857): 164–77.

Luhmann, Niklas. "Einführende Bemerkungen zu einer Theorie symbolisch generalisierter Kommunikationsmedien." In his *Soziologische Aufklärung* 2. Opladen: Westdeutscher Verlag, 1975, 175–92.

————. *Soziale Systeme: Grundriß einer allgemeinen Theorie.* Frankfurt am Main: Suhrkamp, 1984.

Lukacs, Georgi. *The Theory of the Novel.* Trans. Anna Bostock. Cambridge, Mass.: MIT Press, 1978.

————. *The Destruction of Reason.* Trans. Peter Palmer. London: Merlin, 1980.

Luke, Timothy. "Social Theory and Environmentalism: Defining Nature/Society in the 21st Century." Paper presented at the inaugural meeting of the International Social Theory Consortium, 11 May 2000, University of Kentucky, Lexington.

Lukes, Steven. "Methodological Individualism Revisited." *British Journal of Sociology* 19 (1968): 119–29.

Lumsden, Charles J., and Edward O. Wilson. *Genes, Minds, and Culture: The Coevolutionary Process.* Cambridge, Mass.: Harvard University Press, 1981.

Lyotard, Jean-François. *The Postmodern Condition: A Report on Knowledge.* Trans. Geoff Bennington and Brian Massumi. Minneapolis: University of Minnesota Press, 1979.

————. *The Differend: Phrases in Dispute.* Trans. Georges van den Abbeele. Minneapolis: University of Minnesota Press, 1988.

Lyotard, Jean-François, and Jean-Loup Thébaud. *Just Gaming.* Trans. Wald Godzich. Minneapolis: University of Minnesota Press, 1985.

Malinowski, Bronislav. *Crime and Custom in Savage Society.* London: Paul, Trench, Trubner, 1926.

Malkiel, Burton. "Day Trading, and Its Dangers." *The Wall Street Journal,* 3 August 1999, p. A22.

Mandelbaum, Maurice. "Societal Facts." *British Journal of Sociology* 6 (1955): 305–17.

Margolis, Joseph. *Historied Thought, Constructed World: A Conceptual Primer for the Turn of the Millennium.* Berkeley and Los Angeles: University of California Press, 1995.

————. "The Meaning of the 'Social.'" In *The Mark of the Social: Discovery or Invention?* ed. John D. Greenwood, 183–98. Lanham, Md.: Rowman & Littlefield, 1997.

Marx, Karl. *Economic and Political Manuscripts of 1844.* Trans. Martin Milligan. Moscow: Progress Publishers, 1959.

————. *Grundrisse.* Trans. Martin Nicolaus. New York: Vintage, 1973.

Massumi, Brian. *A Reader's Guide to Capitalism and Schizophrenia.* Cambridge, Mass.: MIT Press, 1992.

Matthews, R. C. O. "Darwinism and Economic Change." In *Economic Theory and Hicksian Themes,* ed. D. A. Collard et al., 91–117. Oxford: Oxford University Press, 1984.

McDowell, John. *Mind and World.* Cambridge, Mass.: Harvard University Press, 1994.

McKibben, Bill. *The End of Nature.* New York: Random House, 1989.

Meader, Robert. Introduction to Edward R. Horgan. In *The Shaker Holy Land: A Community Portrait,* xvii–xxii .Harvard, Mass.: Harvard Common Press, 1982.

Miller, Amy Bess. *Shaker Herbs: A History and A Compendium.* New York: Clarkson N. Potter, 1976.

Mitcham, Carl. *Thinking Through Technology: Between Engineering and Philosophy.* Chicago: University of Chicago Press, 1994.

Morgenson, Gretchen. "S.E.C. Chief Wants One Site for Posting All Stock Prices." *The New York Times,* 24 September 1999, pp. A1, C8.

Mosser, Mike, and Carla Cavaletti. "Technology Opens the Door to Day-Trading." *Futures* 28 (1999): 26–28.

Mouffe, Chantal. "Feminism, Citizenship, and Radical Democratic Politics." In *Feminists Theorize the Political*, ed. Judith Butler and Joan Scott, 369–84. New York: Routledge, 1992.

Mumford, Lewis. *Technics and Civilization*. New York: Harcourt Brace, 1934.

Murray, John E., and Metin M. Cosgel. "Market, Religion, and Culture in Shaker Swine Production, 1788–1880." *Agricultural History* 72, 3 (1998): 552–73.

Myrick, Elisha. *Day Book Kept for the Convenience of the Herb Department by Elisha Myrick Harvard Church*, 1849–52. Harvard Shaker Village, Hancock, Mass., manuscript.

———. *A Diary Kept for the Convenience of the Herb Department by Elisha Myrick*, 1853–57. Edward Deming Andrews Memorial Shaker Collection, Winterthur Library, Winterthur, Del., manuscript no. 837.

Nassar, David. *How to Get Started in Electronic Day Trading*. New York: McGraw-Hill, 1999.

Nietzsche, Friedrich. *On the Genealogy of Morals*. Trans. Walter Kaufmann. New York: Vintage, 1969.

Nobel, David, R. *Forces of Production: A Social History of Industrial Automation*. Oxford: Oxford University Press, 1986.

Norris, Floyd. "A New Market, Disturbingly Fragmented." *The New York Times*, 24 September 1999, pp. C1, C8.

Oakeshott, Michael. "Political Education." In his *Rationalism in Politics and Other Essays*, new and expanded ed. 43–69. Indianapolis: Liberty Press, 1991.

O'Neill, John. *Modes of Individualism and Collectivism*. London: Heinemann, 1973.

Parsons, Talcott. *The Structure of Social Action*, vol. 1: *Marshall, Pareto, and Durkheim*. New York: Free Press, 1949.

———. *Societies: Evolutionary and Comparative Perspectives*. Englewood Cliffs, N.J.: Prentice-Hall, 1966.

———. "Interaction." In *The International Encyclopedia of the Social Sciences*, ed. David L. Shils, 429–41. New York: Macmillan, 1968.

Parsons, Talcott, and Edward A. Shils. "Values, Motives, and Systems of Action." In *Toward a General Theory of Action*, ed. Talcott Parsons and Edward Shils, 47–243. Cambridge, Mass.: Harvard University Press, 1951.

Pickering, Andrew. *The Mangle of Practice: Time, Agency, & Science*. Chicago: University of Chicago Press, 1995.

Plato. *The Republic*. New York: Knopf, 1993.

Proctor, William. "New Lebanon: Its Physics Gardens and Their Products." *American Journal of Pharmacy* 18 (1952): 88–91.

Rabinow, Paul. "Artificiality and Enlightenment: from Sociobiology to Biosociality." In *Zone 6: Incorporations*, ed. Jonathan Crary and Sanford Kwinter, 234–52. New York: Urzone, 1992.

Rawls, Anne. "The Interaction Order Sui Generis: Goffman's Contribution to Social Theory." *Sociological Theory* 5 (fall 1987): 136–49.

Rheinberger, Hans-Jörg. "From Microsomes to Ribosomes: 'Strategies' of 'Representation.'" *Journal of the History of Biology* 28 (1995): 49–89.

———. *Toward a History of Epistemic Things: Synthesizing Proteins in the Test Tube*. Stanford: Stanford University Press, 1997.

Richtel, Matt. "Keeping E-Commerce on Line: As Internet Traffic Surges, So Do Technical Problems." *The New York Times*, 21 June 1999, pp. C1, C6.

Ringer, Fritz. "The Intellectual Field, Intellectual History, and the Sociology of Knowledge." *Theory and Society* 19 (1990): 269–94.

Rochlin, Gene I. *Trapped in the Net: The Unanticipated Consequences of Computerization.* Princeton: Princeton University Press, 1997.

Rochon, Diane. "Different Strokes for Different Folks." *Futures* 28 (1999): 10–11.

Rouse, Joseph. *Knowledge and Power: Toward a Political Philosophy of Science.* Ithaca: Cornell University Press, 1987.

———. *Engaging Science: How to Understand Its Practices Philosophically.* Ithaca: Cornell University Press, 1996.

Rueschemeyer, D., and T. Skocpol, eds. *States, Social Knowledge, and the Origins of Modern Social Policies.* Princeton: Princeton University Press, 1996.

Runciman, W. G. *A Treatise on Social Theory,* vol. 1: *The Methodology of Social Theory.* Cambridge: Cambridge University Press, 1983.

———. *A Treatise on Social Theory,* vol. 2: *Substantive Social Theory.* Cambridge: Cambridge University Press, 1989.

Sander, Jennifer Basye, and Peter J. Sander. *Day Trading like a Pro.* New York: Alpha Books, 1999.

Sartre, Jean-Paul. *Being and Nothingness.* Trans. Hazel Barnes. New York: Pocket Books, 1966.

———. *Search for a Method.* Trans. Hazel Barnes. New York: Vintage, 1968.

Sasson, Diane. "A 19th-Century Case Study: Alonzo Giles Hollister (1830–1911)." *Shaker Quarterly* 17 (1989): 154–72, 188–93.

Schatzki, Theodore R. "Social Causality." *Inquiry* 31, 2 (1988): 151–70.

———. "Spatial Ontology and Explanation." *Annals of the Association of American Geographers* 81, 4 (1991): 650–70.

———. *Social Practices: A Wittgensteinian Approach to Human Activity and the Social.* New York: Cambridge University Press, 1996.

———. "Practices and Actions: A Wittgensteinian Critique of Bourdieu and Giddens." *Philosophy of the Social Sciences* 27, 3 (1997): 283–308.

———. "The Social Bearing of Nature." *Inquiry* 43 (2000): 21–38.

Schatzki, Theodore R., Karin Knorr-Cetina, and Eike von Savigny, eds. *The Practice Turn in Contemporary Theory.* London: Routledge, 2001.

Schelling, Thomas C. *The Strategy of Conflict.* Cambridge, Mass.: Harvard University Press, 1960.

Schifrin, Matthew, and Scott McCormack. "Free Enterprise Comes to Wall Street." *Forbes* 161, 7, 6 April 1998, pp. 114–19.

Schwartz, Nelson D. "Meet the New Market Makers." *Fortune,* 21 February 2000, pp. 90 ff.

Searle, John. *Intentionality.* Cambridge: Cambridge University Press, 1983.

Secord, Paul. "The Mark of the Social in the Social Sciences." In *The Mark of the Social: Discovery or Invention?* ed. John D. Greenwood, 59–80. Lanham, Md.: Rowman & Littlefield, 1997.

Simmel, Georg. *Lebensanschauung, vier metaphysische Kapitel.* Munich and Leipzig: Dunker and Humblot, 1918.

———. "How Is Society Possible?" In *Philosophy of the Social Sciences,* ed. Maurice Natanson, 73–92. New York: Random House, 1953.

Simon, Jon. *Foucault and the Political.* London: Routledge, 1995.

Simondon, Gilbert. *Du mode d'existence des objets techniques.* 3d ed. Paris: Aubier, 1989.

Soja, Edward. *Postmodern Geographies.* London: Verso, 1989.

Spencer, Herbert. *Principles of Sociology* 1. London: William & Norgate, 1882.

Spinosa, Charles, and Hubert Dreyfus. "Two Kinds of Anti-Essentialism and Their Consequences." *Critical Inquiry* 22 (summer 1996): 735–63.

Spinosa, Charles, Fernando Flores, and Hubert Dreyfus. *Disclosing New Worlds: Entrepreneurship, Democratic Action, and the Cultivation of Solidarity.* Cambridge, Mass.: MIT Press, 1997.

Star, Susan Leigh. "Power, Technologies, and the Phenomenology of Conventions: On Being Allergic to Onions." In *A Sociology of Monsters: Essays on Power, Technology, and Domination,* ed. John Law, 26–56. London: Routledge, 1991.

Stein, Stephen J. *The Shaker Experience in America.* New Haven: Yale University Press, 1992.

Taylor, Charles. "Interpretation and the Sciences of Man." In his *Philosophy and the Human Sciences: Philosophical Papers* 2, 15–58. Cambridge: Cambridge University Press, 1985.

———. "Lichtung or Lebensform: Parallels Between Heidegger and Wittgenstein." In his *Philosophical Arguments,* 61–78. Cambridge, Mass.: Harvard University Press, 1995.

Taylor, Peter J. *Political Geography: World Economy, Nation-State, and Locality.* London: Longman, 1985.

Thurman, Suzanne. "'No Idle Hands Are Seen': The Social Construction of Work in Shaker Communities." *Communal Societies* (fall 1998).

Tooby, John, and Leda Cosmides. "The Psychological Foundations of Culture." In *The Adapted Mind: Evolutionary Psychology and the Generation of Culture,* ed. Jerome H. Barkow, Leda Cosmides, and John Tooby, 19–136. New York: Oxford University Press, 1992.

Turk, Herman. "Social Organization." In *Encyclopedia of Sociology,* ed. Edgar F. Borgalla, 1894–1907. New York: Macmillan, 1992.

Turner, Stephen. *The Social Theory of Practices: Tradition, Tacit Knowledge, and Presuppositions.* Cambridge: Polity Press, 1994.

Unger, Roberto Mangabeira. *Social Theory: Its Situation and Its Task.* Cambridge: Cambridge University Press, 1987.

U.S. Congress. House Subcommittee on Finance and Hazardous Materials. "The Impact and Effectiveness of the Small Order Execution System." *Hearings Before the Subcommittee on Finance and Hazardous Materials,* 105th Cong., 3 August 1998, serial no. 105–3.

Vincent, Carol. "Do We Need a Stock Exchange?" *Fortune,* 22 November 1999, pp. 251ff.

Vogel, Steven. *Against Nature: The Concept of Nature in Critical Theory.* Albany: State University of New York Press, 1996.

Wahal, Sunil. "Entry, Exit, Market Makers, and the Bid-Ask Spread." *Review of Financial Studies* 10, 3 (1997): 871–901.

Waldenfels, Bernhard. *Ordnung im Zwielicht.* Frankfort am Main: Suhrkamp, 1987.

Walsh, W. H. *An Introduction to the Philosophy of History.* London: Hutchinson, 1951.

Walther, Gerda. "Zur Ontologie der sozialen Gemeinschaft." *Jahrbuch für Philosophie und phänomenologische Forschung* 6 (1923): 1–158.

Watkins, J. W. N. "Ideal Types and Historical Explanation." In *Readings in the Philosophy of Science,* ed. Herbert Feigl and May Brodbeck. New York: Appleton-Century-Crofts, 1953.

Weber, Max. *Basic Concepts of Sociology.* Trans. H. P. Secher. Secaucus: Citadel, 1972.

———. *Soziologische Grundbegriffe.* Tübingen: J. C. B. Mohr, 1984.

Wells, Seth Y. *Remarks on Learning and the Use of Books.* Edward Deming Andrews Memorial Shaker Collection, Winterthur Library, Winterthur, Del., manuscript no. 808.

Wertch, James V. *Mind in Action.* New York: Oxford University Press, 1998.

Wertch, James V., Pablo del Río, and Amelia Alvarez, eds. *Sociocultural Studies of Mind.* New York: Cambridge University Press, 1995.

Williams, Raymond. "Society." In his *Keywords: A Vocabulary of Culture and Society,* 243–47. Oxford: Oxford University Press, 1976.

Wilson, William J. *The Truly Disadvantaged: The Inner City, the Underclass, and Public Policy.* Chicago: University of Chicago Press, 1987.

Wittgenstein, Ludwig. *Philosophical Investigations.* 3d ed. Trans. G. E. M. Anscombe. New York: Macmillan, 1957.

———. *Conversations on Aesthetics, Psychology, and Religious Belief.* Ed. Cyril Barrett. Oxford: Blackwell, 1966.

———. *Zettel.* Ed. G. E. M. Anscombe and G. H. von Wright, trans. G. E. M. Anscombe. Berkeley and Los Angeles: University of California Press, 1967.

———. *On Certainty.* Trans. Denis Paul and G. E. M. Anscombe. Oxford: Blackwell, 1977.

———. "Remarks on Frazer's *Golden Bough.*" In *Philosophical Occasions,* ed. James C. Klagge and Alfred Nordmann, trans. John Beverslvi. Indianapolis: Hackett, 1993, 119–55.

Woolgar, Steve. "Configuring the User: The Case of Usability Trials." In *A Sociology of Monsters: Essays on Power, Technology, and Domination,* ed. John Law, 57–99. London: Routledge, 1991.

Wright, Georg Henrik von. *Explanation and Understanding.* Ithaca: Cornell University Press, 1971.

Wrong, Dennis S. *The Problem of Order: What Unites and Divides Societies.* New York: Free Press, 1994.

Youngs, Isaac. *A Concise View of the Church of God and of Christ on Earth Having Its Foundation in the Faith of Christ's First and Second Appearing,* New Lebanon, N.Y., 1856–60. Edward Deming Andrews Memorial Shaker Collection, Winterthur Library, Winterthur, Del., manuscript no. 861.

INDEX

Lukács, Georg, 182 n. 87
Luke, Timothy, 207 n. 34
Lyotard, Jean-François, 77

Madden, Edward, 62 n. 3
Mandelbaum, Maurice, 133
mangle, Pickering concept of, 109, 119–21, 213–14,
    214 n. 41
Margolis, Joseph, 106 n. 51
Mark of the Social, The (Gordon), 131
Marx, Karl, 178 n. 82
    on individuals, 39, 69
    on natural history and metabolism, 259–61, 263
    on workers and their labor, 99
Massumi, Brian, 90–91 n. 38
Matter-Function, 92, 96
Mead, G. H., 127 n.7
meaning
    in arrangements, 47–54, 99–100
    artifacts and, 99–100, 202
    being and, 47
    definition of, 18
    determination thereof, 50–58, 142
    difference and, 55–56, 55–56 n. 83, 57–58
    function and, 56
    identity and, 18, 47, 53–54, 99–100
    linguistic, 61
    webs of, 142–43, 146, 153
media of communication, 250–51
medicinal herb business. *See also* Hollister,
    Alonzo; Long, James; Shakers
    causal relations and, 97
    constraint in, 223–24
    context and, 62
    deterrorialization in, 249–50
    division of labor in, 34, 86, 155
    early history of, 32–33, 65
    ends in, 81–82, 155, 241, 247–48
    forms of coexistence and, 148
    identity of Shakers involved in, 100
    as knowledge society, 112
    market for, 34–35
    molecular texture of, 104
    new objects and actions in, 107
    orders surrounding, 150–51
    practical understandings in, 78
    practice-arrangement bundles in, 154, 173–74,
        245–48
    as practice-order bundle, 154, 173–74, 245–48

practices in, 73–74
production component of, 35–38, 97
projects and tasks in, 241
rules in, 79, 79 n. 29
teleoaffective structure in, 80–81
use of as example, xviii–xxi
membership, in communities, 84–85
mental conditions
    action understandings and, 135 n. 24
    actions and, 75 n. 22, 229, 230, 231, 232 n. 60
    human life and, 147
    practical intelligibility and, 76, 81
metabolism, of humankind with nature, 259–61,
    263
micro/macro distinctions, examples of, 103 n. 48
Mill, John Stuart, 124
molar, in assemblages, Deleuze and Guattari
    concept of, 102–5, 204
molecular, in assemblages, Deleuze and Guattari
    concept of, 102–5, 204, 234
mongrels, as type of artifacts, 179, 181
monologism, Taylor concept of, 69–70
Mouffe, Chantal, xii
    on difference, 55–56, 55–56 n. 83
    on discourse, 19–20, 23, 50, 141–42, 146, 151
    on subject positions, 50 n. 78
Mumford, Lewis, 180 n. 84
Myrick, Elisha, 52 n. 82, 86 n. 35

Nasdaq (National Association of Security Dealers
    Automated Quotation), 4, 157
    bids and offers, 158, 172 n. 73
    competition and, 172, 172 n. 72
    ECNs, 161–62, 166
    functioning of, 158–59
    information asymmetries in, 160, 161–62, 224
    market, 158, 165 n. 60
    market makers and, 158–60, 161 n. 52, 165, 165
        n. 59, 168 n. 67, 170–72, 172 n. 72
    NASD, 166, 245
    order handling reforms, 160–62, 172, 172 n. 71
    SOES, 160–61, 245
    trading, 158–59, 161, 161 nn. 52, 53
    use of as example, xviii–xxi
"natural beings," definition of, 178–79
natural history
    conceptions of, 256–57
    as evolution of metabolism, 259–61, 263
natural language, 14–15

Printed in Great Britain
by Amazon.co.uk, Ltd.,
Marston Gate.